PUBLISHED ON THE FOUNDATION ESTABLISHED
IN MEMORY OF OLIVER BATY CUNNINGHAM
OF THE CLASS OF 1917
YALE COLLEGE

Elizabeth

EMPRESS OF AUSTRIA

BY COUNT EGON CORTI

TRANSLATED BY

CATHERINE ALISON PHILLIPS

NEW HAVEN

YALE UNIVERSITY PRESS

PRINTED IN THE UNITED STATES OF AMERICA

First published, April, 1936
Second printing, June, 1936
Third printing, February, 1937

PREFACE

MY PURPOSE IN THE PRESENT WORK has been to draw a picture, based upon none but genuine, trustworthy, and hitherto unpublished material, of a woman about whom one of her ladies in waiting, the Landgravine von Fürstenberg, once said: "Neither chisel nor brush can depict her as she really was, or that something about her which had such power to attract and captivate, for it was a thing peculiar to herself. She will live on in legend, not in history . . ."

In these pages my aim has been to bring her forth from the realms of legend into the full light of history, while always endeavoring to keep wholly to the truth. I need hardly insist that I have abstained alike from disparaging criticism and from the "byzantine" adulation of former days. Even when it has been necessary to touch upon delicate subjects, the figures of the Emperor and Empress can stand the full light of truth, and require neither indulgence nor servility. Frau von Ferenczy, a faithful servant of the Empress, was quite right when, in the course of an interview years after the revolution, she said to Hofrat Julian Weiss: "Let all the archives be thrown open! The result will only redound to the honor of the dynasty which is now so often unjustly attacked."

The record of every human creature must contain both light and shadow. In the present work they have been apportioned as my conscience and knowledge of the subject have dictated. When a human life does not turn out successfully, its tragedy lies in the frustration of good intentions. It is easy to judge such lives, but we must try to understand them.

In this work I have tried to help toward an understanding of the Empress Elizabeth by throwing light on the conditions in which she spent her life. Too many people—some of them crassly ignorant of the subject—have darkened counsel and confused people's judgment of this woman by sensation-mongering, romantic embellishments or downright fabrications. What was required was to establish her on a footing of sober truth, and so reveal her to the understanding and judgment of mankind.

I began by reading and collecting all the printed material bearing even remotely upon the subject, but was soon forced to recognize that extremely few printed works could be used at all for any serious work—in point of fact, only three, and these dealing only with fragments of the Empress' life. These are dealt with in detail in the Bibliography. It was soon clear that the work could only be carried out with any prospect of success if it were possible to collate a large number of unpublished documents in both public and private collections. I pursued my researches in country after country, in Austria, Hungary, Bavaria, England, and Switzerland, and succeeded in collecting material from the archives of the imperial house of Austria and the royal and ducal families of Bavaria, as well as from the various state archives and papers in the possession of private individuals, which proved infinitely richer than I could have dared to hope when I started upon my quest.

The documents of the most astounding importance among those which I was able to collect were the correspondence between the Emperor and Empress, the diary in many volumes kept by the Empress' daughter, the Archduchess Valerie, that of the Countess Marie Festetics, who spent twenty-seven years in the closest association with the Empress, and Elizabeth's correspondence with many royal and ordinary persons.

. . . . .

The sources will be discussed in detail in the Bibliography, but I have a debt of infinite gratitude to discharge to all those who have been so good as to lend me such valuable support in my work.

In England, I must express my particular gratitude to Mrs. Violet Borwick, daughter of Captain Bay Middleton, who piloted the Empress in the hunting field, to Lord and Lady Spencer, who, thanks to the kind offices of General Sir Aylmer Haldane, received me hospitably in their delightful home and assisted me in my inquiries, and to Margaret, Lady Langford.

Finally, I would offer my sincerest and heartiest thanks to the directors of the various state archives of which I have made use, and in particular to the Director and Secretary of the Public Record Office, London.

. . . . .

My hope is that this work may be received in the same spirit in which it was written, as an honest, independent, and truth-loving attempt to study the nature of an august lady who was in every respect a unique figure.

E. C.

TRANSLATOR'S NOTE

In view of the extreme inaccuracy of most accounts of the Empress Elizabeth hitherto published, every statement of importance in the original German text of the present work is substantiated by reference to letters, diaries, and other such documents, for the most part unpublished. As such exact documentation was not felt to be necessary for a non-Austrian public, the author has consented to the omission of most of these footnotes, for which those interested are referred to the German edition.

The translator would like to acknowledge her indebtedness to her husband, Professor W. Alison Phillips, for his kind assistance, especially in rendering some of the verses quoted in the book.

CONTENTS

ILLUSTRATIONS

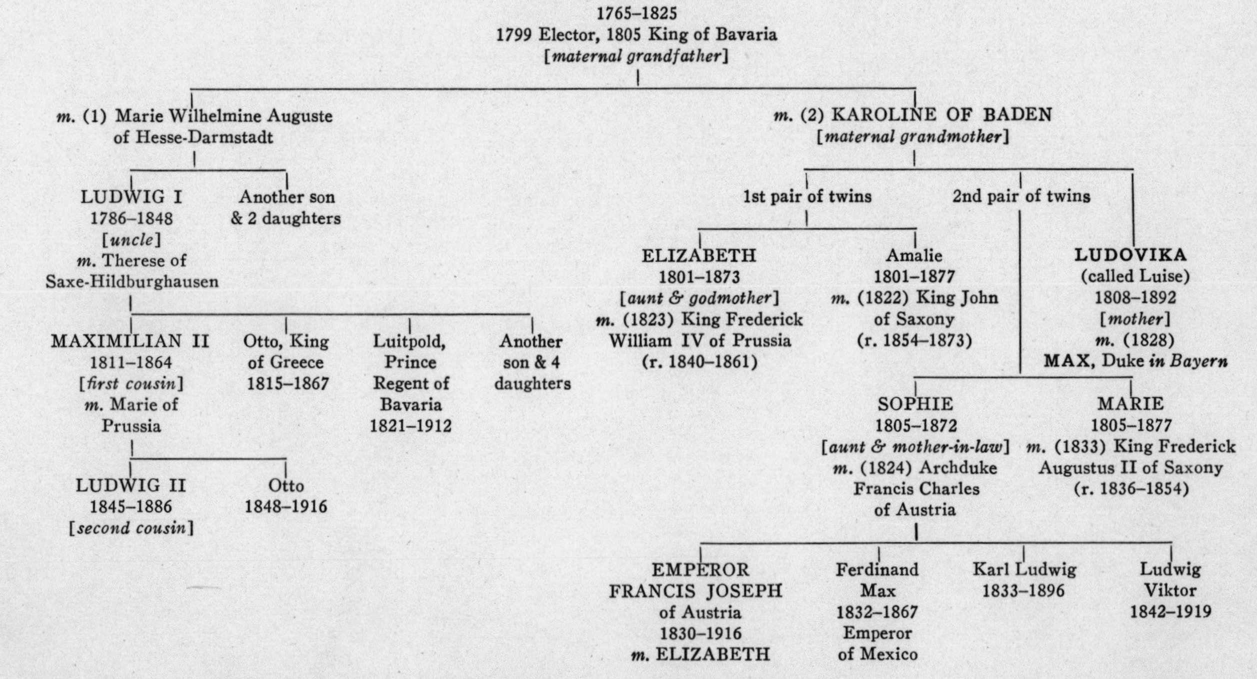

MAXIMILIAN I JOSEPH
1765–1825
1799 Elector, 1805 King of Bavaria
[maternal grandfather]
m. (1) Marie Wilhelmine Auguste of Hesse-Darmstadt
m. (2) KAROLINE OF BADEN
[maternal grandmother]
LUDWIG I
1786–1848
[uncle]
m. Therese of Saxe-Hildburghausen
Another son & 2 daughters
1st pair of twins
2nd pair of twins
ELIZABETH
1801–1873
[aunt & godmother]
m. (1823) King Frederick William IV of Prussia
(r. 1840–1861)
Amalie
1801–1877
m. (1822) King John of Saxony
(r. 1854–1873)
LUDOVIKA
(called Luise)
1808–1892
[mother]
m. (1828)
MAX, Duke in Bayern
MAXIMILIAN II
1811–1864
[first cousin]
m. Marie of Prussia
Otto, King of Greece
1815–1867
Luitpold, Prince Regent of Bavaria
1821–1912
Another son & 4 daughters
SOPHIE
1805–1872
[aunt & mother-in-law]
m. (1824) Archduke Francis Charles of Austria
MARIE
1805–1877
m. (1833) King Frederick Augustus II of Saxony
(r. 1836–1854)
LUDWIG II
1845–1886
[second cousin]
Otto
1848–1916
EMPEROR FRANCIS JOSEPH of Austria
1830–1916
m. ELIZABETH
Ferdinand Max
1832–1867
Emperor of Mexico
Karl Ludwig
1833–1896
Ludwig Viktor
1842–1919

MARIA ANNA, sister of **MAXIMILIAN I JOSEPH**
1753–1824
m. (1780) Wilhelm of Birkenfeld-Gelnhausen
1st Duke *"in Bayern"*
[*paternal great-grandparents*]

PIUS AUGUST
Duke *in Bayern*
m. (1807) Luise Julie, Princess d'Arenberg
[*paternal grandparents*]

MAX, Duke *in Bayern**
1808–1888
[*father*]
m. LUDOVIKA*

(1) Ludwig
1831–1891
m. (1859)
Henriette
Mendel,
created
Baroness
Wallersee
— Marie
Wallersee
(Countess Larisch)

(2) Wilhelm
d. in
infancy

(3) Helene
(Néné)
1834–1890
m. (1858)
Hereditary Prince
Maximilian of
Thurn and
Taxis

(4) **ELIZABETH**
(Sisi)
b. 24-xii-1837
d. 10-ix-1898
m. 24-iv-1854
EMPEROR
FRANCIS
JOSEPH OF
AUSTRIA
(1830–1916)

- Sophie
1855–1857
- Gisela
1856–1932
m. (1873) Prince
Leopold of Bavaria
- RUDOLF
1858–1889
m. (1881) Princess
Stephanie of Belgium
- Marie Valerie
1868–1924
m. (1890) Archduke
Franz Salvator of Austria

(5) Karl
Theodor
(Gackel)
1839–1910
m. (1865)
(1) Sophie of
Saxony
m. (2) (1874)
Maria José,
Infanta of
Portugal

(6) Marie
1841–1894
m. (1859)
Francis II,
King of
Naples

(7) Mathilde
(Spatz)
1843–1886
m. (1861)
Louis
de Bourbon,
Count of
Trani

(8) Sophie
1847–1897
m. (1868)
Duc
d'Alençon

(9) Max Emanuel
(Mapperl)
1849–1893
m. (1875)
Princess
Amalie
of
Coburg

* Second cousins.

ELIZABETH

EMPRESS OF AUSTRIA

I

HOME LIFE

1837–1853

FOR MORE THAN SEVEN HUNDRED YEARS the House of Wittelsbach had ruled over Bavaria. Few princes of this house were ordinary, average men—certainly none of the kings who reigned during the nineteenth century, all of whom had decided leanings toward either poetry, science, painting, or music and worshiped beauty in one form or another.

The Elector Max Joseph, who in 1805 was raised to the rank of King by Napoleon with the style of Maximilian I, was descended from a collateral branch of the House of Wittelsbach. He was particularly attached to one of his cousins, Duke Wilhelm of Birkenfeld-Gelnhausen, who was descended from another collateral branch, and on succeeding to the Electorate in 1799 conferred upon him the rank of a Bavarian Duke, with the title "Duke in Bavaria" (*Herzog in Bayern*), so as not to infringe upon the dignity of the title "Duke of Bavaria" (*Herzog von Bayern*), borne by the older and prouder line. Till then this collateral branch had had no territorial possessions or official princely residence, but now it was better off materially, too, and settled permanently in Munich.

King Maximilian married twice and had no less than

twelve children. Among those by his first wife, a Princess of Hesse-Darmstadt, was Ludwig, afterwards King Ludwig I. He inherited from his mother a gay disposition, a violent temper, and a tendency to eccentricity, but he was a decidedly likable sovereign, with a number of qualities which were to reappear later in more than one member of the Bavarian family; for instance, a mischievous wit, an enthusiasm for art, a love of Greek antiquity, and a strong national feeling. Though not possessed of much literary talent, he wrote poetry and used his royal power to gratify his enthusiasm for all that was noble and beautiful. Nor was his cult of beauty confined to poetry and painting. Few men have been more sensitive to feminine charm, and the famous *Schönheitsgalerie* (gallery of beauties) which he founded contained, side by side with portraits of royal princesses, ladies about the court, and actresses, one of a worthy shoemaker's lovely daughter. It is significant, too, that beside the portrait of the celebated Lola Montez, who played such a fateful part in the King's life, hung that of a beautiful Greek lady, Katharina Botzaris, as testimony to the King's enthusiasm for ancient Greece and for the modern Greeks in their fight for independence, which led him to accept the throne of Greece for his son Otto in 1832.

The "gallery of beauties" also contained a portrait of one of King Ludwig's sisters, the Princess Sophie. Among King Maximilian's children by the second marriage had been two pairs of twin daughters, the younger of which, born in 1805, included Sophie, who was married to the Archduke Francis Charles of Austria in 1824, and Marie, who became the wife of King Frederick Augustus II of Saxony. Of the elder pair of twins, Elizabeth became Queen of Prussia, while Amalie married Prince John of Saxony, who succeeded his brother Frederick Augustus II as King in 1854.

Sophie was distinguished for her imposing personality,

THE ARCHDUCHESS SOPHIE OF AUSTRIA

From an engraving by Kriehuber.

strength of will, and devotion to the Catholic faith. She was also far more ambitious than any of her sisters, one of the younger of whom, Ludovika, had been promised in marriage to Duke Max in Bayern, of the Birkenfeld line, while she was still a child. This marriage, which took place on September 5, 1828, was ominous on account of the close relationship between the bride and bridegroom, who were cousins. The match had been arranged by their parents without consulting their inclinations, and they ended by living apart, though this did not prevent them from producing a numerous family.

Even in his youth Duke Max in Bayern had been restless and fond of travel, and fate was kind to him; for, being exempt from the duties and cares of a sovereign, he was able to indulge his hobbies to his heart's content. For a time marriage kept this restless husband settled in the capital, where a palace was built for him and his wife. His eldest son, Ludwig, was born on June 21, 1831. Both in him and in the other children the psychological effects of inbreeding took the form of an even stronger tendency to shyness, solitude, and nervous restlessness than that which had appeared in a mild form in more than one branch of the descendants of Maximilian I.

The Duke and Duchess traveled about Switzerland and Italy and on returning home in 1834 bought the castle of Possenhofen as a summer residence for their growing family. It is about eighteen miles from Munich on the lovely Starnbergersee, surrounded by wooded hills. The squat building, flanked by four heavy towers, stands in a delightful park with a lovely rose garden stretching down to the shores of the lake. On fine days there is a view across lake and forests as far as the snowy peaks of the Wetterstein Mountains and the Zugspitze. The castle was soon converted into a comfortable residence, known to the ducal family as "Possi."

On April 4, 1834, was born the eldest daughter, who was baptized Helene, but called Néné for short. Three years later, on Christmas Eve, 1837, the Duchess gave birth to another daughter,* who was ushered into life to a due accompaniment of court ceremonial. She was born at forty-three minutes past ten at night, and had hardly come into the world before the Ministers whose duty it was to act as witnesses were introduced into the Duchess' white boudoir, where the midwife showed them the newborn princess. The Duchess' room was full of ladies and gentlemen, who duly admired the baby and noticed that, as in the case of Napoleon, it had been born with one tooth already through. The courtiers interpreted this as a lucky omen, especially as the little Princess was not only a Christmas gift from heaven, but also a "Sunday's child." Queen Elizabeth of Prussia was invited to be godmother, and the child was given her name, but as long as she lived she was known to her family as "Sisi."

Only four weeks after little Elizabeth's birth, her father started out on a long journey in the East. He was particularly eager to tread the classic soil of Greece, for, like Ludwig I, Duke Max was an ardent philhellene and followed the fortunes of his nephew Otto on the royal throne of Athens with tense interest. Yet on arriving there he omitted to visit his kinsman. What he wanted was to know the land and its people, not to take part in court festivities and ceremonies, for which he cared very little even at home. Continuing his travels, he visited Cairo, where he bought four little negro boys in the slave market and took them home with him, where they created quite a sensation. All Munich was present at their baptism, for though his whimsicalities were well known, this one struck the people of Munich as supremely comical.

* The Archduchess Valerie had collected material, partly supplied by the Empress herself, for a biography of her. This material is now in the archives at Schloss Wallsee (see Bibliography). The account of the Empress' childhood is partly based upon this.

After this journey the Duke devoted himself with redoubled energy to his literary efforts, at first concealing his identity under the pseudonym of "Phantasus." His poems were of no great merit; indeed, his literary works dealt with the strangest and most fantastic subjects, though he also indulged in little dialect poems, rhymed jingles, and lively verses, which he sang to the zither, his favorite instrument.

Gay and rather prankish, he knew nothing of royal reserve, and welcomed anyone talented who was also good company, till he became the center of a lively circle drawn largely from the middle classes. He gave banquets and drinking parties and, being himself a good rider and a lover of horses, got up performances in the riding school which he had built adjoining his palace. Here he would himself give displays of horsemanship, or entertain his guests with mounted quadrilles, pantomimes, and hunting scenes.

The Duke cared little for politics. He preferred the rôle of a silent observer and pitied those whose professional duties forced them to take part in them. His researches into history had made him a liberal. Indifferent to his wife, and with no strong family feeling, he made only short and passing visits to his family. Yet he loved the Starnbergersee and the country around it, and imparted his love of nature to his children. His daughter Sisi took after him to a great extent and entered into his hobbies with special understanding. Though he had long left his youth behind him, Duke Max was still overflowing with life and spirits. Yet at times his gaiety would be abruptly overshadowed by a fit of gloom.

The burden of bringing up the children was left to their simpler and more modest mother, who only smiled when she heard that her husband had set up a Round Table of fourteen "knights," over which he presided in the character of King Arthur. One of the most jovial was Kaspar Braun, founder of the well-known comic paper, *Fliegende Blätter.*

These knights varied their copious drinking bouts by a game known as the "*Leberreim,*" which was popular in those days and consisted in finding impromptu rhymes to the verse: "The liver of a pike it is, and not that of a —— (sable),"* or whatever animal seemed to suggest an amusing rhyme.

The Duchess left her husband to follow his own sweet will and concentrated her thoughts upon her children's future. She had no far-reaching political ambitions of her own, but was influenced by her energetic sister, the Archduchess Sophie. She allowed her children to grow up free and untrammeled, so that they had a merrier and more carefree youth than might have been expected in view of the relations between their parents.

The three eldest children were followed by five more, arriving at intervals of about two years, beginning and ending with sons, and with three daughters coming in between. In 1839 was born Karl Theodor, known in the family circle as "Gackel" (cock), who was soon to become the devoted companion of his sister Sisi, his elder by two years. Next came Marie in 1841, then in 1843 Mathilde, jestingly nicknamed "Spatz" (sparrow) because she was so gentle, and four years later Sophie. Last of all came Max Emanuel, known as "Mapperl." They were a very united and loyal family. In winter they romped about the palace in Munich and in summer about the garden at Possenhofen, and their unwelcome tutors and masters had no easy time of it, for lessons were not their favorite occupation, least of all Sisi's.

When she was nine years old, her nurse was replaced by a certain Baroness Luise Wulffen. "Helene's character," wrote the Baroness to a friend in 1846, "is such as to make me feel it desirable to separate her from her sister Elizabeth. Without being a bad child, she has a bad influence on her sister, who is far gentler and very conscientious by nature. But the

* *"Die Leber ist von einem Hecht und nicht von einem —— (Zobel)."*

elder sister dominates her. . . ." The Baroness therefore took tactful measures to keep the sisters apart and threw Elizabeth more into the society of Karl Theodor.

At the age of nine Sisi was not particularly pretty, but she had an irresistible charm and was a general favorite at home. When the children wanted to coax their mother into giving them anything, Sisi was always solemnly deputed as their ambassadress. She rejoiced when they left town for the country, for in her eyes Possenhofen was a paradise, where she could look after her pets, of which she had innumerable quantities, being at one time or another mistress of a roe, a lamb, some rabbits, and a wonderful flock of fowls and guinea fowl. The poor Baroness Wulffen had her hands full, for her little charge was forever escaping from her in the great park. Sisi was never still, and her fondness for drawing was the only thing that would occasionally keep her settled quietly on a campstool. She would sketch her pets, the trees in the park, the distant Alps, or her beloved Possi, and was already beginning to draw clumsy little caricatures of those about her, especially of her governess; but at that time landscape was her favorite subject. She was tormented with piano lessons, but made little progress, for she had not much feeling for music.

Children belonging to the good families in the neighborhood would come and see them, especially the family of Count Paumgartten, with whose little daughter, Irene, Sisi was on the best of terms. The little Countess was rather dreamy and often had the oddest ideas, but this appealed to the Princess. Sisi was secretly beginning to write poetry—very awkward, childish verses, but her little friend thought them lovely. These literary attempts grew more frequent as she became older, for her father's blood was coming out in her. Duke Max did not spend much time with his children, however. He was away so much that they did not miss him very greatly, and once, when a lady asked her whether she had seen her father, who had been back for some days after one of his frequent absences, Elizabeth replied: "No, but I have heard him whistling!"

Duke Max would sometimes appear unexpectedly in the middle of lesson time, but not with any intention of holding an examination. On the contrary, he would interrupt the lessons and carry the children off to the garden amid loud shouts to plunder the fruit trees; or else he would bring a little band with him, and there would be a concert and dancing. If he happened to be in a good temper, the children would take advantage of it by appealing to his paternal authority to obtain something which they had been unable to get from their mother.

They always had breakfast with their mother at eight o'clock sharp, after which lessons went on till two o'clock in the afternoon. But Sisi did not work as hard as her sisters and, whenever her governess turned her back, would sit looking out of the window. She was glad when lessons were over and the children could make expeditions to the other bank of the Isar, or through the park to Bogenhausen, or somewhere else out in the country.

When she was eleven or twelve, Sisi's face was as round as that of any little peasant girl and showed no trace of beauty. As the mother of five daughters, the Duchess Ludovika often had anxious moments of wondering how she was to find good marriages for them all; but in the meantime they led a merry life. During the summer holidays their mother would make short excursions into the mountains, taking the elder children with her. In this way Néné and Sisi, with their two older brothers, saw the Passion Play at Oberammergau, afterwards going on into Austria, to the Aachensee, Jenbach, and Innsbruck.

Meanwhile the state of affairs in Austria was causing their

DUKE MAX IN BAVARIA

From a water color in the possession of H.I.H.
the Countess Waldburg-Zeil.

Aunt Sophie great anxiety. During the 'forties, in the later days of the Metternich régime, discontent had increased alarmingly not only in Hungary and Italy, but in the very center of the Empire. Her heart burning with ambition, Sophie followed the march of events at the side of her weak-willed husband and was far from approving of Metternich's policy in placing the Archduke Ferdinand on the throne, for he was mentally deficient, and she saw clearly that the object of this move had been to secure absolute power for the Chancellor. She felt that his selfish policy was doing untold harm to the prestige of the imperial family and angrily rebelled against it. But since her husband, the Archduke Francis Charles, was the next heir, sooner or later there would have to be a change. Unfortunately, though honest, good-natured, and well-meaning, her husband was quite incapable of guiding the tangled destinies of the Empire with a firm hand; and though she would be at his side with her advice and assistance, she felt that things might be very different if a clever, energetic, fresh ruler were working under her direction. After all, she had no less than four healthy, promising sons. The eldest in particular, Francis Joseph, born in 1830, was a fine young man, and not only the apple of his mother's eye but the hope of Austria. When he grew up, she would be able to seize the right moment for getting rid of Metternich and all his ways.

But events moved faster than she had expected. When the February Revolution of 1848 broke out in France, the people of Vienna could no longer be kept down. On March 30 the Chancellor fled; his system fell with him, and risings took place in Lombardy, Venetia, and radical Hungary, which hoped to secure its independence.

The Archduchess Sophie had long been convinced that changes in the government of the Empire were necessary, but she had not wanted them to come about through insurrection and revolution. She saw that the people were not content with the concessions granted after the fall of Metternich, but were turbulently demanding more. The Archduchess, "the only man in the State," as she has been called, was convinced of the necessity of crushing insurrection not only in the south and east, but also in the capital, by means of the army, which had so far been loyal. She remained firm and unbending, and the direction of the counter-revolutionary measures seemed to fall naturally into her hands. She hated the Italians in the south, who had rebelled at the moment of the Empire's dire extremity, but she hated the Hungarians even more, for in her opinion they were trying to split the Empire in half and incite the army to disaffection. She did not understand Hungary's desire for autonomy, a constitution, and its ancient rights and privileges. She was indignant when the Archduke Stephen, the Palatine of Hungary, consented to the formation of an independent responsible ministry with Count Louis Batthyány at its head, and she admiringly approved the action of General Count Charles Grünne, the Archduke's chamberlain, who asked to be relieved of his office when the Archduke yielded to the Hungarians. She noted the episode carefully and resolved to reward him for it one day.

But the insecurity grew worse and worse. On May 15, 1848, the insurgents prepared to advance in procession on the Hofburg. The lives of the imperial family were threatened, and all, including the Archduchess, were filled with alarm. It was impossible, she considered, to negotiate under such pressure as this, so she did not oppose the flight of the Emperor and his family to Innsbruck, which took place under the pretext of an ordinary pleasure excursion. The Archduchess followed with her three eldest sons, Francis Joseph, her favorite Max, and the amiable Karl Ludwig. In the loyal Tirol, she thought, it might be possible to breathe freely, concert what steps were to be taken next, take measures for suppressing the revolution, and work toward the restoration of the Empire.

Meanwhile the Bavarian sisters stood by one another loyally. It was not far from Munich to Innsbruck, and in June, 1848, the Duchess Ludovika brought two of her sons and her two eldest daughters on a visit to her sister. The cousins now met for the first time, but the eldest, Francis Joseph, took little notice of the others, for he was too much occupied with political events, knowing that the house which was threatening to collapse would one day be his own. Karl Ludwig, however, who was only fifteen, was attracted by his cousin Sisi, who was now eleven. He followed her everywhere, brought her flowers and fruit, and was in despair when the Duchess left Innsbruck with her children. He had quite fallen in love with his little cousin, and she was flattered when he wrote her beautiful letters in a marvelous copperplate hand.

The visit to Innsbruck was followed by a lively correspondence. In June, Karl Ludwig sent Sisi a ring and a rose, and she sent him a ring in return, with which, he assured her rapturously, he would never part. In reply to this she said that she, too, was wearing his ring, and went on to invite him to Possi and to tell him about the circus riders and tight ropedancers whom she had seen. Karl Ludwig wrote still more often in August and October and sent her a watch and chain which she had long desired. But though she thanked him heartily, she never wrote of her own accord, and her letters were like those of any nice little girl, telling him how delighted she was with the two "dear little lambs" given her by her Mamma, which were so tame that they followed her everywhere, and what fun they had on their country excursions or water parties, and how nice it would be if their cousins could be there to share them. As time went on, the correspondence became less frequent, though on New Year's Day, 1850, the Archduke sent his cousin a bracelet, for which

Sisi thanked him in her small, dainty, girlish handwriting, on blue notepaper with a border of flowers and red roses.

The Archduchess Sophie's motherly heart saw the little idyll with approval; but this was no time for idylls. The situation inside the Empire was far too critical. The radicals under Kossuth had gained the upper hand in Hungary. On September 28, 1848, Count Lamberg, the commander in chief of the imperial troops, was murdered in Budapest and open war broke out against insurgent Hungary. Risings also took place in Prague and Vienna.

The Archduchess Sophie had watched these developments with horror and was more determined than ever to take drastic steps to put down revolution. The Emperor Ferdinand seemed to personify the weakness of the imperial house, and he could no longer be tolerated. And now the plans which she had so long been preparing were carried into effect. On August 18 her eldest son, Francis Joseph, had turned eighteen, and his majority was proclaimed. On this occasion Sophie attached General Count Grünne to her son's service as Controller of his Household, to mark her approval of his anti-Hungarian opinions. The Batthyány ministry, the coolheaded liberal minister, Francis von Deák, and Baron Ëotvös, also celebrated as a poet, retired, embittered, into private life. The younger members of the great Hungarian families, among them Count Julius Andrássy, now aged twenty-six, were forced into the arms of the radicals.

On December 2, 1848, the Emperor Ferdinand abdicated and Francis Joseph succeeded to the throne. When the ceremonies were over, he sank sobbing with emotion into his mother's arms. The Archduchess might well take credit to herself for having done her best to prepare her son for his task. For his sake she had even sacrificed her own husband's rights of succession and renounced the outward pomps of an empress for herself; but she meant to be the real mistress, watching over and guiding the young Emperor's first steps. Francis Joseph was shrewd and endowed with a quick understanding. He soon grasped that his duty in life was to work hard, and for this he was well suited by temperament. But he imagined the situation to be simpler than it really was.

He was naturally filled with boundless gratitude to his mother, so that during the earlier years of his reign he was entirely under her influence. The Archduchess Sophie was a politically minded woman and had directed her eldest son's education into like channels. The idea which she had most at heart was that of the greatness and unity of Austria, and what subsequently happened can be traced to this fundamental idea. Francis Joseph had no intellectual tendencies that were likely to make him rebel against her guidance. He had no feeling for music or literature, and even in his early youth his ideas were characterized by clearness and sober realism. For the present, however, he was content to follow his mother's lead.

The task that now awaited her and the men who were devoted to her ideas was to develop the program announced by public proclamation, which was as follows: "In common with my peoples, to fuse together into one great State all the lands and races of the monarchy." But such a common effort was not easy to obtain. It had to be won by armed force. With heavy hearts the rulers in Vienna had to make up their minds to call in the aid of the Tsar, which was bound to lead, sooner or later, to the collapse of Hungary's resistance and the frustration of Kossuth's aims.

In Italy, meanwhile, thanks to the army, which had remained loyal, Radetzky had crushed the risings in Lombardy and Venetia, which had had the support of Piedmont. The King of Sardinia was forced to make peace, and the people grudgingly submitted to armed force. Lombardy and Venetia had been subdued, but they continued to long for their ideal of national liberty and from this time onward opposed a passive resistance even to the most well-meaning efforts of their rulers. But revolution in Italy was handled much more gently than in Hungary, where the brutal Haynau was given a free hand after the capitulation of Világos. Thirteen generals who had taken part in the Hungarian rising were mercilessly hanged or shot. Unfortunately the Emperor Francis Joseph, or rather the Archduchess Sophie, failed to prevent these bloody sentences, for they had been convinced by those about them of the supposed necessity of making a terrible example. Even the Minister President, Count Louis Batthyány, was executed. Innumerable Hungarians were imprisoned, while others, many of whom, like Count Julius Andrássy, belonged to the most noble families in the land, fled abroad. The terrible impression made by these executions and also by the murders committed by the rebels remained like a black cloud between the ruling house with its centralizing Austrian policy, on the one hand, and Hungary with its aspirations toward liberty and a constitution, on the other.

The revolution had now been crushed everywhere, and the way lay open for a policy of reaction. The Austrian Constitution of March, 1849, now recognized only a State "one and indivisible," including the "Crown Land of Hungary," while Lombardy and Venetia became mere provinces. Yet in spite of all, Hungary continued to aspire toward independence, and Count Julius Andrássy, who had been hanged in effigy for the part he had played in the revolution, still cherished this ideal in exile. For the present, however, there was nothing to be done, and Hungary had to submit to the victorious Government in Vienna.

The Government now had a free hand and could once more turn its attention to Germany, where it hoped to check Prussia's aspirations toward hegemony. Thanks to his mother's family connections, Francis Joseph could count upon Bavaria, so he was able to mature plans for overthrowing the March Constitution at home and returning to a régime of autocracy. In this he was in accord with his mother's wishes and those of Count Grünne, who had been appointed his Adjutant General and was in control of the army. The great Austrian aristocracy grouped about the court shared these wishes, too, as did also the clergy, led by Archbishop Rauscher, which was in close touch with the Archduchess Sophie.

But Italy and Hungary merely tolerated the existing situation while waiting for better times. The Archduchess Sophie had triumphed. Whatever may be thought of her policy, her well-directed strength and confidence at a most critical period had achieved what she held to be right and just. But the course she had followed had not made her popular. She was regarded as the head of a "court camarilla," and those about her, especially Grünne, whose power was increasing, were in the habit of referring to her in secret as "our Empress." "The Emperor's mother," as Redlich rightly says,* "was and continued to be the center and directing mind of the whole court." In spite of the assistance given to Austria by Russia, the Archduchess had little liking for that country or its heretic monarch, and her feelings had an influence on her son.

Thus the opening of the year 1853 saw the beginnings of a growing ill-feeling against Russia. Peace ostensibly prevailed within the Empire, but hostility was still alive beneath the surface.

* Joseph Redlich, *Kaiser Franz Joseph von Österreich* (Berlin, 1928), p. 52. English translation, 1929.

II

LOVE AT FIRST SIGHT AND BETROTHAL

1853–1854

THE GRAVEST POLITICAL ANXIETIES NOW seemed to be allayed, and the Archduchess Sophie felt she might now venture on a further step toward the realizing of her long-cherished plans. A favorite idea of hers was that of binding Bavaria, her native land, to Austria through fresh ties of relationship, thus also forwarding the interests of her own family.

The Emperor Francis Joseph was now twenty-two years of age, like a slender, elegant young lieutenant in general's uniform. Being entirely under his mother's influence, he would presumably accept without protest the wife she had selected for him. She had long since discussed with her sister at Munich the project of a marriage between him and the latter's eldest daughter, Néné.

A proposed alliance with the beautiful and clever daughter of the Palatine Joseph of Hungary did not meet with her approval. In her eyes Hungary was a subjugated province and must remain in that position. She regarded it as far more important that Austria should play the leading part in Germany and that a new matrimonial alliance with Bavaria should unite the Empire with one of the three most powerful German kingdoms. Reports from Munich were encouraging. The Duchess Ludovika wrote that her eldest daughter was growing up into a tall and very pretty girl, who knew her own mind and was incomparably more serious and sensible than the rest of her brothers and sisters.

Yet their mother was fonder of the others, and especially of Karl Theodor and Sisi. The latter in particular had developed amazingly. Till lately, in spite of her fascinating personality, she had remained an awkward, not very pretty schoolgirl, but now her appearance, too, underwent a change. Her features became more delicate and maidenly, while her dazzling golden hair, tinged with brown in her earlier years, was becoming astonishingly luxuriant and beautiful, in exquisite harmony with her eyes, as shy as those of a roe. But she was still quite a child, whereas Néné was already a young lady and was now learning to ride, though she was not particularly good at it. No sooner did Sisi see this than she was bent upon having lessons, too, and soon became the third pupil in the riding school. In less than no time she had surpassed her elder sister, for she did not know what fear meant.

As soon as Sisi returned home, she would hurry to her writing table and compose the poems which were her cherished secret. In April, 1853, she was confirmed. The occasion was to be celebrated in the usual way with excursions, theatricals, and games, but a shadow now fell over the festivities. David Paumgartten, her favorite playmate's little brother, was lying at death's door with inflammation of the lungs. For the first time Sisi became conscious of the seriousness of life. She was terribly distressed when her five-year-old playmate succumbed to his illness, and sadly composed some verses in memory of him.

Suddenly, she knew not how, a longing for death came over the young Princess, though her life at home was so merry. The little events of her life, the regular moves from Munich to Possenhofen and back again, were important landmarks in her eyes. She was disturbed by emotions which she hardly understood, and her heart was always restless and agitated.

Tears and laughter are so closely allied, and, though a roguish sprite peeped out from her eyes, tears often won the day; though she was often gay, it was vague longings, love's yearnings and ecstasies that found expression in her letters and in the poems which she preserved as her most sacred treasure in a small manuscript book.* The verses are often written in red ink and illustrated with little sketches.

Sisi was in her fifteenth year when at the ducal court she became acquainted with a young man who made a deep impression upon her, and whose fine brown eyes quite haunted her, as she confessed in a poem.

She would linger by the hedge and wait for him to go by, but at last people began to notice this. Her romance was discovered and came to a hasty end. The young man's portrait was taken from her, and she was ruthlessly cross-questioned to find out how it had come into her possession. The fair dream was over, and she celebrated its passing in a poem entitled "*Vorbei!*" (Past!) The young man was sent away on some mission and stayed away for a long time. When he returned, he was ill, though this was kept a secret from Sisi. But his illness went from bad to worse, and soon the object of her first childish romance also died. This formed the subject of another poem entitled "*An Ihn*" (To Him), beginning with the lines:

Once more the die has fallen
And Richard is no more!

and illustrated with a touchingly clumsy little drawing in which a funeral procession is seen issuing from a gate, with figures like a child's tin soldiers to left and right of the coffin.

Elizabeth's mother observed her little daughter's strange

* This little book is now in the possession of the Empress' granddaughter, H.I.H. the Countess Waldburg-Zeil, at Schloss Syrgenstein (see Bibliography).

behavior with some anxiety. Her merriment seemed to have disappeared. When she was spoken to, her eyes often filled with tears. Horses were now her only pleasure, but she always wanted to ride alone, and sought solitude, which could not be allowed. Her thoughts returned persistently to him who was dead. But soon new impressions came to efface the old, for, after all, she was still very young. Winter came again, and the roofs were covered with snow, but soon a warm wind changed the scene as by magic. How like grief, she thought—and how like love, "which melts away faster than the winter's snow."

Other people now entered her life. There was a young Count F. R. who often visited the ducal court, and once again ecstatic love poems found their way into her book, though this time it was a pair of blue eyes that had touched her heart. One of the poems shows her asking the first rays of morning whether they have kissed her loved one, and praying the golden moon to carry him a nightly message of love. . . . This infatuation lasted for a few months, but since her feelings were not requited this experience too had to come to a painful end, and a final poem confesses that at last she has seen the "hard truth" and knows that he has only friendship to offer her.

But she was too proud to linger over such thoughts. She took refuge with her horses, and as she galloped across country the pains of love faded away. She was allowed great freedom, for among so many children there was no time to worry about her overmuch. Besides, everybody was preoccupied with Néné's future, and great plans were being made for her.

The eldest daughter was to be an empress—empress of the mighty Danubian empire which had now renewed its strength—perhaps even ruler over a greater Germany united with Austria. She must learn languages, dancing, and riding, go a great deal into society, and practice receiving a large circle of people and saying the right thing to them. It was Néné here and Néné there, and little Sisi and her troubles attracted scant attention. Spring went by and summer arrived, and one day their mother announced to them: "In August Néné and Sisi are going with me to Ischl to see Aunt Sophie. Isn't that nice, children? We have been invited, and perhaps the Emperor will be there too."

The Duchess' sister, the Queen of Prussia, was already at Ischl, and great decisions were pending. Francis Joseph knew more or less what was in the air and was so impatient that he left for Ischl with his swiftest horses. On the way there Count Grünne discussed with him the Eastern Question and relations with Russia, but his thoughts were elsewhere, for he was far more curious to know what the cousin was like to whom they possibly meant to marry him. He had not seen her since 1848, though he had heard all sorts of things about her. The journey to Ischl usually took thirty hours on horseback, but the Emperor covered it in nineteen. This delightful spot had been chosen as a summer residence for the imperial family on account of its mineral springs, which had once cured the Archduke Rudolf, Cardinal Archbishop of Olmütz, besides which it had excellent hunting to offer. The visitors did not rent a house at first, and the Duchess Ludovika and her daughters had rooms taken for them in a hotel.

On August 15 they arrived an hour and a half later than they were expected. Their boxes had not yet come, so that they could not change their clothes, but when the Archduchess Sophie looked at Néné and Sisi she saw their dazzling youthful freshness which could not be disguised by their simple traveling costumes. They made a hasty toilet, and the Archduchess sent for her own maid, who dressed Néné's hair carefully, while Sisi gracefully arranged her own. The attendant made a few admiring remarks to the Duchess about both the princesses, but what charmed her most were Sisi's glorious hair and, above all, her charm. At last they all went to the drawing room, where the Emperor was waiting. Their greetings were a little formal, for even Francis Joseph was shy and the Princess Helene was quite embarrassed. She knew very well what was at stake, while the Emperor had that unpleasant feeling which a man has when people are trying to marry him more or less against his will. He saw before him a tall, slender, beautiful girl, but though she was only twenty there was something hard and energetic in her face which was accentuated by her momentary shyness.

The younger sister, on the other hand, was quite unconcerned. She did not like parties and family festivities, especially when foreign relatives were present, nor was she as much accustomed to society as her elder sister, who had been going out for some years past; but she knew, or at least guessed, what was going on, and cast furtive glances at the Emperor and her sister, curious to observe their demeanor. And now all of a sudden she saw that Francis Joseph was not so much interested in Néné as in herself. When he thought himself unobserved, his eyes turned as though spellbound toward Sisi's soft, delicate figure, her bright hair, and the sweet expression on her childlike face, and suddenly his self-consciousness was at an end—but so were his peace of mind and unconcern. Sisi blushed hotly and glanced shyly at Karl Ludwig. But his jealous eye had at once noticed that his brother was looking more at Sisi, whom he himself admired, than at Néné, in whom he ought by rights to have been interested. When they sat down to table, Sisi became quite uncomfortable under the Emperor's constant scrutiny. She was sitting with her governess at the far end of the table, and now turned to her and said in a low voice: "Oh, it is all very well for Néné. She has already met lots of people, but I have not. I am so nervous I can hardly eat."* Early the next morning the jealous Karl Ludwig remarked to his mother: "Mamma, Franzi liked Sisi very much, far better than Néné. You will see, he will choose her instead of the elder one." "What an idea!" said the Archduchess soothingly. "That romp (*Fratz*)!"

But Karl Ludwig was right, for jealousy is clearsighted. Francis Joseph was fascinated by Sisi. On the morning of August 17 the Archduchess Sophie was hardly out of bed when her son came to her room and said excitedly: "Do you know that Sisi is enchanting?" "Sisi?" replied the Archduchess in astonishment. "But she is only a child." "I dare say. But look at her hair, her eyes, her charm, her whole figure! She is delicious!" Not a word about Néné. "Gently!" said his mother. "You know nothing about her yet and must examine her more closely. You have plenty of time, there is no hurry. Nobody expects you to become engaged at once." "No, no! It is better not to take too long over such things," was the reply, and off he rushed in the hope of seeing Sisi again before dinner.

Failing to find her, he returned to his mother and talked excitedly of everything in the world except Sisi, but it was evident that he was thinking of nothing else. At table the same byplay was repeated as on the evening before. His eyes never left her; he almost forgot Néné, who was sitting at his side, and did not speak a word to her, while Sisi, sitting at the far end of the table between Ludwig of Hesse and the Archduchess Sophie, hardly knew which way to look for em-

* This account of the betrothal is based upon a letter from the Archduchess Sophie to her sister, the Queen of Saxony, an incorrect translation of which appeared in Marion Gilbert's *Elizabeth de Wittelsbach*. A copy of it is among the papers of Frau Ida von Ferenczy, now in the possession of Frau Elizabeth von Farkas.

THE EMPEROR FRANCIS JOSEPH
BEFORE HIS ACCESSION, 1847

From a lithograph by Eybl.

barrassment. The Prince of Hesse did not know what was going on. He only saw that his charming little neighbor sat blushing at his side and hardly touched her dinner. "So far Sisi has eaten nothing but some soup and salad," he remarked in surprise to the Emperor's mother. "She must be fasting for some reason or another."

But the embarrassment which was dyeing Sisi's cheeks with such rosy hues was already mingled with a touch of triumph and pleasure at the notice which the Emperor was taking of her entirely of his own accord. The afternoon Francis Joseph again spent with his mother. He was not calm enough for anything else, for she was the only person with whom he could discuss the matter. It was now arranged that at the ball that evening, instead of dancing the cotillion with the elder princess as had been settled, and, indeed, as etiquette required, he was to dance it with Sisi, and anyone accustomed to court balls knows what that means. To dance twice in succession with the same lady in the cotillion almost amounts to a declaration. In the evening the two sisters and their mother appeared at the ball, Néné in a splendid white silk dress with a garland of ivy round her brow, Sisi in a dainty light pink and white muslin dress, with a little diamond arrow holding the golden-brown waves of her hair back from her brow. As she entered the room every eye was upon her, for it was already known that she had bewitched the Emperor, though she did not think he was really in earnest yet. Her manner toward Francis Joseph was as unembarrassed as ever, and she held out her hand to him frankly and without constraint, but it frightened her to be stared at by all those other people. The Emperor did not dance the first or second polka, but said to his mother: "I should like to see Sisi dance." So the Archduchess sent an aide-de-camp, Major Baron Weckbecker, to her little niece, and he asked her to dance the second polka. Sisi danced well, though it was evident that she was fresh from the dancing class. She could feel how Francis Joseph looked at her as if he could not tear his eyes away. Midnight came round, and in accordance with the charming, gay old custom, the leader of the cotillion marshaled the dancers, and the great moment arrived. The Emperor danced with Sisi. And now everyone could see what was happening—everyone, at least, but the person principally concerned. She saw how, in addition to the usual flowers, Francis Joseph offered her all the rest of the bouquets, which he should really have presented to the other ladies with whom he had danced. But when she was asked after the ball whether this had not surprised her, all she replied was: "No, it only embarrassed me."

On the following day, August 18, the Emperor's twenty-third birthday, the rain poured. It was impossible to go out all the morning, so they stayed indoors. Everybody had got up late, except Francis Joseph, who had been unable to sleep and again visited his mother's room early. At luncheon Sisi already sat beside Francis Joseph, and Néné was at the far end of the table where Sisi had sat the day before. The Emperor was radiant, kept looking at Sisi rapturously, and was gay and talkative. After luncheon Néné, the Emperor, his mother, and Sisi went for a drive in a closed carriage, for the weather had improved a little. But the only one who talked was Néné—she talked rather loud, volubly and gaily, but it produced a somewhat forced and artificial impression. The drive did not last very long. When they got home again, the Emperor had a private talk with his mother and requested her to go and ask the Duchess Ludovika to sound Sisi as to whether she would accept him as her husband. "But please beg her not to bring the slightest pressure to bear upon Sisi, for my position is such a difficult one that God knows it is no pleasure to share it with me."

"But, my dear child," replied his mother, "how can you

suppose that any woman would not be happy to brighten your life by her charm and gaiety?" The Archduchess saw that she would have to reconcile herself to the fact that her son's wife would be not the sensible Néné, but Sisi, who was half a child. At the bottom of her heart she felt it to be absurd. An empress ought to be a mature woman, not a child who had still to be educated. But what was to be done? Men are none too ready to allow their mothers to dictate to them whom they are to marry. After all, Francis Joseph was obeying her in part, for he was marrying a sister of the princess she had chosen for him. Besides, she thought, men are all alike. They will always marry a pretty face, even if everything else is as open to question as in this case. The Emperor's mother felt sure that further objections on her part would be useless and might even endanger her plan of a marriage between Francis Joseph and one of her sister's daughters. She therefore decided to yield, though not without certain mental reservations. "I shall take Sisi in hand," she thought, "and form her, so that she may become what I think an empress ought to be." Sophie now informed her sister Ludovika of the Emperor's wish. With tears in her eyes Sisi's mother clasped the Archduchess' hand in great agitation, for up to the last moment she had feared lest her sister's plans might come to nothing. And after all, the fact that they were being fulfilled in such an unexpected way must be ascribed to *force majeure.*

After tea some Tirolese singers gave a performance in the dining room. On going to her room for a moment, the Archduchess Sophie met Rodi, Sisi's governess, and said to her hastily: "This evening the Duchess Ludovika will tell Sisi that the Emperor wishes her to be his wife." In great excitement Rodi hurried to tell Sisi. In the evening her mother came to her and was about to tell her how matters stood, when the child gave her to understand that she knew already.

When asked whether she could love the Emperor, she broke down completely and burst into tears. "How could I not love him?" she replied. "But how can he think of me? I am so young and unimportant. I would do everything to make the Emperor happy, but will it be a success?"

On the following day, the nineteenth, Sisi poured out her heart to her governess, weeping. "Yes, I am already fond of the Emperor," she said, "if only he were not an emperor!" Her future rank alarmed her. She could hardly collect her thoughts and simply could not understand all that had come upon her so suddenly, though everybody around her spoke of it as an unspeakable piece of good fortune. After her talk with Sisi, during which the child wept a great deal and said very little, her mother wrote a touching little note to the Archduchess Sophie telling her of Sisi's consent. It was hardly more than seven o'clock in the morning when the Archduchess sent on the note to Francis Joseph, who hurried in to see her immediately, radiant with delight. Before eight o'clock he was at the hotel, where he first met the Duchess, thanked her and told her how happy he was, then left her unceremoniously and rushed off to find Sisi. She was already up and came to the door, where Francis Joseph threw open his arms, clasped her to his breast, and kissed her as if he were half wild with happiness. Elise of Prussia arrived just at this moment and saw the whole scene. She reported it to the Archduchess Sophie laughingly but enthusiastically, and now the sisters forgot Néné and all their previous plans and only rejoiced that one of their nieces, at any rate, was to be Empress of Austria, so that everything was "all right." Only Karl Ludwig stood apart rather silent amid the joyous turmoil and for a moment it seemed as though he were keeping down a tear. Then he came and wished Sisi the greatest happiness and kissed her hands.

The Emperor next sent for Grünne and his aides-de-camp

and presented them to his future wife. The General, too, thought to himself that this child would be as wax in the Archduchess' hands, even more than the elder sister would have been. The betrothal was now official and need no longer be kept a secret; on the contrary, the Emperor would have liked to proclaim it to the whole world, so happy was he and so enraptured with his fiancée. At eleven o'clock they went to Mass. The priest was already in the secret. All Ischl crowded to the church, which was packed to overflowing. Then the court arrived, the national anthem was struck up, and the Emperor, his mother, and Sisi advanced side by side toward the door. All of a sudden a movement ran through the ranks of the spectators. What had happened? The Archduchess Sophie had fallen back, and little Sisi, fascinating in her shyness, had entered the church before her. She would have liked to muffle her head in a thick shawl, for the curious glances from all these eyes were like the stab of needles. Yet was she not the fortunate girl, the Emperor's chosen bride, the future wife of one of the mightiest of the earth's rulers, and what is more, a handsome, manly young man, fresh and radiant with youth in his glittering uniform? What more could heart desire? In a turmoil of emotion the betrothed couple bent the knee at the most sacred moment of the celebration, and when the priest descended the altar steps at the end of it to dismiss the congregation with his blessing, Francis Joseph took Sisi by the hand, as gently as though she had been some tender flower, and led her up to him, saying: "Please give us your blessing, Your Reverence. This is my future wife."

The rainy day had been followed by a gloriously fine Sunday. Everything was fresh and green, and when the Emperor and his fiancée left the church they were received with a perfect shower of flowers. Sisi grasped her fiancé's hand nervously, and as he looked tenderly at her he was touched to see the confusion betrayed so plainly by her sweet little face, and quickly took her away to spare her the greetings of the crowding, enthusiastic throng.

In the afternoon they again went for a drive through the splendid forests in the neighborhood. It was a little cold and Elizabeth shivered, not so much on account of the chill as of her overwrought state of mind. She had brought no warm wraps with her, so Francis Joseph took his military cloak and wrapped it tenderly around her, whispering in her ear: "You know, I can hardly say how happy I am!" When his mother heard this, she entered into her son's happiness and thought to herself: "Perhaps it is better so—who knows?" Yet the upsetting of her plans rankled a little. "You are right," she said to her son when she was left alone with him for a moment. "Sisi is very pretty, but she has yellow teeth!"

The Duchess Ludovika now telegraphed to her husband and son: "The Emperor has asked for Sisi's hand and awaits your consent. He is staying in Ischl till the end of August. We are all so happy." This telegram produced a great impression, and Duke Max, too, was beside himself with delight. "My wife has done a really good stroke of work there," he thought. But his dear little Sisi? A little romp like that? Yet after all, she had always been a universal favorite and had grown exquisitely lovely of late. He set out for Ischl immediately. The news of the betrothal spread through the whole of Bavaria like a flash of lightning and aroused enthusiasm in every class of the people. In Vienna the joy was not entirely unmixed. There, too, everybody wanted the Emperor to marry. But since the revolution had been crushed, the Archduchess Sophie was none too popular. Her hand was plainly to be seen in this engagement, and people's only consolation was that at least things had not turned out exactly as she had desired.

Portraits of the future Empress were now hastily procured and passed from hand to hand throughout the whole

Empire. Everybody had heard that she was the monarch's own choice, and everybody was thoroughly curious to see what the young girl could be like who had fascinated the first gentleman in the Empire so swiftly and completely.

The betrothed couple spent the closing days of August in unclouded happiness. Sisi had regained a little of her composure and was beginning to enter into her new rôle to some extent, and, though often overcome by sadness and fears when alone, she took a pleasure in the really wild joy of her fiancé, who was more delighted with her every day. He discovered fresh charms and fascinations in her each moment. Everything she said seemed to him clever, sweet, and captivating. Sisi had her portrait painted, while Francis Joseph sat in the room and gazed at her. The artist told him that he had never painted such a lovely face before, and this was no flattery but had all the ring of sincerity. These things produced their effect upon Sisi, and by the end of her visit she felt almost true happiness. It was only with the Emperor's mother that she could not feel quite at home. The Archduchess often cast covertly critical glances at her, or else found fault with her. She even told the Duchess Ludovika that Sisi ought to take more care of her teeth. The little girl felt insulted at this, and even rebellious. But such things were but small shadows in a picture so full of light.

And now arrived the day of parting. Francis Joseph had once more to assume "the yoke," and Sisi must go back to Possi. She always disliked partings, whether from people she loved, her pets, or even places, and found it hard now, but Francis Joseph would not be away from her for long. He was too enraptured with his little fiancée and would certainly rejoin her soon. He was reluctant to settle down again to his affairs in Vienna after his "divine time at Ischl." "It was hard and depressing," he wrote to his mother, "to take a leap from the earthly paradise of Ischl to this writing-table existence and masses of papers with all my cares and troubles."*

On the way homewards and when she was back again in quiet Possi, Sisi thought over her new position. What had happened to her? She had set out for Ischl with no idea of what was awaiting her, and now here she was returning home as an affianced bride. She was to be a great and powerful empress and rule over a gigantic empire with its countless peoples, of whose languages and customs she had no knowledge, and yet she was only a frightened little girl. But all the same, she was firmly resolved to live her own life and follow the desires of her own mind and heart. With her uncontrollable love of freedom and independence, what might not happen? Freedom had been her old love, and now a new love had come to her, so quickly and suddenly. Sisi looked out of the window and watched the flight of the swallows, which she had so often envied because they were free from all earthly trammels, all duties and laws—or at least seemed to be. And she wished she might be one of them, far removed from all that threatened her—from all that seemed so beautiful and mysterious, yet might, perhaps, be so dangerous as well. And once again, as in her early days of girlish romance, Elizabeth confided her longings to her little manuscript book:

O swallow, thy swift pinions lend me,
And be my guide to lands afar,
Happy to break the toils that bind me
And shatter every prison bar.

Oh, could I but with thee be fleeing
Through blue eternities of sky,
How I would praise with all my being
The God, whom men call Liberty.

* For this letter and most of the Emperor's letters to his mother quoted below, see Dr. Franz Schnürer, *Briefe Kaiser Franz Josephs I an seine Mutter, 1838–1872* (Munich, 1930).

How soon would I forget all sorrow,
Forget the old love and the new,
And never fear a sad tomorrow
Nor let the tears my cheeks bedew.

Before this Elizabeth had been left very much in peace and allowed to do what she liked, but now she had suddenly become the center of interest. No less than three artists were engaged in painting her. The best of the portraits was to be for the Emperor. This was urgently necessary, for the portrait by the Viennese painter, Kaiser, was so bad that it made her look like "a white negress," so Francis Joseph had it seized and suppressed at once. At the end of September a courier from Vienna brought her a miniature of him, painted at Ischl and splendidly set in a diamond bracelet. A visit from Francis Joseph was already arranged for the middle of October.

Now, too, the trousseau demanded attention, though Sisi did not take as much pleasure in this as a girl of her age and position might have been expected to do. She saw more and more clearly that she no longer belonged to herself alone. The Archduchess Sophie sent sketches from Ischl to remind her of the happy days there, and on December 29 Sisi thanked her for them in a nice little letter, in which she naturally addressed her aunt by the intimate "thou" and spoke of her impatience to see the Emperor again.

But while she was absorbed in her dreams and feelings, Francis Joseph showed that, however much he might be in love, he was a stickler for correct form and meant everything to be done in due order. He wished to send a formal demand for the hand of H.R.H. the Princess Elizabeth, Duchess in Bavaria, to the court of Munich, and only refrained when his minister in Munich explained to him in great detail that this was unnecessary.

At last, on October 11, 1853, Francis Joseph hastened to his fiancée. He paid a hasty visit to the King in Munich, and then went on to Possenhofen, eager to clasp her in his arms. He was so exuberantly happy that it was a pleasure to see him. He entirely laid aside his imperial dignity and was gay and lively. He romped and played with his fiancée's younger brothers and sisters in the wildest of high spirits, as though he had been a child himself. He found Sisi, if possible, even lovelier and more charming than before, for she was much more natural and at her ease than she had been at Ischl. He had quite a surprise when he saw her on horseback, and was so enchanted that he quite forgot his mother's express instructions that he must warn the Duchess not to let her delicate little daughter ride too much, though riding was such a passion of hers that it would probably have been impossible to restrain her. He wrote ecstatically to his mother about his fiancée, reporting that her teeth were now perfectly white.

On October 15, after his visit to the ducal family, they all returned to Munich, where Queen Marie's birthday was being celebrated with great splendor. In the evening there was a gala performance at the court theatre. The management, with a curious lack of tact, had proposed the opera *William Tell*, the central point of which is the clash between the Austrian bailiff Gessler and the free and noble Swiss hero. The King noticed this, and forbade the performance, so another opera had to be proposed. But the next choice was *Katharina Cornaro*, by Lachner, the Bavarian General Director of Music, which was merely falling out of the frying pan into the fire, for the opera performed before the Emperor and his newly affianced bride as an expression of the delight felt by all Bavaria began with the breaking off of a solemn betrothal and ended with the sufferings of a dying king! As the Emperor and his fiancée entered their box, there was a storm of cheering. Sisi started back nervously and felt so utterly distressed at being the center of attention that those who knew her well almost pitied her.

The following days were occupied by court festivities. At the ball held in the great ballroom of the royal palace, Sisi enchanted everybody, and all wondered how such a prodigy of beauty and grace had gone unnoticed so long. She herself did not share in the general delight. She was unspeakably bored and embarrassed when the whole diplomatic corps was presented to her, though she saw nothing but admiration on every face. The Prussian Minister alone watched things with a grudging eye. "Francis Joseph's visit," he reported, "has caused wild enthusiasm in Munich. Attempts are already being made to exploit this to the detriment of Bavarian friendship with Prussia." The Minister complained of the Emperor's suite, whose attitude, especially Count Grünne's, was calculated to wound Bavarian susceptibilities. Nor did Elizabeth receive a very pleasant impression of her future husband's Adjutant General, whose manner toward her seemed condescending and covertly ironical, a thing which she simply could not endure.

On October 21 Francis Joseph had to go home, which he did with a heavy heart. He had been so happy, especially at Possenhofen, and thanked his mother for having been the author of his happiness so heartily as to efface any recollection she may have had of his own part in it. "I love Sisi more every day," he wrote ecstatically, "and feel surer than ever that no other woman could suit me as well as she does." After the Emperor's visit, the whole court felt proud and delighted, not to speak of the people at large, and so did Sisi's father, Duke Max. His Round Table, known as "Old England," congratulated him in characteristic fashion at a dinner on October 30, 1853, when a collection of twenty-five "*Leberreime*" and poems was performed before him to celebrate the betrothal and the Duke's and Duchess' silver wedding. In the exuberance of the occasion the company rather forgot the respect due to royalty, for a *Leberreim* in honor of the Emperor's future father-in-law made *Schwiegervater* (father-in-law) rhyme most indecorously with *Kater* (he-cat):

The liver of a pike it is, and not that of a tomcat.
We hope the future father-in-law will thoroughly enjoy that!

The incident became the talk of Munich, and Duke Max got into trouble with the royal family. It had to be intimated to him that he was no longer merely a private individual, for since his daughter's betrothal the whole world took an interest in him and his family—a state of affairs as unwelcome to the Duke as to the Duchess, who would both have preferred to live as they had done hitherto.

It now became necessary to instruct Sisi in the history and politics not only of Austria but also of Hungary, for till now she had had few ideas on the subject. In the literary group frequented by Duke Max there was a certain Count John Majláth, a Hungarian, who had made several excursions into history. He became Sisi's tutor and suddenly revealed to her receptive mind a whole world of poetry which was purely Hungarian. Majláth represented to her in glowing colors the chivalrous impulse latent in every Hungarian heart and the strength and courage of this people of dashing horsemen, till, before she had set foot on Hungarian soil, she was fired with the emotions that throbbed in the veins of this ardent patriot. Majláth waited upon the Princess three times a week, and she was always glad to see him, though before this she had always hated lessons and escaped from them as soon as possible.

She showed him delightedly the splendid presents which were arriving from Vienna. On November 19, her name day, one of the palace police attached to the Emperor's person brought her a magnificent brooch, in the shape of a diamond bouquet. On the night between December 20 and 21 the Emperor arrived in Munich after midnight in readiness for Christmas Eve, which was also Sisi's birthday. It was very late when he arrived at the ducal palace, but he insisted upon seeing her at once. By his wish his whole visit was spent entirely *en famille,* so that he could be with Sisi all day. On Christmas Eve they exchanged portraits, each of them having been painted on horseback. When they gathered round the Christmas tree, the Emperor offered his fiancée a bouquet of magnificent flowers which had arrived by express courier from the conservatories in Vienna only half an hour before, together with a parrot from the menagerie at Schönbrunn. Among other presents the Archduchess Sophie had also sent Sisi a garland of roses—perhaps as a reminder that she expected her to be a model of virtue.

But all too soon the political situation made it necessary for the Emperor to return to Vienna. Once again the Prussian Minister had watched the Emperor's visit with a critical eye. He claimed to have observed that Francis Joseph and King Max had not got on any too well, and that the behavior of the Emperor's suite was still causing some annoyance in court circles. "Eyewitnesses assure me," he wrote home, "that during his stay here the monarch closely observed every step and movement of his fiancée, and that the very decided will which is a leading trait in the young Princess' character did not escape his penetrating eye. It appears that in this connection some significant hints were dropped, and since the Emperor's departure people feel that a rather more serious atmosphere prevails in the ducal palace."

Things were not quite so bad as this, though there was an element of truth in his words. The Emperor Francis Joseph noticed on many occasions that his fiancée had a will of her own, and when she wanted something it had to be done, under pain of her displeasure. His accounts to his mother of his visit were certainly a little cooler this time, but he still found Sisi adorable and loaded her with presents. On Christmas Day she had complained of the cold, so on January 16 a special imperial courier arrived with a magnificent fur cloak for her. After all, she was still a child and thoroughly enjoyed all these fine things. But what she liked best was the parrot, as we can see from a tiny lace-edged note which she wrote her former governess, the Countess Hundt. Though about to become an empress, she remained faithful to her childish hobbies, still loving and tending her pet animals and birds, and others might attend to the serious things of life.

The necessary formalities were already being dispatched in preparation for the marriage. In the first place there were obstacles of a legal nature; for Sisi was related to her future husband in the second degree on the mother's side and in the fourth degree on the father's side. Both ties of blood formed an obstacle in canon law, and the former in civil law also. But in the case of great people these things are easily arranged. The Pope was requested to grant a dispensation, and did so without delay.

Next, the marriage settlement had to be drawn up, though all this was Greek to Sisi. "By her father's love and affection," she was granted a dowry of 50,000 gulden, in addition to a trousseau and outfit "suited to her rank." For his part, the Emperor pledged himself to supplement this by a sum of 100,000 gulden, besides which he promised a *Morgengabe* of 12,000 ducats, in accordance with the custom, dating back at least as far as the ancient code of laws known as the *Sachsenspiegel*, by which the bridegroom had to offer his wife a gift on the morning after their nuptial night, in compensation for the loss of her virginity. Francis Joseph also undertook to allow his wife 100,000 gulden a year for her unrestricted personal use, this sum, specified as "pin money" (*Spennadelgeld*), being for her clothing and personal adornment, her charities, and minor expenses. All other expenses were to be provided for by the Emperor. The Empress was further guaranteed an income of 100,000 gulden in the event of widowhood. The Austrian Minister of Finance received an order in the Emperor's own handwriting to have the *Morgengabe* in readiness in newly minted gold and silver coins, "in a suitable casket for offering to the Most Serene bride."

Next, the King of Bavaria had to make a solemn declaration that no obstacles to the Princess' marriage existed, and he seized the opportunity of stating in the deed that, as head of the royal house, he gave his consent to the marriage "with particular pleasure." An inventory of the bride's trousseau and outfit was drawn up in incredibly minute detail, the exact value of every object being entered opposite it. The first group consisted of the ornaments, gold vessels, and jewels, and the second of the silver, but the third, consisting of the wardrobe, was the longest. In it were enumerated seventeen dresses for formal occasions, fourteen high-necked silk dresses, six dressing gowns, nineteen thin summer dresses, pink, violet, corn-colored, and forget-me-not blue, and four ball dresses. Next came sixteen hats and veils, the hats being trimmed with feathers, roses, or violets, and including the garden hat with a garland of wild flowers which had enchanted Francis Joseph at Ischl. Six cloaks, eight lighter mantles, and five capelets of velvet and thick cloth completed the outfit. Then came the rich undergarments, including fourteen dozen shifts, one dozen of batiste with exquisite Valenciennes lace, fourteen dozen pairs of stockings, from the finest silk to the heaviest woolen ones for winter, six dozen petticoats, five dozen drawers, dressing capes, negligees. . . . Then there were the boots and shoes, six pair of every kind, and twenty dozen handkerchiefs of all sorts and colors. Attempts were made to interest Sisi in her outfit, but she could not endure the everlasting fittings and the fuss going on all around her, and slipped away as often as she could. The seamstresses and dressmakers complained that the Princess was never there, and when they did succeed in getting hold of her she wanted to finish with them at once and escape again. People complained that it was difficult to work for her, though it was a pleasure, too, for it was a joy to dress such a slender, enchanting form and adorn it as became an emperor's bride.

On March 15 the Emperor arrived on another visit and handed his fiancée his mother's wedding present, the magnificent tiara, necklace, and earrings of opals and diamonds which she had worn on her own wedding day, and which were as valuable as all the rest of the bride's jewels and ornaments put together. At the same time, however, the Emperor mentioned, as though in passing, that his mother had been quite shocked at being addressed as "thou" in Sisi's last letter. "This must not be done," he said. "Even I, her own son, write to her as 'you,' out of the respect and veneration due to an older woman." Sisi shook her head, for, she thought, an aunt, who was also to be her mother-in-law, ought surely to be called "thou"; however, if the Emperor wished it, it must be right. But her letter of thanks for this splendid present takes its tone from the formal "you." There is a noticeably colder feeling in it, though it says how happy Elizabeth felt at the thought that she could rely confidently on the Archduchess' motherly love always and in all circumstances. But a bitter taste was left behind. She felt that the Emperor's mother was always ready with a reprimand. How good life had been when nobody troubled about her and she could roam about the woods and gardens at Possi. Now there was always something important to be done—usually only some ridiculous formality. For instance, there was her formal renunciation of her rights of succession. The princesses of the collateral line would only become of importance to the succession if the royal and ducal lines of Bavaria no longer possessed a single male representative. And she alone had three brothers! But the family laws of the royal house required that she must take a solemn oath to renounce her claims and sign a deed to this effect in the throne room before everybody. Sisi smiled, and then felt angry, but it was no use, she had to submit to the traditional custom. This was only a foretaste of a thousand similar things which awaited her as Empress, and she was very thoughtful as she returned home after the ceremony.

The day on which she would have to bid farewell to her home drew nearer and nearer. The wedding ceremony had at last been finally fixed for April 24 in Vienna. On April 14 seventeen large and eight small boxes had already been sent on before her. On Easter Sunday, April 16, a great gala concert took place at the royal court of Munich. The diplomatic corps had desired to pay its respects to the Emperor's future bride once more before her departure. This time Sisi appeared with a rich *parure* of diamonds, wearing her new orders for the first time. She looked exquisitely lovely and graceful, but very serious. "The young Duchess," wrote the Prussian Minister, "in spite of the brilliant and exalted position which awaits her at the side of her august bridegroom, seems to be deeply affected at saying good-bye to her old home and exalted family circle, and the expression in which this could be read cast a slight shadow over the Most Serene Princess' face, radiant with all her youthful grace and beauty."

And this time the Minister was not seeing things in too gloomy a light. The nearer the day approached, the more nervous Elizabeth felt at the thought of the strange and unknown destiny awaiting her. Once again before her departure she went out to visit her beloved Possi. With tears in her eyes she bade farewell to the room she had occupied as a girl, to her beloved garden, in which the first leaves and flowers were beginning to appear, her dear mountains, and the lovely lake. She recalled her early friendships, her youthful dreams of love and sorrow, and, as always happened when her feelings were particularly stirred, she took up her pen and wrote a poem expressing her regrets.

At last the day of her departure arrived. On the morning of April 20, in glorious spring weather, Kings Max and Ludwig appeared at the ducal palace to say good-bye to her. All public celebrations had been forbidden, but as the carriages drove along the Ludwigstrasse from the ducal palace to the Siegestor, thousands of people crowded the streets to wave farewell to the departing Princess. She drove in a carriage with six horses to Straubing on the Danube, where the imperial yacht was waiting for her. On one side sat the Duchess Ludovika and Sisi, and crowded on the opposite seat were Néné and the other sisters, while Karl Theodor rode on the box, for, though there was so little room, he would not be prevented from accompanying his little sister on the first stage of her journey at least. When Elizabeth appeared in her dark-colored traveling dress, she was greeted with indescribable cheering. She was very grave, yet sweet and charming, and deeply moved. Tears streamed down her cheeks, and as the crowd thronged round the carriage, cheering and waving to her, she stood up again and again, turned round, and waved farewell to her home, her dear ones, and her childhood. And now a sheet of paper fluttered into the carriage, as though to console her. On it were these verses of the Austrian poet, Johann Nepomuk Vogel:

Rose of Bavarian land,
Starting to blow,
Shall'st by the Danube's strand
Fragrantly glow.

Rose of Bavarian land,
Bear well in mind;
No better gard'ner's hand
E'er shalt thou find.

III

MARRIAGE, HOMESICKNESS, AND GOLDEN FETTERS

VIENNA, THE IMPERIAL CITY, WAS *EN fête*, as though bent upon showing its monarch's bride that her future husband enjoyed the love of his peoples, and especially of his capital. Great things were expected of Francis Joseph, and by making him happy his young and lovely wife would also bring happiness to Vienna. It was true that she was too closely related to him. The daughters of Rudolf of Habsburg had long since inaugurated the series of matrimonial alliances between the Houses of Austria and Wittelsbach, of which Francis Joseph's would be the twenty-second, but the brilliance and splendor of the wedding were to overpower all possible objections.

On April 21 Elizabeth and her family crossed the Austrian frontier, and that evening found Francis Joseph on the landing stage at Linz, ready to escort his fiancée to the dainty lodging, furnished in the national style, where she was to spend the night; after which he drove back to Vienna at full speed. In the capital the most brilliant preparations had been made and everybody was praying for fine weather. There were threatening clouds in the sky, but by the afternoon a strong wind sprang up and swept them away, and the skies were radiantly blue as the flower-bedecked boat bearing the bride drew near the shore at Nussdorf. On the landing stage waited the Emperor and his parents, the chief dignitaries of state, and untold thousands of curious spectators. The boat had hardly drawn alongside when the Emperor leapt across the gap that still remained and, taking his bride in his arms, kissed her rapturously before the whole assembly. Pale and timid, she stepped ashore leaning on her fiancé's arm, dressed in rose-pink silk with a white lace mantle, while myriad throats thundered forth the greeting: "*Hoch* Elizabeth, the Emperor's bride!" For a moment she stood as though rooted to the spot and looked shyly at the cheering crowds, stirred to the depths of her being. Then she collected herself, bowed to right and left, and waved her lace handkerchief, while the sight of her called forth renewed bursts of cheering. Francis Joseph now tried to get her away from the crowds as quickly as possible. They all entered the carriages drawn by the magnificent greys from the imperial stables at Lippiza, and drove rapidly to Schönbrunn, where the rest of the imperial family was assembled to greet them.

Here, too, the palace gardens were packed with solid masses of people, and though Sisi was tired and overwrought, and the excitement and the fatigue of her long journey could plainly be read in her pallor, she had to go out on the balcony and smile and bow and wave her hand, as would henceforth be her official duty. But even inside the palace she found no rest. Her Mistress of the Household was presented to her, the Countess Sophie Esterházy-Liechtenstein, a lady of fifty-six with a rather withered, expressionless face. Sisi looked at her mistrustfully and felt repelled, for there was something of the governess about her. She was, of course, an intimate friend of the Archduchess Sophie, who had chosen her to attend upon the future Empress for good reasons of her own, knowing that she could rely upon her, together with the other two ladies in waiting who were to be Sisi's closest companions, a Countess Paula Bellegarde, who seemed to Elizabeth nice and sympathetic, and a Countess Karoline Lamberg, daughter of the general who had been murdered by the Hungarians on the bridge at Pest in 1848. These ladies were to initiate her into all the ways of the court.

Sisi was prepared to find the festivities, the Spanish ceremonial, and the incredible splendor and pomp of the imperial court trying and exhausting, but she had no idea what really awaited her. When she retired for the night, a bulky manuscript was placed in her hand, entitled "Ceremonial for the public entry of H.R.H. the most august Princess Elizabeth," which she had to study in order that everything should go like clockwork on the following day. Being overexcited, she found it hard to sleep. Her strange bed, her new surroundings, and all that lay before her were too much for her. Francis Joseph was touchingly solicitous and tried to make things easy for her. He kept inquiring what she would like and comforted her when she seemed anxious about how things would go off. "Do not think about it, dearest," he said. "It is all part of our official duties, and you will see how enchanted the people of Vienna will be with my sweet bride."

Early on the morning of April 23 everybody was in gala dress as prescribed by the ceremonial, the ladies wearing crinolines—a fashion introduced in France by the Empress Eugénie. The Duchess Ludovika and her daughter drove in a six-horse carriage from Schönbrunn to the Theresianum, the ancient imperial castle, from which for centuries past the reigning monarch's bride had made her entry into the capital. And now, overcome by the gravity of the occasion, Sisi began to cry and could only be calmed with difficulty. She simply could not endure being stared at, and it would be worse in the glass state coach, drawn by eight horses, in which she was now to be driven all around Vienna like some rare exotic beast. But her weakness was only momentary, and suddenly a hard, resolute expression could be seen on her lovely face, so that for a fleeting moment she was like her elder sister, Néné. Then she stepped into the great, heavily gilded coach, decorated with paintings by Rubens and drawn by the eight milk-white horses bred at Lippiza, and submitted resignedly to a progress which would have filled many another young girl with unspeakable pride and satisfaction. A new bridge across the Wien had just been completed, and the Emperor's bride was the first to cross it. The streets had been transformed into a perfect flower garden, white-robed girls strewed her route with roses, and countless crowds pressed upon the soldiers lining the way. It was a Sunday on which the "Sunday's child" entered her new home in the Hofburg. She made an exquisite picture as she stepped from the state coach, her cheeks flushed with excitement, wearing a rose-pink satin dress shot with silver and adorned with wreaths of roses. As she descended the high steps her diamond tiara caught for a moment in the top of the doorframe, but with a gesture of indescribable grace she rearranged her hair, and for that day at least her work was at an end.

The next day was occupied with preparations for the fateful ceremony. The Mistress of the Household once more presented her with two thick manuscripts. One she had merely to read through, but the other she had to keep and learn by heart. The first was a nineteen-page lithographed program of the wedding ceremonial. She read of all the *allerhöchste* and *höchste* (all-highest and highest) ladies, of those who were *palast-* and *appartementmässig*, of pages of honor and trainbearers, of "generals in attendance" and the "order of the procession" both to the church and back again, as far as the very entrance of the private apartments. "What are *appartementmässig* ladies?" she asked in amusement, and learned that they were those who had the right to appear in the imperial apartments only at stated times and by invitation, as opposed to those who had the privilege of the "great" or "lesser" *entrée*. With a slight shudder she handed the first manuscript back to the Countess Esterházy. The other one bore the title of "Most Humble Reminders" (*Alleruntertänigste Erinnerungen*) and contained an account of the arrangements for the following day. Laughingly the Emperor tried to dispel the cloud which had fallen on his bride's face. "After all," he said, "it will not be so very alarming, and we shall soon forget all about it at beautiful Laxenburg."

At half past six on the evening of April 24 Francis Joseph led his bride to the altar in the Augustine Church. It is impossible to describe the flow and color of the gorgeous spectacle inside the church. The vestments of the great ecclesiastical dignitaries, the military uniforms, the ladies' court dresses and jewels, reflecting the light of thousands of candles, produced a dazzling confusion of varied hues. Suddenly a stir ran through the glittering assembly, and there was a dead silence as the procession approached in state from the Hofburg. The Emperor rode alone at the head of it, tall and slender in his field marshal's uniform, covered with orders, a handsome, manly figure in all the pride of youth, and behind him drove the Archduchess Sophie and the Duchess Ludovika. Between them sat Elizabeth in her white wedding dress, embroidered with gold and silver and richly adorned with myrtle blossom, wearing in her hair the Archduchess Sophie's flashing bridal diadem of diamonds and opals, and at her breast a bunch of fresh white roses. She advanced toward her *prie-dieu* with the utmost grace, looking neither to the right hand nor to the left, deeply serious and as pale as death. She felt as though in a dream, and the Emperor had to give her an encouraging touch and glance before she rose and approached the high altar with her bridegroom. Suddenly, as though from a great distance, she heard the questions of the ecclesiastic who was marrying her and whispered "Yes," almost inaudibly, whereas the Emperor's response rang through the church. And now the golden ring was on her finger and her delicate hand lay trembling with emotion in the Emperor's. At this moment there was a salvo of shots from the infantry drawn up in order in the Josefsplatz. The thunder of artillery was already heard from the city walls, and at the same time all the bells of the Vienna churches began to peal. Suddenly there was silence again. The venerable Prince Archbishop of Vienna, Cardinal Rauscher, approached the altar and delivered an address to the newly married pair. Elizabeth stood there as though under a spell and listened to his long exhortation, which seemed as though it would never end. He spoke of the Almighty, of love and harmony between man and wife, and of the duties and noble tasks of a sovereign. She heard only a word or a disjointed sentence here and there, but suddenly her attention was caught by the words: "The sainted and tender-hearted Augustine speaks as follows: If a woman loves a man because he is rich, then she is not pure: for she loves not her husband, but her husband's money. If she loves her husband, she loves him even if he is poor and deprived of everything."

A slight flush rose to Elizabeth's cheeks, and she looked inquiringly at her young husband. What did this allusion mean? Everybody must know that she had not sought power and wealth, but everything had come upon her without warning, like a miracle, and she had been carried away whether she would or not. And involuntarily she recalled how on the previous day she had seen the venerable ecclesiastic coming out of the Archduchess Sophie's room. Could these words have been intentional? However, the kindly words which followed effaced the momentary feeling of bitterness which his comparison had caused her. She left the church with an even graver face than before, accompanied by fanfares of trumpets and the roll of drums, preceded by pages of honor and dignitaries of state, in a proud procession flanked by the halberdiers of the imperial bodyguard, only to return to the Hofburg and there endure the congratulations of the court. And now she found that an emperor and empress do not belong to themselves. They had to submit to a flood of festivities. Elizabeth went through all these ceremonies in silence at her husband's side. Wherever she appeared she was received with wild applause, but none of it gave her any pleasure. At last she was a woman and an empress—she who so shortly before had been only an unimportant little princess, insignificant, perhaps, but all the freer and more independent for that.

On Friday the twenty-eighth a series of deputations and receptions had again been arranged, but at last Elizabeth struck. She was weary and nervous and felt that she must have a rest. The Archduchess Sophie considered this improper, but Francis Joseph understood her feelings. He put off the receptions and himself drove Elizabeth out in the Prater at noon. The news spread like wildfire, and all Vienna streamed to the Hauptallee. The Emperor had to make a wide circuit and leave the main drive as soon as possible if he wished to enjoy the fresh air with his wife in quiet for half an hour.

Most of the festivities were a misery to Elizabeth, but one of them she did enjoy—the national festival on April 29—for the performance arranged by Renz, the circus rider, in which sixty splendid horses took part, reminded her of her home and her father. Besides, Renz was making a special effort. His troupe, dressed in medieval costumes, rode through the Prater in a brilliant procession, with sixty horses, splendid beasts of every breed. On arriving at the fireworks ground near the third café, they came to a halt and a quadrille was performed with twelve grey and twelve black horses, after which all the riders formed a semicircle and, while forty-four balloons in extraordinary human and animal shapes floated up in the air, Herr Renz gave an exhibition of *haute école* on a splendid grey Arab mare. At the other entertainments Elizabeth could hardly wait for the end, but this time she could scarcely tear herself away and said to the Emperor on the way home: "It really was too lovely! I must get to know that man."

Elizabeth was a mere child, touchingly lovely and very, very young, perhaps too young for her husband's ardent and passionate love-making. She felt it most acutely when, on the morning after she had become his wife in the full sense of the word, the Archduchess Sophie insisted that she must appear at the family breakfast table as she would have done on any other day. Elizabeth protested against what was to her a horrible ordeal,* which she could hardly face, but the Emperor was still so much accustomed to obeying his mother that even he did not venture to raise any objection. He was afraid that in case of a refusal there might be a scene between his mother and wife, so he begged Elizabeth to yield. She did so, but it was a dreadful experience for her, and she returned to her room nervous and in tears, while the Archduchess did not omit to cross-question her son thoroughly.

Elizabeth saw little of the Emperor, who was busy all day. All those around her belonged to her mother-in-law's circle, and the Mistress of the Household and her ladies in waiting were absolute strangers to her. She had not been allowed to bring a single lady with her from home, so that when her husband was not with her she felt lonely and helpless before the secret power represented by her mother-in-law, which made itself oppressively felt even during the earliest days of her married life. For the factors which were ultimately bound to lead to a clash were already appearing. The Archduchess Sophie, with her vigorous and uncompromising personality,

* From an account of the Empress, recorded in the diary of the Countess Marie Festetics (see Bibliography).

was in the habit of crushing the individuality of everybody about her. But though Elizabeth was only sixteen, she had a decided will of her own and an uncontrollable love of freedom, inherited from her father and encouraged at home. Yet she was not allowed to take a single step without her mother-in-law's knowledge. Even at quiet Laxenburg she had to be irreproachably dressed from morning till night and was not permitted to do anything contrary to etiquette or unsuitable for an empress. Of course, Sophie meant all this for the best—of that there can be no doubt. She was far-sighted and politically minded, but nothing could have been more utterly foreign to the young Empress. She found herself virtually a prisoner at Laxenburg, and since the Emperor had to spend all day working at the Hofburg, she felt forlorn in a cold, strange world. She had always dreaded what lay before her, but she had imagined it to be so very different. She missed her home and family and looked back sadly to her carefree life at Possenhofen, for now her whole existence was a series of complicated ceremonies. Realities did not count, appearances were everything, and that was so hard. The Emperor was always kind, loving, and charming to her, but when his mother appeared he always gave way, and besides, he was so seldom there.

Her chief consolation were her pet animals, some of which she had brought with her from Possi. She would sit for hours before her parrots' cage teaching them to talk, and she still found consolation in writing poetry. Just as at Possi she had so often turned to her poetry book as a refuge, so now in these early days at Laxenburg she did the same. Two poems composed at this time,* one entitled "*Sehnsucht*" (Longing) and another "The Captive Bird," sufficiently indicate her feelings.

Her sense of desolation was increased by the Archduchess

* Quoted in full, like the rest, in the German edition of this work.

Sophie's incessant pinpricks, and she felt quite overwhelmed by the entire change that had taken place in her life. Before this she had hardly known what it meant to be brought up by overbearing and irritable elders. When on rare occasions her mother remonstrated with her, she had always done so in the kindest way. But the Archduchess Sophie was of tougher mettle. She regarded it as an obligation to make this little girl, who had turned her son's head, into an empress with a strong sense of duty. In spite of her good intentions her manner was too harsh, and Elizabeth was like a sensitive plant. If anybody was in the slightest degree disagreeable or unkind to her, that person became an enemy in her eyes, and whatever he might do or say afterwards she would always regard him with distrust, though she could be kind and even caressing when she noticed that anybody really liked and appreciated her. This sensitiveness was fostered by her involuntary feeling of pride at the fact that she and no other was the Empress, the first lady in the land. This made her feel even more acutely the restraints to which she was subjected, and she soon persuaded herself that she was in despair. This explains the solemn poem written on May 8, 1854, only a fortnight after her marriage. Of course it was written in a passing mood of depression, but it goes to prove that her character was neither simple nor commonplace, but liable to emotional outbursts which might seriously endanger her relations with the world around her.

O that I had not left the way
That would to freedom me have led!
O that I had not gone astray
On vanity's broad path instead!

Now in a prison cell I wake,
The hands are bound that once were free;
The longing grows that naught can slake.
And freedom! thou hast turned from me!

I waken from a vision rich
Wherein my spirit captive lay,
And vainly curse the hour in which
Freedom! I gambled thee away!

Elizabeth had to keep these verses carefully locked up, for if they had fallen into the hands of her mother-in-law nobody could have foreseen the consequences.

Everything seemed in league to encourage this state of mind. Even the weather helped to make her stay at Laxenburg depressing. May is usually the most beautiful time of year in Vienna and the surrounding country, but that year there were incessant rain and storms, and the heating arrangements at Laxenburg were none too good. Elizabeth caught cold and began to cough. Soon Francis Joseph noticed her unhappiness and, moved by her entreaties, thought of taking her to Ischl as soon as possible and inviting her mother and sister to meet her there. But it was a heavy sacrifice for him to part from his young wife so soon, for in spite of all her moodiness and complaints she bewitched him more every day.

But first, on June 9, 1854, the Emperor and Empress started on a tour through the crown lands of Bohemia and Moravia, which gave them an opportunity to escape from the strained relations at home. The fêtes given in their honor enchanted Elizabeth, especially the wedding procession from the Hanna in Moravia, equally famous for the picturesque costumes of its inhabitants and the fertility of its soil, and the brilliant tournament arranged by the nobility in Prague. On this tour she began to familiarize herself with her duties as Empress, visiting convents and churches, hospitals, almshouses, and orphanages, especially those for women and girls. Her sweet, simple manner and gracious charm delighted everyone and called forth rapturous applause. Everybody envied the young and lovely Empress with her exquisite clothes, and none suspected that she felt herself so hardly used at home.

While Elizabeth returned to Laxenburg, the Emperor still stayed away from Vienna for a time. On June 29, 1854, he received a characteristic letter from his mother, which is typical of the relations between them and of the extent to which the Archduchess concerned herself with the smallest details. Symptoms had appeared which gave cause for hope that Elizabeth might soon be a mother, and Sophie at once began to advise the Emperor how to treat her and urge him to be very tender with her. "But," she added, "I do not think Sisi ought to spend too much time with her parrots, for if a woman is always looking at animals, especially during the earlier months, the children are apt to resemble them. She had far better look in her looking glass, or at you. *That* would have my entire approval."

This genuine motherly anxiety was well meant, but the Archduchess interfered too much. She was almost always at Laxenburg when the Emperor was staying there, for she was afraid that his beautiful young wife would obtain too great an influence over her husband. She was utterly incapable of appreciating her niece's childlike nature, but exaggerated her innocent passion for nature, horses, dogs, and birds into a crime, and was perpetually finding fault.* Elizabeth was never safe, even in her own room, for the Archduchess Sophie was always coming to her apartments to see what she was doing, till the little Empress felt that she was being spied upon. She complained that the Archduchess made an "affair of state" out of the smallest trifles and often scolded not only her but even the Emperor as though they were a pair of school children.

Of course, this was an exaggeration, but Elizabeth worked

* Based upon the Empress' own accounts of her youth, recorded in the diaries of the Archduchess Valerie and the Countess Marie Festetics.

up a perfect hatred of her mother-in-law, into whose power she felt herself to be helplessly delivered. Years later she would complain how miserable her life had been at this time and how helpless she had felt. The Emperor naturally could not be with her during the day, for he always left for Vienna at an early hour and did not return till six o'clock, in time for dinner. Elizabeth would have liked to follow him, but the Archduchess only replied: "It is not proper for an empress to go running after her husband and driving here, there, and everywhere like any young subaltern." On one occasion, however, Elizabeth persuaded her husband to take her with him and was happy to spend a whole day without seeing her mother-in-law. It was so nice to get away from "dreary" Laxenburg for once! But the young couple had hardly returned in the evening when the Archduchess Sophie bore down upon them and gave them a severe scolding—in fact, if Elizabeth is to be believed, she simply "abused" them (*beschimpft*). After that, of course, it never happened again, and Elizabeth remained shut up at Laxenburg. She quite forgot that this was not due to spite on the part of the "nasty" (*böse*) woman, as she called Sophie, but to anxiety for the child that was to be born and whose precious life might prove to be that of the longed-for heir to the throne.

The Archduchess' whole way of thinking was entirely foreign to the Empress. During Elizabeth's first visit to Laxenburg after her marriage a part of the gardens had been closed to the general public and reserved for her use. One day she noticed that it had now been thrown open, so that the public could almost look in at the palace windows. After this, Elizabeth scarcely ever went into the garden again, partly because it bored her to be in full dress early in the morning, with an attendant who was watching her every movement, and partly because she disliked having everybody looking at her now that she was obviously expecting a child.

SELF-PORTRAIT OF THE EMPRESS
SITTING AT HER DESK

From the Empress' sketchbook.

THE EMPEROR FRANCIS JOSEPH
AT HIS DESK

From the Empress' sketchbook, 1855.

But no sooner did the Archduchess notice that Elizabeth was no longer going out than she came to her apartments, forced her to go into the garden, and explained that it was her duty to show herself to everybody, so that the people might rejoice over the hoped-for event. The young Empress felt this to be "simply horrible." In any circumstances she disliked being stared at, but in such conditions she found it absolutely unbearable, so she preferred to stay alone in the castle and cry, though she concealed her misery from her husband as much as she could, so as not to hurt him. She knew very well how dependent he was upon his mother, but she also knew how much he loved her, and did not want to make him a bone of contention any more than she could help. At heart, she said to herself, he, too, "suffered" from his mother's predominance as much as she did; but he could not venture to say anything. For the Archduchess Sophie was her son's adviser in everything, even in matters of high politics. She approved the policy of hostility to Russia already adopted, which was not set off by any real *rapprochement* with the Western Powers, and encouraged the young Emperor in making himself entirely independent of the Tsar, who was so much older than he was. It was not seen till later that thanks to this he would fall between two stools and lose all his friends. For the time being it looked as though Austria were strong enough to defy the Tsar. Elizabeth had nothing to do with such matters. She knew nothing about them and thought that in such things, at least, perhaps her mother-in-law's opinion was the right one.

Besides, the Empress was sufficiently occupied with her own condition. Her pregnancy followed a normal course, and at the end of July they went to Ischl, where the Archduchess Sophie had bought the young couple a villa. There, to her delight, Sisi found her mother, Karl Theodor, and Néné, and the Archduchess Sophie was no longer able to interfere as much as at Laxenburg. The summer went rapidly by, and that winter, in view of the happy event which was expected, Elizabeth did not appear in public. Both she and her husband hoped that the child would be a boy, but they were disappointed. On March 5, 1855, a daughter was born and was of course given the name of Sophie, after the Emperor's mother, who was its godmother, Elizabeth not even being consulted. The baptism was celebrated with the greatest pomp, the whole diplomatic corps being present, with the exception of the Russian Ambassador, for the Tsar was so much annoyed at the attitude of Austria that he did not wish to take part even in a nonpolitical family party. Elizabeth was overjoyed with her first baby, but here again she was reckoning without her mother-in-law, who gave all orders and chose all the child's nurses and attendants, so that the mother could hardly ever be alone with her child. Any orders given by Elizabeth were canceled on the following day, so that instead of being a source of joy the child was only another cause of conflict.

Since Elizabeth took no pleasure in seeing her little daughter if her mother-in-law was always to be present, she finally gave up the struggle and seldom went up to see the child, whose nurseries, significantly enough, were not next to her own apartments. All this was carefully concealed from the outer world, and the people had no idea of the real state of affairs. They only saw the Empress' radiant beauty and splendid clothes and the pomp with which she always appeared in public. Before long she was overwhelmed with requests to intercede with the Emperor, but in replying to these her secretaries were instructed to use the formula: "Her Majesty does not exert any influence." In the summer of 1855 the question of the Concordat with the Pope was under discussion. Elizabeth was a good Catholic; she went to Mass almost every day and had no desire to do anything contrary to religion. But she already observed what an enormous influence the clergy had over her mother-in-law, even in political matters, and how much voice the Prince Archbishop Rauscher had at court. When in the summer of 1855 the Concordat was concluded which transferred certain important rights and powers of the State to the Church, she felt vaguely that in signing it her husband had gone a little too far in divesting himself of his sovereign powers.

Francis Joseph continued to anticipate his wife's desires whenever he could, and on June 21, 1855, arranged for her to pay a visit to her old home for the first time since her marriage. Her whole family came to meet her and carried her off joyously to Possi. Instead of the unformed girl who had left the castle, a beautiful, graceful, and dignified young woman now returned to it. She was in splendid health and went out for walks in all weathers, even when it streamed with rain. Her mother pressed her to confide in her and tell her what was depressing her, and she poured out to the Duchess and Néné all she had suffered at the hands of the Emperor's mother. In the early days her attitude toward Néné had seemed almost apologetic, but now the situation had changed and she would gladly have been the one to stay at her beloved Possenhofen had it not been for the Emperor and her little Sophie. She was touched by her husband's affection, and her baby was more than all the world to her. If only "that woman" were not always interfering between her and the two people whom she loved best!

Even when Elizabeth was away, the Emperor wished her to report to his mother how she and her child were, but her letters were always very formal, consisting of only a few matter-of-fact sentences, beginning "Dear Mother-in-law" and ending even more coldly with "The Emperor and I kiss your hands. Your faithful daughter-in-law, Elise"—not "Dear Mamma" or "Sisi."

The Empress returned to Ischl, and later to Vienna, and the daily struggle went on. Once, on December 14, 1855, she had an alarming experience. She was driving in a four-horse carriage to Schönbrunn with horses which were usually perfectly reliable, but in the Mariahilfstrasse one of the leaders became entangled in the reins, and the beasts took fright and dragged the other two away with them. The coachman was thrown off the box and the four horses bolted with the carriage, in which were the Empress and the Countess Bellegarde. The Countess tried to jump out, but Elizabeth had had a similar experience at Possenhofen and prevented her. The horses turned into a side street, where the driver of a farm wagon, which happened to be passing by, drew his cart across the street. The Empress' horses came down and the shaft of the carriage broke, but Elizabeth and her lady in waiting were unhurt. Pale and nervous, they left the carriage, which was smashed to pieces, and took a cab back to the Burg, where Elizabeth, to the horror of the Emperor, described their adventure and its happy ending.

Dissensions continued between her and the Archduchess Sophie, who had completely taken possession of Elizabeth's baby daughter. Little Sophie was brought up in the Empress Mother's rooms, on a different storey from Elizabeth's, so that if she wanted to see the child she had always to go panting upstairs, and even then she was not alone with it, but, in addition to the servants and attendants who made up what was known as the little Archduchess' "Kammer," she was always faced with her mother-in-law, and often with strangers as well, to whom the old lady was in the habit of showing off the child. And now, when she found herself expecting another child, it tired her to go upstairs. The child arrived at seven in the morning of July 15, and everything went off perfectly well, but Elizabeth was very sad when, in response to her anxious questionings, the Emperor had to tell her that she had borne him another daughter and not an heir to the throne. "Perhaps," he remarked kindly in a jesting tone, "it is because you did not follow the advice of that Rabbi from Pest who wanted you to have his Hebrew poem posted up on your door while the baby was being born." This time the Empress' mother was godmother, though in her absence the Archduchess Sophie acted as proxy. The new baby was given the name of Gisela.

The whole monarchy shared in Francis Joseph's disappointment, for everybody longed for an heir to the throne, as was shown by the innumerable letters he received from the public offering well-meaning advice. The public affection was equally touching, and the Empress was amazed to see a whole roomful of presents sent from every part of the Empire on the occasion of the child's birth.

But exactly the same thing happened to the second daughter as to little Sophie. She was simply removed to the nursery, under the wing of the Archduchess Sophie, and was equally lost to her mother. Again, the physician, Dr. Seeburger, whose advice had to be followed slavishly, was entirely under the influence of the Archduchess Sophie, to whom he owed his appointment. With him too, therefore, there were constant clashes. It was unspeakably bitter to Elizabeth that she could never see her children without meeting with some annoyance. It was an impossible, unnatural state of affairs, and she urged her husband to put an end to it by moving Sophie and Gisela to rooms on the same storey as her own, especially as little Sophie was always unwell and Seeburger seemed quite unable to discover the cause of her sickness. The Emperor adored his wife more and more, for since the birth of her second child she seemed lovelier and more blooming than ever, so this time he gave way. He wrote to his mother that he had made up his mind to move the children to the Radetzky apartments in the Burg, for they were roomier and more convenient and the Empress would not have to go upstairs to them. The letter was sent off on August 30, for both he and the Empress were a little nervous about the effect it might produce, and on September 2 they were starting on a long-projected tour of Carinthia and Styria, during which, for twelve days at least, they would be able to live together without interference from the Archduchess Sophie.

The most enjoyable day of their tour was that on which they climbed the Grossglockner. They stopped at Heiligenblut, one of the highest places in the world and a well-known place of pilgrimage, with a delightful Gothic church. The Empress was overwhelmed with the splendor of the view which lay before them, and the Emperor shared in her enthusiasm. As always happened when he was withdrawn from his mother's immediate influence, Elizabeth gained an ascendancy over him, and this was very necessary, for in answer to the letter of August 30 two very angry letters arrived in close succession from the Archduchess Sophie, reaching the Emperor during the tour. His mother was indignant at the suggestion that the children should be taken from her and brought up elsewhere. Her bitter animosity against the Empress was visible in every word. She even threatened to leave her apartments and withdraw from the Hofburg altogether.

Francis Joseph did not reply at once, for even during this tour he was harassed by documents from Vienna and had always to get up at four o'clock in the morning and spend every free minute dealing with them. But at last he plucked up his courage and for the first time opposed his mother's wishes. He reiterated his desire that the children should be moved, brushed aside her plausible objection that they would

THE EMPEROR AND EMPRESS SHORTLY AFTER THEIR MARRIAGE

From an engraving by Eduard Kaiser. National Library, Vienna.

have no sunshine in the new rooms, and entreated his mother to "judge Sisi indulgently if she is, perhaps, too jealous a mamma, for she is such a devoted wife and mother." He proceeded to use plain language about the painful impression made upon him and Elizabeth when they saw their children positively confined to the Archduchess' apartments and remarked that he had a horror of their being "shown off" (*produziert*) so much, for it only made them vain.

The Archduchess Sophie was filled with consternation when she saw that, slowly but surely, her son was escaping from her power, and realized that soon this might be happening in other than purely personal matters. For the moment Elizabeth had triumphed, but the Emperor's ambitious mother was cut to the heart. The result was that relations between the two became absolutely unbearable, and it was now war to the knife. Sophie could not but see that the influence of the Emperor's lovely wife was increasing, and it was soon evident that her anxiety lest her son might soon cease to listen to her even in political affairs was not without reason. Elizabeth knew nothing about politics and had as yet no ambition to interfere in them, so that Francis Joseph's ideas continued to reflect those of his mother. So far, it is true, these had not been very successful. Thanks to Austria's attitude during the Crimean War, which ended that year, Russian friendship had been lightly but irrevocably thrown away. The words spoken by the Russian Ambassador, Baron Meyendorff, on leaving Vienna in 1854, were soon to prove terribly true. "I am only sorry for the young Emperor," he said,* "for his policy has wounded us Russians so deeply that he can be sure of not having another moment's peace so long as his reign lasts." Again, the Archduchess Sophie's

* Reported in a dispatch from the Bavarian Minister in Vienna, which is now in the Bavarian State Archives.

dream of uniting the whole of Germany with a centralized Austria in a great empire with a population of seventy millions was farther than ever from being realized. And meanwhile ominous unrest was fermenting within the Empire itself, and prospects for the future were gloomy and lowering.

IV

FASCINATION AS AN INSTRUMENT OF POLICY

1856–1858

CONSCIOUS OF AUSTRIA'S DISADVANTAGEOUS position in world politics, the Emperor Francis Joseph began to listen to those counselors who held that an attempt must be made to conciliate opinion in disaffected Hungary and the Lombardo-Venetian Kingdom. He saw how his fascinating wife had enchanted everybody in Bohemia and Carinthia, and hoped that the same thing might happen in Italy. Elizabeth, who did not know the real state of affairs in the south, welcomed the idea of a tour as a means of escaping from intolerable domestic conditions for a few months. The only thing she disliked about it was parting with her children at the very moment when she had emerged victorious from the trying struggle with her mother-in-law, for the children had now been transferred to her own charge. She considered that the Archduchess' bringing-up had not done her daughter Sophie much good, for on returning from Carinthia she had found the little girl pale and thin. So against the advice of her mother-in-law she decided to take the child with her to Italy, leaving only the baby Gisela behind in Vienna.

Letters written from Milan at the time prophesied that the tour would go off smoothly, though it could not be expected to do much toward modifying the political situation, and that the Italians would persist in their systematic opposition to Austrian rule and in their impotent hatred. However, on November 17, 1856, the Emperor and Empress started for Venice, by way of Trieste. Among other places visited by the Empress was the Ursuline Convent at Laibach. She had hardly started her round of inspection when she asked the Mother Superior whether there were not some young negresses in the convent who had come from Eastern slave markets like her father's little black boys. On hearing that there were three, she sent for them, gave them sweets, and played with them, oblivious of everybody else, till she had to be reminded that other visits awaited her and that it was time to go. The Countess Esterházy, Mistress of the Household, was somewhat indignant, but Elizabeth only laughed, which increased the Countess' resentment.

Little Sophie was sent straight to Venice, and on November 20 the Emperor and Empress arrived at the heights of Opčina, commanding Trieste, from which they suddenly caught sight of the pure blue of the Adriatic below them and the port flooded with sunshine and brilliant with flags. There were the usual receptions, reviews, dinners, and gala performances at the theatre. Outwardly everything was brilliant, but while the local notables were being presented to their sovereigns a rather bad fire broke out in the municipal buildings; the fireworks stored there for the illuminations that evening had ignited, whether accidentally or not was not clear. The *bora* was blowing, not very hard, it is true, but hard enough to serve as an explanation of another curious accident which happened, when a gigantic glass imperial crown on the "Galeggiante," a huge state galley intended for the Emperor's use when he visited the harbor, suddenly broke in pieces.* The rumors of sabotage were concealed from the Empress as far as possible, but it was impossible entirely to

* The details of this visit are taken partly from the reports of imperial officials, now in the State Archives, Vienna, and partly from those of the

hide from her that even in Trieste things were not as they should have been and that worse might be anticipated in Venice and Milan.

For months past preparations for the imperial visit had been going on feverishly in Venice. But here, too, difficulties cropped up in the oddest way. The royal palace was being got ready and a carpet had to be laid in the great dining hall. The room was decorated in red and white, and now by some secret influence a green material was sent in for the carpet. Not till everything was ready did the authorities notice that the whole room was now resplendent with the colors of the Italian nationalist flag.

Things were hurriedly set to rights in time for the arrival of the Emperor and Empress on November 25. Here, too, they made their entry on board a splendid old galley formerly used by the Doges on state occasions, which was moored off the Public Gardens; but it was in an alarmingly decrepit state. The authorities had done all they could to produce the outward semblance of a brilliant reception, but on their way from the landing stage at the Piazzetta to St. Mark's the Emperor and Empress had to pass through serried ranks of people, all as silent as the grave. Not a single "*Evviva!*" was to be heard, only the "*Hoch!*" or "Hurrah!" of the Austrian civil and military officers. The English Consul General shook his head. "The crowd's only feeling," he wrote home, "was one of curiosity to see the Empress, whose reputation for marvelous beauty has naturally penetrated even to this place."

With painful emotions Elizabeth followed her husband across the Piazza di San Marco and into the Cathedral, after which Their Majesties proceeded to their residence in

British Consul General, now in the Public Record Office, London, which have been quoted as being less likely to be prejudiced than Austrian or Italian accounts.

the imperial palace, a tastelessly furnished building with a perfect labyrinth of stairs and passages, in which it was quite difficult to find one's way about. The Emperor and Empress frequently appeared in the streets of Venice, but at first the slightest attempt to cheer them was at once suppressed by the bystanders. The masses persisted in their policy of silence, and most of the great noble families stayed away from the city.

On November 29 the Emperor and Empress held a reception, but it was noticed that the Pisani, the Dolfin, the Giustinian, and many other families were absent. Only thirty out of the hundred and thirty patricians appeared to pay their respects to their sovereign. The ladies, who were more numerous than the men, were not likely to forget that evening for a long time. On leaving their gondolas, they had to walk more than two hundred yards before reaching the palace, through a crowd of people who assailed them with abuse and insults. It was impossible to conceal all this from Elizabeth, and when she appeared in the Teatro Fenice she could feel the icy atmosphere, for scarcely anybody saluted her and the Emperor, and the boxes of the most important families remained empty.

The Emperor and Empress were not surprised, for they had been prepared for something of the sort, and they tried to shame the people into good behavior by their example. Elizabeth's sweetness and charm were exerted to the utmost, though she found difficulty in making herself understood. Prince Alexander of Hesse, the Tsaritsa's brother, who was serving in the Austrian army in Italy, says in his diary that she was "*jolie comme un cœur*" (sweetly pretty), but he smiled at the stiff little Italian phrases which she had obviously learnt for the occasion and at her rather halting French. However, despite their political prejudice, the Venetians were not insensible to her beauty. The longer she and the Emperor stayed in Venice, the warmer the attitude of the populace became. People were already beginning to greet them here and there with a friendly salute. The situation really improved when on December 3 an amnesty was proclaimed and the confiscated property of political exiles was restored to them, and on the following day Francis Joseph and Elizabeth were received with loud and repeated applause at the Teatro Fenice.

Pleasant little incidents, which soon became known, played their part in improving popular sentiment. Once while the imperial pair were taking a walk in some *piazza* a man approached them with a petition. "You must present that at the palace," said the Emperor. "I have already tried, Your Majesty, but was refused admittance," replied the petitioner, an ex-officer named Jura, who had been deprived of his major's pension for taking part in the Revolution of 1848. "This is not the place for business," said the Emperor. "Come and see me at the palace." "They will not let me in," was the answer. The Emperor was about to walk on when Elizabeth looked at him imploringly and said: "Do give the man one of your gloves. Then we will give orders that the bearer of it is to be admitted." This was done, the major's pension was restored to him, and the accounts of the affair which soon went around produced a favorable impression.

The British Minister noticed this improvement, which he attributed to the Empress' youth, her rare beauty, charm, and amiability, "but," he reported, "it all remains quite independent of politics." The sympathetic demeanor of the imperial couple could change nothing in this sphere. In such an atmosphere Elizabeth felt what was almost a physical sensation of discomfort. The relaxing climate was not good for her, and she missed her accustomed exercise, for she could not go out in Venice without being almost suffocated by the crowds, besides which there was always a risk of insult or even assassination.

New Year's Day was spent in Venice, and on January 5 they left for Verona, passing through Vicenza. The same thing happened everywhere. The peasantry and the simple people in the towns were not unfriendly, but the upper and upper middle classes received them with calculated coldness and reserve.

Their reception on the eleventh in Brescia, where Haynau's brutality had not been forgotten, was worse than any, and the imperial procession approached the Palazzo Fenaroli amid an icy silence. Tears came into the Empress' eyes as she saw the distress on her husband's face.

Meanwhile in Milan the authorities had made every conceivable effort to prevent the reception of the sovereigns from being marred by an open scandal. Pressure was brought to bear upon the peasantry in the surrounding country to come into the city for the day, thousands of them being paid a lira a head. A report was circulated that on his arrival the Emperor would proclaim an amnesty and reduce taxation, and curiosity and love of a show did the rest.

When the Emperor and Empress arrived, the streets on the way to the palace were crowded with a vast throng. Bunting floated from the balconies, which, by order of the authorities, were filled with people, but not a single "*Evviva*" was heard. The police were powerless against the silence of the vast majority. Their most difficult task, however, was that of filling the great auditorium of the famous Scala. The police had insisted upon every box holder's giving notice whether he was going to use his box or not, and, if not, it was filled by officials or officers. But Milanese society sent servants to occupy its boxes, and only a fifth of the nobility eligible for presentation at court appeared at the performances or receptions. Francis Joseph hoped that his wife's charm and beauty, together with the amnesty and decreased taxation (though his generals advised him against this), would cause the same change of feeling here as in Venice. But in Milan it had no effect. So few ladies of the nobility appeared at the court concerts that two hundred and fifty middle-class ladies were invited, but even of these only twenty-six appeared. "Though the Emperor's visit is officially represented as having been a great success," reported the British Consul General, "the open and ostentatious aversion of by far the larger number of well-to-do and intelligent Lombards is none the less a fact deserving of the most serious consideration."

The Archduchess Sophie listened anxiously to the news from Italy. The strained relations between her and her daughter-in-law were painful to her, for her whole soul was set upon her son's happiness and welfare, and all her actions were to be ascribed to her exaggerated maternal instinct. She now held out an olive branch to the Empress by sending her a portrait of little Gisela. Elizabeth was eager to go home. Life in the hostile atmosphere of Milan was not pleasant, and she longed for her baby. On March 2, when Francis Joseph and Elizabeth left Milan, the streets were no more animated than before, and the people affected absolute indifference.

They were glad to be home again after their not very reassuring experiences, but the Emperor hoped that the tact of his brother Max, whom he had appointed governor in Italy, might make the task of governing that very difficult country easier. Elizabeth's health had benefited by the tour, and so had little Sophie's, though the people of Milan pretended, to her parents' annoyance, that the Emperor and Empress had only brought her with them as a sort of insurance against possible outrages. Elizabeth was wild with joy at seeing her baby again, but was hurt at finding that during her absence the little girl had grown entirely accustomed to her grandmother. She therefore took refuge with her pets, surrounding herself with large dogs and spending much time with her horses, which she petted so much that some of them would follow her like dogs. The Emperor indulged his wife's hobbies to the full, though he himself did not care for animals and was especially indifferent to dogs. He did all he could to persuade her not to ride so often for hours on end, a habit against which his mother never ceased fulminating.

Elizabeth cherished a secret hope that one day she might be able to choose her own ladies in waiting, for she felt the constraint of the Spanish court etiquette more keenly in her daily life than anywhere else. The great noble families of Austria formed an impenetrable rampart round the Emperor and Empress. Nobody who did not belong to these families, however great his personal worth might be, could approach them at all closely. Custom prescribed exactly who were to form the Empress' society: only twenty-three gentlemen belonging to the greatest and most historic families of the land and two hundred and twenty-nine ladies had what was called the "great" *entrée*—that is, the right to appear whenever they wished when the Empress was holding a court. Elizabeth found this intolerable. She liked to talk to anybody who interested or attracted her. The higher nobility were so accustomed to moving exclusively in their own limited circle that they spoke a language full of phrases and family allusions intelligible only to themselves and quite uninteresting to Elizabeth, who had not grown up in this circle. Thus, almost inevitably, the relations between the Empress and this group became strained, and since they favored a centralizing policy and had Greater Austrian sympathies, they inclined toward the views of the Archduchess Sophie. The chief representative of this group in the Emperor's entourage was his Adjutant

General, Count Grünne, who was almost all-powerful, especially in military affairs, till people said jestingly that the colors of the army were green (*grüne*) and not black and yellow, the imperial colors. This coterie disliked Hungary for opposing their ideal of a centralized Austria by obstinately resisting absorption into the unitary state as a mere province and claiming equality with Austria.

Baron Bach, the Minister of the Interior, who, since the crushing of the revolution, had stood for the idea of Austria one and indivisible, now felt that something must be done to conciliate Hungary, if possible, by means of a visit, and win it over by an amnesty and friendly overtures, as had been attempted in Italy. The fundamental idea of the unified Constitution was, however, to remain unaffected, and the Emperor was determined not to depart from it a hair's breadth. But in view of the national character of the Hungarians, the impression produced by the Empress' beauty and fascination was expected to be far greater than in Italy. Their departure was preceded by yet another domestic conflict. Elizabeth wanted to take the children with her at least as far as Budapest, so that she could enjoy having them both to herself, without their grandmother. The Archduchess expressed some anxiety on the score of the little ones' health, but Elizabeth thought this no more than the usual attempt to estrange her children from her and persuaded the Emperor to let her have her own way.

As soon as the prospective visit was heard of in Hungary, signs were at once apparent of the distrust which was felt of Austria and its methods. But though every Hungarian heart was full of smoldering opposition to the political tendencies uppermost in Vienna, the authorities were able to arrange for a magnificent, if not very cordial, welcome to the Emperor and Empress on their arrival at Buda on May 4, 1857, by way of the Danube. Elizabeth was enchanted with the fine natural setting of the Hungarian capital and flattered by the unconcealed enthusiasm for her beauty felt by both the nobility and the people, especially when she appeared on horseback either in the park or at reviews of the troops.

Though the days between May 5 and 13, which the Emperor and Empress spent in Budapest, were fuller than ever of the festivities which Elizabeth so much disliked, she felt remarkably at home there, and the sympathy for Hungarian ways which could be read in her eyes naturally called forth an answering love and cordiality. Rumors of the discord between Elizabeth and the Emperor's mother had long since penetrated to Hungary, and as the Archduchess Sophie's attitude and the part she had played at the time of the revolution were not forgotten, an obscure instinct told the Hungarians that their nationalist aspirations might gain a friend and perhaps even an ally in the Emperor's consort. Efforts were therefore redoubled to make her visit a pleasant one. Greater reserve was shown toward Francis Joseph, for though he had proclaimed an amnesty, it was impossible to bring back to life those who had been executed, and the Emperor still persisted in his resistance to the nation's most ardent desires. But it was not easy to show affection for his consort and antipathy for himself at the same time. Though he declined to receive an address from a hundred and twenty-seven of the Conservative nobility which contained references to a possible restoration of the Hungarian Constitution, yet, as Bach had hoped, part of the cordiality felt toward his wife was reflected upon him, too.

And now a thing happened which seemed to justify the anxiety expressed by the Archduchess Sophie before their departure. On May 13 the Emperor and Empress were to have continued their journey into the interior of Hungary. But Gisela suddenly fell sick. Her parents' departure was at once postponed. Gisela recovered fairly rapidly, but on May

THE EMPRESS ELIZABETH AS A YOUNG WOMAN

From a lithograph by A. Dauthage after the portrait by Einsle, 1858. National Library, Vienna.

19 the same symptoms appeared in Sophie. Dr. Seeburger at first maintained that they were caused by teething, but it was difficult to believe him when the child began to vomit blood and bile. "The little thing cries and screams incessantly in the most heart-rending way," wrote Francis Joseph to his mother. Sophie looked pitifully ill, and her parents were in the greatest distress, especially Elizabeth, who could not help remembering the dissensions which had preceded their departure. But as soon as there were signs of a lasting improvement, she listened to the representations made to her, and the tour was resumed, for the whole country was in a state of expectation, large sums had already been expended on preparations, and the people must not be disappointed.

On May 23 they started for the interior of Hungary. The Empress would have thoroughly enjoyed the sight of the splendid horses and handsome people in their beautiful national costumes who lined the route everywhere, had it not been for her anxiety about her children. When the imperial visitors entered Debreczen on May 28, they received a telegram from Seeburger, which, in spite of all his previous assurances, brought them disquieting news about Sophie's condition. They broke off their tour at once and returned to Budapest by the shortest route. Elizabeth hurried to her little girl the moment she arrived, and found her gravely ill, excessively weak and with eyes already dim. Seeburger was very crestfallen, but when pressed with questions he would only say that he had not given up hope. The young mother was frantic with grief and never left the child's bedside for a moment. But she was powerless to avert the outcome. For eleven hours the Empress followed with anguish every phase of her daughter's agony, while the doctors stood by helplessly and could do nothing. At half past nine in the evening the little girl of barely two could struggle for life no more, and the weeping mother closed her child's eyes.

"Our little one is an angel in Heaven," telegraphed the Emperor to his parents. "We are crushed. Sisi is full of resignation to the will of the Lord." But this was hardly true. Elizabeth was prostrated with despair, blaming herself and everybody else, and it was useless to tell her that the disaster might have happened anywhere and that nobody was to blame.

The tour of Hungary was abandoned, and on May 30 the Emperor and Empress returned to Laxenburg. Politically, however, this sad event produced beneficial results. Everywhere, even in quarters where political discontent was rife, warm personal sympathy was felt for the bereaved parents, and for the moment this obscured the opposition movements in Hungary.

Elizabeth wept from morning till night and talked of nothing but her baby, and she felt her first meeting with the Archduchess Sophie most terribly. Seeing the Empress' grief, her mother-in-law tactfully refrained from comment, but in every order and every word Elizabeth thought she could detect an unspoken reproach, suggesting that the disaster would not have happened if only they had listened to the Archduchess' wise and experienced advice. Elizabeth was now nineteen, but she felt as though she had been married for at least ten years and could not understand that Sophie's attitude toward her was still that of a sensible old mother toward an inexperienced child. So great was Elizabeth's despair that her mother decided to come to Laxenburg with her three sisters to cheer and distract her a little. This was most necessary, for at times Elizabeth's grief assumed very strange forms. She had never cared much for society, and now, with the exception of the Emperor, she would let nobody come near her, but insisted upon always walking and riding alone and withdrew entirely into herself. While she was in this state, there could be no thought of her resuming the tour of

Hungary, so the Emperor decided to return by himself, which naturally did not produce at all the desired effect.

Yet it was harder to persuade the Emperor to adopt harsh measures toward Hungary than it had been before. A number of those who had fled abroad at the time of the revolution now had their return facilitated, among them Count Julius Andrássy, who had been spending his exile in Paris by no means unpleasantly. Liberally supplied with money by his mother, the elegant young Count was an ardent admirer of the fair sex, a welcome guest in the best houses, and the darling of the Parisian ladies. Moreover, he no longer took part in the plots against the Austrian Government carried on in London by Kossuth, but came out openly in favor of a reconciliation between Austria and his native land.

Every move made by the exiles was closely followed in Vienna. Thus it was noted with approval that, furious with Russia for joining in the campaign against his native land in 1848, Andrássy had declared that it was not to Hungary's interest to let the Empire of the Tsars be master of the Danube and Black Sea, a point of view which was in harmony with the anti-Russian tendencies then prevailing in Vienna. Meanwhile, in 1856, the Count had married a Hungarian heiress, the Countess Katinka Kendeffy, the political reputation of whose family in Austria was irreproachable. In 1857 Andrássy was accordingly granted permission to return home with impunity, and his confiscated property was restored to him. All this was eagerly discussed in the bosom of the imperial family, and later in the year news arrived which distracted the Empress from her gloomy thoughts, for she now heard of her sister Marie's betrothal to the Crown Prince Francis of Naples and Sicily.

Yet still the domestic conflict went on, though perhaps less overtly. After the death of her daughter, Elizabeth tried to obtain the removal of Dr. Seeburger, but the Archduchess

Sophie managed to prevent this. The doctor remained at his post, and in spite of her dislike for him continued to treat the Empress. When she had a swelling on the bone of her hand, his method of curing it was to lay two large silver coins on it and bind it up very tightly, hoping that the pressure of the coins would reduce the swelling. Elizabeth endured this for two days, till she began to feel acute pain, when she tore off the bandages and had recourse to ordinary massage. In November the Emperor and Empress again changed their apartments in the Burg, for their old quarters aroused too many unhappy memories and were, moreover, too small for them now. The Empress was given the "Amalienappartement" connecting directly with the nurseries, which was particularly important to her, for by the winter of 1857 she knew herself to be again expecting a child and by this arrangement she was able to spare herself undue exertion. Lately, too, the Archduchess Sophie had become pleasanter, but by this time it was no use, and it still depressed Elizabeth that she had to see her so much too often.

Once more advice was showered upon the Empress from every corner of the Empire as to what she should do during her pregnancy to insure the child's being a boy. She always had these letters shown to her, for she was a little superstitious and longed for a son. Everything unpleasant had to be kept from her carefully, so she was not told when suddenly, on the morning of August 16, those in the castle of Schönbrunn were startled by a loud crash, which shook the very walls. The great luster in the throne room (*Zeremoniensaal*) had fallen down and lay shivered to a thousand fragments. Fortunately nobody was hurt, but this was the second time it had happened in two years. "I shall take great care," wrote the Controller of the Archduchess Sophie's Household, "not to sit under the luster when I am at court." But Elizabeth would certainly have interpreted this as an unlucky omen.

The critical day drew near. On August 21 the Archduchess Sophie, who was at Laxenburg, suddenly received a telegram saying: "Her Imperial Majesty is in labor." She at once left for Schönbrunn, and the first thing she did on arriving there was to have the Blessed Sacrament exposed on the altar of the chapel.* At her previous confinements Elizabeth had hardly uttered a murmur, but at ten o'clock that night she was in such agony that she gave a heart-rending shriek, while the Emperor's mother and the Countess Esterházy fell on their knees weeping and began praying for her. The labor was very difficult, and it was not till a quarter to eleven that night that the Empress was delivered.

"Is it a son?" she asked anxiously in a faint voice. "The midwife does not know yet," replied Francis Joseph, fearing lest the sudden joy might prove dangerous to her. On which Elizabeth said piteously: "Of course! It must be another girl!" "What if it *were* a boy, though?" he said. Elizabeth's beautiful face lit up with joy, but she still suspected them of deceiving her and would not be convinced till she had seen her son.

For the first few days the Empress did not recover very rapidly, for she had such a flow of milk that she could not rest, and she was not allowed to nurse the child herself. This was a grief and made her angry with Seeburger, but apart from this she was indescribably happy. Francis Joseph would have liked to give her all the jewels in the world. He did not think his son very good-looking, but "magnificently built and very strong." When he was congratulated, tears of joy ran down his cheeks, and his love for his wife was, if pos-

* These details are drawn from unpublished letters in the possession of Count Szécsen (see Bibliography).

sible, even greater than before. The Archduchess would now find it more difficult to get her way, for Elizabeth's influence over her husband was more firmly established than ever. But in reality the Emperor's mother rejoiced as much as he did, for in her eyes the child was the best guaranty for her son's happiness and that of the Empire. Her one object now was to bring the child up in accordance with her own views and form him as she had done the Emperor. She had not much confidence in the Empress' educational capacity, perhaps with good reason; but she certainly went too far in trying to eliminate the mother's influence entirely. In view of the Empress' far from pliant character, this attempt threatened serious conflicts for the future.

Everybody concerned meant well and was sure of being in the right, but they were all pulling in different directions.

V

THE ITALIAN WAR AND THE MADEIRA CRISIS

1859-1862

THOUGH SETTLED IN A FOREIGN COUNTRY, Elizabeth had never lost touch with her own home. One after the other her sisters were getting married. First, in August, 1858, Helene was married to the Hereditary Prince Maximilian of Thurn and Taxis, one of the richest princes in Germany, and next came the wedding of her sister Marie, who, to the great delight of the ducal house, was marrying the Crown Prince of Naples and Sicily, so that another of the Duke's daughters would now reign over a European state. She was not so beautiful as the Empress, but resembled her greatly in figure and had a strong and resolute will. Elizabeth traveled with her as far as Trieste and looked on dubiously at the final ceremony of handing her sister over to a Neapolitan royal commissary who was to escort her to her husband in Naples.

Elizabeth would have liked to do all she could to cheer her sister's departure for an unknown land to join a husband who was still more or less a stranger to her. There could be no question of love or inclination—and indeed, the first meeting with Francis in Naples was quite uncomfortable. Marie knew no Italian, the Crown Prince no German and very little French, and even if they had been able to understand each other they would hardly have known what to say.

The Empress now returned home to her unsatisfactory domestic life, but she was beginning to be more alive to her husband's political anxieties. Piedmont evidently intended to take advantage of Austria's isolation after the Crimean War to press her national claims, and continued to agitate for them till Vienna allowed itself to be provoked into issuing a premature ultimatum, which was to lead to war with Sardinia, the ally of France. The decision had been arrived at with undue haste, even Prussia not having been notified beforehand, and now war was imminent.

Up to this time Elizabeth had had no experience of any but peaceful political conditions, but a change now took place. Nervous and impressionable, she saw the future of the Empire endangered, and consequently that of her husband and children, so she did not enter very deeply into the lesser annoyances of her Bavarian relatives, who were greatly upset by the betrothal of her eldest brother, Ludwig, to a beautiful actress, Henriette Mendel. Everybody was indignant, but Duke Ludwig stood firm and at last got his way. Henriette was created Baroness Wallersee, and the wedding took place on May 28, 1859.

Meanwhile in Italy Grünne's favorite, General Count Gyulay, had missed his opportunity of engaging the French and Piedmontese separately before they could effect a junction. His command proved disastrous, and the army was soon in retreat. The Emperor looked on anxiously, till at last he felt that he must leave for the front in person to set things to rights. When he told Elizabeth of his intention, she burst into tears, and before he left exacted a solemn promise that he would be careful. "For my sake and the children's," she said, "think of yourself, too, and not only of your work and the war."

She returned despondently to Schönbrunn, after taking leave of him sadly at the station. On May 31 she appeared unexpectedly at the Church of Our Lady at Maria-Lanzendorf, near Vienna, where there was a famous image of the Virgin, and prayed that her husband's life might be spared. Francis Joseph did not forget his promise to write to her often, and his letters breathe the deepest devotion. "My dearest angel Sisi," he wrote on arriving at Verona on May 31, 1859,* "I am profiting by the first moments after getting up to tell you once again how much I love you and how I long for you and the dear children. Provided only that all is well with you and you are looking after yourself carefully, as you promised me. . . . And do try to find as much distraction as possible, so as not to be depressed. . . ."

But Elizabeth was very melancholy and shut herself away entirely, if only that she might see less of her mother-in-law. She was out riding from early till late and was too restless to settle to any occupation. The Archduchess Sophie shook her head and the Empress' entourage talked themselves hoarse about her strange behavior, especially her old enemy Dr. Seeburger. Once, on happening to meet the Minister of Police, he poured out a flood of complaints and censure of the Empress: "She is unfit for her position both as Empress and as wife," he said, "though she has really nothing to do. Her relations with the children are most perfunctory, and though she grieves and weeps over the noble Emperor's absence, she goes out riding for hours on end, ruining her health. An icy gulf separates her from the Archduchess Sophie, and the Mistress of the Household, the Countess Esterházy, has absolutely no influence over her."

Elizabeth found her only consolation in writing long letters to her husband. Those of May 29 and 30, in which she implored Francis Joseph to let her join him at his headquarters in Verona, bear witness to her depressed state of mind. But the Emperor replied: "For the present, unfor-

*** From an unpublished letter of the Emperor's, which, with the others quoted later, is now at Schloss Wallsee.**

tunately, I cannot comply with your wish, though I should love to beyond words. Women are out of place in the disturbed life at headquarters, and I cannot set my army a bad example, besides which, even I do not in the least know how long I shall be stopping here. . . . I beseech you, my angel, if you love me, not to grieve so much, but to take care of yourself; try to find plenty of distractions, go for rides and drives in moderation and preserve your dear, precious health, so that when I come back I may find you thoroughly well and we may be as happy as can be."

But things were going badly at the front. After the battle of Magenta, which was lost entirely through bad generalship, Milan had to be evacuated and the Austrian troops were compelled to retire within the Quadrilateral. The greatest disquiet was felt in the monarchy, and alarming reports followed in rapid succession. They came to the ears of the Empress, who could hardly control her grief and agitation. Once again she begged to be allowed to join her husband at headquarters, but in the conditions then prevailing this was naturally impossible. "My dear, dear only angel," wrote Francis Joseph, "I beg you, in the name of your love for me, to collect yourself: show yourself in the city often and visit institutions. You do not know what a help you could be to me if you would do this. It will raise the spirits of people in Vienna and maintain the good atmosphere which I so urgently need. . . . Do take care of yourself for my sake, for I have so many worries. . . ."

In spite of the anxiety caused him by Elizabeth's letters, he rejoiced beyond measure when the post arrived. Her letters were always brought him when he woke, and he "simply devoured them while still in bed." Elizabeth's thoughts turned toward Naples, in the hope that it would come out boldly on Austria's side—but she forgot the powerful French fleet. Her sister had hardly been married to the Crown Prince three months when King Ferdinand II suddenly died on May 22 and Marie became Queen, though this did not enable her to help Francis Joseph in any way.

Meanwhile Elizabeth continued to live her ordinary life at Laxenburg, but she slept badly, ate scarcely anything, and spent all day on horseback. She usually rode alone, but was sometimes accompanied by her groom, Harry Holmes, for she liked him and he was an artist in his own line. But the Archduchess Sophie did not consider this proper and complained to the Emperor, so that in the midst of his anxiety about the war he had to cudgel his brains to find out what to do about it. "I have thought over the question of your riding," he wrote to Elizabeth, "and I cannot allow you to ride alone with Holmes, for it is not proper." Finally he proposed that she should be escorted by the Controller of the Imperial Hunts (*Oberstjägermeister*). The letters he wrote on campaign were full of assurances of his love. "I cannot tell you often enough how much I love you and think about you, my angel . . . I love you so vastly." "My dear, heavenly Sisi . . . my only beautiful angel . . ." Such expressions as this recur at every other word. But Elizabeth still felt that in the hour of danger her place was at her husband's side. To calm her nerves she went out riding both in the morning and in the afternoon, and now, to Francis Joseph's alarm, she began to practice jumping regularly. Bad news would throw her into a panic. She felt no confidence in her husband's generals and was in terror of the Emperor and the whole headquarters staff being cut to pieces. Once she rode from Laxenburg to Vöslau and back without stopping, a distance of nearly twenty miles. Francis Joseph implored her not to take such long rides. "Promise me this," he wrote on the eve of Solferino, without even mentioning the impending battle, "for otherwise I shall find you too tired and thin."

Two days later came the news of the defeat. "So I had to

give orders to retreat," wrote the Emperor to Elizabeth. "I rode . . . to Valeggio through a violent storm and from there to Villafranca. I spent a terrible evening there, for it was a confused mass of wounded men, fugitives, carriages, and horses. . . . Such is the sad story of a horrible day, on which great things were done, but fortune did not smile upon us. I am the richer by many experiences and have learned what it feels like to be a defeated general . . . I shall stay here until the army has retired across the Adige and the most necessary arrangements have been made for the future. Then I shall fly to Vienna, where many duties call me. My only ray of consolation and hope now is that I am coming to you, my angel. You can imagine how happy it makes me. . . . Your faithful Franz." But anxious lest his "heavenly, angelic Sisi" should take things too much to heart, he adds: "Only you must not despair, but trust in God as I do, for He will surely rule all things for the best. He is punishing us sorely, and we are only at the beginning of still worse trials, but one must bear them with resignation and do one's duty in all things."

The Italian reverses had their effects in Hungary, too, where the revolutionary elements scented their approaching delivery and began to hope that their long-standing aspirations might now be gratified. Elizabeth had set up a hospital for the wounded at Laxenburg and spent most of her days there. She, too, heard these rumors and saw the approaching collapse of the policy for which she held her mother-in-law responsible—more so, perhaps, than she really was. The last bulwarks of her respect for the Archduchess, based upon a sense of her political superiority, now gave way. Her feeling that the Archduchess Sophie and her creatures, with whom she had surrounded the Emperor, were unable to rise to the greatness of the crisis, but were endangering the very state and dynasty, was confirmed. She realized that complaints and lamentations were useless and that, all other political advisers having come to grief, it was her duty to come forward with advice of her own. Anxious about the attitude of Hungary, she advised her husband to open negotiations with Napoleon III as soon as possible in the hope of ending the war. But then she would remember that she was a wife and mother: "Have you forgotten me among all these events?" she wrote. "Do you love me still? If you did not, then whatever else might happen I should not care." "But, my poor, dearly loved Sisi," replied the Emperor, "you simply cannot imagine how I long for you, and I surely need not tell you again how immensely I love you. You do know it, in spite of the doubts you express in your letters. I am mad with joy at the thought of the glorious moment which will unite me with you once more, my angel . . . I entreat you to be calm and not to give way to vain terrors. It is splendid that you have set up a hospital at Laxenburg, and I thank you with all my heart. . . . Only be strong and endure, and better times will come again one day. . . ."

Meanwhile, it had been suggested to the Emperor that at such a moment he ought not to leave the troops. "My dear, dear angel," he wrote, "you must not think that I have lost my courage and am losing my grip. On the contrary, I have confidence and am endeavoring as far as I can to inspire others with it. . . . I only meant to come to Vienna because I thought that at present I might be more necessary there than here, but since that is not so, I am staying here with my good troops till the middle of July. Do not grieve. . . . Your political plan contains some very good ideas, but for the present we must not give up hope that Prussia and Germany will help us after all, and till then there must be no thought of negotiating with the enemy. . . ."

This time Elizabeth was quite in despair that her husband still did not return. She imagined him in a thousand dangers and thought things to be worse than he told her. She was afraid he might be slain in battle, or make himself seriously ill through overexertion or exposure to rain and storms, or be taken prisoner, or killed in a railway outrage. She completely lost her nerve, and the Emperor had constantly to reassure her. But she could not rest. She rode from morning till night, sat up at night writing long letters to Francis Joseph, her parents, and family, and took a gloomy view of the future. Besides, she worried as to whether her husband loved her. She was hurt when he said he had to return to Vienna on business, and would have liked him to write that it was an irresistible longing to see her that drew him homewards.

Meanwhile the Emperor had received fresh complaints from his mother about Elizabeth's doings. He was on the eve of opening negotiations with Napoleon III, in which Prince Alexander of Hesse had acted as intermediary, and the news from home robbed him of the peace of mind which he so badly needed. "My dearest angel Sisi," he wrote, ". . . I simply cannot tell you how I long for you and how anxious I am about you. Your present alarming mode of life makes me quite desperate, for it is bound to ruin your dear health. I implore you to give it up at once and try to sleep at night, which Nature intended, after all, for sleeping, and not for reading and writing. And do not ride too much or too hard either. It hurt me very much that you did not like my saying I must return to Vienna on account of business. You can well imagine that the one incentive I have for returning and the only pleasure it will offer me is that I shall be able to hold you in my arms once more; but in times like the present one ought not to let oneself be led by the feelings of one's heart, however strong they may be, so much as by one's sense of duty. I have never heard of any meeting with the Prince of Prussia, such as you mention. But I am afraid another interview may be awaiting me; namely, one with that arch-rogue (*Erzschuft*) Napoleon. I should dislike it extremely, but if it can be of any service to the monarchy, even that will have to be swallowed. At present Napoleon seems to be possessed by a prodigious passion for an armistice and for peace. . . ."

But now events moved rapidly. Anxious lest his own country might fall an easy prey to the Prussian army while he lingered in Italy, Napoleon had as much interest in making peace as Austria. This led to the meeting at Villafranca on July 11, 1859, followed shortly afterwards by the signing of an armistice. At last Francis Joseph could return home, embrace his wife, and set his domestic affairs to rights. He found Elizabeth in a state of acutely overwrought nerves, for, though the children were well and happy, the relations between his wife and his mother had become even more embittered. The Archduchess insisted upon having the chief voice in training the Crown Prince for his future duties. The child's nurse was in a most difficult position, for she kept receiving contradictory orders from the mother and grandmother, which was particularly awkward when the Emperor, who was the ultimate court of appeal, was at a distance. Francis Joseph was forced to maneuver constantly between his wife and mother, which was difficult, for both were often right in different ways. But as a result of the war the Emperor began to move further away from the men and ideas with which his mother sympathized and draw closer to his wife's more liberal views. Buol, whose policy had been a hopeless failure, had already fallen, and Count Rechberg had taken his place; but Bach and his centralizing system had fallen, too, and Francis Joseph was drawing nearer to the idea of constitutional government, though he had not yet entirely capitulated. It was high time, for the general situation was most discouraging. Austria had lost prestige in the eyes of the whole world. The course followed after the revolution, of suspending the Constitution, had failed to achieve the desired results, and at the same time mistakes had been made in foreign policy. There was also grave discontent in the army, owing to the blunders made by the higher command in the recent campaign which had led to catastrophe. The all-powerful Count Grünne, who had appointed Gyulay, was held generally responsible, so the Emperor resolved to remove him from his post as Adjutant General and make him Master of the Horse, where he would have no voice in military policy. This amounted to a defeat for the Emperor's mother, since Grünne had been her prime favorite, and it was likely to be regarded by Hungary as a friendly move on the Emperor's part, for Grünne's attitude toward that country's aspirations was well known. Elizabeth observed the change with satisfaction. Every time any part of the structure built up by her mother-in-law collapsed, it opened up the way for her own influence and ideas. But she was yet to learn that the Archduchess Sophie would not so easily admit herself to be worsted, though her influence might be temporarily shaken.

By the beginning of 1860 the young Empress was living in a state of incessant agitation. Three confinements in the space of four years, the vicissitudes of the war, and her constant feud with the Archduchess and her clique had undermined her health. And now another thing happened which she felt most acutely, for she had a very strong family feeling. The idea of a united Italy had taken great strides since the campaign of 1859, and her brother-in-law's position suffered in proportion. The King and Queen of Naples knew not a moment's peace. Sporadic risings broke out, and in May Garibaldi started out on his famous expedition of the Thousand, which at a single blow severed Sicily from the Kingdom of Naples, and, when Palermo fell on June 6, 1860, showed the whole world that the Bourbon régime had feet of clay. Appeal after appeal for help went forth from Naples to the courts of Europe, and naturally to Vienna among them. Elizabeth implored her husband to intervene, but since his unsuccessful campaign the situation was such that no assistance could possibly be given. On June 13 Dukes Ludwig and Karl in Bayern arrived secretly at Laxenburg on a visit to the Empress, and discussed every possible and impossible plan for helping their sister, but all in vain. The Dukes were able to observe the state of Elizabeth's nerves and general health, and to see what a pitch the antipathy between her and her mother-in-law had reached.

It was a long time since she had spent much time with her dear ones in Bavaria, and she now promised to pay them a visit in July. At Possenhofen, too, everybody was very much upset about the fate of the Queen of Naples. They heard that the King reigned but did not govern and was quite unfit to cope with the emergency. Garibaldi was already thinking of crossing over to the mainland from Sicily. The Austrian minister reported that the King of Naples had hardly anybody left upon whom he could really depend. Yet the Queen was in favor of his defending his crown by arms at all costs. Then, on August 21, Garibaldi landed in the south of the peninsula, and everywhere both army and people went over to him. King Francis looked on apathetically, but his twenty-year-old queen was admirable in her energy and courage. She was said to have told her husband that if he did not place himself at the head of the troops which still remained loyal, she would do so herself.

Meanwhile the magic name of Garibaldi was doing its work, and all that remained to the King was to retire into the fortress of Gaeta. For his own part, he would have preferred to throw up the whole thing. He only put up a defense in order to secure a successful retreat, and because he was shamed by the demeanor of his wife, whose courage rose as the danger increased, a characteristic in which she resembled her sister the Empress. Elizabeth felt the deepest sympathy with her sister's fate, and the consciousness that she herself had to sit by with hands folded increased her nervous irritability.

Meanwhile, as the wounds of the year 1859 began to heal, the Archduchess Sophie gradually regained her influence in Vienna. The October diploma, which still embodied the idea of a unitary empire while granting a central parliament, was not irreconcilable with her views. Francis Joseph himself confirmed this when he wrote to her on October 21, 1860: "We are going to have a little parliamentary life, it is true, but the power remains in my hands." This being the case in politics, it was hardly to be expected that his mother would consent to resign control in things domestic. The clashes between her and Elizabeth became more and more frequent, till toward the end of October, 1860, they were of almost daily occurrence. Elizabeth reproached her husband bitterly for not taking her part in everything; but at times she seemed to him too nervous and erratic, and he felt that such an important matter as the education of the Crown Prince was better left in the hands of his mother, who had trained him himself for the throne so carefully. Thus Francis Joseph was torn between his mother, to whom he owed everything, and his wife, whom he loved beyond words; and, moreover, as was only natural, he was also exposed to innumerable temptations from attractive women. The fact that he was not always insensible to these was felt as a slight by his young wife, conscious of her own dazzling beauty. She completely lost her balance. The interminable war had worn out her patience, everything seemed unbearable, and she saw enemies on all sides. Her health displayed alarming symptoms, which at first seemed inexplicable and brought her to such a pass that she resolved to put an end to the whole situation. She went to her husband and told him that she felt ill and wanted to go to a southern climate in order to escape the winter. Francis Joseph proposed Meran, Arco, or some sunny place on the Adriatic, but the Empress shook her head and replied: "No, no! I must go far, far away, right out of the country."

She wished to go abroad, so as to show people that she really meant to break away, and she mentioned Madeira as being sufficiently remote. There, on an island, far away in the ocean, where eternal spring reigned, she might try to regain her physical and mental equilibrium. In her despair Elizabeth forgot her duty as wife and mother, as empress and first lady in a great empire. She was quite unconscious of the violent sensation which her sudden departure to such a distant land was sure to make, for it had all the appearance of a flight. The Emperor was shocked. He had anxiously watched the change in his wife during the last few months, and had been so depressed that Count Rechberg had noticed it and wondered what could be happening. Francis Joseph had always been chivalrous toward women, and the antipathy between his wife and mother had cut him to the quick. And now he was in the gravest anxiety, for the Empress was seriously ill. Doctors were called in and examined her thoroughly, but no very definite symptoms were to be found, except the sore throats from which the Empress often suffered, but that was not a sufficient pretext for a voyage to Madeira. They would have to be described as an incipient affection of the lungs, or perhaps a tuberculous affection of the throat.

It so happened that there was no Austrian ship available at the moment, but Elizabeth refused to wait and said she must start at once. A request was sent to Queen Victoria, who placed her yacht at the Empress' disposal for the voyage from Antwerp to Madeira and invited her to pay her a visit. Elizabeth, looking pale and wasted, thanked the British Ambassador for the yacht, but declined the invitation, on the ground that she wished to preserve the strictest incognito. The Countess Esterházy was left behind with the children. On November 17 Francis Joseph escorted his wife through Munich to Bamberg, after which she went on alone to Antwerp, where the Queen's yacht was waiting for her.

The news of the Empress' sudden illness and departure made a deep impression on the public, which was entirely taken by surprise, especially as it was rumored that her illness was really serious. Suggested remedies at once began to pour in from every corner of the land. One man asked permission to send several bottles of water from a "miraculous spring." A Berlin brewer named Hoff did not even ask permission, but at once dispatched a large case of malt extract "in order that she might be better nourished." Even the Archduchess was quite affected by this sudden decision. She naturally judged her strange daughter-in-law's apparent flight severely, but for the rest, it was playing into her own hands, for Elizabeth was leaving her a free field to exert her influence over the Emperor and bring up the children according to her own ideas, thus regaining all the ground she had recently lost.

The great world received the news of the Empress' grave illness very seriously. All the crowned heads vied with one another in offering their services. Count Carvajal, whose birth and wealth made him a sort of king in Madeira, offered her his own villa. He did not know that the Empress dreaded being involved in a number of social and other duties. She had rented a small villa, buried in flowers. Money was no object, for the Emperor had provided her with unlimited credits. The yacht *Osborne* had a very stormy voyage from Antwerp to Madeira, and it was observed that, ill though she was, the Empress bore the unusually rough passage better than any of the other passengers. Nobody appeared at mealtimes, but Elizabeth was not in the least inconvenienced by the tossing waves.

Soon the yacht neared the island. As they passed the lofty black basalt cliffs of Cabo Girão, suddenly Funchal, the capital, lay before them, rising in terraces on the slopes of a high, cloud-capped mountain. Far above it the towers of the church of Nostra Senhora do Monte, a place of pilgrimage, peeped out from the pine and chestnut woods. The whole population had crowded into the town to enjoy such a great event as the arrival of the lovely young Empress who had so suddenly fallen ill. Many expected to see a pale, wasted form, or thought she would have to be carried ashore, but nothing of the sort happened. Elizabeth disembarked with a very grave face, it is true, but to all appearance fresh and well and braced by her sea voyage. On the Molo stood a Portuguese grandee with a letter of welcome from Dom Pedro. He thought the Empress looked very well and could not help wondering a little, for the only symptom to be noticed was an occasional slight cough. He at once conducted her to her villa. Elizabeth was in raptures. High on top of a sheer cliff was a marvelous tropical garden, in which stood a house with a fine veranda supported on columns, up which glorious creepers with purple and yellow bells climbed luxuriantly. From the great windows there was a view out to sea, and an intoxicating fragrance was wafted from the garden. On the very edge of the cliff stood a summerhouse buried in flowers, looking straight down to the sea, some hundred feet below. The picturesque prospect was framed in a setting of laurels and palms. During the first few days Elizabeth was enchanted by the scenery. For a time she forgot her cares and illness, and her melancholy moods did not return till the monotony of everyday existence once more asserted its sway and she gradually grew accustomed to her lovely surroundings. She now began to feel homesick for her husband and children. On Christmas Eve, in particular, which was her birthday, and when her suite did all they could to reproduce home conditions for her, her thoughts were with her family. In reply to the New Year's wishes which reached her, she wrote sadly: "May it be a better one for us all than the last. I am often dreadfully agitated at present." Elizabeth was thinking of her mother and of the sister who was in such extremities in Gaeta. It was a long time since she had had any news from her, and she waited expectantly for the Emperor's messengers, Uxküll, Latour, and Louis Rechberg, who went to and fro with letters, and whose duty it was to report to the Emperor how Elizabeth was. Their impressions varied. Her mental condition made her physical state seem even worse than it really was. "I am terribly sorry for the poor Empress," wrote Count Rechberg to his aunt,* "for, quite between ourselves, I think she is very, very ill. Her cough seems in no way better than before her voyage here, though as a rule she does not cough much. . . . But mentally she is terribly depressed, almost to the point of melancholia, though in her condition this could hardly be otherwise—she often shuts herself up in her room all day crying. I cannot imagine what the reason can be, but she has not received a single letter from the Queen of Naples since arriving here. She hoped I would bring her one, and cried the whole day after my arrival, when she saw that she was to be disappointed. She eats alarmingly little, and we, too, have to suffer for this, for the whole meal, consisting of four courses, four sweets, coffee, etc., does not last more than twenty-five minutes. She is so depressed that she never goes out, except for an hour's ride at a footpace, but simply sits at the open window."

* From an unpublished letter in the possession of the Countess Gabriele Rechberg.

Elizabeth spent most of her time with the eight ponies that had been bought or hired for her, passing the time as best she could with what had delighted her in early childhood. Here she could give way to her love of animals and flowers and indulge her childlike side, which was one of the secrets of her inexhaustible charm, together with the fascinating archness of a nature essentially gay. To all who were nice to her, and paid her what she called "little attentions" over and above what was due, she always wanted to give some pleasure in return. The following letter to her brother-in-law is typical of many: "Dear Ludwig," she wrote,* "didn't I send you a dried sea horse in my last letter? Please be very kind and have a really nice, exact copy of it made for me in gold, of the same size. . . . I want it for Mittrowsky, who dried it for me and is always bringing me all sorts of sea creatures, of which I am very fond. A little time ago I sent for a big dog from England. You see, I am increasing my menagerie, though I am afraid all my little birds will not survive the voyage. . . ."

In all her letters home Elizabeth complained that she was getting no news from her sisters, not even from those in Bavaria. Marie of Naples could not write, of course, for she was beleaguered in Gaeta, where she was bearing herself with the greatest courage. The diplomatic corps had retired to Rome, and it had been proposed to the Queen that she should accompany them, but she had refused. She showed high powers of endurance and was an inspiration to the garrison, and when the general in command of the besieging forces offered to have a distinguishing sign placed on the Queen's palace and the hospitals so that they should be spared during the bombardment, she persuaded her husband to accept the offer on behalf of the hospitals, but to decline it for her

* The Empress' letters to the Archduke Ludwig Viktor are now in the archives at Schloss Wallsee.

palace. After five months, abandoned and betrayed by everyone, the monarch had to capitulate on February 13, 1861. The King and Queen withdrew to Rome and took refuge in the Palazzo Farnese under the protection of the Pope, just as in 1848 Pius the Ninth had sought protection in the Kingdom of Naples. Their marriage had not turned out very well from the first, and now they had to live a life of inaction as exiles. When Elizabeth heard the news, she deplored her sister's loss of her throne, but was at least relieved from tormenting uncertainty.

For the rest, the Empress had benefited in both body and mind from her stay in Madeira, that ever-blooming garden with its splendid air, its beauty and peace, where camellia trees thirty feet in height were covered with bloom in February. The couriers and other visitors found her looking much better as time went on. Her cough had almost disappeared and she was in better spirits. She often listened to the tunes played on her favorite mechanical musical instrument, which had been given her as a Christmas present. She was already beginning to talk of going home and looked forward to seeing her husband and the children, for she had felt the separation keenly. But she dreaded the meeting with the Archduchess Sophie, to whom she had not written, even when the Archduchess sent her a beautiful statuette of St. George as a friendly overture. She merely asked the Archduke Ludwig Viktor to thank his mother for it. "I kiss her hands," she wrote, "but I do not write to her simply because I feel that my letters must bore her, for I have written so often to you and there is not much to say about this place." Her mother-in-law would have been prepared for a reconciliation, but Elizabeth no longer desired it.

On April 28 she started on the homeward journey, after distributing presents, money, and orders broadcast, and all Funchal regretted her departure. She sailed for Spain on the comfortable English royal yacht in glorious weather. She had asked that there should be no official reception at Cadiz and wandered unrecognized through the beautiful town. On the next day, May 1, she took an ordinary train to Seville, but though she had begged that she might be allowed to preserve the strictest incognito, the Duc de Montpensier, brother-in-law of the Queen of Spain and a great lover of pomp and ceremony, could not bear to lose such an opportunity of cutting an important figure in public, and came to meet her at the station covered with orders, afterwards conducting her to his state coach with its six horses, which was waiting in readiness, and offering her his palace at Sant' Elmo. The whole thing was only an annoyance to Elizabeth. She wanted to see Seville in peace and not take part in any ceremonies, so she declined the offer of his palace and confined her relations with the Duke to the minimum required by politeness. The King and Queen also invited her to Aranjuez, but she did not think of accepting. She had had enough of the Queen's brother-in-law and his self-importance already, and preferred to go and see a bullfight at Seville on May 5. The Spaniards were most curious to see the beautiful Empress of whose illness the whole world had heard, and since they were themselves fond of ceremonies, etiquette, and pomp they could not understand why the Empress should be so anxious not to receive all the tokens of respect due to her rank. But they could observe no trace of illness about her. Everybody was captivated by her beauty and dazzling appearance. The Austrian Ambassador in Madrid, who had gone to meet her at Cadiz, reported to Vienna: "Her Majesty pleased everybody extraordinarily. Her gracious dignity and elegant simplicity could not fail to produce a great effect and impress people here, where stilted emotionalism alternates with the most unseemly informality."*

* From an unpublished report in the State Archives, Vienna.

She continued her voyage past Gibraltar and the Balearic Islands to Corfu, every place vying with the next to make her visits as pleasant as possible, though it never occurred to them that they would have succeeded far better if they had simply paid no attention to her.

Spoiled though she had been by all the fine landscapes she had seen in Madeira and on the way back, Elizabeth was in ecstasies when, on May 15, 1861, after a brief visit to Malta, the *Victoria and Albert* entered the Bay of Gasturi in Corfu. The green rolling hills on all sides were covered with orange trees in bloom, cypresses, and laurels, while a sea of an incomparable blue encircled with a girdle of foam its craggy shores, which were simply smothered with golden broom. Mighty fortifications, dating from the days of Venetian domination, towered above them, and to the east, on the mainland, lay the snow-covered mountains of Albania.

Corfu is one of the Ionian Islands, which were then under British rule. Elizabeth would gladly have stayed there longer and explored the enchanted island in all directions, but the Emperor had traveled to Trieste and was on his way to meet her on board the yacht *Phantasie*. With tears in his eyes Francis Joseph welcomed his wife after their long separation, and, after a visit to Miramar, they returned to Vienna. Everybody found the Empress looking fresh and blooming. But she had hardly arrived when she had to bow to the demands of court ceremonial and hold courts at which for hours on end she received the ladies eligible for presentation.

It was a great joy to her to see her children again after being deprived of them for so long, but of course she found that they had fallen entirely under the influence of the Archduchess Sophie, and when she ventured to raise objections she was roundly given to understand that she had been away such a long time that somebody had had to take care of the children, so the system of education introduced during her absence must still be followed. She did not enjoy a single day's peace. The old antipathies blazed up again, and she was more than ever conscious of the coldness and scarcely veiled hostility of the court, which was entirely on the side of the Emperor's mother. Elizabeth declared that she would stay no longer in the Burg, where the Archduchess Sophie was mistress, so as early as May 23 Their Majesties moved to Laxenburg. It was soon heard that the Empress wished to live a very quiet and retired life, for the courts she had held, her journey, and the change of climate had affected her health and she required the greatest care. The Prussian Minister already reported that there was some talk of her again spending the next winter in the south. The state dinners and courts announced for the next few days were suddenly canceled. On June 18 it was rumored that the Empress' condition again gave cause for the gravest apprehension, for she was coughing badly, had no appetite, and was very weak. And sure enough, the doctors once more advised her immediate departure. She had scarcely been home four weeks and now she had to go south again. The wildest rumors went the round in Vienna. Something was obviously wrong. The Empress had appeared looking fresh and blooming, yet on the very next day it was heard that, in the opinion of her doctors, nothing but immediate departure could avert the gravest consequences. The Empress' proposed visit to Munich for the marriage of her sister Mathilde to Count Louis of Trani, the eldest brother of King Francis II of Naples, which was to take place on June 5, was not paid. The Bavarian Minister even reported* that there was small hope of her recovery and spoke of a mortal illness. He alleged that Dr. Skoda, who was treating her, was incompetent and had told him that if the Empress stayed in Vienna she would have hardly six weeks more to live. Her departure was fixed for

*** This unpublished dispatch is in the Bavarian State Archives.**

the twenty-third, and her old family doctor from Munich was called into consultation and examined her. The British Ambassador did not know what to make of it. "The Empress," he wrote, "must be very ill indeed, and she is quite aware of her dangerous condition. She is forbidden to speak, so as to avoid any unnecessary irritation of the throat, and since His Majesty often has business in Vienna, Her Majesty spends her days almost alone." Count Rechberg told the Ambassador that the Empress was going to Corfu. "I never heard that spot recommended by the doctors before," replied Lord Bloomfield, "as a summer resort for invalids of that sort, for there is malaria there, too." "Nor did I," said Rechberg, "and for that reason I cannot understand why Meran was not chosen or some suitable place inside the Empire." It was hard to know what was really going on—whether it was simply a case of illness or whether the domestic dissensions in the imperial family had caused the Empress' health to give way again. But all Vienna was undeniably depressed, and the Emperor seemed in the deepest distress.

On June 23 Francis Joseph escorted Elizabeth back to Trieste, whence she was accompanied to Corfu by the Archduke Max, arriving on June 27. Even on the voyage she had felt much better, the fever had abated, and she had no need to consult her physician, Dr. Skoda, who had accompanied her. The Lord High Commissioner placed his palace and country house at her disposal, but she chose the latter, for there she would find it easier to live in the strict seclusion which she desired. She had asked to be spared all formal visits. Dr. Skoda returned home early in July and reported that the alarming symptoms had greatly abated, that Her Majesty coughed less and was free from fever. Elizabeth took long walks in the laurel woods and went sailing far out to sea. She also bathed, which was rather curious in one supposed to be suffering from a lung complaint. "My life here is even quieter than in Madeira," she wrote to the Archduke Ludwig Viktor. "What I like best is to sit by the shore on the great rocks; the dogs lie down in the water and I look out at the lovely moonlight on the sea." She was disturbed by a visit from Count Grünne, who had been somewhat tactlessly sent to Corfu to report upon her health. She gave him a cold and almost hostile reception, for she regarded him as nothing but a spy of her mother-in-law's. Grünne was fully aware of this, and the accounts he gave of his visit in Vienna were not very favorable to the Empress. They were repeated to her, and now her old antipathy for the General as one of the Archduchess Sophie's most trusted adherents rose to such a pitch that, if she had been capable of hatred, she would certainly have hated him.

Meanwhile her Bavarian relatives had been greatly alarmed by all that was going on. The Duchess Ludovika was puzzled. Like everybody else, she received the most contradictory accounts of her daughter's health, so she resolved to send the Count and Countess of Thurn and Taxis to Vienna to find out the real state of the case. Count Max Thurn and Taxis stayed with the Emperor and joined in his hunting parties, while Helene went on to Corfu, where she arrived on August 23 to Elizabeth's great delight. This was the first occasion on which the sisters had spent any length of time together since they were married. The shadow that had once lain between them had long since disappeared, especially when Helene saw that, after all, her sister's lot was not so very easy. She found her sister pale, with a slight puffiness about her face, and was shocked to see that she ate scarcely anything, but at last succeeded in persuading her to eat meat several times a day. She joined her in expeditions by land and by sea, during which the Empress had an opportunity of pouring out her heart to her sister and complaining of all that had caused her illness and second flight from home. Helene offered her services as mediator, and on returning to Vienna at the end of September reported everything to the Emperor.

Elizabeth's departure to such a distant place for the second time had been most unpleasant for the Emperor. He naturally heard that everybody was attributing these odd happenings to reasons the discussions of which could not but be painful to him, even though they were not true. Quite apart from his love for his wife and his desire to live in peace with her and the children and to come back to a pleasant home after his laborious day's work, he had to think of his own prestige, and that of his house, which were bound to suffer so long as people could indulge in theories about the reasons for the Empress' actions. The transition from her dangerous state of health in Vienna to her astonishingly rapid recovery in Madeira and Corfu had been too abrupt. But now Helene had paved the way toward improved relations. "I should like to spend the early days of October," wrote Francis Joseph to his mother, "in paying a rapid visit of a few days to my dear Sisi in Corfu. I feel the greatest longing to be there after such a long separation." Early on the morning of October 13 the Emperor arrived in Corfu, to find his wife in far better health. He explained all his troubles, begged her to be reasonable, and promised to take her part more actively than he had done before in the matter of the children, and, if necessary, to oppose his mother. Elizabeth longed for her little ones. She wrote constantly to Gisela* and Rudolf, and her letters always ended with some such expression as: "Do not forget your Mamma" or "Think of your Mamma often."

The Emperor and Empress now arrived at a compromise.

* The Empress' letters to the Archduchess Gisela are in the possession of H.R.H. Prince Konrad of Bavaria.

She would not return to Vienna again, for her nerves and health did not permit it, but she would return within the frontiers of the Monarchy. So it was agreed that Elizabeth should go straight to Venice, where the children would shortly follow her, of course without the Archduchess Sophie. The Emperor was greatly pleased with Corfu, though what interested him most were the military works carried out by the English. He returned home with his mind at rest, hoping that now everything would be in order and that he would be able to visit Venice much oftener than distant Corfu, besides which a certain political advantage might result from the Empress' visit to Venice. The idea was growing far too prevalent that, since the loss of Lombardy, Vienna now intended to dispose of Venice, too, by exchange or sale.

On October 26 the steam frigate *Lucia*, with Elizabeth on board, arrived at Venice, where she was met by three of the Archdukes, among them Johann Salvator and the young Ludwig Salvator, who, though only twenty-three years of age, was greatly interested in art and science and was therefore known as the "learned" Archduke. In the evening the Piazza di San Marco was illuminated by order of the Sindaco, but the people pointedly avoided it and took no part in the demonstrations of joy. The Empress, however, wanted only peace and quiet and led the same retired life in Venice that she had in Madeira and Corfu, passing her time in reading. She was, however, unable to go for walks, for, though she did not look ill, her feet were very swollen and her features still showed the same puffiness. Her joy knew no bounds when on November 3, 1861, Rudolf and Gisela arrived in Venice. But disagreements at once began with the Countess Esterházy, who had received instructions from the Archduchess Sophie about the treatment of the children during their visit, instructions with which Elizabeth disagreed. At the end of the month Francis Joseph arrived, too. Both he and his wife could not help noticing how coldly they were received. It was obvious that the people were quiet only because they were kept in order by the troops, and that they had nothing but contempt for Austrian rule. When Francis Joseph expressed his surprise to the governor at the way in which the Venetian nobility avoided him and his wife, attempts were made to induce some of them to appear at the palace, but in vain. Elizabeth began to feel very ill at ease in Venice. Her health had not improved, and her constant dissensions with the Mistress of the Household, whose friendship she had failed to win, rankled in her mind, till at last she succeeded in persuading the Emperor to remove the Countess Esterházy from her position and replace her by her former lady in waiting, Paula Bellegarde, who had meanwhile married Count Königsegg-Aulendorf; the Count at the same time became Controller of the Empress' Household. The Archduchess Sophie naturally felt this to be aimed at herself.

In March the Emperor paid another visit to Venice. Elizabeth had discovered another pastime to distract her leisure. "I am getting together an album of beauties," she wrote to her brother-in-law, "and am now collecting photographs for it—of women only. Please send me any pretty faces that you can hunt up at Angerer's or any other photographers' . . ." Later on a request was sent to the Minister for Foreign Affairs to ask all Austrian ministers and ambassadors abroad to look for portraits of beautiful women and send them to the Empress. Rechberg passed on these instructions to the Ambassador at Constantinople, adding that in addition to portraits of Oriental beauties the Empress desired some of beautiful women in Turkish harems. This was most embarrassing, for in view of the manners and customs of the country it would have been as much as his life was worth to ask for such photographs. As he said, nobody would believe that he really wanted them for his Empress. He did, however, succeed in obtaining a few, but he thought with a smile that the Empress no doubt wished to compare them with her own portrait and see how much more attractive she was herself.

In the second week of April the Duchess in Bayern arrived in Venice to see with her own eyes what was really the matter with her daughter's health, for she had long since heard that there was nothing wrong with her lungs. In May the Emperor again arrived on a visit, after which Elizabeth returned home with the Duchess, staying at Reichenau so as to avoid Vienna and the Emperor's mother. There she was joined by Dr. Fischer, who had known her since her childhood and had always considered that her case had been wrongly diagnosed. He expressed the opinion that Elizabeth was suffering from acute anæmia. Since there was nothing wrong with her lungs, it was no longer of any advantage to her to remain in the south, and a hydropathic cure at Kissingen was far more advisable. The Empress, whose beauty had been affected by the swelling of her features, had greater confidence in Dr. Fischer, so it was decided that, on leaving Reichenau, she should at once go on to Kissingen for the cure. Elizabeth was inclined to take any illness more seriously than was really necessary, and this made things difficult for the doctors, who always found on examining her that her constitution was on the whole excellent, hardy and vigorous, so that it could only be a question of time and nerves before the lovely young Empress, who was only twenty-five, was entirely restored to health and free from all fear of possible complications. And, as a matter of fact, her visit to Kissingen, where she lived in retirement in a small villa, did her good. In July she paid a visit to Possenhofen, where she was deeply touched at seeing the Queen of Naples and the newly married Count and Countess Trani after all their sad experiences. But the accounts she heard of the Queen of Naples' marriage were not very satisfactory, for the Queen had separated from her husband and seemed unwilling ever to return to him. .

On August 14 Elizabeth returned quite suddenly and unexpectedly to Vienna, her lady in waiting, the Princess Helene Taxis, having to be summoned by telegram. "Now we have her back in this country," she wrote to a former lady in waiting,* "just as we had two years ago; yet how many things lie between—Madeira, Corfu, and a world of troubles. . . . She was received with an enthusiasm such as I had never heard before in Vienna. On Sunday there is to be a choir festival (*Liedertafel*) and a torchlight procession at which fourteen thousand people have expressed their intention of being present. *His* expression as he helped her out of the carriage I shall never forget. I find her looking blooming, but her expression is not natural, it is as forced and nervous as it can be, her color so high that she looks overheated, and though her face is no longer swollen, it is much thickened and changed. The fact that Prince Karl Theodor accompanied her proves how much she dreads being alone with *him* and all of us. . . ."

The reception given to the Empress in Vienna was incredible. The joy and enthusiasm at her return reached such a pitch that in court circles it was regarded as in some sort a demonstration in favor of the liberal Empress as opposed to the Emperor's reactionary mother. And now Elizabeth settled down, first at Schönbrunn, and resumed her old accustomed life. She enjoyed having the children with her, especially the little Crown Prince, who, as the Princess Taxis wrote about this time, "has become charming (*ravissant*), jolly, natural, clever, and very good-looking." Elizabeth's feet were now less swollen and allowed her to go for long

* The letters of the Princess Helene Taxis here quoted are in the possession of the Count Szécsen. This lady should not be confused with the Empress' sister Helene, Hereditary Princess of Thurn and Taxis.

walks both in the morning and in the afternoon. Gradually, too, she started riding again. She greeted her favorites in the stables enthusiastically. For the moment the Archduchess Sophie was away, so there was no need to fear any clash between them. Yet at first Elizabeth felt so ill at ease in the atmosphere of the Court of Vienna that she asked her sister the Queen of Naples to join her when her brother Karl Theodor had to leave. But the Queen was not the most desirable companion for her, for she only upset Elizabeth by her complaints about her unhappy marriage.

Oblivious of the demands of etiquette, Elizabeth lived according to her own inclinations. Her ladies in waiting noticed this; indeed, they found it hard to accept things calmly and observed her every movement. "She does not seem at all anxious to let us attend her now," wrote the Princess Helene Taxis from Schönbrunn on September 15, 1862. "She walks and drives out a great deal with His Majesty, but when he is not here she stays alone here in the part of the garden at Reichenau which is closed to the public. However, God be praised, she is at any rate at home, and inclined to remain here; that is the main thing. She is very nice to him—before us, at least—talkative and natural, though *alla camera* there may be many differences of opinion—that is often plainly to be seen. She looks splendidly, quite a different woman, with a good color, strong and brown; she eats properly, sleeps well, does not tight-lace any more, and can walk for hours, but when she stands there is a vein in her left foot which throbs. The Queen of Naples does not look well—that household seems to be going badly."

It was now hoped that the Empress would recover her health entirely, and her household, in particular, longed to see her leading an ordered and regular life again. The varying moods to which Elizabeth had been subject during the last few years, her despair at her ill-health, and her shrinking sensitiveness had made their life anything but an easy one. The Countess Karoline Lamberg had married in 1860, just in time to escape the dissensions and travels of the next few years. "I can only congratulate you," wrote the Princess Helene Taxis to her, "upon not having had to go through these two years of martyrdom with us. Now we are settled in Schönbrunn, and the thought that we are 'settled for good somewhere'* seems quite strange. It was hard for her to give up her recent traveling about, and I quite understand this. When one has no inward peace, one imagines that it makes life easier to move about, and she has now grown too much accustomed to this. For the rest, Helene (Elizabeth's sister) is coming here for a fortnight while the Emperor is away hunting, for he will not give that up. . . . She still exerts a calming influence, for she is so sensible and orderly herself and tells her the truth. She (the Empress) went out riding at Reichenau, and has done so here once at seven in the morning, alone with Holmes. The walk has naturally become a gallop, but she does not want to trot yet. She simply refuses to let herself be accompanied by Grünne and Königsegg. The former has been entirely ignored and avoided so far. Otherwise, thank God, things are going on well. . . . I believe, indeed, that she has moments of despair, but nobody can laugh like her, or has such childlike whims. She says herself that it is not unpleasant to her to see us occasionally, but it is odious to her to have us in waiting. . . ."

The Emperor left nothing undone that might make life at home as pleasant as possible for his wife. He was most attentive, sent for the most beautiful horses for her, and anticipated her every wish. Provided only that her health could be thoroughly restored during the next few years, and the Archduchess Sophie would keep herself a little more in the background, all might yet go well.

* In English in the original letter.

VI

DOMESTIC BROILS AND FLUCTUATING MOODS

1863–1865

GRADUALLY THE EMPRESS BEGAN TO ACcustom herself to Court life once more. In the middle of February, for the first time in three years, she appeared at a small court ball (*Kammerball*) to which only two hundred and fifty guests were invited. Everybody was surprised and pleased to see how blooming she looked. Her features had lost their puffiness, her smile had returned, and her charm was as great as ever. Yet there was no end to the gossip which went on round her, and when it was not about herself it was about her family. Elizabeth remained deeply attached to her home. Recent events had only drawn the bonds closer, and she took a special interest in everything concerning her brothers and sisters. The Queen of Naples' marriage came to a crisis. She refused to live in Rome any longer with her husband, and in October, 1862, suddenly retired to the Ursuline convent in Augsburg without a word of warning, prepared to stay there till further notice. Her relations at once did all they could to patch up the marriage again, at least outwardly. The news of this flight was all the more upsetting for the Empress because the courtiers were already comparing it with her own visit to Madeira and Corfu and were only too glad to attribute the strangest tendencies to the whole ducal house of Bavaria, and being oversensitive she was apt to suspect malice even where none was intended. An atmosphere of icy coldness gradually grew up about her at the Court of Vienna, and she naturally gravitated toward the Hungarian nobility, for, knowing her opposition to the old state of affairs, the homage they paid her was tinged with expectancy. She was flattered by the skilful references made both verbally and in writing to the power which the charming Queen of Hungary's beauty and fascination were known to exert over her husband, and the hopes which were consequently entertained of it; but she regretted her ignorance of the Magyar language.

The first time she seriously felt the lack of it was when she found it hard to make herself understood by the Crown Prince's nurse, and it was from her that she learned her first scraps of Magyar. In February, 1863, however, she began to study the language in earnest, throwing herself into it with characteristic energy. The hours which had to be spent in attending to her lovely hair, more than a yard long, which was now gradually darkening to a golden brown, she devoted to learning lists of words. She also spoke Magyar to her maid while dressing, before proceeding to the physical exercises with dumbbells and other apparatus which kept her supple and in good condition and would, she hoped, soon make her fit to ride again. She had portraits of all her splendid horses painted by the artist Zellenberg and hung in one of her sitting rooms, which she called her "riding chapel" (*Reitkapelle*) and would show to all lovers of these noble beasts.

Since, however, she was not yet entirely restored to health, the doctor insisted that she must take the cure at Kissingen again this year. She was always welcomed there like a fairy queen, and would appear daily on the promenade, where she showed a special solicitude for those who were seriously ill. Thus she would walk almost daily with the blind Duke of

Mecklenburg, acting as his guide, and she also interested herself in a crippled Englishman named John Collett, whose social position was by no means exalted, and who was taken out regularly on the promenade in his wheeled carriage. He was very well read and, like everybody else, was fascinated by the Empress, till before long the unfortunate man was madly in love with her. At first he did not know who she was and took her for a lovely English girl, but before long he discovered her real identity. He would send her books and flowers, and even poems of his own composition. "There is one quite small thing," says one of his letters to the Empress,* "which would give me real happiness, and that is a lock of your hair. If I am wrong to ask you for such a thing, please forgive me. I should value it not because you are an empress, but because you really exert a most wonderful power over me, and I value your friendship so very highly for its own sake alone." John Collett was touched to find that an empress, and, what is more, an enchantingly lovely woman, should take such an interest in a poor cripple. These three people became inseparable—the young Empress, the blind Duke, and the cripple in the wheeled carriage—and would talk about God and the universe, life and death, happiness and suffering; and John Collett wrote in a shaky and scarcely legible hand a touching little poem calling down blessings on Elizabeth and beginning with the words:

May God preserve the lady fair and true
Whose pitying heart can feel for others' pain.
For thou, at least, kind Queen, hast not passed through
The trying fires of suffering in vain.

On July 25 the Empress started on her homeward journey. She had hardly left before John Collett tried with his almost failing hand to write and thank her for the sunshine

* These letters are in the archives of Schloss Wallsee.

which she had brought into his life. Elizabeth always answered his letters. She wrote that she had had his two favorite songs set to music and often had them sung to her in the evenings when she returned from her ride. But his request for a lock of her hair was refused, on the ground that she had made a vow never to give any of her hair to anybody. "Thank you," she wrote, "for the little poem. You ask me to criticize it. I can only say one thing, which is that you value me too highly and I do not feel myself half worthy of what you think and write about me. . . . You are in such pain and so weary, and yet you do not forget to pray for me, and that is so kind of you. Please do not cease to do so, and pray God that he will grant a wish of mine—my one and only wish, for which I pray morning and night and every day during Mass," by which Elizabeth probably meant her hope of a complete recovery.

While Elizabeth was living this life of her own, Francis Joseph was at the Conference of Princes (*Fürstentag*) at Frankfurt, at which, by Bismarck's desire, Prussia was not represented, so that the antagonism continued which was ultimately to lead to the fratricidal war for the hegemony of Germany. Elizabeth now threw herself with ardor into the study of Magyar, and Francis Joseph reported to his mother that Sisi was making incredibly rapid progress in the language. But the Archduchess watched her daughter-in-law's growing sympathy for Hungary with a jaundiced eye, as was to be seen even in the smallest externals. On one occasion the Emperor and Empress appeared in the central compartment of the imperial box at the theatre, while the Archduchess Sophie took up her place in the one next them. Elizabeth was wearing a gold-embroidered headdress of the kind generally worn by the wives of Hungarian magnates. When the Archduchess Sophie caught sight of this, she began staring at Elizabeth through her lorgnette in the most

THE EMPRESS WITH HER DOG,
"SHADOW," *c.* 1864

From a photograph.

ELIZABETH, *c.* 1863

From a photograph in the possession of H.I.H. the Archduke Theodor Salvator.

marked way, actually standing up and bending over the front of the box to have a better view of her. Then she sank back in her place and shook her head half in amazement and half in annoyance. This little scene had not been lost on the public. A sensation ran through the theatre, and everybody started whispering, till the Empress, followed by her husband, rose and left the theatre before the end of the performance.

A few days after this incident, sad news arrived from Munich. Elizabeth's friend, King Maximilian II, the poet and scholar, died suddenly and unexpectedly on May 10, 1864, and was succeeded by his eighteen-year-old son, Ludwig II, who was totally unprepared for the duties of his new position. He had always taken a great interest in poetry and knew most of Schiller's plays by heart, but he was entirely unfamiliar with the business of politics. Two qualities he had in common with Elizabeth: a shrinking from society and a love of riding. But the relationship between them was too distant for the characteristics of one branch of the family to justify the drawing of any conclusions as to the other. Their only common ancestor, as may be seen from the genealogical tree (pages xii and xiii), was Ludwig's great-grandfather, King Max I of Bavaria, who showed no particularly abnormal mental symptoms. Elizabeth's mother was the child of the second marriage of King Max I. Moreover, the seeds of the insanity which was afterwards to appear in both of the sons of King Max II were first introduced into the Bavarian royal house through the wives of the successors of Max I. Elizabeth, moreover, belonged to an older generation than her cousin Ludwig II, who was eight years younger than she was.

King Max's death was followed shortly afterwards by that of his sister, the Archduchess Hildegarde, wife of the Archduke Albrecht. At three o'clock on the morning of April 2 the Empress was roused from sleep and informed that the Archduchess was dying. She at once hurried to her bedside and stayed with her to the end. "It was the first time," she wrote to Collett, "that I had seen the death of a grown-up person. It made the most terrible impression upon me. I had no idea that death could be so hard, that the struggle with death is such a fearful one. To think that everyone has to go through it! How enviable is the lot of those who pass away from this world of mourning while still unconscious children. Yes, life is a hideous thing, in which nothing is certain but death."

Soon, however, another event occurred to distract her attention from her mourning. For years past Francis Joseph's younger brother, the Archduke Ferdinand Max, had cherished the chimerical idea of founding an empire in Mexico, having become involved in the schemes of the Emperor and Empress of the French and a number of unscrupulous Mexican exiles. This project was now to be realized. The Archduke and Charlotte had refused to listen to any advice to the contrary. Elizabeth was one of those who shook their heads over the proposal. She simply could not understand the anxiety of her brother- and sister-in-law for a crown, for in her opinion they should have been only too glad not to have one. While Charlotte was staying in Vienna during the last few weeks before their departure, Elizabeth showed her every possible mark of affection, though making no secret of her own opinion.* But this was of no avail, and on April 14 their ship set sail, bearing the Archduke and Archduchess toward a more than problematical future.

Summer found the Empress once more at Kissengen, taking her annual cure, and afterwards with her family at Pos-

* See a letter to Elizabeth from the Empress Charlotte of Mexico, Chapultepec, April 10, 1865, which says: "I do not forget how much heart you showed toward us this time a year ago."

senhofen. While at Kissingen, she received a visit from the young King Ludwig II of Bavaria. She was curious to see him again, for she had heard that he was wonderfully handsome with his noble face, framed in dark brown hair, and his flashing blue eyes with their strange fascination. Accounts of him varied greatly. Some were enthusiastic about him, while others detected something in him which was, to say the least, strange. He had intended to make only a short visit, but was so pleased with Elizabeth that he spent four weeks in Kissingen. The homage which he paid to her was not, however, of the kind usual between a young man and a beautiful woman. He looked upon her without desire, as upon some fair heavenly vision, and what attracted him were her views upon life and the originality of her whole nature.

Meanwhile the Schleswig-Holstein campaign had begun, in which Austria took part with Prussia, and on her return home Elizabeth had further opportunities of showing her kind and pitying heart by visiting the wounded in the hospitals. It was a pleasure to her to speak to the Hungarian soldiers in their native language, however haltingly. She was already beginning to read Eötvös and Jôkai with the dictionary and to dip into Hungarian history books. What she now wanted was a Hungarian lady to whom she could talk and, above all, whom she could trust. A certain Countess Almássy was commissioned to find a suitable young lady and drew up a long list, including many names drawn from the great Hungarian nobility, but not forgetting an old friend of her own, Marie von Ferenczy, belonging to a good family of the Hungarian gentry at Kecskemét, one of whose brothers had five daughters and a crippled son. Thus it was that the name of little Ida von Ferenczy—a lovable, modest, and gentle girl, though not pretty—came to figure among so many great and noble names. When the list was submitted to the Empress, her eye at once fell upon the simplest name.

"I should find it much easier," she thought, "to attach such a girl to myself." She asked for her photograph, and, on obtaining further information about her, remarked: "Yes, I am sure I shall like her."

Trembling with anxiety, Ida Ferenczy awaited her first meeting with her Queen. She was a girl with a natural, healthy, cheerful, bright disposition, and a true Hungarian patriot. She little thought that she was the very type for whom the Empress was looking—a simple creature, if possible unspoiled by etiquette and court intrigues and far removed from the narrow circle of the court aristocracy. What the Empress wanted was somebody who would serve *her* and not the Emperor's mother.

In November, 1864, the Countess Königsegg, Mistress of the Household, presented Ida von Ferenczy to the Empress, who had just returned from riding. Blushing crimson, the young girl stood gazing at her Queen in deep emotion, while the Empress, with that incomparable charm which made it so easy for her to fascinate people when she wished, looked searchingly at her and said in Magyar: "I am greatly pleased with you. We shall be much together."

It was not altogether easy to find a place for this new lady in the strictly graded court hierarchy. Owing to her comparatively modest birth, it was not thought desirable to make her a maid of honor at once, in case this might offend others belonging to greater families. The expedient was adopted of making her a member of an institution for ladies of noble birth, in Brünn, which would give her the right to be called "Frau," and she was appointed "Reader to Her Majesty." Elizabeth immediately put her on her guard and strictly forbade her ever to say a word about what they said or did together. This, she said, was the *sine qua non* of a satisfactory relation between them. Elizabeth was right, for Ida Ferenczy had only been there a few days when the Archduchess Sophie's principal lady in waiting presented herself and the moment she had been introduced said: "Pray consult me in everything and confide all Her Majesty says to me." During the early days Elizabeth put Ida through a perfect cross-examination daily to find out whether she had really been won over to her mother-in-law's party.

At first the ladies in waiting were very kind to the "new one," but soon they noticed Ida's reticence toward them, and at once their attitude changed. But the Empress soon discovered that she had found what she had always longed to find—one who was devoted to her body and soul, and to her alone. Soon Ida had become a friend whom she addressed by the intimate "thou" and trusted implicitly, and for whom she always rang when she needed someone with whom she need not fear either spying or gossip. And so the young "*nemes lány*" (girl of noble birth) from Kecskemét acquired a real influence over the Empress, and not only taught her Magyar, but also fostered her affection for Hungary.

Since her third cure at Kissingen, Elizabeth again enjoyed excellent health. Her pristine beauty had returned; indeed, as a woman of twenty-seven, she was even lovelier than as a girl. Winterhalter, portrait painter to the courts of Paris and London, who had painted nearly all the royal ladies and beauties of his day and was now at the summit of his fame, painted her twice. One portrait was a full-length figure, in state robes and all her jewels; the other, the more intimate one with the hair loose, which Francis Joseph had hanging in his study opposite his writing table. On returning to Paris to paint another portrait of the Empress Eugénie, the artist told her of Elizabeth's beauty and the interesting conversations he had had with her during the sittings. The Empress had long desired to meet her "colleague" in Vienna, if only to find out whether she was really as lovely as people said, and outshone herself. She requested the French Ambassador in Vienna to sound the authorities as to whether, in the event of the Empress' visiting Kissingen again in the following year, a "personal and most respectful overture on her part" would be acceptable. Though the proposal was put forward very discreetly, Elizabeth would not hear of it. She of course disliked nothing more than visits, court festivities, and ceremonies, but sometimes they were not to be avoided, especially when they took place at her own home. In February, 1865, her favorite brother, Karl Theodor, went to Dresden to marry the Princess Sophie of Saxony, and, whether Elizabeth liked it or not, she had to attend the wedding. Dresden was enraptured with her, and both the court and the people were so carried away that she was greeted with ovations wherever she appeared. "You simply cannot imagine," wrote the Queen of Saxony to the Princess Mary Hamilton,* "what enthusiasm was aroused here by the Empress' beauty and amiability. I never saw our quiet Saxons so moved before (*en émoi*): old and young, high and low, serious or frivolous, nice and nasty, they were all simply off their heads (*rein weg*) about her, and still are—her visit was epoch-making (*elle a fait époque ici*)."

The enthusiasm was, however, one-sided. Elizabeth did not feel well and could hardly wait till it was time to go home. "I shall really be glad," she wrote to her little Rudolf, who was now seven years old and a particularly bright child for his age, "when I am back with you all again. I do not like it here at all—I feel quite depressed, for I would so gladly go home, yet I have to stay here for another four days." On March 28 she went on to Munich, where Ludwig II met her at the station in person, though Elizabeth had asked that there should be no official reception. The King was at that time a center of public attention, for, though he had only been on the throne a year, he was already seen to be so fan-

* From a letter in the possession of Prince George Festetics.

THE EMPRESS

From a sketch by Winterhalter, 1864, in the possession of Count Königsegg, Munich.

tastic that the old conservative diplomatists who were watching him had one shock after another. The Austrian Minister in particular, Count Blome, shook his head over the King's doings. Even in the autumn of the previous year the Minister had expressed grave doubts about Ludwig's behavior and "the fact that the crown was now on the head of an utterly inexperienced prince, scarcely more than a boy." "The young King," he reported at this time,* "is still a problem. His conduct is full of amazing contrasts, and it is hard to see how he will turn out. At present it is evident that childish ideas and romantic enthusiasms preponderate." The Minister described the King's bedroom at Hohenschwangau, lit by a mechanical nightlamp, which could, if desired, represent all the changes of the waxing and waning moon, and whose dim light fell upon a little fountain. "So far, fortunately," Blome slyly added, "only the scenery of the ballet has penetrated into the royal sleeping apartment." He saw with amazement how the King was simply lost to the world as he watched Schiller's *Kabale und Liebe* at the theatre and sobbed violently as he followed the action of the drama. "If my judgment of the young prince is correct," he said, "Nature has endowed him with more imagination than understanding, and his bringing-up has largely neglected the heart. Grave symptoms can be observed of exaggerated self-esteem, headstrongness, and lack of consideration. The King cannot bear any advice unless he has asked for it. . . . Literary men and artists are received in audience more than any other class of the public. . . . His Majesty's chief tastes are for music and literature, and since he has no real musical talent, the former is concerned more with the words than with the

* This and the following letters and dispatches are now in the State Archives, Vienna, as are also the Empress' letters to the Crown Prince Rudolf here quoted, and, in general, all the letters addressed to him, unless otherwise stated.

music. It is the text of *Lohengrin* and the other operas by Richard Wagner, based upon the old German saga cycle, which is the cause of his preference for Wagnerian music." The Minister was incensed at the relation between the composer and the young King, and referred to it as a scandal which was getting worse and worse. Wagner's "impudent demands for money" and "improper expressions" infuriated him. The artist, he said, was showing quantities of letters in the King's handwriting, in which he was addressed as "thou" and loaded with the most extravagant eulogies! "What can one say?" said Blome. "It cannot but lead to a decrease in the respect due to the sacred person of the monarch. Moreover, the King has so far taken no pleasure in the society of ladies, or in associating with the feminine sex. If thus divorced from the practical world, it can be understood that the imagination will play an increasing part."

The Empress hardly knew what to think of her royal cousin. In her old home she heard decidedly kinder opinions expressed about him than were current in official circles. "Yesterday," she wrote to her little Rudolf, "the King paid me a long visit, and if Grandmamma had not come in at last, he would be here now. He is quite reconciled to me. I was very nice, and he kissed my hand so often that Aunt Sophie, who was peeping through the door, asked me afterwards whether I had any hand left. He was wearing an Austrian uniform again and was all scented with *chypre*. . . ." Shortly afterwards Elizabeth received the Austrian Minister, Count Blome, who told her the most extraordinary stories about the King. But on returning home she told the Emperor, who had read Blome's reports from Munich with growing anxiety, that in her opinion they were too severe, for she did not like people to express such adverse opinions of the King of her native land.

In July the Emperor and Empress took up their customary residence at Ischl with the children. The Empress was not at all pleased with her son's appearance. She found him pale and thought he was growing too quickly, and she felt sure that his crowded timetable of studies was far too exacting, for though he was advanced for his age both physically and mentally, he was overexcitable. Since 1864, when he entered his eighth year, the boy had been in the charge of Major General Count Gondrecourt, and from that time his physical condition had noticeably deteriorated.

Elizabeth would have liked to dispense with her annual cure at Kissingen this year, but Dr. Fischer insisted that she must take it. Shortly before leaving she made a brief excursion with her husband to Hallstatt and Gosaumühle. She was now a splendid walker again, unresting and untiring, and Francis Joseph even proposed that on her return he should take her chamois-shooting with him.

During the first few days at Kissingen Elizabeth felt lonely and depressed and telegraphed for her great sheep dog, of which she was very fond. "I am so happy at having Horseguard here," she wrote to her daughter Gisela.* "He was frightfully glad to see me, and almost crushed me in his arms. . . . I walk a great deal in the wood, for people follow me about too much on the promenade. I have had a very kind letter from the King, in which he says that the doctors have forbidden him to come here . . . so I shall be able to live here quite quiet and undisturbed." During her tedious cure Elizabeth had leisure to write letters and improve her Magyar by reading. She felt the separation from Ida Ferenczy greatly, for even during this first year she had become very much attached to her. "I think of you (*dich*) a great deal," she wrote to her, "during the long process of hairdressing, during my walks, and a thousand times a day. . . .

* The Empress' letters to the Archduchess Gisela are in the possession of H.R.H. Prince Konrad of Bavaria.

But now I am just horribly depressed. . . . Life is tedious enough here. I have not yet found any gay society, or is there any prospect of such a thing. I go for a great many walks, which occupy almost the whole day . . . and I also read a great deal. . . . Now and then I even play the organ. . . . And now God be with you, dear Ida. Don't get married in the meantime either to your Kálmán or to anybody else, but remain true to your friend E."

The Empress was unspeakably delighted to see her family again on her return, and her faithful Ida, too. The only pity was that the latter could not join in the long walks of which Elizabeth was so fond, for she was small and delicate and had a slight weakness of the heart.

But the atmosphere at the court of Vienna was the same as ever, to judge by a letter written in December, 1865, by the Landgravine Fürstenberg. "I really hardly know," she wrote,* "how anyone is to remain in a good humor when surrounded by nothing but people complaining, lamenting, and in desperation, for everyone around me, both high and low, is more or less discontented and out of temper. So this is the much-vaunted court life! And one has to try and find a bright side to look upon!" She gives, however, nothing but good accounts of the Archduchess Sophie. "My mistress (*die Herrin*), who is really kind hearted and considerate, notices when one pays her attentions and likes doing kind things for one. . . . She takes an interest in everything, and it is incredible how much she knows, so that one learns a great deal. . . ."

The Landgravine was still critical of Elizabeth, and in the quarrels then going on about the education of the children, and especially the Crown Prince, she was entirely on the side of the Archduchess Sophie, who perhaps overdid her well-

* The Landgravine von Fürstenberg's letters are in the possession of the Countess Gabriele Rechberg.

meant efforts to turn the Crown Prince into a highly educated, able man, thoroughly well prepared for his duties. Seeing that she was again not to be allowed to have any voice in the education of her own child, the Empress was bitterly jealous and so failed to recognize the Archduchess' good intentions. In her opinion General Gondrecourt's methods of training could hardly fail to turn her Rudolf "practically into an idiot" (*Trottel*). "It is madness," she said in after years to her lady in waiting, the Countess Marie Festetics,* "to frighten a child of six with water cures and try to turn him into a hero." For instance, on one occasion Gondrecourt left the child inside the Tiergarten at Lainz, near the gate, slipped out quickly himself, and then shouted through the gate: "Here comes a wild boar!" The child naturally began to scream, but the more he cried the more they tried to frighten him, till he became so nervous that, as the Empress said, it was positively dangerous to his health. Even the Archduchess Sophie did not like such methods as these, but Gondrecourt was her protégé, so Elizabeth held her responsible for it all. When the Empress heard of the wild boar incident, she felt that this was too much, and summoning up all her courage she went to the Emperor. But Francis Joseph hesitated. He saw what trouble and thought his mother had devoted to bringing up his son, and he placed more reliance upon her judgment in this matter than upon that of his young wife and could not make up his mind to oppose her. But now Elizabeth took an extreme step. "I cannot stand by and see such things going on," she declared. "It must be either Gondrecourt or myself. . . ." With these words she left the Emperor, went up to her room and wrote him what amounted to an ultimatum:† "It is my wish that

* These words are quoted in the Countess' diary, October 15, 1872.

† The correspondence of the Emperor and Empress is now at Schloss Wallsee.

full and unlimited powers should be reserved to me in all things concerning the children, the choice of those by whom they are surrounded and of their place of residence, and the entire control of their bringing-up; in short, I alone must decide everything up to their majority. I further desire that everything concerning my own personal affairs, such, for instance, as the choice of those about my person, my place of residence, all changes in domestic arrangements, etc., etc., should be left for me alone to decide. Elizabeth."

The Emperor now saw that his wife was in deadly earnest and gave way. Gondrecourt was removed from his position, the exclusive charge of the Crown Prince was transferred to a physician, Dr. Hermann Widerhofer, and Colonel Latour von Thurnberg took charge of his education. The Empress' relations with the Archduchess Sophie were, of course, hardly improved by all this; indeed, her life during the next few months was to be made very difficult for her. Every attempt was made to estrange the Emperor from the Empress. The latter went so far as to say that people had tried to ruin her, by offering her, with devilish cunning, opportunities for wrongdoing, for the purpose of coming between her and the Emperor.*

But Elizabeth was no longer a young girl. She was a woman of twenty-eight, who not only knew her own mind but was also growing daily more conscious of the power given her by her beauty over her husband and the whole outer world as well. This increased her self-reliance and influence, but also her responsibility. Formerly the education of the Crown Prince had been conducted on, perhaps, too conservative lines, but now this state of affairs was entirely reversed. It became too liberal, and the Archduchess Sophie's religious influence was superseded, while at the same time Elizabeth

* The Empress' own words are quoted in the diary of the Countess Marie Festetics, October 15, 1872.

failed to stop that systematic cramming of the Crown Prince with lessons of every kind which was making him incredibly precocious. It was a tragic situation. Everybody meant so well and, with the resources of the whole Empire at their disposal, might have chosen the noblest and most learned persons to train the child in the best possible way, and yet they all went wrong.

However, it was not in the Empress' nature to be always unhappy and distressed. On the contrary, she was often ready for hearty laughter, merriment, and nonsense. After all, she was young and, Empress though she was, meant to get some enjoyment out of life. She exulted in her successful attempts to influence her husband and showed her gratitude by greater cordiality toward him. On his name day nothing would please her but that the whole court should get a little "tight" (*einen kleinen Schwips bekommen*). "We laughed a great deal at table," she wrote to her son, "for I made all the ladies drink Papa's health in a whole glass of champagne; Königsegg was quite worried, Paula (Königsegg) was inclined to get too lively, and by the end of dinner Lily (Hunyady) could hardly stand."

The Empress now received regular reports from Latour on her son's progress, and this was a great joy to her after having been left in ignorance for so long. In politics she followed with the greatest interest Deák's efforts to present the case for Hungary in the press that Easter, for gradually Ida Ferenczy's influence was making itself felt. There was already some talk of a visit of the Empress to Budapest, and the appointment of fourteen Hungarian ladies in waiting (*Palastdamen*) was an intimation that in that country the court was likely to have a thoroughly national character.

When the Kingdom of Italy was proclaimed in 1861 and formally recognized by Bavaria, among many other states, Elizabeth was indignant, for she judged all questions from the point of view of family interest, and this recognition affected the rights of her sister Marie, the dethroned Queen of Naples. She did not hide her feelings from the Bavarian Minister in Vienna, Count Fugger, who immediately informed his sovereign. Ludwig II at once wrote and begged her not to be annoyed with him, for, he said, no other course had been open to him.

"Dear Cousin," she replied,* "rest assured that, whatever my own views may be, I should never cherish bitterness or anger against you. I cannot deny that I was very much surprised at the recognition of Italy by Bavaria, of all countries, for every ruling house which has been driven out contains some member of the Bavarian royal family. However, I assumed that the reasons which led you to take this inexplicable step must be so important that, in view of the important interests and sacred duties which you represent, my modest opinion of your action cannot be taken into consideration. I quite see this, so I am doubly touched by the friendly impulse which prompted you to write to me, and I beg that, whatever may arise, you will be assured of the deep love which attaches me to my home and the cordial and sincere friendship which I feel for you in particular. . . ."

When Elizabeth felt that she could no longer bear life in Vienna, her old home always offered her a refuge, and on December 13, 1865, another crisis arose quite suddenly and unexpectedly. The Emperor was away at Buda when she noticed a recurrence of her old symptoms and decided then and there to go to Munich. She telegraphed to her husband for his consent, but in such terms that he could hardly have withheld it. Nobody was informed of her decision, not even the Archduchess Sophie or the Minister of the Imperial House. She wanted to consult Dr. Fischer, and since he was

* The original letter is in the private archives of the Bavarian royal house, Munich.

unable to wait upon her she must needs go to him in order to set her mind at rest. Great astonishment was felt among the public at the Empress' sudden departure immediately before Christmas and her own birthday. The Prussian Ambassador saw in her decision a touch of that caprice which, he said, "is not altogether unusual in the princesses of the Bavarian 'ducal' line."* Francis Joseph was quite alarmed. He at once sent instructions to the Minister in Bavaria to request the King not to go and meet the Empress in state at the station, so that her visit might remain as private as possible. While still in Buda, he received a letter from his wife saying that she would return at latest by the twenty-third, in time for her birthday and Christmas; yet in spite of this she stayed in Bavaria till the end of the year. It was not till December 30 that she returned to Vienna, accompanied by her mother and to some extent reassured about her health, to spend New Year's Day of the fateful year 1866 among her children and at her anxious husband's side.

* From a dispatch in the Prussian State Archives, Dahlem.

VII

KÖNIGGRÄTZ, ELIZABETH, AND HUNGARY

1866–1867

SINCE THE DISASTROUS CAMPAIGN OF 1859 the Hungarian question had been in a state of seething unrest. The power of the Crown had been weakened, and Hungary never ceased agitating for the restoration of its old historic rights and the Constitution of 1848. Toward the end of 1865 there seemed some possibility of a rapprochement between the Vienna Government and the aspirations of the nation beyond the Leitha. A militant association of patriotic but moderately minded Hungarians had been formed in Budapest, whose aim was to obtain satisfaction for the Hungarian demands while maintaining the connection with Austria. At the head of it was the advocate Francis von Deák, a man of sixty-two, esteemed in his country by both high and low for his cool political sense, his reasonable attitude during the Revolution of 1848, his modesty and uprightness, and his powers as an orator. In opposition to Kossuth's separatist plans he maintained that a total separation from Austria would mean death to Hungary, from which there would be no resurrection. Such being his views, he was a natural mediator.

Deák's views were also those of Julius Andrássy, who was aware of the Empress' Hungarian sympathies. Ida Ferenczy, with whom he was in close touch, told him how hard the Queen was trying to master the Magyar language, and of the antagonism between her and the Archduchess Sophie, especially over the Hungarian question. When Andrássy first met the Empress he, too, was impressed by her incomparable charm. Elizabeth had heard much about him, from Ida Ferenczy among others, and looked with some curiosity at the "*beau pendu*" of 1848, who turned the heads of all the women and was the perfect type of a Hungarian nobleman, with his picturesque, fur-trimmed magnate's uniform, his tall, slender figure, and noble face.

After eleven years of marriage, Francis Joseph was well known to be as much in love with his wife as ever, and Andrássy saw in this a possible means of overcoming his hesitations. Francis Joseph was still convinced that nothing but a strongly centralized constitution would secure the future power and existence of the monarchy. So long, however, as nothing was done to interfere with such vital common factors as the army, finance, and foreign affairs, he was not altogether averse to considering the wishes of the Hungarian nation, for this would safeguard Austria's position as a Great Power while conciliating Hungary. During the winter of 1865 negotiations went on promisingly; the Hungarian Parliament was summoned, and on December 12 Francis Joseph, without the Queen, arrived in Budapest to open it. On December 17 deputations from both the upper and lower houses waited upon their sovereign and, prompted by Andrássy and Deák, expressed the desire that they might soon have an opportunity of welcoming to their capital "the honored and dearly beloved mother of the country, the august Queen." The Emperor nodded his consent, whereupon Francis Deák proposed that both houses should send deputations to congratulate the Empress upon her approaching birthday.

Just as the deputation was about to start, it was heard that the Empress was staying in Munich on account of ill-health, so the ceremony had to be postponed and the group was not received by her till January 8. The Hungarian representatives, almost all of whom belonged to the great Hungarian nobility, appeared at the Hofburg with the Cardinal Primate at their head, wearing their picturesque magnates' costume, and with the tall form of Julius Andrássy towering above them all. Elizabeth received them, attended by her Mistress of the Household and eight newly appointed Hungarian ladies in waiting and wearing a Hungarian national costume of white silk with a lace apron, a richly laced velvet bodice, and a Hungarian cap trimmed with lace, above which flashed a diamond crown. Her lovely face was flushed with excitement, and as she scrutinized the deputation her eyes rested upon Andrássy, who was looking at her with an expression of dazzled wonder.

The Cardinal Primate opened his address by speaking of the love and unbounded loyalty felt by the Hungarian nation for the Queen, the mother of the heir to the throne, and concluded by expressing a hope that they might welcome her in their capital—the sooner, the better. Elizabeth replied in Magyar, clearly and with perfect fluency, though with a slight, rather English, accent, thanking them cordially and holding out the possibility of a visit. The Hungarian phrases flowing so easily from the lips of the Queen—and such a lovely, fairylike queen—were greeted with the wildest enthusiasm. Never before had such a thunderous "*Eljen!*" rung through the Marmorsaal of the Hofburg.

Elizabeth soon responded to this invitation, for by January 29 she was in Budapest. The entry of the "hereditary" (*erblich*) royal pair, as they were officially styled before the coronation, went off without a hitch. In front of the imperial carriages rode the imposing mounted contingents from Pest and Buda, known as the *Banderien,* with their magnificent horses. But the task awaiting the sovereigns was no easy one.

They had first to break down the social barriers which had existed between Hungarians and Austrians since the Revolution of 1849 had been crushed. Even in that hospitable society it had been impossible during the previous fourteen years for an officer in Austrian uniform to enter the military club or any great lady's drawing room.

On February 1 a deputation from both houses of Parliament presented an address of welcome to the Emperor and Empress, and so warm were the terms in which the nation's thanks for Elizabeth's visit were expressed that it was plain to everybody, and above all to herself, that this was no mere official ceremony, but a sign of genuine personal affection. This was a thing to which she was quite unaccustomed, for in Austria she had always felt herself to be pursued with enmity and was consequently on the defensive. But now her heart was touched by the warmth of her welcome, and she felt an answering sympathy.

She again spoke in Magyar, which met with the same prodigious success as it had in Vienna in January, so that even the Emperor's reply to the loyal address did not produce such a chilling effect as it would otherwise have done; for it contained an unequivocal warning that Hungary must not indulge in exaggerated hopes and should put forward none but feasible proposals.

Even here, however, Elizabeth characteristically found it hard to fulfil the duties of her rank, as can be seen from her letters to the children. "I am having a most unrestful time here," she wrote to her little son on February 6, "but I do manage to go to the riding school every day. . . . If only you two were here, I would not mind staying for the whole winter, but as it is, I shall be very glad to be back with you soon. . . . Now I must close, and begin dressing for the city ball (*Bürgerball*), which will be very hot and tiring. I am speaking almost more Hungarian than German here."

"There is a great deal to do here," she wrote to her little daughter; "the constant dressing and undressing is dreadfully tedious; the court which I held for the ladies was very tiring, with all the standing and talking." Affairs of this sort were too exhausting for her, and warning symptoms of her old malady reappeared. At times, when things were too much for her, she would burst into tears as soon as she was alone. But both she and Francis Joseph enjoyed the prodigious effect produced everywhere by her beauty and her knowledge of Magyar, which now became the fashionable language at court, till the members of the Household, who would never have dreamed of learning it before, began laboriously murdering the language. Everything good that happened—amnesties, the restoration of confiscated property, and so forth —was attributed to the Empress by public opinion; but when Francis Joseph intimated that he could not yet give full satisfaction to Hungary's aspirations, this was ascribed to the evil influence of the court of Vienna, his mother, or the Austrian ministers, whose influence the Empress had not yet succeeded in checking.

Meanwhile the visit of the Emperor and Empress to Hungary had been viewed with mixed feelings in Vienna. "I hear," observed the Emperor in a letter to his mother, "that people in Vienna are again gratifying their usual taste for being afraid—this time lest I might make concessions here, or consent to the formation of a ministry, etc. Of course I have no idea of doing anything of the sort . . . but Vienna is grumbling as usual. Heaven preserve one from orthodox circles (*Gutgesinnte*) in Vienna! Things here are progressing slowly, but with firmness on the one hand and confidence, friendship, and right handling of the Hungarian character on the other, we shall manage. Sisi is a great help to me with her courtesy, tact, and discretion and her excellent Hungarian, in which people feel more inclined to listen to an occasional admonition from such fair lips."

The Emperor did not yet realize how far his wife's enthusiasm for Hungary had gone. On one occasion, when visiting the girls' school kept by the *Englische Fräulein* in Budapest, she spoke Magyar to the Mother Superior, who, being an Italian, did not understand a word. "I hope," said Elizabeth, "that next time I come, you will answer me in the Hungarian language." Scarcely more than a fortnight later she returned, whereupon the Mother Superior feigned illness and took to her bed; but Elizabeth went to her room, said something in Magyar, which she did not understand, and then left her—and shortly afterwards the Mother Superior had to retire. Elizabeth was always seeing Andrássy, and liked talking to him better than to anyone else, and he was glad to see that he was gradually winning her over to his own way of thinking. On one occasion she said to him quite spontaneously: "I am speaking in confidence, so I can tell you what I should never say to anybody else. If the Emperor's cause goes badly in Italy, it pains me, but if it goes badly in Hungary, it is death to me." On March 5 she left the capital with her husband after a stay of six weeks, and her farewell words at the station were: "I hope soon to be able to return to my dear, dear Hungary." And she pronounced the word "dear" with such charm and feeling that tears came into the eyes of all those present.

Attempts were now made in Vienna to counteract the Hungarian influences at court. A police warning was actually received by the Minister of the Interior* accusing the Empress' reader, Ida Ferenczy, of being the creature of the Left Wing of the Hungarian Parliament and hoping to influence the Empress in favor of their views. But Hungary

* Now in the State Archives, Vienna.

was not the only source of anxiety. Germany, too, was giving cause for serious alarm, and the great question of who was to enjoy the hegemony of Germany urgently demanded a solution. Bismarck was making every effort to cut the Gordian knot by excluding Austria from Germany, if necessary by force of arms.

It was already clear that the Chancellor had concluded an alliance with Italy, and in March and April, 1866, it became evident that war could no longer be avoided. Elizabeth dreaded the possible reactions upon her native land and family. She knew that nothing was farther from Ludwig II's ideas than to take part in any warlike projects of Bismarck's, but it was doubtful whether he would prove a good ally to Austria.

Elizabeth would have liked to pay a visit to her old home, for all sorts of things had been going on at Possenhofen. She had long been anxious about a marriage for her sister Sophie. Duke Philip of Württemberg had been thought of, but that had come to nothing. And now, in March, 1866, the Emperor's brother, the Archduke Ludwig Viktor, went to Possenhofen to ask for Sophie's hand and was warmly received by the Duchess Ludovika. The young people, however, were not attracted to each other. "The Emperor never thought she would have him," wrote the Empress to her mother. "If only she could find a husband whom she loved and who made her really happy. But whom?"

Next a Spanish prince wished to marry the Princess Sophie, but the Empress knew from her husband that this suitor was "a rough fellow and a *mauvais sujet*" and did not consider the Spanish court at all desirable. She would have preferred Ludwig Viktor. "He is really a good fellow," she said, "and perhaps after all something may come of it."

Elizabeth was delighted when in April the court moved from the Burg to Schönbrunn. "The weather is glorious now," she wrote to Frau von Ferenczy, "and I am glad to leave the city and enjoy greater freedom, especially as I have permission to go to the stables by myself when I like." Besides, it enabled her to escape the traditional drive through the Prater in which the Emperor always took part on May Day to please the people of Vienna. "This year," she wrote to her mother, "I am not celebrating May Day in the usual wearisome fashion, but have excused myself on the ground of my cough and am remaining quietly here, which is beyond comparison pleasanter than being walked up and down the avenue in a carriage with one of the Archduchesses and gaped at by hundreds of people . . . I am not going to Füred,* for times are so depressing, with war at our very doors, that I do not like to leave the Emperor." During these anxious days, indeed, Francis Joseph was always glad when he had a few hours to spare and could take a walk through the woods to Hainbach with his wife on Sunday afternoon like any simple citizen.

By May 8 the whole Prussian army was ready for war, and Austria too began to mobilize in both the north and the south. Meanwhile the King of Bavaria was quite oblivious of wars and rumors of war, and on May 21 paid a secret visit to Richard Wagner in Switzerland. "I hear that the King is off again," wrote Elizabeth to her mother. "If only he would think a little more about government, now that times are so bad!" "It would really be a blessing," she said in another letter, "if the King of Prussia were to die. It would save so much unhappiness." During these sad days she made a number of vows, and on June 9 went to Mariazell to give thanks for the fulfilment of a wish and make another vow, "for," she wrote, "God knows there is enough to pray for!"

On June 15, 1866, war was declared, and by the following

* A Hungarian watering place which the Empress had thought of visiting.

day Prussian troops had already crossed their frontiers. Elizabeth read the newspapers in an agitated and disconsolate frame of mind and wrote the Emperor long letters every day. She was far more uneasy than in 1859, for Bavaria now entered the war on the side of Austria, though without enthusiasm and merely because it felt morally bound to do so. Had the decision rested with the King, this would certainly not have happened. During the days preceding the declaration of war Ludwig II had retired to the Roseninsel in the Starnbergersee, and for three days his ministers could not obtain access to him. One evening fireworks were actually seen on the island.

When things began to look serious, the Empress left Ischl to be near the Emperor and to equip a hospital at Laxenburg, as in 1859. She was most uneasy about her family. "I am anxious beyond words about my brothers," she wrote to her mother, "and often wish that they had been sisters. . . . They say that the first time one goes to a church one's prayers are answered, and yesterday I did go to one for the first time. You are right when you say that the newspapers make one even more nervous. They only tell one the really important things belatedly, and most of their news consists of lies and a lot of gossip and argument, which do nothing to change the march of events. But of course one goes on reading them, because at present one has no intelligence left for anything else."

Elizabeth left the children at Ischl, promising to write regularly, and arrived in Vienna on June 29. Ill-disposed people in the entourage of the Archduchess Sophie watched her actions sceptically. "At least she is here," was the Landgravine Fürstenberg's caustic comment, "and it would be wise not to expect more."

But in spite of what people said, Elizabeth was trying wholeheartedly to support her husband, for it was characteristic of her that, though exacting and headstrong in times of peace, when the seriousness of the situation demanded it she displayed energy and spirit. She wrote pages to Rudolf, who was now eight years old and precocious enough to take a keen interest in the war. "In spite of the depressing times and all he has to do, dear Papa is looking well, thank God, and is filled with a calm and confidence in the future which command admiration, though the Prussian troops are terribly strong and their needle guns are having a prodigious success." Elizabeth kept the Emperor company whenever he had a free minute, spending the rest of her time visiting the hospitals, where she was untiring in her efforts to cheer and comfort the wounded, though she was saddened by the sight of one of the "only too efficient guns."

Once she saw in the hospital an infantryman named Joseph Fehér, a gipsy, whose right arm had been shattered by several bullets. The doctor said that it would be impossible to save his life without amputating, but Fehér shrank from the operation. Elizabeth did her best to persuade him, and said on leaving him that when she returned next day she hoped to find that in his own best interests he had consented. The soldier persisted in his refusal, and Elizabeth redoubled her efforts. At last he said: "If Your Majesty will be present at the operation, I will consent." Elizabeth shrank for a moment, but then replied firmly that she would. She sat by his bedside, holding his uninjured hand with infinite compassion while preparations were being made. Not till the man had been given the anæsthetic did she leave the operating theatre and make her round of the wards, leaving orders that she was to be sent for when the time came, so that when the soldier recovered consciousness she was still sitting by his bedside. On opening his eyes, the first thing he saw was the Empress' lovely, pitying face.

But the news from the front grew worse and worse, and

Elizabeth had to write sadly to her son's tutor that the army of the north had suffered terribly in the recent battles, and that though a few corps still remained intact, the army and headquarters were retiring for the present to Moravia. "You can see from all this," she wrote on July 1,* "that things are not going very well for us. The Emperor is splendid, always calm and collected. . . . This is bad news, but we must keep up our spirits. Tell Rudolf as much as you think fit."

And now, at seven o'clock on the evening of July 3, Count Crenneville, the Emperor's Adjutant General, brought him the decisive telegram: "Battle at Königgrätz, the army defeated and in flight toward the fortress, in danger of being surrounded there." The Emperor and Empress felt the shock profoundly. They sat together late into the night of July 3, waiting for fresh messengers of disaster to arrive from the theatre of war, and realized that the whole effect of the Archduke Albrecht's victories in the south would now be undone. The Emperor was deeply affected, but he and his wife continued to hold their heads high. Elizabeth had only one thought—how she could best support and console her husband. She wanted to telegraph to Rudolf's tutor again on the evening of July 3, but the Emperor did not wish it. On the following day, however, she wrote to Latour. "None can tell what will happen now," she concluded. "God grant that peace is concluded; we have no more to lose, so it would be better to meet ruin honorably. How terrible it must be for you and Pálffy to have to bear it quietly at Ischl. I understand it only too well, but God will reward you for making this heavy sacrifice and not abandoning the poor child whose future is so gloomy. Our poor Emperor! He is indeed sorely tried."

She received agonized telegrams from her mother, asking

* From a letter in the State Archives, Vienna.

what was to happen next, how the Emperor was, whether he would stay in Vienna or would have to flee. "We still feel as though we were in a dream," replied Elizabeth on the morning of July 5. "One blow on top of another . . . and then we are told we must trust in God! I have no idea what will happen next. . . . It is best to have no time to think, but always to keep moving. I spend my mornings in the hospitals, and I am especially glad to be with the Hungarian soldiers. The poor fellows have nobody here who can talk to them. . . . The Emperor is so overwhelmed with business that really his only relaxation is for us to sit together for a while in the evenings by the open window. . . ."

The Mistress of the Household, who did not understand any Hungarian, was annoyed when Elizabeth talked Magyar in the course of her visits to the hospitals, for instance to Count Bethlen, who had been wounded at Jičin and was in hospital at Laxenburg; for, she thought, what might the Empress not be saying to him?

These events were, if possible, an even greater blow to the Archduchess Sophie than to the Emperor and Empress, for she saw the ruin of all her dreams and desires. The whole political structure she had tried to build up had collapsed and her proudest hopes were at an end. She now judged her daughter-in-law more justly, as may be seen from a letter which she wrote the little Crown Prince: "I am sending you a few words in haste, my dear child," she wrote, "to tell you for your consolation that your poor dear father, God be praised, is well, physically at least, and your dear Mamma remains at his side like his good angel, is always near at hand, and only leaves him to go from one hospital to another lavishing consolation and help on every side."

Even her entourage began to change their attitude. "The Empress spends her whole day in the hospitals," admitted the critical Landgravine Fürstenberg, "and is really a perfect providence, entering into everything, attending to everything, taking thought for everything, in a motherly, affectionate way. God be praised! At last! . . . It was high time that she should try and win the hearts of the public, and she is going the right way to work to do so."

It was an unusually hot July, but the Empress would not think of going to the country. She would sit by the Emperor's writing table all day, and his aides-de-camp could not repeat often enough what a comfort she was to their poor sovereign and how she tried to cheer and console him as the bad news came in. But the enemy was advancing and might shortly reach Vienna. At a ministerial council on July 9, 1866, arrangements were discussed for moving the Emperor and the principal officials to Buda. Elizabeth was to precede them, the ostensible object of her journey being to visit the hospitals, but it was really a preliminary to the flight of the court and had the further intention of appealing to the chivalry of the Hungarians, as had been done at an equally critical moment by Maria Theresa. None could be better fitted for such a mission than Elizabeth.

It was now evident how fortunate it was that the Empress had not shared the anti-Hungarian views of the Archduchess Sophie and her circle. When Elizabeth arrived in Budapest with Ida Ferenczy, she was received with enthusiasm. Andrássy and Deák were at the station to meet her. "It would be cowardly," said Deák to his friends, "to abandon the Queen now that she is unfortunate, after our friendly approaches recently when things were going well for the dynasty." He and Andrássy escorted the Empress to the castle in Buda and had a conversation with her in which they explained how the radical, revolutionary elements on the Left, representing Kossuth's principles, meant to take advantage of the terrible plight of the crown. Now, they said, was the moment for prompt action, so as to take the wind out of these people's sails by concessions such as they themselves had long been recommending.

Elizabeth saw that action was necessary. She hastily took a villa in the mountains near Buda (the Villa Kochmeister) and then, on July 12, returned to Vienna to fetch the children. She reported to the Emperor what she had seen and heard, and implored him to make Julius Andrássy Minister for Foreign Affairs. Impressed both by the Count's good looks and by his brilliant abilities, the Empress saw in him the only possibility of keeping Hungary attached to the dynasty and preventing the monarchy from breaking in half. Francis Joseph, however, in spite of his heavy burdens, was still cautious, for he could not yet see his way clearly. Whatever course they adopted, he said, might have grave consequences. He must first take counsel with his ministers.

But time pressed, and even the next day might be too late; Elizabeth urged him agitatedly to grant her request, but all he said was: "Take the children to Buda and be my advocate there. Hold people in check as best you can, and we shall find a way." The Emperor did not go to Pest, for he was hoping for the intervention of Napoleon III, to whom he had ceded Venetia, and he was afraid that in Hungary the pressure brought to bear upon him would be too great. On the thirteenth his wife and children departed for Buda, and at the same time the jewels and precious objects in the treasury in Vienna were removed to the armory in Buda.

On the very day after her arrival Elizabeth wrote to the head of the Hungarian chancellery in Vienna,* asking him to propose to the Emperor that he should summon Deák to his headquarters in Vienna, where he might perhaps achieve what she had failed to do. She could no longer look on, she said, while those at the head of the Government in Vienna got

* The Empress' correspondence with George von Majláth is now at Schloss Wallsee.

things into still greater confusion. George Majláth enjoyed her confidence, for he was one of those whom she had immediately attracted and now, having failed to persuade the Emperor, she turned to him again: "I will be frank with you," she wrote. "One thing above all others I ask of you: be my deputy with the Emperor and take over my function of opening his eyes to the danger into which he will irrevocably fall if he persists in refusing all concessions to the Hungarians. Be our savior, I implore you, in the name of our unhappy fatherland and of my son. I also count upon the friendship, a little of which I perhaps only imagine that you feel for me. The concession which I tried to obtain from the Emperor, unfortunately without success, is that he should remove the men at present forming the Government and appoint Julius Andrássy Minister for Foreign Affairs. This would be a concession to Hungary without compromising ourselves by yielding for the present. His popularity in the country would have a calming effect and inspire confidence and keep the kingdom quiet until circumstances permit us to settle internal affairs. . . . If it is absolutely impossible to induce the Emperor to do this, let him at least make Andrássy Minister for Hungary. The great necessity at the moment is for the country to be kept calm and induced to place all the strength it can command at the Emperor's disposal by a man who is himself a guaranty of a better future. . . . I commit the whole matter to your charge. . . . Had you always been the only one, how different the position would be now; but since we have got so far, do not retire, at least, without having broken the influence of Count Esterházy, without succeeding in getting the Emperor to remove the man whose well-meant but ruinous advice is bringing so much misfortune upon us. I have turned to you without reserve. I can only give my confidence fully or not at all. If you can accomplish what I failed to do, millions will bless you, but my son shall pray for you daily as for his greatest benefactor. I am not trusting this letter to the post. You may keep the messenger as long as you wish, but do not let him return without an answer. *Isten áldja meg,* Elizabeth."

Majláth replied that the Emperor, too, was convinced of the necessity of taking drastic steps in dealing with Hungary, but was only afraid lest like causes might lead to like effects. He did not want a one-sided solution such as had been attempted in 1848, and desired to avoid even the appearance of having initiated these measures under pressure of external conditions.

In view of the state of feeling in Buda the Empress could not understand this hesitation. She had just had a meeting with Andrássy in the apartments of her Mistress of the Household, and while still fresh from this interview drafted a most serious letter to the Emperor with her own hand.

"I have just returned from the Königseggs'," she wrote, "where I had an interview with Andrássy—alone, of course. He set forth his views clearly and plainly. I quite understood them and arrived at a conviction that if you will trust him —and trust him entirely—we may still be saved, and not only Hungary but the monarchy, too. But *in any case* you must talk to him yourself, and at once, too, for any day matters may take such a turn that he would no longer undertake it after all; at such a moment it really requires great self-sacrifice to do so. Do talk to him immediately, then. You may do so without reserve, for I can assure you that you are not dealing with a man desirous of playing a part at any price or striving for a position; on the contrary, he is risking his present position, which is a fine one. But like any man of honor, at a moment when the State is approaching shipwreck he, too, is prepared to do all in his power toward saving it; what he possesses—his understanding and influence in the country—he will lay at your feet. For the last time I beg you in Rudolf's name not to lose this, the last moment. . . .

"I have asked Andrássy to tell you the truth quite frankly and inform you of everything, though unfortunately it is not cheering. Please telegraph to me, immediately upon receipt of my letter, whether Andrássy is to leave for Vienna by the night train. I have arranged with him to be at Paula's again tomorrow, where I am to tell him the answer. If you say 'No,' if at the last moment you are no longer willing to listen to disinterested counsels, then you are behaving ——ly [word defective in original] to us all. You will then be relieved forever from my future ——[the original reads '*B. und Sk.*'*], and nothing will remain to me but the consciousness that, whatever may happen, I shall be able to say honestly to Rudolf one day: 'I did everything in my power. Your misfortunes are not on my conscience.'"

The tone of the letter is very grave, too sharp, indeed, for an Emperor weighed down by so many anxieties. But the danger had been represented to her as so urgent that she believed she had to be severe in her husband's interests.

The Hungarians knew how to strike while the iron was hot and did not realize that Elizabeth was already won. Two days after her letter to her husband had gone off, the post brought her what was apparently a private letter in a strange handwriting. She opened it and looked hastily for the signature, but there was none. It was an anonymous letter in which the Queen was addressed as the "guardian angel of Hungary upon earth" and requested to intervene. Peace, it said, could only be achieved if the monarch would restore the laws of 1848 to the fullest extent, appoint a Hungarian ministry, and have himself crowned King of Hungary. The ministers recommended by the anonymous writer were Deák, Ëotvös, and Andrássy, three names which she now heard on

* Perhaps "*Bitten und Sekkaturen,*" "prayers and teasing."

every side. Anxiously she awaited the answer to her request. And now she received a telegram from the Emperor hurriedly composed in cypher: "Have summoned Deák in secret. So do not commit yourself too far with Andrássy."

The news of the Empress' visit to Budapest had reached the ears of Kossuth, too. As leader of the Hungarian exiles in Italy, recent developments had filled him with far-reaching hopes, and he at once saw the danger with which her visit might threaten his plan. On July 16 he wrote angrily from Florence to Count Csáky: "The expressions of sympathy with the Empress on the occasion of her visit to Pest produced a bad impression here. It is very important, extraordinarily important, that a national demonstration should be made in the opposite sense. The national passiveness of the Hungarians is most depressing."

The Emperor had read the Empress' letter with deep emotion, and now made up his mind to summon Julius Andrássy. Meanwhile on the sixteenth Elizabeth again discussed the situation with the Count in detail and gave him a letter to deliver to the Emperor, in which she summed up the whole situation in Hungary and repeated her former request. She concluded this note with a description of the Villa Kochmeister and the great glass door leading from her room into the garden.

Next day she received a letter from Francis Joseph by courier. "Beloved angel," he wrote, "Pray most fervently to God that He will enlighten me, so that I may do what is right and my duty. Well, today I am expecting G. A. (Gyula [i.e., Julius] Andrássy). I will listen to him quietly and let him talk and then examine him well to see whether I can trust him. The old man (Deák) is no longer in Pest and has got to be fetched from the country, so that he can be here tomorrow or the day after. Though I should prefer to talk to Andrássy alone first; for the old man is very clever, of course, but never had much courage. The situation here is unchanged. Napoleon is still acting as mediator, but has done nothing with the Prussians yet. . . . They may attack any day now, but they will not get across the Danube so easily as all that. . . . I must close now, and set to work. Farewell, my angel, I embrace you and the dear children with the greatest longing for you both. God protect us, God protect Austria. Your ardent lover, Franz."

At midday on the seventeenth Andrássy was received in audience by the Emperor and handed him Elizabeth's letter, after which he developed his views quite frankly for an hour and a half and asked the Emperor to discuss matters with Deák first and foremost. Francis Joseph said that he had already sent for him, and requested Andrássy to wait till he arrived.

Quite early in the morning of the following day the Emperor wrote his wife an account of this interview with Andrássy. "I found him, as I had always done before, not definite enough in his views, and lacking in due consideration for the rest of the monarchy. In view of the present decisive moment he wants too much and offers too little. He is a good, honorable, and highly gifted man, but I fear he is not strong enough and has not enough resources in the country to carry his present views into effect. Then, according to his own constitutional theory, he would resign, and I should be faced with the alternative of the extreme Left or martial law. First of all, though, I must have another talk with the old man, and then with both of them together, before I can come to any decision.

"I am very grateful to you for your whole description of the Villa Kochmeister, which must be very pretty. But I do not at all like the glass door into your room, for people are certainly able to see in while your washing is going on, and that worries me. So do have a large curtain made to cover the whole door. I beg you to take care of your health and spare yourself, or else I shall have you getting seriously ill, and that would be terrible . . . *Dein treuer Männeken* (Your faithful little husband)." Elizabeth's daily letters were the greatest joy to Francis Joseph, for, he said, she and the children, whom he "clasps to his heart with the deepest love" in every letter, were now his only consolation.

At seven o'clock on the morning of the nineteenth Deák was duly received in audience by the Emperor. He had very secretly taken a room at a modest little inn called the Gasthof zum Hasen at Meidling under the name of Advocate Ferenczy—which throws a revealing light upon the part played by the Empress' reader; then he drove to the Hofburg in a one-horse cab. "We discussed all conceivable eventualities for an hour very frankly in great detail," wrote Francis Joseph to his wife. "I have never found him so calm, clear, and sincere. Far clearer than A. and taking the rest of the monarchy far more into account. Yet I received the same impressions from him as from A. . . . Deák inspired me with high esteem for his honesty, frankness, and devotion to the dynasty, and confirmed me in my conviction that, had not this luckless war intervened, I should have come to an understanding with the Parliament before so very long, and along the lines upon which we were proceeding. But courage, resolution, and endurance in misfortune have simply not been granted to the man. He absolutely refused to meet A. and left at eleven o'clock as secretly as possible. Today I mean to talk to A. alone so that the threads of the negotiations may not be broken off, for, once external affairs are settled, it will certainly be possible to do something with him. *Adieu,* my Sisi. Embracing you and the children, I am your little one who loves you vastly (*Dein dich ungeheuer liebender Kleiner*)."

Meanwhile the Prussians were advancing all the time. On

July 18 King William set up his headquarters at Nikolsburg, and the Prussian campfires were already visible from Vienna. Francis Joseph hoped that the negotiations for an armistice might be successful and looked forward to them anxiously. Besides, he was troubled about his wife's health, "which," he wrote, "is getting worse and worse." As soon as an armistice was concluded, he hoped that the Empress and the children might be able to return to Ischl, where he would perhaps be able to pay them frequent visits. "For," said the Emperor, who signed his letter "Your poor little one" (*Dein armer Kleiner*), "I too should be the better for a rest one of these days."

The armistice was concluded and conversations about the preliminaries of peace began. "The negotiations will be difficult," said Francis Joseph, "since the King in particular seems quite intoxicated with his success. . . . May God's blessing rest upon them, for in view of the condition of the northern army and after the losses we have suffered, little is to be hoped from a prolongation of hostilities." He admitted that something must be done in Hungary, but did not want to make any changes before peace had been concluded. Things of that sort, he said, should not be done in too much of a hurry; the Hungarian constitutional question must be solved with reference to the rest of the monarchy.

In the meantime Elizabeth had again been feeling very ill and overtired, so she summoned her old family doctor, Hofrat Fischer, to Buda, which pleased and reassured Francis Joseph. "I am so anxious about you," he wrote to her, "and only hope that if any long armistice or peace is concluded, you will completely recover in the mountain air. . . . In any case, we are severing our connection with Germany altogether, whether they demand it or not, and after the experiences we have had with our dear German associates (*Bundesgenossen*), I regard this as a piece of good fortune for Austria."

Both Elizabeth and Francis Joseph continued to be good correspondents. He was quite upset and ashamed if a single day went by without his having written—as for instance on July 24—and begged Elizabeth "in contrition" (*zerknirscht*) to forgive him. But if he was anxious about her health, she was equally so about his. In spite of all the misfortunes which had come upon him and his country, Francis Joseph had remained perfectly well physically. "I am often amazed myself," he said, "to find how calmly I can bear such events and such a run of unspeakably bad luck and distress without my health being ruined."

Till now the Emperor had not ventured to advise Elizabeth to leave Buda with the children. But on July 26 the preliminaries of peace were signed, and since Vienna was no longer threatened by the enemy, Francis Joseph's first thought was that he could now see his wife. "Now I should like to ask for something very nice," he wrote on July 28. "If only you could pay me a visit! It would make me endlessly happy. I simply cannot get away from here at present, much as I should like to come to you all. . . . I long for you so, and perhaps you, too, would be glad to see me again at such a sad time. You might leave the children there for the present. . . . It would be a great comfort to me. . . . The Prussians are evacuating the whole of Austria and Hungary. In the preliminaries the integrity of Austria and Saxony is safeguarded, we are severing our connection with Germany entirely and paying twenty million thalers. I don't know what the Prussians are doing in the rest of Germany, or what they are going to steal; that is no further concern of ours. . . . I am glad that you can ride again. It will do you good."

Meanwhile Count Andrássy had paid a visit to Deák, who had, so to speak, run away from him. He went to see him on his estate at Puszta Szent-László and received assurances of his support, which was of such moment. He then returned to Pest, waited upon the Empress again, and informed her that Francis Joseph was raising great difficulties and that Belcredi in particular, the Austrian Minister President, was obstructing everything. He went back to Vienna, where the Emperor received him on the twenty-ninth in a noticeably more friendly spirit than the first time. Andrássy reported the outcome of his conversations with Deák, which contained the essential points of the *Ausgleich* (compromise) arrived at later. Yet in spite of his assurances that the new government would endeavor to bind the nation to the interests of the sovereign and the crown, the Count made no progress and the Emperor still said that he wanted to examine the question more thoroughly.

In accordance with Andrássy's advice, Elizabeth now considered that the moment had come to exert personal pressure upon her husband, and, since he, too, urgently desired to discuss things with her, on July 30 she decided to leave for Vienna. That same evening she sent word to Andrássy from Schönbrunn that she wished to speak to him on the following day. "It is certain," noted the Count in his diary, on receiving this invitation, "that if success is achieved, Hungary will have more cause than it knows to be grateful to the 'beautiful Providence' who watches over it." While he was writing this, Elizabeth was urging her husband to grant Hungary's wishes, but he quoted Belcredi's objection to the effect that concessions to Hungary might make a bad impression upon Bohemia, which had suffered, on the whole, more than any other part of the country from the effects of the war. There was a sharp difference of opinion, and Elizabeth became almost nasty. She continued to insist on the subject, till the Emperor, too, was vexed.

On July 31 Andrássy waited upon the Empress and found her depressed, for she had to admit that she had achieved nothing. She took a very gloomy view of the future and already foresaw the collapse of the whole Empire. "I shall continue to work toward the way of deliverance which you have shown me," she said, "but I have lost all hope of seeing my activities crowned with success."

All she could obtain was that Andrássy was again allowed to lay before the Emperor his ideas on the new form to be given to the monarchy as a whole. But now peace was in sight and pressure from the external enemy had slackened, so it was easier to feel that the state of affairs in Hungary was not so critical as had been alleged by Deák, Andrássy, and the Empress.

After a short stay in Vienna Elizabeth left for Buda again on August 2. In spite of everything Francis Joseph was very sorry to let her go. "My dear angel," he wrote, "here I am alone with my many worries again, and longing for you. Come and pay me another visit soon, that is, if your strength and health allow it, for though you were quite disagreeable and teasing (*sekkant*), I love you so infinitely that I cannot exist without you. Take great care of yourself and be careful when you are riding, for I am very anxious about you. . . . The damned Hungarian Legion* is once again advancing on Hungary. I only hope our troops will get to it in time and cut it to pieces. *Adieu,* my Sisi, think lovingly of me and come back again soon."

Now that the consequences of the unsuccessful campaign began to be visible, Francis Joseph was "melancholy and depressed, absolutely numbed," and had to pull himself together with an effort if he was not to flag at the important moment of the peace negotiations. He longed for his wife more than ever and touchingly signed his letters "*Dein einsames Männeken*" (Your lonely little husband).

* The Klapka Legion, which was taking part in the Prussian operations.

But Elizabeth was still cross with him for not giving way to her over the Hungarian question. She took this as a personal defeat and felt it particularly keenly because Andrássy had witnessed it. Francis Joseph's repeated hints that she might soon visit him again met, therefore, with no response. On August 5, indeed, she wrote to him in very formal terms, as though to punish him, saying that she could not come, as Schönbrunn was unhealthy at that time of year, and only Ischl could be thought of for her and the children—if that.

This time Francis Joseph was seriously annoyed, and his reply has an unprecedented note of bitterness. Even the opening words are less affectionate than usual. "My dear Sisi," it runs, "most heartfelt thanks for your letter of the fifth, the whole tenor of which is merely intended to prove to me by a host of arguments that you want to remain in Buda with the children, and intend to do so. Since you must see that I cannot leave here at a moment when there is a recrudescence of hostilities in Italy and peace negotiations with Prussia are still in progress, and that it would be contrary to my duty to adopt your exclusively Hungarian point of view and slight those lands which have endured unspeakable sufferings with steadfast fidelity, and which now, if ever, require special consideration and care, you will understand that I cannot pay you a visit. If you find the air here unhealthy, so be it; I should be as little able to visit you at Ischl as in Buda, so I must simply make the best of it and continue to bear patiently the lonely existence to which I have long been accustomed. In this respect I have learned to endure a great deal, and in the long run one becomes accustomed to it. I shall waste no more words on this point, for otherwise, as you most justly remark, our correspondence would become too boring, so I shall wait quietly to hear what you decide later."

This letter reached Elizabeth at a moment when she was already feeling rather nervous and unwell. She tried to allay her inward unrest by riding for hours on end in the country around Buda. Ida Ferenczy, who did not ride and so was unable to accompany her, saw Elizabeth's restless, unsettled state of mind with anxiety. The Empress answered the Emperor's angry letter quite briefly, without entering into its contents in detail, but merely describing her rides.

In the course of one of these she passed close by Gödöllö, a country place about eighteen miles from Budapest. Elizabeth had heard a great deal about it, and about a monument which the first owner had had erected to his favorite grey horse, so she was very eager to see it and asked Francis Joseph if she might not pay the place a visit, especially as there was a hospital there for the wounded.

Francis Joseph's annoyance had not been of long duration, and now he again expressed his alarm at hearing that Elizabeth was injuring her health by excessive riding, for she was getting even thinner and hardly sleeping at all. He recalled how exactly the same thing had happened in 1859. "If you wish," he replied, "you may go and visit the wounded at Gödöllö. But do not look over it as though we wanted to buy it, for I have no money at present, and we shall have to economize enormously in these hard times. The Prussians have devastated the imperial estates abominably, too, and it will be years before they recover. I have reduced the sum allotted for the expenses of the court next year to five millions, so that more than two millions will have to be saved. Nearly half of the stables will have to be sold, and we shall have to live very simply. . . . Your sad *Männeken.*"

This letter touched Elizabeth. She felt sorry she had been so severe, and wrote on August 8 that she would be in Vienna about the thirteenth, this time staying a whole week. Francis Joseph was delighted. "And now I have three more days in which to rejoice over seeing you again, and then almost eight happy days during which I shall have you all to myself, and we shall be together as much as possible. . . . Be nice to me when you come, for I am so depressed and lonely, and I need you to cheer me."

When Elizabeth returned to Vienna, she felt an icy atmosphere in her entourage, as well as in the demeanor of the Archduchess Sophie, whom she avoided as much as possible. People wanted to make her feel it for having been away from the Emperor so long and, above all, for showing such a preference for Hungary. This time not only the court but also the Government were against her, and, though the Empress' intervention in favor of Hungary had been kept strictly secret, even the people noticed with disfavor her lengthy absence in Buda, which could no longer be attributed entirely to the war. Belcredi was especially indignant because it upset his plans, and said that Elizabeth had taken advantage of the Emperor's state of mind while he was being assailed by bad news to give still more marked support to those "specifically and selfishly Hungarian efforts" to which she had long lent her patronage, though so far without success.

Elizabeth did not discuss the Hungarian question with Francis Joseph so much during these days. Andrássy had advised her not to, so as not to vex the Emperor; but, he said, when the right time arrived they could begin again and lead the monarchy slowly but surely toward the *Ausgleich*. Elizabeth's visit was comforting to Francis Joseph, for the nearer they approached to peace, the worse the internal difficulties of the country became. He was therefore quite unhappy when she returned to Pest on August 19. He felt that she was too cheerful at leaving him, and before twenty-four hours had elapsed he wrote telling her how lonely and dejected he was and how much he longed for her. "There are still difficulties over the peace negotiations," he continued, "and it will be even longer before we get the damned Prussians out of the country. It is enough to make one despair."

It was particularly painful for him to face all this alone, for, as he said, when Elizabeth was there he could at least talk to her and she often cheered him, though now and then she was rather "*sekkant*" (teasing). "Yes, how I miss my treasure—and what a treasure!" he wrote to her. "Do not leave me alone so long, my Sisi. Do not leave me to pine so long, but come back to me."

The Peace of Prague was signed on August 23, and Francis Joseph could now think about going to Ischl, so as to have himself "patched up into a usable condition again" by the good air and his favorite sport of shooting, for, he added, in his present state he was good for nothing.

On September 2 Elizabeth accordingly returned from Buda with the children, but the influence of her visit to Hungary lingered with her. Not content with talking Magyar with her reader, she felt a desire to resume the regular study of the language. Ida Ferenczy's attention was now drawn to Max Falk, a very well-read and cultivated Hungarian journalist. He was summoned to the palace and arranged to read the works of Hungarian writers with the Empress. Elizabeth was most conscientious and wrote out her exercises as punctiliously as any child at school. Ida Ferenczy was present at the lessons, which frequently led to a debate on burning questions of Hungarian politics. Falk was also an advocate of the *Ausgleich*, besides which he managed to give expression to his own liberal Jewish ideas. They often discussed the subject of revolution, and the Empress was quite prepared to maintain that a republic was the best form of state, for she had no need to learn liberal views from Falk, having imbibed them in the schoolroom.

In September Francis Joseph was faced with the difficult problem of choosing a Minister for Foreign Affairs. He did not intend to give this important post to Andrássy, because he feared the impression this might produce in Vienna. But an Austrian would not consent to an *Ausgleich* with Hungary, to which he was being slowly but surely won over, largely by his wife's influence. He therefore thought of choosing the Saxon statesman, Baron Beust, who had left his own king's service after the unsuccessful outcome of the war.

Every possible expedient was adopted for countering Andrássy's influence. It was known that the Empress was still pushing his claim, so one day she received an anonymous letter, warning her against the Count as an "unusually vain man." She immediately showed him the letter, and when he asked whether she was at all inclined to believe it, she said "No," adding that if she had been, she would not have mentioned it to him, but observed for herself whether it was true. She was also able to tell him that the Emperor had actually joined her lately in drinking the health of the "old gentleman" (as they called Deák).

After this they went on to speak of Beust. "What do you think of him?" asked Elizabeth. "I can hardly think," replied Andrássy, "that a foreigner is capable of infusing new life into the monarchy. One has to have been born in a country and lived in it to be able to save it. I hope Your Majesty will not take it amiss and think me lacking in modesty if I voice my conviction that at the present moment I alone can be of use." "How often I have told the Emperor so!" cried Elizabeth, hardly allowing him to finish his sentence, and she dismissed him with repeated assurances that she would make every effort to complete her husband's conversion. She had, moreover, met Beust at the time of her visit to Dresden and found him personally uncongenial. Yet in spite of all her efforts she still failed to obtain the appointment of Andrássy as Minister for Foreign Affairs. Beust took office on October

30 and at once declared that the Government's first task must be to arrive at a settlement with Hungary, so the Austrian Belcredi had gradually to give way.

At the beginning of 1867 another deputation from both houses of the Hungarian Parliament waited upon Their Majesties in Vienna, but it is significant that they were received by the Emperor and Empress separately. The Emperor was not looking well. The disasters of the past year had left their mark on him. He read his answer to the address and paused on reaching the word "*Ausgleich*," but there was a profound silence, without any sign of applause. The deputations next proceeded to the Empress, who answered them cordially in Magyar.

Francis Joseph was more nearly approaching his wife's views on Hungary, especially as Beust did not think the dual system at all likely to endanger the position of the monarchy as a Great Power, but believed, on the contrary, that it would be on a far stronger and more powerful footing with a contented Hungary. So at the end of January Elizabeth felt that she could go with a quiet mind to Zürich, where her sister the Countess of Trani had just had a daughter. On the twenty-second she heard of the betrothal of her sister Sophie to King Ludwig II, at which she was particularly pleased, because attempts to arrange a match for the Princess had broken down so often; so she decided to pass through Munich on her way to Switzerland. King Ludwig, who had a feverish cold, rose from his sick bed to go and greet her at the station as she passed through.

The Empress enjoyed herself in Zürich, but complained to the Governor and Dr. Escher, the President of the Executive Council, who had been invited to meet her, that whenever she went for a walk crowds of schoolboys followed her about and made her quite nervous. She wrote to her "sweet little Rudolf" telling him about the "excellent things" in the pastry cooks' shops and "Tante Spatz's" baby girl. "On the whole," she said, "the baby in her swaddling bands (*Wickelkind*) is not as revolting (*abscheulich*) as babies so treated usually are. But near at hand it does not smell very nice." "I like the little thing best," she wrote to her mother, "when I neither see nor hear it, for, as you know, I cannot appreciate little babies." She missed her usual opportunities of speaking Magyar, but devoured Hungarian books to prevent herself from losing ground in the language. "I hope I may soon hear from you," she wrote to her husband, "that the Hungarian business has at last been cleared up and that we shall soon find ourselves in Ös-Budavára (near Budapest). As soon as you write and say we are going there, my heart will be at rest, for then I shall know that the longed-for goal has been reached."

About this time Beust became Minister President, Belcredi retired into private life, deeply offended, and the way now lay open toward the *Ausgleich*. On February 18 Francis Joseph's rescript was read out in the Hungarian Chamber of Deputies, appointing Andrássy Minister President for Hungary and restoring the Hungarian Constitution. Taxes and military contingents were now voted punctually, and the majority of the nation ranged itself on the side of Deák and Andrássy, though Kossuth called them traitors and accused them of betraying their country. Rejoicing in this event as a personal triumph, Elizabeth had returned to Vienna on February 8. In token of her gratitude she was now particularly charming to her husband, but as she gained popularity in Hungary she lost it in Austria. The Emperor Francis Joseph had not welcomed the *Ausgleich* very cordially, but after the failures of 1859 and 1866 he no longer had entire confidence in his own judgment. The Empress' liberal opinions began to gain ground as the influence of the Archduchess Sophie decreased. And the coronation in Budapest, which was fixed for June, was so arranged as to be a striking triumph for Elizabeth.

In March she went into mourning because of the death of her brother Karl Theodor's wife, and therefore did not accompany the Emperor to Pest on March 12, when he was received with indescribable enthusiasm. Francis Joseph was stirred at the sight of the masses of people lining his route to the castle in Buda. "I had no idea," he remarked to Andrássy, "that Pest had so many inhabitants." On this occasion the Count informed Francis Joseph that in its joy and enthusiasm at the reconciliation with its sovereigns, and in the hope that the King and Queen would now make longer and more frequent visits to the country, the Hungarian nation had bought them a summer residence in the country. It was remembered in Pest that during her last visit the Queen had greatly admired Gödöllö, so that was the place chosen. Francis Joseph also learned that plans were being made for crowning Elizabeth at the same time as himself, though the custom was that the Queen should not be crowned till some days after the King.

"It was an enormous pleasure to me," she wrote to him, "to hear that Gödöllö is to be our property, and I can hardly wait for the moment when it will be in readiness and we are able to reside there. At present my curiosity is even greater. If only I could see it soon. It was a pleasant surprise, too, that we are to be crowned together; it will not be so tiring as it would be if the whole thing were going to last several days."

She now devoted the whole day to studying Magyar. "I am much pleased with Falk's manners," she wrote to her husband, "and hope that at last I shall make real progress. You need not be jealous of him, he is the living image of the typical Jew, but very clever and agreeable." Elizabeth was impatient at finding that even now she had not mastered the language, but she was well on the way toward it. She was constantly reading poetry, including the poems of Ëotvös, who had now become a minister. "What a pity," she remarked, "that Ëotvös has written so few poems." "It is indeed," replied Falk, "but there is one not included in the collected poems, for it is suppressed." "What do you mean—suppressed? Why? What is it about?" Falk then read her "The Standard Bearer," which tells how, when the flower of Hungarian manhood lay dead on the field of Mohács, the flag, the symbol of freedom and independence, remained standing, and how it had been kept flying all down the centuries and would be to all eternity.

Hearing that Falk was in regular correspondence with Ëotvös, the Empress asked him to show her his letters. In this way she learned many things which would hardly have come to her ears in any other way. Later she corresponded with Ëotvös herself, asking him to send back her letters corrected.* She was particularly interested in all works which had been banned or formed the subject of legal proceedings. Once the conversation turned upon Count Széchényi, that great Hungarian of tragic fame, and the Empress remarked: "I have heard of a work of his, called a '*Blick*' or something of the sort. What is it about?" She was referring to Széchényi's *Blick auf den anonymen Rückblick* (Glance at an Anonymous Writer's Retrospect), which ridiculed Bach's pamphlet entitled *Rückblicke.* It was of course suppressed and could only be smuggled into the country with great difficulty. "Have you got a copy?" asked Elizabeth, and, since Falk did not reply at once, she continued: "Ah, then you *have* got it! Well, please bring it to me." "But, Your Majesty . . ." stammered Falk. "Perhaps you think I ought not to read such books!" remarked the Empress, and, walk-

* Specimens of these letters are preserved in the Elizabeth Museum, Budapest.

ing over to her writing table, she picked up a slender brochure entitled "The Collapse of Austria, by a German Austrian,"* published at Leipzig in 1867, and strictly prohibited, of course, inside the monarchy. This extremely radical little book, which went so far as to assert that the existence and peace of the European nations and states depended upon the collapse of Austria, and closed with the words that Austria's downfall was a European necessity, made a profound impression upon the Empress, who was still deeply affected by the catastrophe of the previous summer, especially since the author savagely attacked her greatest enemies at Court, Grünne, Gondrecourt, and Belcredi. Falk was startled to see such a pamphlet in the Empress' hands, but he regularly brought her all sorts of prohibited books, including the history of Hungary's struggle for liberation, by Bishop Michael Horváth, who was ultimately granted a pardon at Elizabeth's request.

The influence of this liberal Jewish journalist was greatly disliked at the court of Vienna, though nobody knew exactly what was going on; but none ventured to take any overt steps against him, for this would have meant an open attack on Elizabeth. An adroit attempt was made to eliminate him at the end of April, when the court moved to Schönbrunn, but it was long before this proved possible.

At last all obstacles to the *Ausgleich* were removed, and on May 8 the Empress accompanied Francis Joseph to Budapest, where she was literally buried in flowers on her arrival. "For three centuries," wrote Ëotvös, "we had tried faith, then again and again hope, till only one possibility remained: that the nation should be ready to love some member of the reigning house from the depths of its heart. Now that we have succeeded in this, I have no more fear for the future."

* *Der Zerfall Österreichs. Von einem deutschen Österreicher,* Leipzig, 1867.

The enthusiasm of every class of society rose to incredible heights as the coronation drew near. Ëotvös, who had always been in opposition till now, attended the Empress and rejoiced at these demonstrations as though he had been the Controller of her Household; and in response to little Rudolf's inquiry whether on her arrival in Pest there had been "a really loud cheer" (*ein recht grosses Eljen*), she was glad to be able to answer that there had been.

On May 11 the Emperor and Empress drove out to Gödöllö, where alterations were going on busily in both the castle and the grounds, and the Empress was particularly delighted with the shady park and the splendid opportunities for riding. She thoroughly enjoyed the races at Pest, and took a childlike pleasure in the sight of the peasants riding bareback.

Such was her interest in Hungarian politics that she sent for Horváth to explain certain things in his *War of Liberation*, and remarked with reference to the executions of 1849: "I was not yet a member of the dynasty at that time, when a number of things were done in the name of my husband, then quite a young man, which he regrets more than anybody. Were it in our power, we two should be the first to recall Louis Batthyány and the martyrs of Arad to life." She had just read Kossuth's open letter to Deák condemning the whole system of the *Ausgleich* and feared lest it might create difficulties again at the last moment; but Horváth assured her that Kossuth was out of date and nobody listened to him any more. Subsequent events seemed to confirm this view. Elizabeth followed the political struggle with tense interest, reading the daily reports of the Parliamentary debates and public speeches. "I see more and more," she wrote playfully to Francis Joseph, "that I am extraordinarily clever, though you have not a sufficiently high opinion of my superior intelligence."

Some apprehension was felt as the coronation day approached. Deák received threatening and abusive letters, and there were rumors that the Left intended to create a disturbance during the ceremony. But careful precautions were taken.

The festivities began on June 6. Elizabeth now saw herself at the goal of her desires and felt sustained by the love of the whole Hungarian people; yet a slight shudder came over her when she thought of the endless succession of fêtes that she would have to attend. "It becomes a fearful burden," she wrote to her mother, "to dress up first thing in the morning in a court train and crown and hold courts and receive presentations all the time—and then this appalling heat! How delightful it must be at Possi just now. The coronation takes place on Saturday at seven o'clock in the morning; the days before and after it are crammed with tiring ceremonies; the balls and the theatre will be the worst of all, for at present it is no cooler even at night."

While according to ancient custom Elizabeth was herself mending the mantle of St. Stephen, which was to be placed upon Francis Joseph's shoulders at the coronation, darning the holes in the coronation stockings, and putting a lining into the crown, which was far too big, she heard the appalling news of the death of Mathilde, the Archduke Albrecht's eighteen-year-old daughter, who, in attempting to hide a forbidden cigarette which she was smoking, had set her thin cambric dress on fire and been burned to death in a moment. This tragic event threw the court into mourning, but the coronation festivities had already started and could not now be postponed.

On the evening of June 7 there was a careful rehearsal in the parish church at Buda, and Elizabeth had many satirical comments to make upon it. In the evening she tried on the magnificent costume of white and silver brocade scattered with jewels, patterned with lilac blossoms, and worn with a black velvet bodice, a masterpiece created by Worth in Paris for the comparatively modest sum of five thousand francs. She showed herself to the Emperor, who was so enraptured with her appearance that he embraced her.

At seven o'clock on the morning of June 8, 1867, a coronation procession of unexampled brilliance moved off from the royal palace. The great ones of the land, in numbers never seen before, dressed in their magnates' costumes and riding on noble horses with trappings which gleamed with gold, assembled to do honor to the kingdom, but at the same time to display their own pomp and power. The Emperor, wearing the uniform of a Hungarian marshal and riding on horseback; Elizabeth, looking bewitchingly lovely in the national costume with a diamond crown on her head and driving in the state coach drawn by eight horses; the Life Guards, with leopard skins floating from their shoulders, riding on their grey horses, made a picture which recalled the proudest splendors of the kingdom and the aristocracy in the most sumptuous days of the Middle Ages.

Elizabeth's ideas were too modern for her to enter into this aspect of the occasion, but, like everybody else, she was awed by its solemnity. Tears rose to her eyes as Andrássy, representing the Palatine, with the assistance of the Prince Primate, placed the crown of St. Stephen on the sovereign's head in the cathedral and laid the mantle of St. Stephen upon his shoulders. But when, according to ancient custom, the same crown was held over Elizabeth to crown her Queen of Hungary, she forgot all her weariness and dislike of ceremonies and thrilled with the consciousness of this great moment and the unbounded love which she read in the eyes of the glittering assembly. She was stirred to the depths when the *Te Deum* thundered forth, and as she and her husband laid the thick gold coins bearing their own effigy upon the golden plate, her eyes again filled with tears. A roar of cheering went up from the multitude as the royal couple left the church. While the Emperor mounted his horse and rode off toward the Coronation Mount and the platform where he was to take the oath, followed by a procession in which rode the princes of the Church, clad in their magnificent robes, with coronets and miters, and while the Minister of Finance scattered gold and silver coins among the people, Elizabeth hastily changed from her heavy coronation robes into a simple white tulle dress, and took the steamer over to the other side of the Danube, to the Lloydpalais, where she looked on from a flower-decked window at the procession and the ceremony which followed. Amid all this splendor what interested her most were the fine horses, but she had some difficulty in repressing a smile when two unfortunate bishops, who had never been on horseback in their lives, involuntarily parted company with their mounts as salvos of musket fire were heard and cannon thundered out the salute.

She looked anxiously at the Emperor, whose splendid horse was also a little restive but was held in check by its skilful rider. She watched while her consort raised his finger in taking the oath, then galloped up the Coronation Mount on his milk-white horse, and brandished his sword toward the four points of the compass. Not till the state banquet was over were the exhausted Emperor and Empress at last able to retire to their private apartments.

On the fifth day of the festivities Their Majesties were each presented with a coronation offering of five thousand gold ducats in an elaborate silver casket. It was, of course, anticipated that they would use the money for the good of the country in some way, but nobody had expected it to be set apart for the widows, orphans, and disabled men belonging to the *honvéds* who had fought against Austria. And, whether rightly or not, all Hungary was convinced that this suggestion, too, was to be attributed to Elizabeth.

What she most enjoyed were the natural products presented to them as offerings. A long procession of young men and girls, dressed in the national costume, brought them glorious flowers, fruits of incredible size, a model in confectionery of the Coronation Mount with the Emperor on it, a crown of St. Stephen made of pastry, enormous richly decorated hams, two huge live fish, each weighing sixty pounds, slung on a pole, appealing little lambs and calves, and last of all a fascinating cream-colored foal for the Crown Prince, with its mane and tail plaited with tricolor ribbons in the colors of the Reich.

Despite the fears which had been felt, the six strenuous days of festivities had gone off without accident. Elizabeth had captured the imagination of all who had seen her. The *Pester Lloyd* spoke of the Queen as one of the noblest of earth's creatures. Everybody agreed with Deák, who was presented to her on this occasion, when he said that their lovely sovereign was a perfect emblem of graciousness and reconciliation. Even the Archduchess Sophie's ladies in waiting admitted this, though their praises had a little sting concealed in them. "The coronation is over," wrote Theresa Fürstenberg. "Her Majesty looked quite supernaturally lovely during the solemn act, as moved and absorbed as a bride. I rather felt, too, as if, in *one* respect, she did interpret it in this sense." A comprehensive amnesty roused the greatest enthusiasm. Almost all the exiles returned home, with the exception of Kossuth, whose organ, the *Magyar Ujság*, merely dismissed the festivities with a tardy reference of four lines among the "News of the Day." "The coronation," it remarked laconically, "went off as arranged on the eighth of the month. Except for certain slips (*Entgleisungen*) which may be attributed to the restiveness of the horses, there were no accidents to record."

But now the proud days at Budapest were at an end, and

none too soon, either, for they were an intense strain upon the Emperor and Empress. On June 12 they set out for Ischl, in the hope of finding a little rest there and avoiding possible demonstrations of the popular feeling in Austria, where the coronation had been viewed with more than mixed feelings. The events of the past year had, indeed, exalted Elizabeth into a half divine being in the eyes of the Hungarians, but for that very reason had injured her popularity in Austria.

VIII

NEW INTERESTS IN LIFE

1867–1871

THE EMPEROR AND EMPRESS NOW HOPED to enjoy an untroubled spell of rest at Ischl after all their exertions, but they were bitterly disappointed. The month of June, 1867, brought several heavy blows. On the nineteenth Francis Joseph's brother Maximilian was shot in Mexico, and so ended the adventure which had led this idealist and his ambitious wife to destruction. The impression produced by this tragedy was immense, especially on the Archduchess Sophie, for Max had been her favorite. Though she had long dreaded this terrible event, she refused to believe that it had really happened. She seemed to age suddenly, her spirit was broken, and, though fond of society before, she retired into herself and nursed her sorrow in secret. But while Elizabeth shared her grief, even this blow failed to draw the two women closer together.

A still severer shock to the Empress was caused by the news that the Hereditary Prince of Thurn and Taxis, her sister Helene's husband, had died on June 26. The marriage had been a singularly happy one, and when the Emperor and Empress went to Regensburg for the funeral, they found the widow distracted with grief. She sought consolation in redoubled piety, which earned the warm approval of the Archduchess Sophie.

On July 2, after a short stay at Possenhofen, Elizabeth returned to Ischl, where she found a letter from the King of Bavaria, who had accompanied her part of the way from

LUDWIG II AND THE DUCHESS SOPHIE
IN BAVARIA AT THE TIME OF
THEIR BETROTHAL

From an engraving.

Munich and had once more been captivated by her. "You can have no idea, dear cousin," he wrote in his exaggerated manner, "how happy you made me. The hours recently passed in the railway carriage I reckon among the happiest in my life; never will their memory fade. You gave me permission to visit you at Ischl; if the time which will be so happy for me is really approaching, when my hope of seeing you will be fulfilled, I shall be of all men upon earth the most blest. My sense of the sincere love and reverence and faithful attachment to you which I cherished in my heart even as a boy makes me see heaven upon earth, and will be extinguished by death alone. I beg you with all my heart to forgive the contents of these lines, but I could not help myself. . . ."*

Elizabeth returned no answer. She had heard a great deal at Possenhofen about her future brother-in-law's strange behavior toward his fiancée, and felt that this unusually cordial letter of the King's was only a prelude to confidences which she would have to hear at Ischl. The last thing that she wished was to be involved in the business of this marriage; what she wanted was peace and to keep all potentates away from Ischl, especially the highly disconcerting King Ludwig II. So she persuaded Francis Joseph to write without saying a word about the projected visit, which was a very broad hint indeed.

The peace of her life at Ischl was now threatened from another quarter, for the papers announced that her aunt from Prussia was expected. In this case, she was determined to leave Ischl, inconvenient though it might be. She had not forgotten the events of the previous year and wrote to the Archduke Ludwig Viktor: "I will have no dealings with Prussia."

Before Maximilian's death the Emperor and Empress had meant to accept Napoleon III's invitation to visit him in

* This letter is now at Schloss Wallsee.

Paris. Elizabeth had disliked the idea, and now the matter had settled itself, for it was clearly impossible for Francis Joseph to go to Paris in view of the fact that it was Napoleon who had hounded on his brother into the adventure which had had so bitter an ending. Napoleon and Eugénie desired, however, to pay a penitential visit to Salzburg; and Beust, who was working hard to effect a *rapprochement* between Austria and France, urged that Elizabeth should be present, too, because he knew how anxious Eugénie was to make the acquaintance of her beautiful imperial rival. Elizabeth raised objections, saying that she was not feeling well and was in pain. "Perhaps I am with child," she wrote to the Emperor. "While this uncertainty lasts, the thought of the Salzburg visit is very depressing. I am so utterly miserable that I could cry all day. Comfort me, dear soul, for I am in great need of it. I take no pleasure in anything, I do not want to ride or go for walks either, everything in the world is insipid (*Pomade*). Why could you not come here early today, or tomorrow, which is a holiday? What have you got to do in Vienna? Or are you enjoying yourself so much at Laxenburg (you know with whom!) that you cannot tear yourself away?" She meant that he must be holding very enjoyable audiences, since he was always receiving beautiful girls. The Emperor denied this, and earnestly begged his wife, for reasons of state, to take part in the meeting at Salzburg if her health made it in any way possible. The Empress submitted with a sigh.

The meeting at Salzburg was watched by the world with intense interest, not only because of its political importance, but because the two beautiful Empresses were to appear together in public for the first time, thus making it possible to judge which was the lovelier. The people of Salzburg gave the Emperor of the French a very cold reception, and a sharp order was needed before the town council would present an address of welcome. People were astonished to see that the Empress Eugénie, though not of royal blood, had not only beauty in common with Elizabeth, but also an innate dignity. But on the whole, Elizabeth triumphed all along the line. The Empress of Austria's beauty was of so fascinating and charming a quality that no one, not even the Empress Eugénie, could vie with it. It was now observed that the latter was a head shorter than Elizabeth, and that her Paris dress, with its skirt coquettishly looped up to show her little foot, was not quite in keeping with Austrian ideas of what was suitable for an Empress. The Empress Elizabeth got on well enough with her, but there was no question of any such intimacy as was described in the tales which circulated among courtiers and journalists. The two women had too little in common. The Empress of Austria did not care for Eugénie, who in turn was never at ease owing to her depressing sense of her own humble origin. But in her dealings with Elizabeth she showed much tact, treating her with a certain deference without loss of dignity.

Both Francis Joseph and Elizabeth were heartily glad when the festivities were over, for the heat had been excessive and the Emperor felt no pleasure in renewing his acquaintance with Napoleon III, whom he called "the arch-scoundrel of Villafranca." Elizabeth now left for Zürich, where she met her sister, Queen Marie of Naples, and the Count and Countess of Trani, but an outbreak of cholera soon drove the sisters to Schaffhausen, where they admired the falls of the Rhine. The Empress had been constantly ailing and had gradually come to the conclusion that she was expecting another child. She longed to see her children, who were general favorites at court, though the Landgravine Fürstenberg, who could never resist a dig at Elizabeth, said they were such dear little creatures, such good, amiable children, that they seemed to belong only to their father.

Elizabeth also longed for her handsome sheep dog, Horseguard. This love of dogs, which she had inherited from her mother, was also a target for the Landgravine Fürstenberg's sarcasm, and she wrote home to her sister that Elizabeth "lives for her dogs, always having some on her lap, at her side, or in her arms, and kills fleas at table and even on the plates!" She added, however, by way of consolation, that the plates were at once changed. When Elizabeth saw a beautiful dog in the streets, she had no hesitation in speaking to absolute strangers. She met a gentleman with a great mastiff at Schaffhausen; the man recognized her and, to her great surprise and delight, greeted her with the words "God bless you!" in Magyar, whereupon she entered into conversation with him. Her joy in dogs, and especially large ones, was now a matter of common knowledge, but this taste was not shared by the Emperor, who found the great beasts "more than fatiguing." Elizabeth appointed her own kennel man, who proudly styled himself "the official charged with the care of the imperial dogs," but appeared in the books as a "supernumerary court indoor servant" and was tersely referred to as "the dog boy" (*Hundsbub*) by the ladies in waiting. Offers of dogs came to her from all quarters, but for the most part they were too small for her liking. "I am almost afraid," she wrote to Ida Ferenczy, "that there is no dog in existence as large as I want."

"Which will be gladder to see me again," she wrote later, "you or Horseguard? . . . Kiss your friend Monica, though I do not know her, since you write that she is so beautiful." For Elizabeth loved all nice-looking people and sought them out wherever they were to be found. In Zürich, too, she discovered a pretty child, about whom she wrote to the Crown Prince Rudolf. "We have made the acquaintance," she said, "of a little girl twelve years of age, who is ill, but very beautiful, with magnificent hair. We talk to her, and often I even kiss her! You can imagine how beautiful and sweet she must be!"

Elizabeth was so charmed with Schauffhausen that she persuaded the Emperor to come there and fetch her home, stopping in Munich on the way, where they heard strange stories about the King of Bavaria. The Austrian chargé d'affaires reported that the King was behaving in a quite abnormal way and that his extreme excitability undoubtedly pointed to mental derangement. He sought solitude, spending most of his time in aimless moonlight rides among the mountains, and the constant postponements of his marriage were due to his feeling that he could not bear to give up his solitary life in a world of dreams; but the ducal family was already indignant at his behavior. As for the intended bride, whose heart had never been in this engagement, Ludwig and his eccentricity frightened her. The King seldom visited her, and when he did, it was usually unannounced and at night. The Duchess Ludovika could do nothing to prevent this, but whenever there was a prospect of such a nocturnal visit she had Possenhofen or Kreuth lighted up from top to bottom and made all the servants stay up. And so they all waited till the King deigned to appear, even if it were at midnight or in the small hours of the morning.* But whenever the date of the wedding was touched upon, the King kept silence. In fact, the breaking-off of the betrothal was not due to the amiable Princess Sophie, whose disposition was then still a joyous one, but to lack of natural feeling on the part of her fiancé. At last Duke Max intervened. He wrote to the King that these constant postponements, and the rumors to which they inevitably gave rise, were no longer compatible with the dignity of his house and his daughter's honor, and that, if the wedding did not take place on No-

* This information was personally communicated to the author by H.R.H. the Duchess Henriette de Vendôme, Princess of Belgium.

vember 28, Sophie would release him from his engagement. The Princess received the King's reply four days later. "Dear Elsa," it began—the style being as usual taken from Wagner's opera—"Your parents desire to break our engagement, and I accept the proposal. . . . Your Heinrich."* The entry in his diary under this date (8 October) is as follows: "Sophie got rid of (*abgeschrieben*). The gloomy picture dissolves. I longed for freedom. I am athirst for freedom, now that I live again after this torturing nightmare." And on the day on which the marriage was to have taken place he added: "Thanks be to God, the fearful thing was not realized."

This affair made a deep impression, not only in Bavaria, but throughout the whole European world. The sensation was especially great in Bavaria, where the future Queen's Household had already been chosen and arrangements had been made for the marriage on the King's wedding day of a thousand poor couples, for whom dowries were to have been provided from the royal bounty. The people were disappointed and angry, and gossip said that the King had thrown the life-sized marble bust of his fiancée out of the window into the courtyard. Meanwhile the King himself moved daily from one palace to another, or went off into the mountains, so that neither his ministers nor his family ever knew where to find him.

When the Empress Elizabeth heard the news, which evidently came to her as a complete surprise, she wrote to her mother in great indignation: "You can imagine how angry I am with the King, and the Emperor is, too. No words can describe such conduct. After what has happened I cannot conceive how he will ever be able to show himself in Munich again. I am only glad that Sophie takes it as she does; with

* From a communication of Count Trauttmansdorff to Beust, in the State Archives, Vienna.

such a husband, God knows, she could never have been happy. I now redouble my wishes that she may find a good one at last, but who will that be? . . ." At the same time, in view of the naturally strained relations between the ducal and royal families, she suggested that the Duchess should send Sophie on a visit to her at Vienna for a while. But the Princess did not want to come, and the Duchess thought it better that she should live for a time in complete retirement. Elizabeth and Francis Joseph were not of this opinion. "We do not consider," wrote the Empress to her mother, "that there is any need whatsoever for Sophie to go into retirement, for she has nothing to be ashamed of; it is only the King who has, and, for the very reason that he and the Queen Mother would probably prefer not to see her, if I were in her place I would go to the theatre quite often and, in general, live exactly as before, the only difference being that, naturally, nobody belonging to our family would go to court. . . ." And Elizabeth resolved to do all she could to secure another suitor for Sophie as soon as possible, if only to show the King how indifferent they were to him and his conduct.

Meanwhile the question of the Emperor and Empress' going to Paris had again been raised, for they had to return the Salzburg visit. But Elizabeth absolutely refused, and it was therefore decided to inform the world that, in the doctors' opinion, she was in the third month of another pregnancy. The Empress excused herself on these grounds in a letter to Eugénie, with assurances of her regret, while at the same time writing to her mother that she did not in the least regret not going to beautiful Paris.

The Emperor Francis Joseph therefore went alone and thoroughly enjoyed his visit. He had expected great things of Paris and the International Exhibition there, but he was "struck all of a heap (*paff*)," for, he wrote to Elizabeth, he "had never thought it would be so overwhelmingly beautiful." He was in Paris at the same time as King Ludwig II of Bavaria, who had found it expedient to leave his realm for a while after the scandal over his engagement.

"The Empress is always inquiring after you," Francis Joseph reported to Elizabeth. "At present she is principally occupied in trying to keep King Ludwig at arm's length, for he has been here now for three days and is still pressing her for a kiss. For the rest, he is as jolly as a boy (*kreuzfidel*). . . ." "She has arranged with Ludwig to go up with him today in the balloon which makes daily ascents from the Exhibition Gardens. There is no danger, as the balloon is a captive one; but the Emperor is to be told nothing about it. *You* would not do a thing like that behind my back. . . ." "On the whole, I am enjoying myself very much. Yet I have an infinite longing for home and for you all, my only real happiness. I am sure you will be very nice to me and I will comfort you in your sorrows and do my best to cheer you. . . . The Empress actually did go up in the balloon with Ludwig, and was enchanted with it. One cannot but be lost in astonishment at all the imposing, beautiful, and useful things one sees. It is like a dream. . . ." And he added next day: "Little Napoleon is an intelligent, but very little chap (*Bub*). He has lots of freckles and wears red stockings like a cardinal. We have something better to show. I have seen a great many little ladies (*Dämchen*) and very pretty ones. But my thoughts are only of you, my Angel, you may set your mind at rest."

Elizabeth was well content that her husband should enjoy himself in Paris, though he, too, complained of being tired. "I am glad I am not there," she wrote to her mother. "After all, everything is so much easier and simpler for gentlemen." But in spite of all, Francis Joseph longed for home: "This is my last letter before we meet again, for which I am all impatience," he wrote, adding in French: "Where is one better off than in the bosom of one's family?" and ending with: "I embrace you, my glorious, passionately beloved wife, together with the children, and remain, your *Männeken.*"

The Emperor looked forward to enjoying a little rest on his return from Paris. But he found none in Vienna, for he was immediately overwhelmed with Government business of all sorts, audiences, festivities, visits to exhibitions, and the like. He now began to appreciate Gödöllö, the coronation gift of the Hungarian nation, as Elizabeth did, finding it "a refuge to which he could retreat when the Viennese annoyed him altogether too much." Thus the new country house became a fresh bond of union between them. The peace of Gödöllö, in contrast with the never-ending rush of Vienna, was particularly grateful to Elizabeth as her condition made itself increasingly felt. Much resentment was now felt in Vienna owing to rumors that the child was to be born in Hungary and not in Austria, and that if, as was hoped, it were a son, it was to be called Stephen, after the patron saint of Hungary. Despite the opposition of Viennese court circles, Andrássy urged the Emperor to accede to Elizabeth's wish that the child should be born on Hungarian soil, but great indignation was felt at court when it was announced that on February 5 the Empress would leave for Hungary on a visit of several months, though as a rule people were glad of her departure. The dislike felt for her went to such lengths that the Landgravine Fürstenberg reports with horror to her sister a remark let slip by an aristocratic lady in an unguarded moment, to the effect that the Empress deserved to have a miscarriage. Again, when on February 18 the court ball took place without her, people said that it had only taken place at all thanks to the absence of this "eternally obstructive element." The children remained in Vienna, and the Empress was delighted to hear that little Rudolf was now a keen and courageous rider, nor was she unduly concerned when Latour reported that he was too apt to make light of religious matters.

As the time of her delivery approached, Elizabeth became more and more restless. She longed for her husband. "I am going on well," she wrote, "but I need your company to cheer me up." The Emperor had great hopes of a son, but the Empress was convinced that the child would be a girl and had already thought of names for her. She intended to call her Valerie, and her prophetic instinct was justified, for on April 22 she gave birth to a little daughter. Francis Joseph described the baby in a letter to little Rudolf, who was full of curiosity. "She is a beauty," he wrote, "with great, dark blue eyes, a nose which is still a bit too fat, a very tiny mouth, enormously fat cheeks, and such thick dark hair that it could be dressed already. Her body is very plump, too, and she hits out vigorously with her hands and feet."

Elizabeth was determined to keep her child entirely to herself. The Archduchess Sophie's influence was now at an end, and this time the baby could not be taken away from its mother. She would not let it out of her sight, but jealously defended her rights and allowed nobody to approach it without her express permission. She had never been able to regain her full influence over the other two children, who were much older, and her obvious preference for the new baby soon led to its being nicknamed at court "the one and only one" (*die Einzige*). Only three weeks after the birth of the little Archduchess the Jewish Women's Society of Vienna begged permission to enrol her as an honorary member.

The Empress' recovery from her fourth confinement was slow. On June 9, 1868, though still far from well, she left Hungary for Ischl. What upset her most was that she was not yet allowed to ride and was in consequence "often fearfully melancholy, and would like to cry all day." When his wife was in these moods, the Emperor always advised her to go home to Possenhofen, for he had learned by experience that she recovered her spirits among her brothers and sisters. On August 9 Elizabeth arrived at Garatshausen on the Starnbergersee, where the ducal family had gone through a very uncomfortable period of strained relations with King Ludwig since the unfortunate affair of the broken engagement. Such a situation could not be allowed to last indefinitely, and efforts were made to bring about a reconciliation, which the King's peculiarities made none too easy. If anyone could effect it, Elizabeth could, for the King still thought most highly of her—indeed, she had been the chief reason for his betrothal; for if he could endure living with a wife at all, he would have preferred a sister of the Empress.

Meanwhile his eccentricities were becoming still more marked. His chief occupation during the day was now photography, but at night he would ride round and round the brilliantly illuminated court riding school. Elizabeth was most amused at the story of his "ride to Innsbrück." He had appeared at the riding school, armed with maps, ordered two horses, one for himself and the other for a groom, and while these were being saddled sat down at a table and reckoned the number of times he would have to ride round the course in order to cover the requisite distance. Then he mounted and started riding round and round the riding school, with the unhappy groom behind him, going on all night, from eight o'clock in the evening until three in the morning, which was about the time it would have taken him to reach Kufstein. Then he dismounted, ate a frugal meal, and began again, riding day and night as long as his horse held out, till he had reached what his calculation of the distance indicated to be the end of his journey, whereupon he went home satisfied.*

* Count Trauttmansdorff to Beust. Vienna, State Archives.

When the King and the ducal family met at last in May, 1868, it was quite accidentally and in comical circumstances. While riding round the Starnbergersee the King had been thrown from his horse, which ran away. Though uninjured, Ludwig would have had to walk all the way home had he not met a peasant's cart which gave him a lift. As chance would have it, while seated in the straw in this one-horse cart with mud on his clothes, he met the ducal family driving along the road in two fine carriages. The peasant drew toward the side of the road deferentially, and the King, who never drove out as a rule except in opulent coaches drawn by magnificently harnessed greys, appeared to his former fiancée in this modest guise for the first time since breaking off the engagement.

The Duchess Ludovika would no longer allow the name of Wagner to be mentioned in her presence, and adopted the views of those who regarded "the whole Wagner business" as a dangerous craze of the King's. But great satisfaction was felt when on August 13 Ludwig paid a visit to the Empress Elizabeth at Garatshausen and also met the whole ducal family. Meanwhile the Emperor Francis Joseph had also arrived. Having heard curious stories about King Ludwig from all quarters, he purposely cultivated his society in order to form his own opinion of him. The result was not reassuring, and the Emperor and Empress began to ask themselves anxiously what would be the end of it all.

An eligible suitor now appeared for the Princess Sophie in the person of the handsome Prince Ferdinand of Bourbon-Orleans, Duke of Alençon, a grandson of King Louis Philippe. This time it was decided to make no delay, but to celebrate the wedding in September; and so the gay and vivacious Sophie, who had rapidly recovered from her broken engagement, now found a home of her own. She was, however, somewhat surprised when, on the eve of the wedding, while the guests were already assembling, her late fiancé, Ludwig II, suddenly appeared unannounced and stayed for a few minutes.

The Empress Elizabeth had of course taken her daughter Valerie with her to the Starnbergersee. From the very first she had been overanxious for her baby's welfare. There was a stormy scene with the wet nurse one day, for Valerie's digestion was rather upset, and Elizabeth ascribed this to the woman's milk. "I am terribly alarmed, really horrified," she wrote to Ida Ferenczy, and at once telegraphed for another nurse, "for, believe me, I do not know a moment's peace. It is a horrible feeling when one knows that one's dearest treasure upon earth is surrounded by untrustworthy persons." A battle had still to be fought with the old nurse, who was at once dismissed, for, as Elizabeth said, "not even the Lord God can get on with her"—though when the nurse was questioned, she said the same of the Empress. She simply could not understand such a panic because the baby was sick for a day. She did not know that Elizabeth trembled for this child because it was really her own, and hers only.

In her letters to Ida Ferenczy Elizabeth gave rein to her feelings, for she knew Ida to be a faithful soul to whom she could safely write all that was in her mind. Thus she complained that she could not have luncheon alone with Dr. Balassa of Pest, who had been called in to attend Valerie, because this was not considered proper. Or she would mention, for instance, that Prince Leichtenstein, whom she calls the *szépherczeg* (the handsome prince), had made a very favorable impression upon her sister, the Queen of Naples, and she would like to know what impression she had made upon him; or again, that she had given up all hope of getting rid of her Mistress of the Household, the Countess Königsegg, and much besides of the same sort. She never forgot to send a thousand kisses to the horses, confessed that she rather shuddered at the thought of Schönbrunn, and begged her reader to get Andrássy, whom she always calls "our friend," to arrange for some hunting at Gödöllö.

The Emperor had now returned home and wrote her somewhat chaffing letters. On happening to mention his Adjutant General, Count Bellegarde, he added in brackets "Don't blush now!" for at first Bellegarde seems to have shown a marked weakness for the Empress, but had met with little encouragement. So when the Count arrived at Possenhofen early in September on a mission from the Emperor, Elizabeth wrote to Francis Joseph: "Bellegarde has arrived. You may set your mind at rest, I am not flirting with him or anyone else."

After a visit of nearly six weeks Elizabeth returned by way of Vienna to Hungary, where she was to remain until Christmas Eve. To the great indignation of the Viennese she had preferred to spend exactly three quarters of the year which followed the conclusion of the *Ausgleich* in Hungary in the undisturbed peace of Gödöllö. But whenever Valerie suffered from the inevitable childish complaints, the Empress was beside herself. "You will pity me from the depths of your heart," she wrote to her mother on October 5, 1868, "when I tell you what I have suffered during the past week and the mortal terror I have endured. My Valerie has been ill, and since I love her as much as you do Gackel, and get just as upset about her as you used to do when he was a baby, you will be able to imagine what a state I was in. . . . But God be praised, she is much better. . . ." And this indisposition arose from the baby's cutting her first tooth! Yet it was enough to make Elizabeth distribute two hundred gulden among the members of the "Imperial-Royal Nursery" as Valerie's attendants were styled.

The Empress was always flying from one extreme to another. She would turn sad, melancholy, and even desperate on the least provocation, only to change abruptly to irrepressible mirth, impish humor, and the spasmodic fits of laughter which caused her such agony to stifle on solemn ceremonial occasions. She was highly diverted by Valerie's new wet nurse, who would sing all manner of *csárdás* in a deep mannish voice, yet had a terror of mice, of which there were plenty at Gödöllö. One actually found its way into the Empress' room. "Yesterday evening," she wrote to the Emperor, "there was a great hunt in my old room. The children, women, lackeys, and chambermaids were all chasing a mouse with brooms, sticks, and dusters; it was a regular steeplechase, in the course of which the unhappy mouse fell into Horseguard's drinking bowl, but jumped out of the water again; at last Wallner (the footman) caught it, after it had crept under Bally's skirts, and wrung its neck. . . ."

Elizabeth was quite disconsolate when the quiet, idyllic life at Gödöllö came to an end and she had to migrate to Budapest at the beginning of December, where, in accordance with the terms of the *Ausgleich*, the Delegations of Austria and Hungary were meeting to settle the affairs common to both halves of the monarchy. Here she had to be seeing people all the time, while the dinners, visits to the theatre, receptions, and invitations hardly left her time to breathe. Now and then she found some compensation when she discovered an interesting personality with whom she could converse among the crowd of those eligible for presentation at court.

Thus, when Maurice Jókai was presented to her, she said to him: "I have long wished to make your acquaintance; your works have been known to me for some time. I consider *Kárpáthy Zoltán* the finest of them"—a work in which Jókai embodies the spirit of national idealism. The Empress' prolonged conversation with the poet attracted particular attention, for he was a deputy of the Left, which was hostile to the Government, and editor of the *Hon*, a paper representing the same views. He begged permission to present the Queen with his next work, and with the happy conclusion of the *Ausgleich* in her mind she said to him: "I think you will have more time to devote to poetry, now that political questions are being given a holiday." "I have reason to be grateful to poetry, too," replied Jókai, "for I owe to it the gracious favor shown me at present, which my political activities would not, perhaps, have earned me."

"I understand nothing about politics," replied Elizabeth with a smile, whereupon Jókai responded with ready wit:

"The highest stroke of policy is to win the heart of a country, and Your Majesty understands perfectly how to do that."

The poet like many another was dazzled by his Queen. When she spoke, he said, her every feature spoke, too, especially her eyes, whose glance outshone the brilliance of the diamonds she wore. "We see in her," said Jókai, "not the Queen, not the woman, but the genius of our land." All Hungarians said the same, it was the general opinion, and no flattery. When Elizabeth met the poet again later, she asked him:

"Have you done much work since I saw you last? The more you write, the more I shall have to read."

"Your Majesty," he replied, "is the first lady in the land in supporting literature too."

"And you are still working?"

"To me work is life."

"Then you are a happy man!"

It was no mere desire to please that made Elizabeth say this; it expressed her real feelings. She loved and read the Hungarian poets, Petöfi, Ëotvös, Arany, Jókai, and others, with deeper interest than did thousands of ladies to whom they spoke in their own mother tongue.

It was about now that she heard of the sudden death of

Dr. Balassa, who had attended her and her little daughter during the past year. Elizabeth sent a message of warm sympathy to the widow and asked her to come and see her in Budapest as soon as she felt strong enough to share her sorrow with others. To those whom she found congenial and who served her devotedly Elizabeth was always loyal. Though she never forgot the least insult or slight, she never failed to be aware of real love and attachment.

In the meantime the Empress had dismissed the Count and Countess Königsegg-Bellegarde, the last survivors of the Household chosen for her by the Archduchess Sophie, and appointed Baron Francis Nopcsa Controller of her Household. He too was a Hungarian, which naturally caused general indignation at the court of Vienna, for the Königseggs had made themselves generally popular there, and it was well known that their retirement had not been altogether voluntary.

The German and Slav papers were already complaining that Elizabeth now lived in a world which was wholly Hungarian, that she always spoke Magyar, admitted only Hungarian ladies to her intimacy, and had even chosen no nurses for little Valerie but those who could sing Hungarian folk songs to the little "royal girl" (*Königsmädchen*). Elizabeth therefore met with no very cordial reception when she returned to Vienna on Christmas Eve after spending two hundred and twenty days out of one year in Hungary. No sooner was she back in Vienna than she began to pour out her complaints to her mother. "I am desperate at having to be here," she wrote in January, 1869, "and long for Buda all the time, where it is so much more beautiful and pleasanter in every respect." When in the following March she returned to Hungary after a short trip to Agram, she felt happy and contented, though even in Buda she could not live in complete seclusion if the Emperor did not happen to be there, for she had occasionally to receive people and perform the duties of her rank, if only the most necessary ones. "I am living now," she wrote to the Emperor, "like the nun in the snail shell, who thought she was quite hidden till the abbot came and wished her good morning."

Meanwhile Count Julius Andrássy made use of Ida Ferenczy more and more when he had any communication to make to the Queen of Hungary. From this time onward, indeed, the correspondence between them became a regular one, and Elizabeth was drawn still further into the sphere of Hungarian interests. She embroidered the first colors for the newly established *honvéd* force, which was of revolutionary origin. And even Francis Joseph began to be noticeably affected by this trend of ideas.

The Emperor visited his wife at Buda as often as his engagements permitted, and she was always unhappy when he had to leave her again. "You are quite slipping away from me, my dear little one," she wrote in April, 1869, after such a parting; "during the last few days I had trained you so nicely, but now I shall have to begin all over again when you return. . . ." "You know me and my habits," she wrote some days later from Gödöllö, "and my *extinction de roi.* But if you do not like me as I am, well, I must be pensioned off."

It was, indeed, high time for Elizabeth to return to Vienna, if she was not entirely to forget that she was Empress of Austria as well as Queen of Hungary. She loved basking in the adoration of Ida Ferenczy, who was now in constant attendance upon her, and whose name for her beloved Empress was "the dewy flower" (*taufrische Blume*)—an appellation which Elizabeth herself used with a touch of irony at her own expense. Every evening Ida was at her bedside; in fact, she had grown so much accustomed to this that she could scarcely rest without this "soporific" (*Einschläfern*).

In July of this year, 1869, the Empress rented Garatshausen, her brother Ludwig's country house, for six months, as she felt most contented in the familiar surroundings of her homeland. She admitted to Ida Ferenczy that she was rather indolent. "I am living here with a perfectly vacant mind, as I love to do," she wrote to her. "I am speaking so little Hungarian at present that I quite regret it. Your dewy flower is not particularly loquacious and confines herself to absolute essentials." Ida Ferenczy had to keep her informed about the Emperor's state of mind, how her favorite horses were, and so on, and was always being urged to write more often, because, the Empress said, it was a bad habit only to answer letters, and positively discourteous. Elizabeth's own chief occupations were bathing, riding over to see her various brothers and sisters, reading, and taking little Valerie out for drives. She showed a marked taste for holidays abroad and seized every excuse for traveling. Her sister Marie, the Queen of Naples, who had been reconciled with her husband and was now in Rome, entreated her to come and bear her company at her first confinement. The Empress begged Francis Joseph's permission to do so, a most inopportune request in his eyes, for the political situation was very critical. A French force was occupying Rome and endeavoring with some difficulty to protect the temporal power of the Pope against the onslaughts of the new Kingdom of Italy. But he could deny her nothing.

In spite of her congenial family life in Bavaria, Elizabeth confessed to Ida Ferenczy that she sometimes suffered from "a terrible Hungarian homesickness." She was overjoyed to hear that "our friend," as they both called Andrássy, was coming to Munich from July 26 to 28 and proposed to take this opportunity of waiting upon her. This was even more of a pleasure to her than usual, because of her longing for

Hungary. "But do not be alarmed," she wrote to her confidante, "I shall not fall upon his neck, for all that."

The Archduchess Sophie had announced her intention of coming on a visit to the Duchess Ludovika on July 21. Valerie's new English governess, a Miss Throckmorton, did not know the Archduchess yet and had no idea of the strained relations between her and the Empress, so Queen Marie of Naples undertook to enlighten her, adding a warning that, if she wanted to get on well with Elizabeth, she must on no account say anything to offend her Hungarian predilections.

The Empress' thoughts now dwelt chiefly upon her visit to Rome. "Everything depends now," she wrote to her faithful Ida, "on whether my husband allows me to absent myself for such a long time. My greatest sacrifice will be leaving my dear 'Ballerina' behind! What a pity I cannot take all my favorite horses with me. Kiss her for me from top to toe, but take care she does not kick you in the stomach, for she is a treacherous creature at times."

On one occasion the real master and mistress of Garatshausen, Duke Ludwig and his morganatic wife, Baroness Henriette von Wallersee, *née* Mendel, came to dine with her informally there, neither the relations, who were still sulking at the Duke's marriage, nor the suites being invited. "I was glad enough to dispense with my entourage," wrote Elizabeth to Ida ironically. "I can imagine how they swore, but I could not offend such exalted personages by seating them at the same table as my sister-in-law!" The Empress already showed particular kindness to her brother's little nine-year-old daughter Marie, who was as lanky as a beanstalk and ran about the garden in muddy shoes and stockings, but was lively and merry and had ridden ever since she was five—a special recommendation in Elizabeth's eyes. In spite of her relatives, she determined to attach the child to herself and watch over her future.

Elizabeth was a singular compound of a spirit of revolt with a melancholy which would change when least expected to impishness and frank enjoyment. At times her mood would be deeply serious, critical, ironical, and even cynical, and then again she would be thoroughly childlike. Her love for her little daughter absorbed her utterly, and with her she became a child again. Once a strolling showman appeared with a tame bear, which delighted little Valerie immensely, and still more Elizabeth. When it had danced for her, she threw an apple into the lake and the bear jumped in after it, splashing about happily in the water and swimming around like a man. When a steamer approached, the beast took fright, uttered a loud roar, and made for the shore in a series of mighty bounds. It was so tame that it would let itself be stroked and ate out of their hands. Elizabeth would have liked to keep it and take it back to Austria, and gently hinted in a letter to Francis Joseph that the price of it would be seven hundred gulden. Guitar and zither players and performers on the mouth organ were also attracted to Garatshausen, till the Duchess said to her daughter: "My dear Sisi, you are getting exactly like your father with your passion for mountebanks."

Pressure of affairs made it impossible for Francis Joseph to come to Garatshausen, and he begged Elizabeth to return to Ischl soon. She consented, adding as a proviso: "Since I am prepared to do your will and make sacrifices, I hope you will do the same for me." When the Emperor asked how matters stood with regard to Ludwig II, she replied: "Thank God, we neither see nor hear anything of the King of Bavaria; he has always got the fidgets (*Zappel*) and is perpetually on the move." She sighed as she made up her mind to return to Austria and Ischl. "Except for you and my horses," she complained to her friend Ida, "I meet with nothing but unpleasantness wherever I go."

The chief topic of conversation at court at this time was the Emperor's impending journey to Suez for the opening of the Canal. This was fixed for November 16, 1869, and it was announced that the Empress Eugénie would represent her husband at the ceremony. For a moment there was a question whether Elizabeth should accompany the Emperor, but she shrank from the inevitable festivities, besides which she had no great liking for the Empress Eugénie. Francis Joseph thought it better, too, for one of them to remain behind with the children, so it was finally decided that he should travel alone. On October 26, 1869, he took leave of the Empress at Gödöllö. At the last moment she regretted that he was going without her, and wrote to him that she thought of nothing all day but of him and the beautiful journey that lay before him. She was so anxious that she persuaded him to take a physician with him. On that same day Francis Joseph wrote to her saying that he was being "parted from everything he loved on earth."

From such small indications as these the Archduchess Sophie perceived that the Emperor and Empress were on excellent terms, and for this she gave Elizabeth full credit. She now treated her with great consideration, and it was now the Empress who, by her conduct toward her mother-in-law, put herself in the wrong.

The Emperor's first stopping place was Constantinople, where he paid a visit to the Sultan Abdul Aziz, finding him "the most charming host imaginable." He sent the Empress long descriptive letters every day. She was very envious when she read his account of the Sultan's stables. "You would have begun with them, I feel sure," he wrote, and proceeded to describe the superb grey Arab mares, the Sultan's favorite horse, a thirty-year-old grey which he still rode, the remaining eight hundred royal horses, and so on. She laughed at his account of the Sultan's little son, who had a hundred and fifty horses of his own, but was so vicious and spoiled that he "thrashes the Sultan's aides-de-camp with a horsewhip."

When Elizabeth read these descriptions and the accounts of the pleasant, mild weather in the south, she felt a "terrible longing" for a milder climate, for winter was now setting in. She, too, wrote the Emperor long letters almost daily and hoped this would convince him that she was "thinking enough about him, though unable to express this in an amusing way." Andrássy, who accompanied the Emperor, also wrote regularly to Ida Ferenczy, and thus indirectly to the Empress.

From Constantinople Francis Joseph proceeded to Jaffa, and thence to the Holy Places. The Sultan had provided a brilliant escort. Hundreds of Turkish soldiers mounted on dromedaries, and Bedouins on magnificent greys awaited him in a camp where the tents were embroidered with silk and gold. Then the whole caravan set out for Jerusalem. On coming to the Jordan, the Emperor had a number of bottles filled with water to take home, for it was an ancient custom to baptize the children of the imperial family in the water of the Jordan. Andrássy bathed in the river, for he had heard that whoever did so would be able to work miracles, and, as he remarked, "That may be very useful to my country." The Emperor sent his wife all manner of souvenirs of the Holy Places, such as a metal bottle of Jordan water taken from the spot where Christ was baptized by St. John the Baptist and a box made of stone taken from the Holy Sepulcher.

From Jaffa the Emperor continued his journey to Suez, where for the first time he found letters from the Empress, telling him about her new dog, Shadow. "I envy the Sultan his wild animals," she wrote, "but I had rather have a negro. Perhaps you will bring me one as a surprise, for which I kiss you over and over again in anticipation. . . . So now you are happily united with your beloved Empress Eugénie. It makes me very jealous, too, to think that you are playing the charmer for her benefit while I sit here all alone and cannot even take my revenge. . . . I am lazier than ever and dread the very thought of having to bestir myself. But I should like to go to Constantinople, all the same. . . ." Francis Joseph was able to reassure her. The Empress of the French, he reported, had lost much of her beauty and seemed to him to have grown very stout. He described an enormous ball in the Khedive's palace, to which were invited all the guests, of whatsoever degree, assembled for the opening of the Canal. Some thousand people were present, so that the crush was indescribable, and even the Emperor Francis Joseph, with the Empress Eugénie dressed in bright red and wearing a crown, on his arm, had great difficulty in making his way through the press. The arrangements were quite unworthy of the grandiose setting, and they had to wait an eternity for supper. "There was only one thought in all our minds," he wrote to his wife, "how to get out (*Aussi möcht ich*), and the Empress and I did all we could to hurry up the supper. We were bound to wait for it, as the most magnificent preparations had been made, the menu consisting of more than thirty dishes." This was quite enough to cure Elizabeth of her envy. She liked traveling well enough, but if it had to be paid for in this way she had rather do without it.

Meanwhile news had been received that Queen Marie of Naples was expecting her child some time during the month of December. Elizabeth, therefore, set out for Rome, arranging to break her journey at Miramar so as to meet her husband there on his return from the East. She arrived in Rome on the eve of the opening of the Vatican Council, and found the city full of dignitaries of the Church assembled from all parts of the world. She stayed at the Palazzo Farnese as the guest of the King of Naples, who, she said, "wore himself out with efforts to be amiable."

The Empress was present at the opening of the Council on December 8, 1869, watching the proceedings from the box reserved for sovereigns. The impression it made on her was that of "an ocean of miters." The religious ceremonies lasted for seven hours, but one was more than enough for Elizabeth. Next day she was received in audience by the Pope in the Vatican. He was most talkative and friendly, but she understood very little of what he said, for he spoke Italian, and she wrote to the Emperor that all the "shuffling-round-on-one's-knees" (*Auf-den-Knieen-Herumrutschen*) struck her as "really comical." On the twelfth Pius IX returned her visit at the Palazzo Farnese. "This again," she reported to Francis Joseph, "was accompanied by awful ceremonies. The whole Household was assembled, and we waited on our knees at the foot of the staircase. . . . Since the conversation was in Italian, I had no occasion to exert myself. When he left there was a repetition of the ceremonial. By the steps the Pope pulled a scarlet cap down over his ears and donned an ermine-trimmed scarlet mantle, in which he reminded me of the Empress Karoline Augusta. . . ."

Elizabeth took advantage of her strict incognito to avoid, as far as possible, receiving royalty, members of the diplomatic corps, and the like. On the other hand, under the guidance of Baron Visconti she visited all the sights of Rome. On December 24 the expected event occurred, and Queen Marie was delivered of a little daughter on Christmas Eve, Elizabeth's own birthday. The Empress showed great solicitude for her sister and was with her night and day, with the result that she caught a cough through walking about the cold palazzo, with its mosaic floors, in her thin night attire. She attempted to cure it by drinking asses' milk, but the effective cure came when the Roman nobility invited her to take part in a great hunt in the Campagna. She thoroughly enjoyed herself, riding with the Princes Doria, Odescalchi, Piano, and a good many others, who all admired the enchanting horsewoman; and Elizabeth was full of enthusiasm, though she found the going far less easy than in Hungary. Her "great favorite here" was Count Malatesta, who had been attached to her suite. All Francis Joseph's fears for her safety proved groundless, and not a single misadventure occurred while she was in Rome.

From Rome Elizabeth traveled straight to Buda, which again caused great indignation at the court of Vienna. There had already been some ill-feeling at her having raised the salary of her reader, Ida Ferenczy, from eighteen hundred to three thousand gulden, besides granting her an allowance for traveling expenses. For Ida was regarded as Andrássy's instrument, and Valerie, it was said, was being brought up as the "daughter of the Hungarian King." Indeed, the Empress wrote to her mother that the dear little mite of two spoke Hungarian better than any language so far, and it was already possible to understand what she wanted to say.

June found the Empress back at Ischl. But her peaceful country life, interrupted only by such innocent amusements as performances by trained dogs, a clever horse, and the like, was abruptly broken by the news of the critical relations between Prussia and France. This meant that Francis Joseph could not come to Ischl. "It would be too sad," wrote the Empress to him, "if war were to break out again." But he assured her that this would not be such a bad thing as she supposed, for it would be all to the good if the arrogance of Prussia were humbled by Napoleon III, and the favorable moment had arrived. Elizabeth's point of view now changed. She had been affected to some extent by the hostility to Prussia prevailing at the court of Vienna since 1866, and now, like Francis Joseph, she looked forward to a victory for the French in the impending war.

The Empress had wanted to visit her family in Bavaria, but this was rendered impossible. She would not stop at Ischl on any account, since this would have meant spending the whole summer with her mother-in-law, and that, as she wrote to the Emperor, she simply could not endure. At such a time, moreover, she did not want to be too far from the railways and all facilities for receiving news, so it was decided that she should stay at the village of Neuburg on the Schneealp, where the Emperor could reach her in five hours. She shared her mother's fears, for her brothers Ludwig and Karl Theodor were going to the war, and she was curious to know whether they now sympathized with Prussia.

The news of the affair of Saarbrücken was at once telegraphed to her by the Emperor as a great French victory. "The French have at least made a good beginning," she replied. "Is that a place of importance? I am curious to know how the Prussians will explain this affair." "If this sort of thing goes on," she wrote a day or two later, "the Prussians will soon be back in Berlin again. I am already enjoying the prospect of hearing from your own lips what you think of it all. So do come very soon." But now news arrived in rapid succession of German victories at Weissenburg, Wörth, Spichern, and Mars la Tour. Since the court of Vienna had seriously considered intervening on the French Emperor's side at the right moment, disillusionment was now correspondingly bitter, and the news of the successive victories of Prussia gave reason to fear that she might next turn upon Austria and rend her to pieces. "We may possibly vegetate for a year or two more before our turn comes," wrote Elizabeth to her husband. "What do you think?"

The Archduchess Sophie was naturally the person most deeply affected at thus seeing all her hopes shattered in the evening of her life. Besides, the denunciation of the Concordat with Rome, in the conclusion of which she had played a part, was now being contemplated. In melancholy mood she complained to the little Crown Prince of the heavy burdens she had to bear. "I am delighted that the Bavarians have distinguished themselves so," she wrote to him, "but as one of their blood (*Stammverwandte*) I can only regret deeply that this did not happen in the year '66, and that they are now fighting and shedding their blood like true German Michels for the utter ruin of their independence and autonomous existence."

But worse was still to come. On September 1 Sedan capitulated, and the Emperor Napoleon III surrendered his sword to the King of Prussia. On the fourth the Republic was proclaimed in Paris, and the Empress Eugénie had to make a hazardous escape from France. In writing to his mother the Emperor Francis Joseph described the catastrophe as a terrible one and the rejoicing of the King of Prussia, "with his arrogance, vanity and hypocrisy," as "shameless." As for Elizabeth, "the news of the Republic," she wrote to the Emperor, "did not surprise me much, I only wonder that they did not do it long ago. When you come here I hope you will tell me all the details of the Empress' flight. That interests me greatly. . . ."

The Archduchess Sophie was cut to the heart by the war and its consequences, and she told the Crown Prince how deeply she sympathized with Louis Napoleon and his wife. The results of the war of 1866 had made such an indelible impression upon her that she quite forgot the wrongs inflicted on Austria by Napoleon III in 1859 and on herself personally in the affair of Maximilian of Mexico. But in addition to everything else, the battle of Königgrätz had destroyed her influence over the Emperor Francis Joseph and the Government of Austria and Hungary, and even in her declining years the ambitious woman could not recover from this.

Events were to deal the Bavarian family yet another blow. On September 20, the "*venti Settembre*" famous to every Italian, the troops of the Kingdom of United Italy entered Rome, and the King and Queen of Naples, who had been trying to hatch conspiracies against the Italian Kingdom, were forced to make a hurried flight from the Eternal City. From this time onward they led a wandering life, always cherishing vague hopes that they might one day recover their Neapolitan throne.

Elizabeth, who was secretly proud of the distinguished part played by her native country in the war, now believed that peace would be speedily concluded, enabling her to go quietly to Meran with her children. But her journey, by way of Salzburg, Kufstein, and Innsbrück, which she had never visited before, developed into a triumphal progress. Every evening bonfires blazed on the heights. At the railway station at Innsbrück she was given a brilliant reception, in the middle of which she caught sight of a large dog. Immediately—so the Princess Gisela reported to the Crown Prince—she had eyes only for the man who held it in leash. She made a sign to him, and the next day the dog was hers. In Meran she stayed at the Villa Trauttmansdorff, where there was an array of ancient armor and the walls were hung with family portraits, and little Gisela, who was now fourteen, wrote to her brother Rudolf that it was a good place in which to play at ghosts.

Soon the King and Queen of Naples and the Duke and Duchess of Alençon arrived in Meran on a visit to the Empress. She was devoted to all her sisters, especially the Queen of Naples, who greatly resembled her. Indeed, the Empress' sisters seemed to take pains to emphasize their resemblance to her, whether in figure and habits or by the veils, coiffure, and dress which they adopted. This was also true of the Duchess of Alençon, though she was considerably smaller than Elizabeth. So far did the sisters carry this imitation that the Queen of Naples always had a dog of the same breed and size as the Empress', and with a similar collar. The King of Naples looked on with a tolerant smile. He accepted his fate in a matter-of-fact spirit, remarking, "For me kingship is a thing of the past." As for Elizabeth, having no horses with her at Meran, she went for long walks at a very rapid pace which, to the horror of her ladies in waiting, often lasted for four or five hours.

One result of the campaign in France had been an entire reversal of Austrian policy with regard to Prussia. It was now clearly impossible to cherish any thoughts of revenge for the events of 1866, even in secret, and the Emperor William's visit to Ischl on August 11, 1871, was proof that Francis Joseph and his Minister for Foreign Affairs had accepted the changed situation. The little Crown Prince, who was also present on this occasion, was now gradually beginning to take part in everything. His chief interest was in natural science, and he pitied "those fellows" who could take no pleasure in it. He was especially fond of observing animals and studying their habits. But, whereas his mother loved them dearly, always had them about her, and never treated them with anything but kindness, Rudolf, though only twelve, was already shooting every creeping or flying thing. His tutors did nothing to restrain him, for they thought that, in view of the Emperor's passion for shooting, his son must learn to be a good shot as soon as possible; but all this killing of animals while still a child undoubtedly had the effect of making him callous in later life. There are some drawings of his dating from between the years 1867 and 1871, in which the little Crown Prince represents himself as shooting at a bird on a tree, a family of hares, or a covey of partridges, and in every case the blood is represented by a great splash of red. Elizabeth's influence on her son was not sufficient to enable her to check this tendency.

In the middle of March the Empress left Meran and went to Buda for five days. She was met at the station by the Archduchess Klothilde, wife of the Archduke Joseph, who was attended by the Countess Marie Festetics. In reply to Elizabeth's inquiry the Archduchess said that the Countess was her new lady in waiting, who had been recommended to her by Deák and Andrássy. Recognizing her to be an exceptionally clever and keen-witted woman and devoted to the cause of Hungary, they desired to introduce her to the court, in order to have a trustworthy friend and patriotic ally there.

The Countess fell under the Empress' spell at once. "She is the most beautiful creature I have ever seen," she noted that same evening in her carefully kept diary, "full of royal dignity, and yet wondrously winning, with such a soft voice. Her eyes are too delightful." The Empress had a long and friendly talk with her, especially about their mutual friends Deák and Andrássy. On March 19 there was a great dinner at the Archduchess', at which Elizabeth appeared in a low-necked purple dress with her hair hanging down below the waist. The Countess noted in her diary that there was something suggestive of a lily in her appearance, and that she looked sometimes like a girl and sometimes like a woman. She was astonished when, on exchanging a few words with her cousin Count Gustav Bellegarde, who shared the views of the Archduchess Sophie, she heard him make some rather disagreeable remarks about the Empress; and when she begged him not to spoil her pleasure, he only laughed.

The Countess carried away with her some bitter feelings about courtiers, for she was unaccustomed to the atmosphere of courts. She had been brought up in the country, and now, in her thirty-second year, she looked with critical eyes at all that went on around her. "There are many clever people there," she noted in her diary, "among them Andrássy, Eotvös, and my old Deák. Then there are pleasant people, then merely kind people, then elegant people, as well as parvenus, idlers and gossips, beautiful, amiable women, friends, relations, male and female cousins. The sum of all these, together with stupid and pushing people, is called 'the great world.' "

Having met the critical Countess twice during her stay in Budapest and taken a great fancy to her, the Empress talked to Andrássy about her. And so it came about that when in July one of her ladies in waiting, the Princess Helene of Thurn and Taxis, married and resigned her position, Elizabeth begged that the Countess might be appointed in her place. Marie Festetics felt some misgivings, but on July 4, 1871, Count Andrássy called on her and urged her to accept. "You must go," he said; "there is no room for hesitation. It is your duty to make this sacrifice for your country. A person whom God has endowed with plenty of intelligence ought to show gratitude for it, and the Queen stands in need of someone faithful."

"But does she deserve it?" asked the Countess. Whereupon Andrássy looked at her with such an expression of astonishment that she blushed. "What a question to ask!" he said in a grave voice. She now told him with some reluctance what she had heard and especially what Bellegarde had said; whereupon Andrássy replied: "You regard me as a friend, do you not? Well, I should advise you to accept unconditionally. The Queen is good, clever, and pure. They abuse her because she loves our country, and that they will never forgive her. For the same reason they will persecute you, but that is of no account. In this way you will be able to serve both the Queen and your country, and it is your duty to accept. Deák has written to me to the same effect.

Besides, such an offer cannot possibly be rejected. It is not done." Thus it was that Marie Festetics came to the Empress.

Elizabeth spent the months of October and November, 1871, at Meran with Valerie, the little Crown Prince Rudolf being again unable to come. In place of her lady in waiting Lily Hunyady, who had also married, she took the Countess Ludwiga Schaffgotsch, who seemed pretty and congenial. "The most beautiful things about her," wrote Elizabeth to the Emperor, "are her eyes and a long black moustache." The new lady in waiting at once had a foretaste of what the Empress meant by "going for a walk," and returned home half dead from a walk that Elizabeth had called "a little stroll." But she smiled at the Empress' excessive fears for Valerie's health. The slightest bleeding at the nose threw Elizabeth into great agitation, and whenever she heard of illness anywhere—smallpox, scarlet fever, and the like—she trembled for fear of infection. Toward the end of November a few cases of scarlet fever were reported from Vienna, so when the Emperor proposed to visit Meran, Elizabeth was alarmed lest someone in his suite might possibly carry the infection. "We live so very close together here," she wrote to her husband on the twenty-ninth. "Only think what might happen if illness were brought into the house. . . . It is terribly hard for me to ask you not to come, but it would certainly not be a useless precaution. . . ." So the Emperor stayed away.

He had already asked what the Empress would like for her birthday, which was always celebrated with particular pomp, because it fell on Christmas Eve. The answer he received was an astonishing one: "Since you ask what would give me pleasure," she wrote on the fourteenth, "I beg for either a young royal tiger (Zoological Gardens in Berlin, three cubs) or a locket. What I should like best of all would be a fully equipped lunatic asylum. So now you have choice enough." This last request was not intended as a joke, but was put forward quite seriously, for the Empress had long interested herself in the insane. Arrangements for the care of lunatics in Vienna were very bad, and Elizabeth had made repeated efforts to remedy this state of things. It would involve great expenditure, but she never relaxed her efforts and seized this opportunity of recalling the matter to the Emperor's attention in this somewhat original fashion.

Meanwhile, during the Empress' absence, one of her most heartfelt wishes had been fulfilled; on November 9 Andrássy replaced Beust as Minister for Foreign Affairs. This was inevitable in view of the outcome of the war of 1870–71, for all thought of revenge for Königgrätz had now to be given up, while a reconciliation with the new Germany was all the more essential owing to the strained relations which still subsisted with Russia. The Empress herself was the first to recognize this.

In a letter dated from Vienna on August 14, 1867,* and addressed to Bismarck, Freiherr von Werther, the Prussian Ambassador, had characterized Andrássy as intelligent and energetic, but had added that, as a statesman, he held amateurish views about everything outside the borders of Hungary. This may be taken as representing the general opinion of the new Minister for Foreign Affairs held by the foreign diplomats accredited to the court of Vienna. By Russia his appointment was naturally regarded as an unfriendly act; Andrássy had been a Hungarian rebel in 1848 and cursed the Russian intervention, so that the Empire of the Tsars was bound to feel some mistrust when he was charged with the conduct of the dual monarchy's foreign policy. For Elizabeth it was a personal triumph, while Vienna received the news of the appointment with mixed feelings. It looked

* Now in the Prussian secret State Archives, Dahlem.

like a fresh step toward the "Hungarian foreignization" (*Überfremdun*) of the monarchy, which was laid to the charge of Elizabeth. With the exception of the Countess Schaffgotsch, the only Austrian who now remained in the immediate entourage of the Empress was the newly appointed Mistress of the Household, the Countess Marie von Goëss, *née* Countess Welsersheimb, an amiable, sensible, somewhat retiring elderly lady of great tact, with an even disposition, whom Elizabeth troubled less than she did the ladies in waiting. All the rest were Hungarians.

The Countess Marie Festetics entered upon her duties on December 21. The Empress, wearing a blue dress and with a great hound at her side, received her standing in the middle of the room and greeted her with the words: "Well, I think we shall get used to each other." Then she made some little jokes and talked about anything and everything, remarking in the course of their conversation: "Andrássy told me that you are straightforward and truthful, please be so with me, too. If you want to say anything to me, say it honestly and frankly; if you want to know anything, ask *me* and not anyone else. When they abuse me, which is a habit of this house, do not believe them. Make friends with nobody for the present. Ida you can trust implicitly. She is not a court lady, and I do not want her to become intimate with them; they will only seek her friendship out of curiosity. In your case it is different. I know your character from Andrássy. We leave on December 27. I shall take you with me."

The Empress spoke clearly and with decision. Her expression was now sad, now arch, now gay, now serious. Marie Festetics left the room with her mind in a whirl. What would life be like with this fascinating woman, who was, among other things, an empress?

IX

THE EMPRESS' INTIMATE LIFE

1872–1875

IN THE COUNTESS FESTETICS THE Empress Elizabeth had found not only a lady in waiting but an extremely intelligent companion. The Countess accompanied Elizabeth and the Archduchess Valerie to Meran in the winter of 1872, and living in such immediate contact with her mistress was able to study her character at close quarters.* On the very first morning she was summoned to attend Elizabeth while her hair was being dressed. The Empress' hairdresser, Angerer, had recently married, but not wishing to part with her, the Empress had promoted the husband, a clerk named Feifalik, to be her own secretary. Frau Feifalik was of very humble origin, her mother having been a midwife, but she had acquired such skill as a theatrical hairdresser that the Empress found her indispensable, for the care of those luxuriant tresses was no light task. The Empress grieved over the loss of a single hair, so Frau Feifalik invented an ingenious device by which the hairs left in the comb were drawn out by an adhesive substance which she kept hidden under her apron and she was able to show her mistress a perfectly empty comb. Even the washing of this mass of hair was a serious undertaking which occupied the greater part of a day. Conscious of being indispensable, the hairdresser was apt to

* Except where otherwise indicated, this chapter is based mainly upon the diary of the Countess Festetics.

presume and had a thousand pretensions, which the Viennese call "*Faxen.*" She had always borne the ladies in waiting a grudge for their superior rank, and viewed this new one with suspicion.

For her part the Countess Festetics felt that she was regarded as an interloper and a "spy" of Andrássy's, and from the first this hardly promoted pleasant relations between her and the rest of the Empress' entourage. Their Hungarian nationality was naturally a bond between her, Baron Nopcsa, and Ida Ferenczy, but even in their case the mutual sympathy was far from perfect. The two ladies soon came to love the Empress and were both a little jealous of her favor. Efforts were also made to set them against each other, and both received abominable anonymous letters, which, though doubtless consigned to the wastepaper basket, could hardly fail to leave a sting behind.

When the Empress returned to Vienna, Marie Festetics was able to obtain a closer insight into the relations existing within the imperial family. Every Friday the Archduchess Sophie gave a large dinner party, and at one of these, on January 21, 1872, the new ladies in waiting were presented to her. The Countess Festetics was impressed by the nobility of the Archduchess' bearing, which was both kindly and imposing, but noticed that, though she herself was received with the barest inclination of the head, the Austrian Countess Schaffgotsch was honored with a long and friendly conversation, while the Archduke Ludwig Viktor did not even trouble to have himself introduced to the Hungarian lady. After dinner the Empress asked her whether she had felt hurt. "No, Your Majesty," she replied, "I was more annoyed." "One has to get used to that sort of thing," replied the Empress. "Anyone attached to me is naturally persecuted. I am quite surprised that the Archduke did not at once take your education in hand, for he likes to teach everybody manners except himself." The Archduke Wilhelm's attitude was quite different. "Don't let yourself be influenced by all the gossip," he said kindly; "be true to the Empress, she is good and noble."

The antagonism to Hungary in the Emperor's military chancellery was still as inveterate as in Count Grünne's day. The anti-Hungarian Count Bellegarde, a handsome, intelligent man with the air of a *grand seigneur*, had a knack of making people look ridiculous by a mere word or two, which amused the Emperor and therefore influenced him. His little sarcasms were frequently aimed at Andrássy, and Francis Joseph received them without protest and with a slight smile. But this attitude naturally led to sharp differences of opinion with the Empress.

On January 23 a telegram from Meran announced that Valerie, who had been left behind there, was a little unwell. This threw the Empress into a state of great anxiety, and as soon as the two court balls were over she and the Emperor hurried to Meran. At that time legends were circulated to the effect that they had quarreled, that the Empress had locked her door upon her husband, and so on. After the Emperor had left, the Countess took long walks and drives with her mistress and got to know her more thoroughly, coming to the conclusion that Elizabeth was very decided, thoughtful, and highly original, but somewhat embittered in her views. She noted how, whenever possible, the Empress avoided those with whom her rank forced her to come in contact and preferred solitude or the society of some intimate who was sympathetic to her.

"Are you not surprised," asked the Empress suddenly one day, "at my living like a hermit?"

"I am indeed, Your Majesty, for you are still too young."

"Yes, I am," replied the Empress, "but I have no choice but to live like this. I have been so persecuted, misjudged, and slandered, so hurt and wounded in the great world. God looks into my soul. I have never done what was evil. And I thought to myself that I would seek society that would leave me in peace and offer me enjoyment, without upsetting me. I have withdrawn into myself and turned to nature, for the forest cannot hurt one. It has been hard, of course, to be alone in life, but in the long run one grows used to anything, and now I enjoy it. Nature is far more grateful than men."

A little while later the Countess accompanied the Empress on an excursion to the "*Eremit*" (Hermit), one of the most beautiful and wildly romantic walks in the neighborhood of Meran. Suddenly Elizabeth asked her whether she would like to be a hermit. "Oh, no!" she replied. "Yet peace is so precious," said the Empress, "and one can only strive for and win it far from the world, far from mankind. Of course that leads to musing and brooding." She went on to talk about the days of her young womanhood. Her tone was melancholy, but suddenly some jest would break through the sadness, revealing her humor. It was remarkable how different she was from most other people in almost every way. It was her eyes that laughed first, then the mouth; and her eyes had a radiance that went straight to the heart of those she looked at. She was entirely swayed by her sympathies and antipathies. She was never commonplace, and everything about her revealed the contemplative cast of her mind. "It is a pity," noted Marie Festetics, "that she fritters away her whole time on what are essentially idle fancies and feels compelled to do simply nothing. She has a tendency to intellectual indolence and at the same time a craving for freedom which makes any restraint irksome to her. When she is dining with a small party she is charming, provided that no unsympathetic element is present. But if there is, she freezes everything about her."

After spending about a week at Meran the Empress left for Budapest, where the rapturous reception given her by an enormous crowd was sufficient proof of her continued popularity in Hungary. A surprise awaited her at the royal palace. The Archduchess Gisela, though hardly sixteen, had become engaged to Prince Leopold of Bavaria, the second son of Prince Luitpold, afterwards Prince Regent. The marriage was open to certain objections. It seemed to the Empress "much too soon," and the degree of consanguinity was very close, Prince Leopold's mother being an Austrian Archduchess. But the field of choice was limited, for the bridegroom had to be a Catholic and of royal blood, so "since there are so few Catholic princes," as the Emperor Francis Joseph wrote to his mother on April 7, "we had to try and secure the only one to whom we could give Gisela with confidence." Elizabeth was less upset than might have been expected, for Gisela had been estranged from her by the Archduchess Sophie from her earliest childhood and had never meant so much to her as little Valerie. But though Gisela was unusually tall and well developed for her age, the Empress could not quite reconcile herself to the fact that the child of yesterday was now engaged to be married, and decided that the marriage must be postponed for at least a year. Of course it did not take very long for it to be said that she was marrying off the child in a hurry because she did not want to be seen about with a grown-up daughter!

At the end of April Elizabeth returned to Meran, where she heard that, as the result of a severe chill contracted on May 10, the Archduchess Sophie had been suffering from "nervous symptoms," such as a tendency to somnolence and trembling of the hands and feet. The Empress was summoned to Vienna, where she arrived on the sixteenth. The Archduchess grew worse and worse, but her mind remained perfectly clear and she took an affectionate farewell of every member of the imperial family. On the evening of the twenty-sixth she seemed better, and Elizabeth, who had been at her bedside until half past eleven at night with the other members of the family, went home to the Hofburg to snatch a brief rest. She had hardly arrived when a footman rushed in with the news that Her Imperial Highness was dying, and His Majesty begged her to come at once. The coachman drove to Schönbrunn as fast as he could go. Elizabeth was in mortal fear lest the Archduchess might die before she reached her bedside, when it was certain to be said that her absence was intentional. When at last she reached Schönbrunn she asked breathlessly whether Her Imperial Highness was still alive, and was relieved to hear that she was.

The whole court was assembled: the family, the Ministers of the Imperial Household, and the members of the Household; but the death agony was long-drawn-out. The Countess Festetics, who sat waiting in a corner, justly remarked that death was not a court ceremony, and that great people should be allowed to pass over into the world beyond in peace, in the same holy quietness as beggars. The Empress agreed with her and felt that this traditional formalism was bound to stifle all real feeling.

The Archduchess survived the night and was still alive at seven o'clock. Hours passed by, the Archdukes left the sick-room, and a voice was heard announcing that Their Imperial Highnesses were going to dinner. But Elizabeth, the "heartless" as she was called, remained seated in the chamber of death, though for ten hours she had eaten nothing. The Emperor only left his mother's bedside for a brief moment, but the Empress stayed there all the time till, at a quarter to three in the afternoon, death put an end to the Archduchess Sophie's sufferings. As usual, Elizabeth showed herself very sweet and good at the critical hour. In the presence of death all hostility was forgotten and faded away. She thought only of more recent years, during which the Archduchess' attitude toward her had entirely changed, and she admitted to herself that she, too, was not exempt from blame for the misunderstandings which had caused a lifelong estrangement between her mother-in-law and herself. But those circles in Vienna which had never been able to understand and appreciate Elizabeth remarked: " 'Our Empress' is now lost and buried."

Soon after the funeral the Empress left Schönbrunn for Ischl, where she was to spend the summer. Even her somber mourning garments could not cast a shadow over her glorious figure and enchanting face, and every time Marie Festetics went for a walk with her, she became more enraptured. "It is a joy to be with her, and even to follow her," she wrote. "It is enough to gaze upon her. She is the very incarnation of the word charm. Sometimes I think of her as a lily, then again as a swan, a fairy, or an elf. And then after all I think: 'No! She is a queen! From the crown of her head to the sole of her foot, a queenly woman! Fine and noble in all things.' And then again all the gossip comes into my head, and I think there must be a great deal of envy behind it, for, to sum it all up, she is bewitchingly lovely and full of charm. But I am struck more and more by the absence of any pleasure in living which I feel in her. There is an atmosphere of calm about her which is very striking in one so young! Her voice is generally tranquil and soft, only rarely excited. Now and then, when she speaks of the merciless way in which she has been treated, there is a slight quiver in it. How can anyone hurt a person looking like her?" The Countess proceeds to give an example of this treatment. "In order to annoy me," the Empress confided to her one day, "the Archduke Ludwig faithfully retails to me all the lies people tell about me. He hates me, of course, and that is his way of trying to hurt me. Now I never see him alone and will not receive him. He has gossiped so much and told such lies that he has really spoiled my life. He abuses everybody, and me too. He says odious things and then pretends that it was I who said them. But I will not see him now, so I live in peace."

The Empress would talk like this in her frequent moods of depression and melancholy, but fundamentally her disposition was a cheerful one and her keen sense of the ridiculous often made her almost incapable of repressing the paroxysms of helpless laughter with which she was overcome even on the most solemn and ceremonious occasions. One evening at dinner, for instance, Prince Lobkowitz, one of the Emperor's aides-de-camp, was seated opposite her, fidgeting negligently with a toothpick, when, as ill luck would have it, it flew out of his hand and across the table, straight into the Empress' soup plate. At first she tried to ignore what had happened, but it was too much for her, and she shook with laughter till the tears streamed down her face. The Emperor turned and asked what she was laughing at, as he would like to share in the joke. The unhappy aide-de-camp sat looking utterly crushed, turning appealing eyes upon the Empress, till she felt so sorry for him that she replied with a mischievous smile: "Oh! something just occurred to me."*

It did her good, said the Countess Festetics, to see the Empress laugh so heartily, just as she did when she took her children on excursions in the neighborhood of Ischl. The Crown Prince, a nice attractive boy with great soft, brown eyes, laughed and chattered with his mother and thoroughly enjoyed life, incredibly precocious and nervous though he was for a lad only fourteen years old. Elizabeth had succeeded in having him taught Magyar by Bishop Hyazinth von Rónay, who had taken part in the rebellion of 1848 as

* *"Es ist mir etwas eingefallen."* The point of this witty answer is inevitably lost in translation. In German *einfallen* means both "to occur" and "to fall in."

an army chaplain on the Hungarian side and been forced, like Andrássy, to go into exile in London. The Bishop was astonished at the young Crown Prince's ultraliberal ideas, which, though crude and immature, were startling enough as set forth in an essay written in December, 1872, for his tutor, Latour.* He explained, for instance, that man is nothing but an ennobled animal; that from time immemorial aristocrats and priests had worked hand in hand to keep the people stupid in order to share in ruling them; that the "best society," as it styles itself, is nothing but a festering abscess on the body of the state, and so on. There was speculation at court as to where the young Crown Prince could have picked up such ideas as these, and it was thought that they might be traced to certain remarks of Elizabeth's which the child had misunderstood and exaggerated. But the Crown Prince was so little in his mother's company, and so fully occupied all day under the superintendence of excellent tutors, that his views could hardly be ascribed to Elizabeth's influence only. His nervous, unusual tendencies were doubtless inborn, and were possibly due to the fact that his parents were so closely related. Yet the Archduchess Gisela, on the other hand, had developed into a simple, quiet, and sensible woman.

Little Valerie was rather a shy, nervous child, who shrank from contact with anybody, and this made her mother all the more devoted to her. If the child so much as went for a walk, there was a solemn leave-taking, and when she returned the Empress asked over and over again whether anything had happened to her; for she never ceased to dread some accident to her remarkable little girl, whose shy, intelligent expression was called disagreeable by those who did not know her.

* The essay is in the State Archives, Vienna. See also Mitis: *Das Leben des Kronprinzen Rudolf* (Leipzig, 1928), p. 23 *seq.*

In the middle of September the Empress went to Possenhofen, where she found her sisters, Queen Marie of Naples and the Princess Helene of Thurn and Taxis, who had brought her four children. The Princess Helene, notes the Countess Festetics, had grown very stout, neglected her dress, and looked rather like a caricature of Elizabeth. The children were "enchanting," but a little too much in awe of their mother. The fourth sister, Mathilde, Countess of Trani, had a beautiful figure, but none of Elizabeth's winning ways, and rather resembled a feeble copy of her. Of the brothers, Duke Karl, though not handsome, was the most distinguished. The youngest, Prince "Mapperl," was strikingly goodlooking, but less intelligent. They were all as shy as Elizabeth and her little daughter Valerie—evidently a hereditary trait. They were a very united family, and the Countess further notes that Elizabeth's old home was simple, but well run, neat and orderly without ostentation, and with good and wholesome, if somewhat old-fashioned food, but no trace of the "beggarly" domestic arrangements about which ill-natured persons in Vienna spread tales.

The most interesting news to be heard at Possenhofen was about the King. He still behaved strangely and did his best to avoid the capital. Only when Elizabeth was there did he emerge from his retreats, and nothing would restrain him from coming to see her. On September 21, 1872, he announced his intention of paying a visit to Possenhofen, at the same time intimating that no one must be present but Elizabeth. The Empress gave orders, however, that he was to be received on his arrival by Baron Nopcsa, the Controller of her Household, and the Countess Festetics. He arrived punctually in a magnificent four-horse carriage with postilions, and rapidly exchanged the cap which he wore on one side of his beautiful wavy hair for the stiff Austrian shako. He was wearing the Grand Cross of the Order of St. Stephen, put on upside down, and the sash, which in Austria was worn at the waist, across his shoulder, though the correct way had been explained to him. Marie Festetics thought him "a handsome man, with the bearing of a stage king or a Lohengrin in the wedding procession." Elizabeth greeted him very cordially and was about to present her lady in waiting; but he gave her a piercing glance with those wonderful eyes, whose expression would change so rapidly, now soft and dreamy, now lit with a quick sparkle of malice. Then suddenly the burning, sparkling eyes grew cold and an expression of positive cruelty came into them. The King accompanied the Empress into the house, his heavy step contrasting with her elastic tread, which gave the impression of floating rather than walking.

Elizabeth and Ludwig were both handsome and had certain traits in common, including a love of solitude, a tendency to indulge in occasional fits of brooding, and a passion for riding. Yet they were so fundamentally different that the Empress found it hard to talk to the King. His presence made her feel ill at ease. She remembered that his brother was already insane and that the King himself showed, to say the least, strong symptoms of the same disorder, and she was terrified lest the same disaster might befall her, for, after all, she too belonged to the Bavarian family. She was, however, somewhat reassured when she found Ludwig's conversation quite normal.

At the end of September the Empress returned to Buda, where she went for long walks among the neighboring hills, her favorite spot being the summit of the Blocksberg, a rocky promontory, with a glorious view, rising precipitously above the Danube. Some isolated outbreaks of cholera in the city drove her away at the end of October, and she went to Gödöllö, where preparations were now being made for riding to hounds. She had succeeded latterly in inspiring the Emperor with her own taste for this sport and the two would ride together for hours through the forests in the neighborhood of the palace. The Empress was in her element following the hounds, and felt a sense of triumph when men were being thrown all around her, while she herself proudly negotiated all obstacles. The hunting was difficult, and one had to ride "devilish well." She sent Francis Joseph detailed reports of every run. "The meet was at the racecourse," she wrote to him on November 22, 1872. "I drove to it in a carriage, so that there was no expense (to set your All-Highest mind at rest). It was a very fine run, with the fox on ahead, and the hounds after him. Holmes,* Pista, and I always led the field, so we had no need to hurry and could take our time over jumping the very numerous ditches. Of those behind us, the following came down: Elemér Batthyány, horse killed on the spot, Sárolta Auersperg fell over him, neither of them hurt, one of our grooms with the fast grey, no harm done. Before the run Béla Keglevich and Viktor Zichy were thrown, the latter *while standing still.* Old Béla Wenckheim was delighted, he said it was all part of a good run. But the fox ran to earth; they dug all around the spot for a fearfully long time, but in the end left the poor beast in peace." Sometimes the Empress was in the saddle from eleven o'clock in the morning till half past five in the afternoon, and when there happened to be no meet, she would ride horse after horse for hours at a time in the little riding school at Gödöllö.

Andrássy often came out to Gödöllö and received accounts of what was happening in the house from his confidante, Marie Festetics, who told him about all the grumbling, abuse,

* Holmes, who was sixty-two at this time, had charge of the Empress Elizabeth's hunting stable at Gödöllö, which then contained twenty-six horses, one pony, and one donkey. "Dear" Mr. Holmes, as the Empress called him, had an exceptional knowledge of horses and was himself a keen rider. It was he who trained the Empress' mounts and prepared them for the hunting field.

and gossip that went on in Elizabeth's entourage and how she had constantly to be defending her mistress. The Empress seemed to her to be positively treated like an outlaw. Though she was the Emperor's consort, people might say what they liked about her with impunity. To which Andrássy justly replied: "Yes, but you know it is not easy to find such a nice little theme every day." Besides Andrássy, the Countess Festetics visited the other great man to whom she owed her position, Francis Deák, who, in a room in a hotel, was leading a life of loneliness and suffering which was to end only with his death. The Empress sent Deák presents of books and flowers and asked if she might visit him; indeed, his sufferings cast a shadow over her hunting season, which was usually so gay.

A meet in the beautiful surroundings of Gödöllö was a lovely sight, and loveliest of all was the Empress herself, who looked her best among the gentlemen in pink, her magnificent figure set off by her close-fitting riding habit, sitting her splendid mount with perfect mastery and grace. Andrássy often joined the hunt, and on October 5 expressed his feelings about her in a confidential letter to Frau von Ferenczy. "You can imagine," he said, "how enthusiastic the young people are when they see her. Sometimes they express this feeling by following her too closely, like dolphins around a ship, and nobody can prevent this. . . . Yesterday it was quite dark and rained when we went home. My cab happened to be there, and I offered it to Their Majesties. His Majesty accepted, but only for the Queen, and so I had the good fortune to escort her to the station. When we arrived it was crowded with people waiting to see Their Majesties. Imagine their comical faces when the Queen stepped out of a cab with me and I conducted her to the waiting room. They did not recover till the Emperor and the Archduke Wilhelm arrived after us. You see what an old gentleman

THE EMPRESS HUNTING

From an oil painting by Emil Adam.

your friend has become, to be trusted to escort beautiful ladies through night and mist. I must admit, however, that a long drive in the dark over a bumpy road may be a delicate matter even for the most sensible paterfamilias; this one, it is true, lasted only a few minutes, and in so short a time as that not even Adalbert Keglevich or your friend Pista could forget who it was that had been intrusted to their care."

The Empress was always in the best of spirits after a run, and charming to the Emperor, who never ceased to adore her and escaped from Vienna to Gödöllö as often as possible. But no sooner was she at home again and surrounded by courtiers than this good humor vanished in a trice. When she went for a walk in the park she had a horror of meeting them, and would wear a thick blue veil and carry a big sunshade or a fan, which always accompanied her even on horseback. "Let us hurry away," she would say, turning down the nearest bypath, "I can absolutely hear what they are saying." "Yes, that Bellegarde hates me so much that I break out into a perspiration when he so much as looks at me. I can feel who likes me and who does not." All this, the Countess Festetics remarks, was often pure imagination, and the Empress suspected people who would have honored and even idolized her if she had not seemed to distrust them.

In other respects Elizabeth knew as little of the world as a child. She had no idea of the value of money. On December 15, 1872, she made an excursion to Pest with Marie Festetics, descending in the funicular railway like any ordinary person to the Kettenbrücke, the suspension bridge connecting Buda with Pest. On the way down she asked the Countess whether she had any money with her. "Yes, Your Majesty." "How much?" "Not very much, twenty gulden." "But that is a great deal," said Elizabeth. . . . She wanted to go to Kugler's (Gerbeaud's), the world-famous confectioner in Pest, to buy things for Valerie, and succeeded in reaching the shop unrecognized. She made her purchases with the zest of a child, and when a large parcel had been collected asked if it would cost twenty gulden, only to discover that it was a hundred and fifty!

Though Marie Festetics was entirely under the Empress' influence and devoted to her heart and soul, she was by no means blind to her faults. She was particularly concerned about the indolence to which Elizabeth constantly gave way. She simply could not understand the principal fault with which the Empress was reproached—that of being wanting in any sense of her high destiny, or pride in being a sovereign and the consort of an Emperor. This was all part of Elizabeth's character and inborn nature, which even such strong external influences as those of the court of Vienna were powerless to alter. In some respects she was in advance of her age, both intellectually and in her attitude toward matters of hygiene. She was careful to preserve the slender lines of her body and hardened it by sport and gymnastics. Etiquette and traditional forms, the pride and exclusiveness of birth, were ideas to which she could never reconcile herself, for her early training had been far too free and unfettered. Besides, she had an inner emotional life of her own which could never find an outlet in the atmosphere of the court, exclusively concerned with externals. She was in constant revolt against the caste spirit of those about her and against partisan considerations of any kind, and this led to innumerable conflicts. Her free, romantic youth had developed in her a passion for liberty, on which no other influences made any impression. Thus in judging her it is hard to hold the balance even. She would have liked to see all men contented and happy, and indulged in incessant dreams and broodings which were dangerous in her position. She wanted to get to the bottom of everything and had too inquiring a mind. She needed occupation, and since that of an empress was antipathetic to her temperament, all her faculties lay fallow. Whenever she did take up anything, she threw herself into it wholeheartedly, for she never did anything by halves. Her exaggerated solicitude for little Valerie, for instance, had become a standing joke, so that the child was nicknamed the "*Extramädel*" (special child).

Elizabeth was always in search of occupation, for she was by nature active. She failed to impose her personality upon the court, though she had a clearer insight than most of those about her and a better grasp of the situation prevailing at the moment, while the fact that she had no desire to dominate gave her an advantage over all the vain and pushing people with whom she was brought into contact. She herself had no ambition or desire for popularity and no wish to make use of her power and rank, but would have liked to be her husband's guardian angel and wanted every happiness and good fortune for him, for was he not the father of her son who would one day inherit his mighty empire and proud rank? Such was the Empress Elizabeth as pictured in the diary of the Countess Festetics during the year 1873. Such was this woman, with her almost supernatural beauty, whose inestimable virtues and exceptional qualities were often ignored—sometimes deliberately so—on account of her little sins of omission and her peculiarities.

The Empress was certainly very sensitive, and the gossip that came to her ears embittered her. She did not defend herself with the same weapons, but followed the dictates of her nature by withdrawing into silence and solitude. "What she finds painful today," wrote Marie Festetics prophetically, "will become easy in time, and she will do less and less; people will attack her more and more, and for all her riches she will become poorer . . . and no one will remember that she was driven into this loneliness." She describes the Emperor as quick of apprehension but totally lacking in imagination. Overwhelmed with work, to which he devoted himself with a wonderful sense of duty, he was open to none but positive impressions and could never understand the world of dreams in which alone Elizabeth could exist. In spite of his worship of her he did not understand this side of her nature. She was hurt when he characterized her enthusiasms as "scaling the clouds" (*Wolkenkraxlerei*), and at such times a wall seemed to rise up between them.

On February 9, 1873, Elizabeth lost one of her few remaining friends at court, the Empress Karoline Augusta, sister of the Archduchess Sophie and fourth wife of the late Emperor Francis I. She had always taken Elizabeth's part, but could do little to help her, for she lived in complete retirement at Salzburg so as not to overshadow the Archduchess Sophie, who could not bear the title of Empress. Her death caused Elizabeth genuine sorrow.

The charge that the Empress was too neglectful of her duties as sovereign was certainly unjustified so far as the year 1873 was concerned. She was to be seen everywhere, in orphanages and lunatic asylums as well as at the impressive ceremonies of Holy Week, the Corpus Christi procession, and the washing of the feet on Maundy Thursday, on which occasions the imperial court had always displayed great pomp. She may have heaved a sigh, but she played her part admirably. Robed in her long black gown, she bent down to wash the feet of the old women; knelt before the Holy Sepulcher on Good Friday; walked with a lighted candle in her hand, amid the pealing of bells and the roll of drums, in the great procession which seemed to represent as in a pageant the whole splendor of the ancient House of Habsburg. Nobody appreciated what it cost her to perform these ceremonial duties which did such violence to her nature. For her a ceremonial meant running the gauntlet of curious eyes for hours together, and not till she had driven out in the Prater, or changed into her habit in the riding school and gone for a gallop on one of her splendid horses did she recover her spirits. But even then crowds surrounded her at every turn and never tired of gazing at her beauty.

At times the Empress would ride with some cavalier as her escort, and often with Andrássy. As a rule they were on excellent terms, but occasionally there were storms, for with him, too, she liked to have her own way.

On April 20, immediately after Easter, the wedding of the Archduchess Gisela took place. The Empress attended the ceremony in a dress embroidered in silver, with a diamond crown on her hair, looking more like a young girl than the bride's mother. But she bore herself with imposing dignity, and it was not till the words "I will" were spoken that she was seen to be in tears. The "heartless woman" (*Frau ohne Herz*), as she was called, was weeping at parting from the child who had never been really her own. The festivities which followed the ceremony were a torture to her; receptions, concert, enormous dinner parties, and a gala performance at the theatre seemed like so many stations of the cross. *A Midsummer Night's Dream* was the piece chosen for the gala performance, and Elizabeth wondered why a play had been chosen to celebrate a royal wedding in which a princess falls in love with an ass; while Prince Leopold jestingly asked his wife: "Is this intended as an allusion to me?" It was explained, however, that *A Midsummer Night's Dream* was the "*usus*" at all weddings, and the young couple were duly amused at this remarkable custom. They were received with special honor in Munich, for the bride was the daughter of the lovely Empress whom King Ludwig idolized. They were driven from the station to the palace in the King's famous gala coach drawn by six white horses; this was the first occasion on which anybody had been allowed to see it. With its rich wood carvings and beautifully painted panels it had cost no less than fifty thousand gulden.

The wedding festivities were hardly over before another "rush" (*Hetze*) began. For several months past preparations had been in progress for a splendid Universal Exhibition in Vienna. Great personages from all parts of the world, including the German Crown Prince and Princess and the Prince of Wales, had announced their intention of being present at the opening ceremony. In pursuance of Andrássy's policy of a *rapprochement* with Germany, the German princes were to be singled out for attention. They were staying at Hetzendorf, and it was arranged that they were to proceed to the Exhibition buildings in the Prater in a splendid procession following that of the Emperor and Empress. Francis Joseph's immediate suite was to assemble in the Empress' apartment at eleven o'clock, and duly did so; but the Empress failed to appear. Though it was not yet quite eleven, the Emperor began to pace restlessly up and down. At this point a message was brought to Count Grünne, the Master of the Horse, saying that the Crown Prince and Princess' procession was already passing along the Ringstrasse. The Count informed the Emperor, who grew purple with rage. "It is beyond belief," he said, "that such a thing should be possible! My orders were that the Crown Prince was to arrive after me, and now this infernal mess (*die Schweinerei*) has been made! He will arrive before me, and I shall not be there to receive him. Who was it that allowed the carriage to start earlier, contrary to my orders?" White to the lips, the Count replied quietly, "It was I, Your Majesty."

The Emperor, beside himself, made a threatening movement toward the Count, saying, "You shall answer for this!" But suddenly the Empress was at his side. She had entered the room unnoticed while everybody was watching this painful scene in an embarrassed silence. She laid her hand on the Emperor's arm, and, as though she had touched him with a magic wand, the angry words died on his lips, and she looked at him with such tenderly imploring eyes that his threatening frown disappeared. Then she took him by the arm. "Please let us waste no more time," she said, in a calm, gentle voice; "let us go." The Emperor docilely followed her advice, and in a minute or two they were all seated in the carriages. Marie Festetics was a witness of this scene. . . . "And yet," she comments in her diary, "did not the Empress once say to me, 'That man (Grünne) has done me so much harm that I do not think I shall ever be able to forgive him, even on my deathbed'?"

The Crown Prince's procession was hastily informed of what had happened, and stopped under the railway bridge in the Prater, tactfully pretending not to see the imperial carriages drive past. In a few minutes everybody had assembled in the gigantic Rotunda of the Exhibition and then, and not till then, did the German Crown Prince drive on, looking like Lohengrin in his white Guard's uniform with his silver eagle-crowned helmet glittering in the sunlight.

The Emperor delivered the opening address in his sonorous voice, the bands struck up the Austrian national anthem, flags were dipped in salute, and the Exhibition was opened. For three hours the Emperor and Empress went round with their guests, inspecting the exhibits of the various countries, and were received everywhere with loud enthusiasm. When Elizabeth entered the Hungarian pavilion there was a frantic outburst of cheering, which drew a blush to her cheek. Everyone was pleased that the Prussian guests should see how popular and beloved the Emperor and Empress were in Vienna.

Elizabeth got on very well with the Crown Princess Victoria (formerly the English Princess Royal), whom she found sensitive, attractive, intelligent, and modern in her views. She even presented her with her portrait, a thing she never did except for those whom she found really sympathetic, no exception being made in the case of royalty—rather the reverse, indeed. But the two women understood each other at once, and their meeting was the beginning of a lifelong friendship.

The Empress found the festivities that were inseparable from the Exhibition most exhausting and sought refreshment in nature whenever possible. The spring was a beautiful one, and she liked going for walks early in the morning in the green, blossom-scented Prater. At six o'clock in the morning, while Vienna was still asleep, the Empress and Marie Festetics would walk to the Lusthaus and back, for at that time there were no idle sight-seers and curious crowds. If she went out later, she was at once followed by a train of people, which always annoyed her and made her nervous. Not that she was afraid of assassination, for few sovereigns have been so fearless. But she was as shy as any roe and was forever complaining that everybody else might enjoy themselves as they liked, but that she could not even take a walk in peace. There were even people so lacking in feeling as to actually push themselves in between her and the picture she was looking at at an exhibition and stare at her through their lorgnettes, or even examine her through field glasses from a short distance away. When such a thing happened Elizabeth flushed hotly and left the room without a word, never to return. When she attended the races, which, with her fondness for everything connected with horses, she loved doing, she had no such alternative. On the way to the Freudenau she had to pass through a serried mass of people stretching from the Hofburg to the racecourse, all waiting to catch a glimpse of her. She was received with enthusiasm all the way and bowed her acknowledgments, but by the time she reached the crossroads at the Praterstern, when four kilometers of the principal avenue still remained to be traversed, she said to the Countess Festetics, who was sitting beside her: "Marie, I cannot go on, I am quite seasick already." And she had actually turned pale. "One must have seen it to understand," comments the Countess. Once at the races, however, she quickly recovered, for she was happy, and it was evident from her demeanor that she would have loved to be mounted on one of the thoroughbreds racing past over the green turf.

Elizabeth played her part valiantly at all the festivities and banquets. Indeed, nobody at court spared himself during this time, for sovereigns and royal personages were now streaming to Vienna from all the ends of the earth, and the lesser the potentates, the greater the importance they attached to their rank. But the mightiest monarchs in Europe came, too, among them the Tsar Alexander II, though his attitude was very reserved and his face hardly ever lit up with the faintest spark of amiability. Elizabeth's charm alone availed to melt him, and she also cast her spell over his suite, including Prince Gortchakoff, the lively little man who enjoyed such power in Russia and was so hostile to Austria. There was a Prince Dolgoruki in the Tsar's suite, who had long greatly admired the Countess Festetics and now asked her hand in marriage. This was exceedingly unwelcome to Elizabeth. "I will allow you to make yourself agreeable," she said to her, "but not to fall in love, still less to get married. I do not want you to leave me for the sake of a stranger." This sounds thoroughly selfish, but Marie Festetics felt flattered, and succeeded, after a struggle, in overcoming the dawning attachment. The Empress had her way, and Prince Dolgoruki abandoned his suit.

For the rest, the Russians had sharp eyes. "You have enemies here at court," said Count Shuvaloff to the Countess

Festetics one day, "you and that adorable woman the Empress. I believe they take it amiss that you are both fond of the Hungarians." The Countess merely laughed and thought to herself, "They have excellent spies." Then she hurried down to a banquet, at which the whole company, including the Emperor and Empress, was already assembled, but the Prince of Wales and Prince Arthur had not yet arrived. Both of them were charming and very popular, but wherever their engagements might be—whether at dinner, in the riding school, the Prater, or the Exhibition—they were "always late."

The Emperor and Empress had no rest. Even Francis Joseph felt the strain. "I am tired out," he said one day, "and should like to grant myself sick leave for a time." It was a sign of the enormous change that had taken place in the relations between Austria and Germany during the last few years when on June 24 the German Empress Augusta also arrived, bringing an autograph letter from the Emperor William. Her tall figure gave her a certain dignity, but she was very much painted and generally made-up, and her carriage was rather pompous and theatrical. In strong contrast with Elizabeth, she spoke in a loud voice with much exaggerated sentiment, so that only a few minutes had gone by before she was known among the courtiers as "the foghorn." The Empress Elizabeth shone all the more brightly in comparison, but before long the Empress Augusta's real and essentially noble character won people over, in spite of her eccentricities, and the reaction in her favor went so far that, by the time she left, the members of the suites were holding her up as a model of all that a sovereign should be, and insinuating, as usual, that she was an example to Elizabeth.

Various absurd incidents occurred to break the monotony of the occasion. Thus, at a great banquet in the Kaiserpavillon, Elizabeth had ordered for the last course an excellent chocolate cream, served in small pots, and as each course was served she warned her ladies not to eat too much, but to leave room for this cream. At last the great moment arrived. The fat little restaurateur had reserved himself the honor of serving the Empress in person, and came tripping fussily across the polished floor with a silver dish in his hands, when he suddenly slipped and lay sprawling on the ground, while the precious contents of the little pots went trickling away in all directions. The Emperor, with his accustomed good nature, sprang up to go to the poor fellow's assistance, but Elizabeth merely remarked softly: "Only see that he doesn't scrape it up and offer it to us." A fresh supply was quickly brought, however, but all the Empress said was, "Oh, well, then it will just be served up to somebody else." Then followed a visit to the circus. What she enjoyed most of all were the horses and the performing monkeys, for there she could laugh till the tears streamed down her face.

So far the royal visits had been, on the whole, nothing but a burden, but the Shah of Persia, who arrived on July 30, provided entertainment for the whole court. The Shah had heard of the Empress' beauty, and, accustomed as he was to collecting around him all the loveliest women in his realm, was particularly curious to see her. When His Persian Majesty first met her, she was wearing a white dress with a train, embroidered in silver, and a purple velvet sash, with a circlet of flashing diamonds and amethysts on her flowing hair. Marie Festetics noted that she had never seen her look more lovely. On entering the room the Shah, who looked a typical Oriental potentate with his black hair and beard, remained standing before her for a moment, dumbfounded. Then he put on his gold-rimmed eyeglasses, examined her calmly from top to toe, and regardless of the Emperor, who was looking on with amusement, walked all around Elizabeth, exclaiming at intervals: "*Mon Dieu, qu'elle est belle!*" In fact, he was so absorbed in gazing his fill that at last the Emperor had to pluck him by the sleeve and remind him to offer the Empress his arm and take her in to dinner. At first he did not understand, but at last it dawned upon him, whereupon he took Elizabeth by the hand and walked with her into the banquet hall, swinging her arm to and fro. She was vastly amused, and the Emperor was in mortal terror lest at any moment she might be unable to restrain her laughter.

Matters were even worse at table. Behind the Shah's chair stood his Grand Vizier, with whom he kept up a conversation in Persian. The fish was served with a green sauce in a silver sauceboat with a ladle. This looked suspicious to the Shah, for it was suggestive of arsenic, so he took a ladleful, tasted it, and calmly replaced the ladle in the sauceboat with a grimace, while Elizabeth tried desperately to concentrate her attention upon a portrait of the Emperor Francis I hanging on the wall opposite. The Shah bowed to her and insisted upon her taking his glass of champagne, drinking out of it, and clinking glasses with him. He did not eat much, for most of the items on the menu seemed to him pretty dubious. But now a footman appeared with a great silver bowl full of fragrant strawberries. The Shah calmly took it out of the man's hand, set it before him, and proceeded to eat the whole contents down to the very last berry.

But the episode which most delighted the Empress was one which concerned old Count Crenneville, formerly the Emperor's all-powerful Adjutant General and now his chief chamberlain, who had been attached to the Shah. Once, when His Persian Majesty was driving in the Prater in an open carriage, he made Crenneville, who was in gala uniform, sit, not beside him, but on the little seat with his back to the horses. And since the Shah found the sun too much for him, he handed Crenneville in the most friendly way a white umbrella for him to hold over the autocrat's head. The full beauty of this episode can only be understood by those who knew Count Crenneville.

Elizabeth drove out to Laxenburg to see the Shah's three favorite horses, whose manes and tails were dyed rose-pink, and over which His Persian Majesty's Master of the Horse had to keep guard in person. But while everyone else laughed at the Shah, Elizabeth thought him an original, and was particularly pleased by the fact that he was quite at his ease and said and did exactly what he liked. He never spoke an amiable word to anyone who was not brought face to face with him, and only gave presents or decorations to those who took his fancy. Thus, when he presented his portrait set in diamonds to the Emperor and Count Andrássy, it was pointed out to him that it was customary to confer some special mark of distinction on those of the Emperor's brothers who happened to be present. "No, I don't want to," he replied calmly; "I only give my portrait to those whom I like." As for the Empress, he called her a goddess and told Andrássy she was the most beautiful woman he had ever seen. "Such dignity, such a smile, such kindness!" he said. "If ever I were to come back again, it would be solely as a mark of my respect for *her*."

On August 12 there was a fête at Schönbrunn, with a display of fireworks at the Gloriette. The Shah was enchanted. But while the Countess Goëss was presenting the old ladies to him at the tea party which followed, he suddenly remarked in French: "Thanks, that's enough." On the morning of his departure he had the Countess Festetics roused at four o'clock and commissioned her to express his gratitude to the Empress once more and tell her that her image would never fade from his memory. The period of his visit had indeed been a lively one and served as a theme for witticisms for some time to come.

Elizabeth now returned to the country with great relief and devoted her time to her children. The Emperor spent a short time at Ischl, too, but returned to Vienna when the King and Queen of Saxony, to Elizabeth's annoyance, announced their intention of visiting the Exhibition. "Was it really worth while to go back in such a hurry just because of the Saxons?" she wrote. "You could so easily have made them come at the same time as the Serbians and Greeks. You spoil everybody so much that you do not even get any thanks for your excessive politeness—quite the reverse, in fact. You really agree with me, but you will not admit it, as always happens when one has done something stupid. . . ."

Meanwhile the financial world had been alarmed by a panic on the Vienna Stock Exchange, and the Exhibition, which had already suffered from the cholera scare, closed with an enormous deficit. Elizabeth did not understand the deeper significance of this, but her confidence in the policy of the Ministers, and above all in their economic insight, was badly shaken. In these days she once more proved herself a faithful consoler of the Emperor, who took these troubles very much to heart.

In September a visit was expected from the King of Italy, as a definite step in the new direction given to Austrian policy under Andrássy's guidance. The Empress returned to Schönbrunn for the occasion; but when the King arrived she was suffering from gastric fever and so sick that she was unable to receive him, to his great disappointment, for she was the only person who roused his curiosity. Andrássy was greatly put out, too, because it was sure to be misinterpreted and give rise to all kinds of gossip. People remembered how Elizabeth had canceled engagements on account of the Queen of Naples, and so on. This time, however, it was not "shamming sick" (*Schulkrankheit*), a habit of which the Viennese amiably accused her. "Heaven knows," comments the Countess Festetics, "she had given proof enough during the Exhibition that she does her duty. She had looked forward eagerly to the horse show, but had been unable to visit it because she had been in bed for ten days."

As soon as Elizabeth was well enough she fled to Gödöllö, where she hoped to recover rapidly. It was now October, the leaves were falling, and the forest of Haraszti was bright with autumn colors. At the end of the month she was still only allowed to take gentle rides in the park on a pony. To provide herself with a little amusement she mounted Ida Ferenczy and Marie Festetics, who had never ridden anything in their lives, on two donkeys presented to her by the Khedive. She would watch the Emperor wistfully as he rode off in pink to the meet at the head of his guests, with Prince Leopold at his side, who looked ten years older than his father-in-law. The Empress was still far from well, and on the night of October 20 the Emperor was so anxious about her that he asked Hofrat Widerhofer for God's sake to tell him what was the matter with her, for she was looking dreadful. But her illness was not so bad as all that. She had a strong constitution, and the rest at Gödöllö did her good. She would have recovered still more rapidly had she not been vexed at the sight of the everlasting bickering that went on all around her. There were, as a matter of fact, three courts: one attached to Francis Joseph; another which the Empress had gradually managed to choose in accordance with her own wishes; and a third around the Crown Prince, who, though only fifteen years old, was already behaving like a grown-up person, so that his gentlemen had become less dependent on his parents than before. These three courts waged war upon one another, which caused endless unpleasantnesses.

On December 2 Their Majesties had to go to Vienna for the silver jubilee of the Emperor's reign. The celebrations were beautiful and impressive, but at the same time very wearing. In the evening there were to be elaborate illuminations; the Empress wanted a little fresh air first, so she went for a walk with the Countess Festetics along the Ringstrasse. She had often done so before without attracting attention, but on this occasion she was recognized and surrounded by a cheering crowd. At first all went well, and she smiled her thanks. Soon, however, thousands of people began to stream up from every direction, and it was impossible either to advance or to go back. The circle around Elizabeth and her companion grew narrower and narrower. The Countess begged and implored, both ladies were terrified and could hardly breathe, and the police were helpless. Suddenly the Countess began to scream: "You are crushing the Empress! Help! Help! Make way! Make way!" At last, after about an hour, some gentlemen succeeded in opening a narrow lane through the crowd to a carriage, into which Elizabeth was helped, half-dead with agitation and utterly exhausted. The carriage could only advance at a footpace, owing to the dense masses of people, and was a long time reaching the Hofburg. When at last it arrived, the Empress thanked the Countess with an enchanting smile. "It was really you who saved me," she said. This was enough to fill the Countess' heart with a glow of emotion. "No one in the world," she noted in her diary, "can look at one as she does when she says anything kind, and such a look and such words make one feel happy always."

On December 3, the day after the celebrations, the Empress returned to Gödöllö. The shortness of her stay in Vienna on such an occasion was resented in certain quarters there, a newspaper article commenting on the fact that "that strange woman the Empress" preferred to stay anywhere rather than in Vienna. Shortly afterwards, when a deputation from the "Concordia" society of journalists waited upon the Emperor to congratulate him on his silver jubilee, he expressed a hope that in future the Press would not concern itself with the private and family life of the Empress—an obvious allusion to the article mentioned above.

The year 1874 opened with a sensation, for the lovely young Empress, who did not look anything like her age, now became a grandmother. Both she and her daughter Gisela, who gave birth to a daughter on January 4, had married at the age of sixteen. She at once started for Munich, though there had been several cases of cholera there, but declined an invitation to stay in the palace, owing to her dread of being left alone with King Ludwig. On the day after the baptism she suddenly appeared in Marie Festetics' room and announced that she was going with a doctor to visit the cholera hospital. "I am going alone," she said, "because I cannot take upon myself the responsibility of letting anyone attend me." The Countess was aghast. She tried to dissuade the Empress, but in vain. When they reached the hospital Elizabeth wished to leave the Countess in the carriage; but she protested. "I beg Your Majesty," she said, "not to shame me by refusing to let me attend you." In the hospital they saw some harrowing sights. But the Empress went from bed to bed and, with her usual captivating charm and sweetness, spoke a few words of comfort to the sick and dying. Overanxious though she might be when the Emperor and her children were concerned, she was entirely heedless of danger to herself.

It was never her custom to announce her visits to hospitals beforehand, so that all preparations likely to disturb the patients were avoided. She came and went without a sound, with infinite kindness in her eyes. She found one young man who was in his death agony. "I shall soon die now," he gasped. "Oh, no," said the Empress. "God is good and He will help you." "But I have the cold sweat of death upon me," said the young fellow, stretching out his hand to her. She touched it and answered: "Why should you think it is the sweat of death? Your hand is warm. That must be a good, salutary perspiration." The sick man smiled and said with deep feeling: "I thank Your Majesty a thousand times. Perhaps the good God will grant me my life. God bless Your Majesty." The sick man, the Empress, the Countess, and the doctor were all in tears. A few hours later the poor fellow was dead.

On returning home the Empress changed all her clothes, washed herself, and threw away her gloves; nor did she visit Gisela that day, but only went for a short walk in the park. Two mornings later she did not feel quite well, which caused a panic in the Household, but fortunately nothing came of it. All Munich was talking of the Empress' courage in visiting the hospital.

She spent a lot of time with her sister, the Queen of Naples. The Empress, says the Countess Festetics, was undoubtedly wittier and more original than her sister, and her character was finer, but the Queen of Naples was both clever and energetic and thus acquired considerable influence over the Empress. She was forever relating the advantages of her own existence as a "Queen on the retired list" who could do whatever she liked and live wherever she liked, and this encouraged Elizabeth's distaste for her own burdens. In recent years the Queen had been much in England and she continued to sing the praises of that country and the glorious hunting to be had there. The Prince of Wales had already told the Empress about it during his visit to Vienna, so that she was gradually developing a longing to know this rider's paradise.

On January 17 she paid a visit to Ludwig's mother,

who talked to her with childlike levity about things which seemed of no importance at the time but acquired a grim significance afterwards. She described, for instance, how she had been alarmed by rain falling in her room, although the sky was cloudless outside. At last the mystery was cleared up: the pond in the King's winter garden on the roof was leaking. She talked as though having a blue lake on the roof, with moonshine and other embellishments, was the most natural thing in the world. While she was giving a humorous account of this, a handsome young fellow with dark eyes and hair burst into the room. It was Prince Otto, whose mental condition was growing worse and worse. Shortly after this the Empress rose to leave. The Prince gave her his arm and conducted her to her carriage, but she whispered anxiously to the Countess, "Please keep an eye on him. I feel as though he were going to throw me down the stairs."

In spite of a swollen face and the cholera scare in Munich, King Ludwig could not deny himself the pleasure of coming from his country palaces over and over again to visit Elizabeth, which was certainly no pleasure to her. Toward evening on January 17 he appeared again. The Empress was tired and sleepy and wanted to go to bed, but the King stayed for hours and it seemed as though he would never go. She summoned the Countess Festetics repeatedly, but the King did not take the hint. Finally, she took him with her to the lady in waiting's room, which he heartily disliked, as he always wanted to be alone with the Empress. But even this failed, and Elizabeth returned with him to the drawing room in a thoroughly nervous state. At last she came running out by herself and called to the Countess: "Save me, Marie, and think of some means of getting him away. I cannot stand it any longer." After a while, the lady in waiting accordingly tapped at the door and was encouraged by an unusually loud "Come in." "Your Majesty commanded me to knock at half past ten," she said, "as Your Majesty has to rise early tomorrow morning. I did not venture to disturb Your Majesty earlier, but now it is after half past ten and I fear Your Majesty may have a headache. I hope this will excuse my presumption in disturbing Your Majesty." She said this with an apologetic expression, but the King looked at her very disagreeably, remarking: "One forgets all about time here." He had been talking to Elizabeth about his broken engagement and his love of solitude, and how people misjudged him.

He had scarcely gone when Elizabeth came to Marie Festetics. "Thank God," she said, "that it succeeded. But it was dreadful. I am terribly sorry for the poor King. I am fond of him, but I am still fonder of my bed. Yet I believe there is a certain resemblance between him and me, and a tendency to melancholy and a love of solitude are all part of it." "God forbid that there should be any real resemblance," replied the Countess, "Your Majesty simply wants to excuse everything on the plea that it is a family idiosyncrasy for which nobody is responsible." Whereupon Elizabeth looked rather taken aback and then laughed. "It is bold of you to say that," she said, "though there is something in it. But I pity the poor King from the bottom of my heart." "Yes," comments the Countess in her diary, "a King is indeed pitiful when he is not mad enough to be shut up, yet at the same time so abnormal that he can have no intercourse with sensible people in society. During this visit he ought to have seen long before he did that the Empress was absolutely distracted and hardly knew what to do with him. But it was enough for him just to gaze at her."

It is curious that Ludwig's mother had no clear idea of what awaited her sons. On her last visit Elizabeth had expressed a wish to see a hospital again. And now, on January 18, the Queen Mother suddenly proposed that they should go together to visit—a lunatic asylum. This interested Elizabeth, for in view of the frequent signs of mental disease in her family, she was anxious to learn more about it, and accepted the suggestion with a certain eager curiosity. The visit was carried out with great thoroughness. Elizabeth heard the unfortunate patients now laughing horribly, now raging and screaming, now weeping bitterly, now singing. One girl with red hair displayed her skill as a pianist. She struck a note three times and then began to rattle violently up and down the keyboard with her beautiful white hands. Another woman looked hard at Elizabeth. "You are an empress," she said, "and yet you wear a woollen dress? How disgraceful!" A painter smilingly showed them a drawing of a stag with a church balanced on its antlers, and a tree on top of the church instead of a cross. And so it went on for two hours. It made a deep impression upon the Empress, whose face was white and grave. The Countess was deeply affected, and the only one who remained unmoved was the Queen Mother, who had two sons on the verge of madness. "Marie," said Elizabeth to the Countess when they had returned to the carriage, "it has had a terrible effect on me. I had not imagined it would be so sad. I was astonished at the Queen. It seemed almost to amuse her. But of course the poor thing is used to it."

On January 22 Elizabeth was back again in her beloved Pest and could enjoy the fine view from the royal palace at Buda. On the following day the Emperor arrived, too, and scolded her a little for visiting the cholera hospital in Munich. Next she made her first appearance as a grandmother at a court ball in Vienna, radiant with youth and beauty. On February 11 the Emperor left for St. Petersburg to return the Tsar's visit. He was to be away till the twenty-second, and for a moment Elizabeth was in doubt whether to remain in Vienna or return to Hungary. But since the

Emperor's visit to Russia was rather unpopular in Vienna and Elizabeth knew that her frequent journeys to Hungary had caused a good deal of ill-feeling, she decided to remain where she was.

On Shrove Tuesday the first masked ball took place in the great hall of the Musical Society (*Musikverein*). These assemblies were attended by ladies and gentlemen, and even young girls, belonging to the highest society, and the Shrove Tuesday ball was the most aristocratic of all. Everybody was saying how splendid it would be this year, and Elizabeth suddenly took it into her head that she would like to go to it in disguise. Only Ida Ferenczy, her indispensable hairdresser Frau Feifalik, and her waiting woman Schmidl were let into the secret, and they had to take an oath that they would not betray it. In the evening they all went to bed as usual, but as soon as the whole house was asleep the Empress got up, put on a great auburn wig and a domino with a train, which had imprudently been made of an unusually beautiful, heavy yellow brocade. Then she put on a mask with a long lace veil, so that her face and even her neck were absolutely concealed, both in front and from behind.* Ida Ferenczy, who wore a red domino, was to address the Empress as Gabriele, so that, in case any suspicions were aroused, they would fall upon Gabriele Schmidl, whose tall, slender figure resembled that of the Empress.

The two ladies entered the ball room, seated themselves in the gallery, and looked down at the merry, noisy throng be-

* The description of this charming episode is based on the account given by the Archduchess Valerie of what the Empress and Ida Ferenczy told her about it, as well as on information supplied by the person principally concerned in it, Herr Friedrich List Pacher von Theinburg, who unfortunately died on May 12, 1934. This gentleman was good enough not only to describe the episode to me personally, but also to place at my disposal the correspondence which he subsequently had with the Empress, as well as with her lady in waiting.

low. They sat together so quietly that nobody came near them, and by eleven o'clock Elizabeth was beginning to feel bored. Then an idea occurred to Ida Ferenczy. "Please, Gabriele," she whispered, "choose somebody in the ball room whose appearance you like and who does not belong to court society, and I will bring him up to you. At a masked ball one has to talk to people and mystify them." "Do you think so?" replied the Empress, and began to look about the ball room. Presently she noticed walking about by himself an elegant young man whose face she had never seen before. She pointed him out to Ida Ferenczy, who at once hurried down, slipped her arm suddenly into his from behind, and began merrily questioning him as to who he was, whether Count X. was there, whether he knew Prince N., and so on—all to ascertain the young gentleman's social position and find out whether he had any connections with the aristocracy. The results of the little examination were satisfactory, for it was evident that he was not connected with the court at all. Then, of a sudden, the domino asked point-blank whether he would do her a service. "With pleasure," he replied. "I have a beautiful friend here," she said, "who is sitting up in the gallery all alone and is terribly bored. Would you not care to entertain her for a while?" "Why, of course!" he replied. Whereupon the red domino led the young man up to the yellow one, who had been watching the little comedy with great amusement. The two were now brought face to face, and a rapid cross-examination ensued on both sides. Fritz Pacher, who was an official in a Government office, was a shrewd observer, and the heavy silk domino, together with the wearer's whole appearance and every word she uttered, made him aware that he was in the presence of a lady of the highest rank, so he only ventured upon a few tentative and embarrassed remarks, at the same time puzzling his brains to guess who she could be. Meanwhile the yellow domino had risen and stood, a tall and commanding figure, by the balustrade, gazing down at the rout below. Then she said abruptly: "You know I am quite a stranger here. You must explain things to me a little. Let us begin at the top. What do people say about the Emperor? Are they content with his government? Are the consequences of the war entirely healed?" To which Fritz Pacher gave cautious but sound answers, interpreting popular sentiment.

Suddenly she asked: "And do you know the Empress, too? How do you like her and what do people think and say about her?" Elizabeth was convinced that nobody would suspect her of being at the ball, so she ventured this incautious question. It flashed through the young man's mind that he must be standing beside the Empress, and that she was asking him about herself. But then he felt serious doubts, and after hesitating a moment said with animation: "Of course I only know the Empress by sight, from seeing her riding in the Prater. I can only say that she is a wonderful, gloriously beautiful woman. It is generally regretted that she has so strong an objection to letting people see her, and is far too much taken up with her horses and dogs. This is certainly doing her an injustice, for I know that a passion for dogs and horses is a family trait, and there is a story that her father, Duke Max, once said: 'If we had not been princes, we should have been trick riders!' " This criticism amused the Empress. "Tell me," she said, "how old do you think I am?" Upon which the young official gave the Empress' exact age. "You?"* he said. "You are thirty-six years old."

The Empress gave an involuntary start and said in a somewhat embarrassed tone: "You are not very polite," after which she immediately changed the dangerous subject. The conversation began to languish, till at last the lady in

* The full familiarity of this conversation is difficult to give in English, for both in it and in some of the letters exchanged later *du* is used.

the yellow domino rose and said: "Very well, now you may go." But the young man was not to be so easily dismissed. "That is most kind of you," he said ironically. "First you send for me to come up to you, then you squeeze me dry, and now you give me my dismissal. All right, I will go, since you have had enough of me. But one thing I think I may venture to ask of you—that we should shake hands at parting." And with these words Fritz Pacher held out his hand. Elizabeth did not take it, but looked at him in astonishment. "Very well," she said, "you may stay. Sit down and then escort me down into the hall."

From this moment the invisible barriers between them disappeared. The yellow domino had been stiff and formal, but now she seemed to have turned into another person. Elizabeth started talking about God and the world and discussing political and social conditions of Austria in an ironical vein. She took her companion's arm and leaned lightly upon it and for two hours they wandered through the hall and adjoining rooms chattering uninterruptedly. Though proud of the sensation created by the truly regal apparition on his arm, Fritz Pacher did not feel quite at his ease. He carefully avoided paying court to her in any aggressive way and said nothing capable of being misinterpreted. It was evident to him that he had a great lady on his arm, for he noticed how unaccustomed she was to being pushed and bumped against in a crowd. When people failed to make way she actually trembled in every limb. Young aristocrats who were present began to take an interest in the couple, for they felt sure that the lady belonged to their own world; but only one of them seemed to suspect her identity, and that was Count Nicholas Esterházy, a great sportsman and Master of the Fox Hounds at Gödöllö.

Elizabeth obtained exact information from her companion as to his name, profession, origin, and career. She found his frank criticisms of public affairs entertaining and often agreed with his views. And when at last conversation turned upon Heine, Elizabeth's favorite poet, the young official won her heart, and she said some nice things to him, telling him how sympathetic, sensible, and intelligent she had found him.

"For the most part," she said, "people are never anything but flatterers, and anyone who has learned to know them as I have cannot but despise them. But you seem quite different. I know now who you are, but do tell me, who do you think I am? Where do you place me?"

"You? You are a great lady, a princess at least. That is obvious from your whole bearing."

Elizabeth laughed, and he gradually became bolder, begging her at least to take off her glove and let him see her hand, even without any ring, for the hand is so characteristic of its owner. But Elizabeth refused.

"You will get to know me some time or other," she said, "but not today; we shall meet again. Would you perhaps come to Munich or Stuttgart, if I were to arrange to meet you there? For you must know that I have no home and am constantly traveling."

"I will, of course, go anywhere you may command," he replied.

Fritz Pacher was torn between a thousand thoughts and emotions. Was this the Empress or not? "In any case," he reflected, "I am in the presence of a clever, cultured, and interesting woman with a strain of originality. So much is evident. Nothing commonplace makes any impression upon her."

And so the hours sped by. It was long past midnight: the red domino had drawn near several times and kept pressing toward them, but the yellow one took no notice. At last, however, the parting had to come. Elizabeth had learned Pacher's address and promised to write to him soon, saying that they would be sure to meet again. "But just one thing you must promise me," she said. "Escort me to my carriage, but do not go back into the ball room afterwards. Your hand upon it!"

The young man did exactly as the figure in the yellow domino asked. The red domino now joined them, and the three descended the great staircase of the foyer together. Here they had to wait a little while a cab was summoned, and now his curiosity suddenly got the better of him. "I should really like to know who you are though," he said, and bending toward her, tried to lift the lace veil attached to her mask and see the lower half of her face; whereupon the red domino, in consternation, shrieked and threw herself between them. At this moment the cab was announced. A hearty handshake was exchanged, and in an instant the masks had entered the carriage, which at once drove off, and the whole haunting vision vanished into the darkness.

"Heavens!" said Elizabeth to Ida in alarm, "supposing he were to find out who I am. We must not drive straight to the Hofburg. He may be following us." So Ida Ferenczy ordered the coachman to drive a long way out into the suburbs, and there made him pull up at the entrance to an alley, where she got out, looked about until she was satisfied that nobody was following them, and then ordered the cabman to drive straight to the Hofburg.

Meanwhile the youthful hero of this adventure, who was twenty-six years old, returned to his modest home in an exalted state of mind and knew no peace for the next few days. He spent his time roaming about the Prater in the hope of meeting the Empress. He walked round and round the Hofburg on the chance of seeing her drive out. On one occasion he did succeed in raising his hat to her as she drove past quite close to him. She glanced at him, and for a moment her face showed a trace of agitation. The carriage had hardly gone by before she looked through the peephole at the back, but at once let the flap fall again.

A week later Fritz Pacher received a letter from Munich. The date in the top right-hand corner is in the Empress' handwriting, but the rest is obviously disguised. "Dear friend!" it ran, "You* will be surprised at receiving my first note from Munich. I am spending a few hours here on my way through and am using the brief moments of my stay here to send you the promised sign of life. With what longing you must have waited for it. Do not deny this with your honest German nature. But have no fear, I am not demanding any declarations, I know as well as you do what has been passing in your mind since that night. You have talked to a thousand women and girls before, and even believed that you were amused by them, but your spirit had never met its kindred soul. And at last, in a gorgeous dream, you found what you had been seeking for years, only perhaps to lose it forever. . . ."

Fritz Pacher replied at once and asked Gabriele whether she ever thought about him, and, if so, there were a thousand things he would like to know: how, where, what, when. He wanted the yellow domino to tell him how she spent her time, who formed her society, whether he had any cause to be jealous, and so on. He took the letter to the head post office, where it was to be called for. Two days later, in answer to his inquiries, he was told that the letter had been claimed. This little adventure provided Elizabeth and her reader with mirthful conversation for weeks to come. Ida Ferenczy was particularly delighted because the Countess Festetics, who plumed herself on her highly confidential relations with the Empress, had no idea of what had taken place.

On February 27 the Emperor Francis Joseph and Count

* Here the conventional "you" and not "thou" is used.

Andrássy returned from St. Petersburg, both fairly satisfied with the results of their visit. Their reception had been brilliant, though the real feelings of the Tsar and of Russia toward Austria had undergone no essential change, for bygones were not so readily forgotten. Something, however, had happened with regard to Count Bellegarde. The Emperor had given orders for it to be broken gently to him that he must ask to be allowed to retire. The Count believed this to be the work of the Empress and the Countess Festetics, on account of his anti-Hungarian views and the fact that, out of jealousy of Andrássy, he had allowed himself to be drawn into court intrigues against him. As a matter of fact they had no hand in his downfall, which was due to other causes. Elizabeth's report to the Emperor of the farewell audience which she granted him was very brief: "Bellegarde came today to take leave of me," she wrote on March 9, 1874, "but as he asked no questions I said nothing, which was at least more convenient."

The Empress had become very reticent by now. "I am so careful what I say about others," she said to the Countess Festetics, "because I have suffered so much from what people have said about me. Now, indeed, I believe only what I hear myself. I do not want to do anyone any harm, but it is very painful, Marie, when one has done nothing, to be made the target of malignant gossip, as I have always been. A sort of indifference has come over me. I am very cautious, I avoid contact with people, which can be nothing but agreeable to them, for they do not like me, and it is easier for me."

"I cannot deny," replied the Countess, "that everything is not as it should be, but Your Majesty does not know how many people are devoted to you and how happy they are when they see Your Majesty."

"Oh, yes," said the Empress, "they are curious enough.

When there is any sight to see, everybody rushes to look at it, whether it is a monkey dancing on a hurdy-gurdy or myself. So much for their love! I am not so ready to believe in fidelity, I am not so vain as to imagine all that, and it is wiser to miss something than to deceive oneself."

The only thing that distracted Elizabeth from all these unpleasantnesses was her perfectly innocent little adventure at the masked ball. She was determined not to keep the promised assignation, but planned to continue the correspondence, so her letter of February was followed by another in March, ostensibly written from London, which she did not really intend to visit till late in the summer.

"Dear friend!" it ran, "How sorry I am for you (*du*)! Without news of me for so long, how desolate your life must have been, how the time must have dragged! But I could not help it. My spirit was tired out, and my thoughts had lost all buoyancy. Many a day I have sat for hours at the window gazing out into the dismal fog, only to turn freakish (*pudelnärrisch*) once more and plunge from one amusement into another. You wonder whether I thought of you? I know what my thoughts were, and that is enough for me. I am not bound to satisfy your curiosity, conceited creature, so you shall hear nothing on that point. People praise London so highly, but I only know that to me it is intolerable. Shall I describe the sights to you? Read Baedeker, and that will save me the trouble. You want to know what I do and how I live. It is not at all interesting. A few old aunts, a spiteful lap dog, many complaints about my extravagance, and my sole recreation a lonely drive in Hyde Park every afternoon. In the evening a party after the theatre, and there you have my life in all its soulless desolation and desperate boredom. Yes, Fritz, even you would be a distraction here! What do you say to that? Are you less vain, for one day at least?—Only think of my weakness, I am homesick, homesick for sunny, light-hearted Vienna, but, catlike, for the place, not for the people. And now sleep well, the clock before me points to past midnight—Are you dreaming of me at this moment, or are your songs full of longing going forth into the stilly night? In the interest of your neighbors I hope it is the former.

"My cousin has returned to her parents, so in future send your letters to the following address: Mr. Leonard Wieland, General Post Office, London.

"With cordial greetings,

"GABRIELE."

Elizabeth gave this letter to her sister, the Queen of Naples, who was about to start for England, and commissioned her to send for any further letters that might be addressed there. This, she thought, would be the best way of destroying all traces of the further correspondence and of keeping it from the knowledge even of her ladies in waiting. For when she had mentioned her first letter to Herr Fritz Pacher to Ida Ferenczy, the latter had at once expressed her misgivings and begged the Empress not to continue a correspondence which might so easily be misinterpreted. This further letter raised a perfect storm of emotion in the breast of the young man to whom it was addressed. In his reply he tried to penetrate the mystery, while pretending that it was no mystery to him; whereupon in April there came another letter from Elizabeth, ostensibly written in London:

"Dear Friend, I have been away in the country for a week and only found your letter on my return. It amused me, and that is why I am replying so soon. Besides, I am curious about this mad business. You ask a frightful number of questions, but at the same time you seem to think that you know everything perfectly. Why should my name not be Gabriele? Have you an aversion to that beautiful, archangel's name? Of course Friederike would be prettier, but it is too late to change now. Then again, you seem to have got it into your head that I am not in London. If only I could be back in Vienna! For I assure you that I was much better amused there. Perhaps I may be able to go there for the month of May, but I hardly think so; in fact, I fear I may be detained here for the whole summer and autumn. In that case you might include England in your holiday trip and pay the yellow domino a visit, if we have not tired of each other by that time. You will like being here, there is so much to see, so much that is interesting, particularly for one in your profession. And since you were once a farmer, how these nice country houses will appeal to you. From the wealthy lord's great establishment down to the simplest farmer's cottage, good taste is everywhere combined with what is practical. Yes, the country is beautiful; but I hate London, it makes me melancholy and I cannot rid myself of the spleen. I have said farewell to my old aunts and am now staying with my brother. This does not interfere with the real object of my stay here, and I am delivered from that boring society in which I include the lap dog; for, even at the risk of incurring your displeasure, I must confess that I have no feeling at all for dogs. To this you must ascribe the fact that I have no idea to what breed your own dog belongs. In order to enlighten me, you might send me a photograph of yourself with your faithful companion. And so you wish to know what I am reading—I read a great deal, one day with another, but quite unsystematically—indeed, my whole life is unsystematic. Only very seldom do I come across a book that really appeals to me, written as it were from my own soul, but lately one has come into my hands, and I thought I must write to you about it: *Deutsche Liebe* by Müller. Please read it and tell me what you think of it; it pleased me tremendously. Do you know, you are very indiscreet? You ask me for nothing less than my biography—it certainly would not bore you, but I must know you better first. But this much I will tell you today, that the most memorable time in my life was a winter which I spent in the East, and that my sweetest memories are bound up with that wondrous land of legend. While I am writing these lines you are probably on the shores of one of the Italian lakes, which are no less beautiful in their own way. I know them, too, but my visit to them lacked that atmosphere of happiness which so richly pervaded my stay in the Orient. I know that there, too, you will still be thinking of me, in spite of your mother and sister. Unconsciously and unintentionally I have woven myself into your life. Tell me, do you wish to break the bonds? It can still be done now, but later, who can tell?

"With cordial greetings,

"GABRIELE."

The descriptions of England and the reference to her dislike of dogs were an attempt to put Fritz Pacher on a false scent, and so was the reference to the East, which she had never yet visited, unless she was alluding to her visit to Corfu. But the young man did not wish to seem a dupe, so in his reply to this letter he hazarded an unmistakable reference to the person of the Empress, and even ventured to say that her name was neither Gabriele nor Friederike, but could and should be Elizabeth! He was punished by the abrupt cessation of the correspondence. No yellow domino made its appearance on Shrove Tuesday. Elizabeth saw

Pacher in the Prater and at a flower show, but only as one of the public. She may have acknowledged his salute somewhat more graciously than that of others, but she never spoke to him; and soon the march of events obliterated the memory of this little episode.

On April 29 the Empress' brother, Duke Karl Theodor, married, as his second wife, the lovely and charming Maria José, Infanta of Portugal. Elizabeth was greatly pleased with this marriage and heard from all quarters that it was the best choice her brother could possibly have made. She was unable to attend the wedding, but sent a magnificent present. When she came to know her sister-in-law during her next visit to Possenhofen, she was enchanted with her. "I like Marie immensely," she wrote to the Princess Gisela, "I consider her a rare beauty and am never tired of looking at her." The reason why the Empress was unable to attend the wedding was that Valerie was ill again, and there were also unpleasant scenes among the child's attendants.

At the end of July, in response to an invitation from her sister, the Empress decided to take her daughter to the Isle of Wight, for the sake of the sea bathing. She was determined to do her best to avoid any official reception. This was her "holiday," and she meant to enjoy it in peace. Above all, she was anxious to escape from the political intrigues which were now at their height in Vienna. First there was the Bohemian party, which blamed Elizabeth for the fact that the Emperor had not had himself crowned in Prague; then there were the people who did not consider her pious enough and regarded her as the sole obstacle to a greater subordination of State to Church; then there were the "absolutists" and "centralists," who wanted to revert to the policy of the Archduchess Sophie, and held Elizabeth solely responsible for undermining it. But as a matter of fact, after the *Ausgleich* Elizabeth no longer used her great influence over the Emperor in favor of any further political plans whatsoever. Her one desire was that everything should go well for her husband and children, and whenever she could she helped the Emperor with her clever brain and delicate tact; besides which the Emperor liked to discuss everything with her and set high store by her judgment.

On July 28 the Empress started for the Isle of Wight, traveling by way of Strassburg and Le Havre. At Strassburg she wanted to see the cathedral, but was afraid of being recognized, which always made her unhappy and prevented her from enjoying things to the utmost. So she went there some hours before the appointed time and found nobody but a little old woman, who conducted her to a priest. He acted as her guide around the cathedral, and when they came to the tombs of the Habsburgs, delighted Elizabeth by talking of the Habsburg lip as a sign of degeneracy. Meanwhile Frau Feifalik, the hairdresser, emerged from the Empress' lodging and was greeted with respectful salutes, which she acknowledged by bowing to right and left. The Empress laughed as she watched this scene from a distance, and then she gave the old woman a piece of gold, but the old dame would not accept it, for she had guessed by now who it was that she had conducted. "The honor and the joy," she insisted, "are reward enough for me." "Your Majesty sees," said Marie Festetics, "that there are good people in the world, after all." "Yes," replied the Empress sadly, "the people here do not hate me."

For political reasons Elizabeth did not stop in Paris, and arrived in the Isle of Wight on August 2, 1874, accompanied by the Countess Festetics and Ida Ferenczy. The island was at its loveliest, with its splendid oaks and laurels, magnolias and cedars, and masses of flowers; and Steephill Castle, Ventnor, where she stayed with her suite, was a charming spot.

The Empress had hardly arrived before the Queen of England drove over from Osborne to visit her. Queen Victoria had never seen her before and knew her only from photographs and pictures, none of which, as she now found, did her justice or even gave the remotest impression of her loveliness. Many reports about the Empress' unsociability and moroseness had been current at the English court, so her visit had been anticipated with some apprehension. For her part Elizabeth was interested in the celebrated John Brown, who had been the Prince Consort's favorite servant, and was therefore given such a privileged position by the Queen. As for little Valerie, the Queen frightened her. "I have never seen such a stout lady," she said.

The Empress' impressions are contained in a letter written to her husband from Steephill Castle, Ventnor, on August 2: "The Queen was very kind," she wrote, "and said nothing that was not amiable, but she is not sympathetic to me. The Prince of Wales was kind, nice-looking and as deaf as a post, and the Crown Princess, who is staying three or four miles away from her mother, was just as usual. Their quarters are small, but pretty, and they are prolonging their stay here. She is coming to see me tomorrow. I was most polite, I may say, at which everybody seemed astonished. But now I have done my duty. They understand that I want to be quiet, and they have no wish to intrude. . . ." A few days after her first visit, however, Queen Victoria invited Elizabeth to dinner. The Empress excused herself in a polite letter, and wrote to Francis Joseph that she thought the Queen too would be glad to be thus relieved of exertion. But this was not the case. On August 11 Queen Victoria paid another visit to Elizabeth and renewed her invitation by word of mouth. The Empress again declined it, and this led to a slight coolness. "I did so," she confessed in a letter to her mother, "because that sort of thing bores me."

The Empress preferred to roam about London incognito. At this time of year society was out of town. "Everybody is away," she wrote, "and the streets with the finest houses seem as though dead." But that was what she liked, for it meant that at least she was not interfered with. She had to call on one or two people, indeed; among others the Duchess of Edinburgh and the Duchess of Teck. In the evening she would mount the famous white coronation horse from Budapest, which she had brought with her, and go for a ride in Hyde Park with Count Beust, the Austrian Ambassador. Horses were brought from all quarters for her inspection, and they were naturally not cheap ones. "The one I should most like to have," she wrote to Francis Joseph, "costs twenty-five thousand gulden!" And she hastily added: "So it is naturally out of the question."

Accompanied by Marie Festetics, she began a frenzied sightseeing of the gigantic city, as though she wanted to see everything at once. She visited Madame Tussaud's famous waxworks, where she found a figure of her husband. "Vastly amusing," was her opinion of the show, "but very gruesome in parts." She stayed there more than an hour and a half and could hardly tear herself away. She also visited Bedlam, at that time the largest lunatic asylum in the world, ten times the size of the one in Munich. Here Elizabeth found herself in a whole world of disordered minds. According to the Countess Festetics, the deepest impression was made upon her by a young girl whom she saw seated on the grass under a blossoming tree in the beautiful garden making wreaths, which she then placed solemnly upon her head with a calm composure indicative of megalomania. Next, a madman spoke to the Empress, begging her to set him free. "Why are you here?" she asked. "The Jesuits hate me," he replied, "and as an excuse for locking me up, they accused me of having stolen St. Peter's purse in the street. Of course that would have been a serious crime. But it's not true," he added with a sly smile, "because you see, I am St. Peter myself." The Empress listened to him with tense interest and replied quite calmly: "In that case you will be sure to get out soon."

After this visit the rush began again. The Empress made an excursion to Melton and Belvoir Castle, where the Duke of Rutland had his kennels, and on August 26, 1874, she hunted for the first time on English soil. She spent the night at Melton and visited the stables, with the result that the idea of passing a whole hunting season there took such possession of her that the possibility was seriously discussed. Several gentlemen from Austria-Hungary joined in the hunt, including Count Tisza, Count Tassilo Festetics, and the two brothers Baltazzi, the sons of a Levantine banker, who had first come into prominence at Vienna on the occasion of the Empress' marriage. The Countess Festetics regarded these two gentlemen with suspicion, for they did not belong to any of the noble families of Austria-Hungary and were said to have "smuggled" themselves into court society through their sister, the wife of the Austro-Hungarian diplomatist, Baron Vetsera, whom she had met at the Embassy at Constantinople. "Great caution is necessary," notes the Countess. "They are clever people, brothers of a Baroness Vetsera who suddenly made her appearance in Vienna, intelligent, rich, and all having the same beautiful, interesting eyes; no one knows exactly where these people come from with all their money, but they are pushing and make me feel uncomfortable. The brothers are devoted to sport, ride splendidly, and shove themselves in everywhere; but they are dangerous to *us*, because they are quite English, and because of the horses!"

The two days' hunting was so exhausting that even the men were dead beat and could hardly stand after it. But Elizabeth was in her element, and enjoyed herself so thoroughly that she did not feel in the least tired, and laughed heartily when, in spite of all his efforts and his unbounded respect for her, Count Tisza kept nodding with sleep in her presence. She was quite sorrowful when it was time to return to the Isle of Wight, but the passage over the Solent enchanted her, though it was very rough and her companions very seasick. She herself was a splendid sailor and began to crave a long sea voyage. The passion for travel, an inheritance from her father, stirred in her blood. "What I should like best would be to pay a short visit to America," she wrote to her mother. "The sea tempts me whenever I look at it."

At Ventnor she resumed her sea bathing. Whenever the Empress entered the water, crowds would gather on the neighboring cliffs and watch her through field glasses. To guard against this a little stratagem was devised. Marie Festetics and one of the maids had to put on flannel bathing gowns exactly like the Empress' and enter the water at the same time. "It is such a pity you cannot come," wrote Elizabeth to her husband. "After all those maneuvers you might really take a fortnight off to see London, then dash up to Scotland (*einen Rutscher machen*) to visit the Queen, and then have a little hunting in the neighborhood of London. We have horses and everything here, so it would be a pity not to use them. Do think it over for a day or two before, with your usual refractoriness, you say no. . . ." She also told the Emperor that Lady Dudley had presented her with a hunter, though she had tried to prevent this, explaining that it was not customary for her to accept presents. The lady was not to be denied, however, and sent her the horse, which was a beautiful creature, but very large. The Empress wrote to Francis Joseph: "Even you would look like the dot on an *i* on its back."

She now took frequent rides with the daughter of the English riding master Allen, who owed his position to the Queen of Naples' recommendation, and whom Elizabeth called "if possible, an even more perfect gentleman" than old Holmes. She was well content that the Queen was now at Balmoral, and not at Osborne, so that she was spared further visits. As for Francis Joseph, he followed the Empress' accounts of her stay with great interest, but it was impossible for him to join her; every hour of his time was already engaged for months ahead. Elizabeth regretfully accepted the situation. "I beg you not to let your plans be upset," she wrote to him on September 26. "Sport is so essential to you as a recreation that I should be inconsolable if my return were to deprive you of even one day of it. I need no demonstrations to convince me of how much you love me, and it is because we do not put each other out that we are so happy together. . . ."

She now decided to return home, not wanting to be separated from her husband for such a long time. On the way to Vienna she proposed to visit Possenhofen, though she was alarmed at the prospect of having to meet Ludwig II. "If only the King will leave me in peace!" she wrote to the Emperor shortly before leaving.

On arriving at Boulogne the travelers found a gale raging. The howling of the wind drowned the roar of the waves. It was a wonderful spectacle, and, in order to enjoy it better, Elizabeth and the Countess Festetics rashly went down to the seashore. In a moment their umbrellas were turned inside out and they themselves thrown flat on the sand by the wind. They struggled to their feet with difficulty, but could not advance a step, and were almost worn out when a coast guard hurried up, gesticulating furiously, and, having no notion who they were, seized hold of an arm of each and dragged them away. It was not till he found a gold coin in his hand that he became more agreeable, and explained that on such days as that nobody was allowed on the shore, and that if a policeman had seen them there, it would have been as much as his place was worth.

On her way home Elizabeth stopped at Baden-Baden, where the German Emperor and Empress were at the station to meet her. Their daughter, the Grand Duchess of Baden, went into raptures over her beauty, whereupon the Emperor William rubbed his left side and said: "It is better not to look at her too long, for it warms one's heart far too much."

She next went on to Possenhofen, where she was fated not to escape the King of Bavaria. This time he made himself particularly agreeable, after his own strange fashion, not only to her but also to her ladies in waiting. At about half past one in the morning he sent the Countess Festetics an elegant bouquet of a hundred roses, delicately graded from deep crimson to pure white, the aide-de-camp who brought it having strict orders to present it in person. The Countess was awakened and was in agonies at such a compromising situation, especially as the house was built of wood and the Empress' room was immediately underneath her own. They left on the following day, and since King Ludwig was to be at the station in Munich to see them off, the unfortunate Countess had to take this bouquet, the size of a small table, into the compartment with her, where it proved a great trial on the journey. The King, who seemed to Elizabeth to have grown excessively stout, told her about the special performances for which he was preparing in his theatre, the most interesting of which in the Empress' eyes was a spectacle laid in the days of Louis XIV, with a great hunting scene in which innumerable dogs were to take part. The culminating sensation was to be a downpour of rain, with real water. After some few minutes' conversation, the King asked the Empress' permission to accompany her a little way on her journey, an unwelcome proposal, for he got on her nerves, and produced a more and more sinister impression upon her as it became increasingly evident that his brother Otto was on the verge of complete insanity. Marie Festetics had to come to her aid, which she did by explaining to the King that the Empress' hound, Shadow, was so bad tempered that he would not tolerate anybody he did not know. Her Majesty, she said, was in terror lest the dog might bite him. At last the King understood and allowed her to start without him, but his beautiful eyes, with their strange suggestion of cruelty, haunted the Empress and her companion for a long while.

The Empress spent the closing days of the year riding with the Emperor at Pardubitz and hunting at Gödöllö; and then, after the turn of the year, came the carnival celebrations on Twelfth Night, involving those public appearances for which the Empress had such a profound distaste. It is curious that she should have found court balls such a torture, and her aversion at least shows that the excessive vanity attributed to her was largely a myth. Those in attendance on her were always in transports of delight at the sensation produced by her appearance, though she was now thirty-seven years old. After one such ball, Marie Festetics, whose enthusiasm for her knew no bounds, compared her with a swan, a lily, a gazelle, or the legendary Melusine. "At once queen and fairy, yet very womanly, majestic yet childlike, girlish yet august, gracious and dignified—that is what she is, speaking objectively and without exaggeration. What a pity that no picture can render this, and that people exist who have not seen her. I was proud to see the Empress so much admired! But such a ball is terribly fatiguing for her. To go on talking for four hours in all that heat and noise! And not a soul gives that aspect of it a thought. People feel it quite natural that she should work like a machine."

But it all cost Elizabeth a struggle, and she had to fight

for the right to gratify her insistent desire to live apart from the world. The blue veil and the fan were used more and more often. When she stepped into her carriage she sent away everybody who chanced to be near. In the gardens she would retreat to the pergolas, where no one could see her, and when not actually "in harness," as she called her gala dress, she hid herself whenever she could. People misinterpreted this, for, oblivious of her inborn shyness, they imagined that she was doing something which she wanted to hide. They would have been far less imaginative if she had not behaved so mysteriously. Marie Festetics racked her brains to think how she could help her. The Countess had already received several offers of marriage and had refused them all; but she often wondered whether she was doing right to sacrifice love, a home, and a life of her own for the sake of the Empress. But then she would remember how Elizabeth had adjured her not to leave her, and resolved never to surrender the flag which Andrássy and Deák had placed in her hands. For the Empress did really stand in need of support and of trustworthy women friends. She had a calendar, of the simple sort used by the Hungarian peasants (*István Bácsi Naptára* or Brother Stephen's Calendar), in which she occasionally entered remarks or little poems which had pleased her, or sometimes verses of her own. In March she composed a quatrain reflecting her mood of the moment entitled "*Ruhelos*" (Restless):

Great wishes must to greater wishes yield,
And never can content the heart possess.
For when you think your happiness attained
Lo, it has ceased to be your happiness.

When Marie Festetics reproved her, telling her that she ought not always to yield to her whims, but should control herself and try to find contentment by accepting her limitations, the Empress' reply took the form of entering in her calendar some verses entitled "*Selbstbeherrschung*" (Victory over Self):

> *And must I, then, myself constrain?*
> *Would this, then, profit me?*
> *But who would vanquished be, I pray,*
> *Should I the conqueror be?*
>
> *A foolish robber, sure, is he*
> *Who thinks to gain more pelf*
> *By lying ambushed in the woods*
> *Only to rob—himself!*

Her preference for Budapest and her dread of returning to Vienna remained unchanged: "I am really desperate at the thought of it," she wrote to her mother in January, 1875, "life is so quiet here without relatives and other plagues (*Sekkaturen*), whereas there there is the whole imperial family. Besides, here I am as untrammeled as in the country, I can go for walks and drives alone, etc." Francis Joseph was an exception to these strictures, for at this time Elizabeth was on the most cordial terms with her husband. She was uneasy when, in April, 1875, the Emperor went to Trieste and Venice to return the King of Italy's visit, and then, for political and military reasons, proceeded to Southern Dalmatia, which was reputed to be half uncivilized and revolutionary. Elizabeth wept bitterly when they parted. "I have a presentiment that something is going to happen to you," she said. On the evening of April 2 Marie Festetics was at the theatre, when the Empress sent for her to come home, on the ground that she felt impelled to write a letter that very night to General von Beck, who was accompanying the Emperor. In this letter, which was dictated to the Countess, she held the General responsible for the Emperor's life and begged him not to leave his side for an instant.

The Empress now redoubled her physical exercise, as she always did when nervous and overwrought. She was at the height of her mania for horses. No longer satisfied with hunting and practicing systematically in the riding school for several hours a day, she aimed at higher things, hoping to attain the perfection which she had witnessed in the circus. It so happened that Ernst Jakob Renz, founder of the famous circus of that name, was in Vienna with his troupe. The son of a tight-rope dancer, he had succeeded in raising his profession to a high, really artistic level and developed his circus into a world-famous spectacle where people marveled at his glorious horses, trained to perfection. The public was most enthusiastic about his daughter Elise, and so was the Empress. One of Renz's trainers, named Hüttemann, entered her service. A small circular riding school was built next the royal stables, and three real circus horses were procured, among them the famous "Avolo," who would kneel down with the Empress on his back. Elizabeth began taking lessons from Fraülein Elise Renz. The only thing she feared was that her absent husband might object on the ground of public opinion, so she hastened to assure him that Fraülein Elise was "most respectable," and, according to the German Ambassador's accounts, gave lessons to the ladies in Berlin. Elizabeth was constantly going to the circus, either alone or with Valerie, and on such occasions the performances lasted a long time, for Renz would introduce a number of extra turns in her honor, which she enjoyed like a child. Not only the horses, but wild beasts, too, roused her to enthusiasm, but she was bored by pantomime and things of that sort.

On May 15 the Emperor returned from Dalmatia, to Elizabeth's great joy, for, in spite of all the gossip, she was still very much devoted to her husband. But her nature being no ordinary one, those who could only judge others by themselves readily found something to object to in her. Now that

Gisela was married, and Rudolf, who was seventeen, was increasingly absorbed in the training necessary in view of his future duties, she felt lonely and out of her element, and this ministered to her inborn craving for foreign travel.

X

RIDING IN FOREIGN PARTS

1875–1882

DURING THE SUMMER OF 1875 THE EMpress was asked to ascertain whether the Princess Amalie of Coburg would consent to marry her youngest brother. Marie Festetics successfully conducted the negotiations, and the betrothal took place. "So Mapperl is soon to be a husband," wrote the Empress to her mother. "Queer taste for one so young as he is to forfeit his liberty, but one never knows how to value what one has till one has lost it. . . . Of course you will not go to the wedding on account of your head. Nor shall I, for I am too lazy and shrink from seeing people . . . (*menschenscheu bin*) . . ."

After short visits to Garatshausen and Ischl Elizabeth felt a desire to travel, and Valerie provided an excellent pretext. Widerhofer had once more prescribed sea bathing for the Archduchess, and this time they wanted to go to France for a change, to some quiet little watering place in Normandy. The Emperor objected that the monarchy was not on the best of terms with the new republic, which harbored anarchists of every sort. "Something will happen to you there," he said; "and besides, they will not be exactly delighted in Berlin." The Empress insisted, but the Emperor's remark gave her food for thought, and between May 22 and June 8 she made her will, after which she started for Sassetôt-les-Mauconduits in Normandy, strong in the conviction that nobody would touch one who, like her, had never injured anybody in her life. Karl Linger, her secretary, who was in charge of her traveling arrangements, had gone on ahead and taken a simply furnished château belonging to a rich shipowner, with a park full of great trees and masses of hydrangeas. Elizabeth took some of her favorite horses with her, and she bathed early every morning, walking down to the sea from her bathing hut, accompanied by her two big dogs Mahomet and Shadow, between screens of sail cloth to shield her from curious eyes. In the afternoons she went on long expeditions to châteaux and country places in the neighborhood, most of which, like Sassetôt itself, had been in the hands of *nouveaux riches* since the revolution. "Democrats, republicans, and *parvenus*," commented the Countess Festetics, "lead a scandalous life there. A perfect rabble, with all the vices of the old nobility and none of its virtues." Elizabeth soon found that she could not go about here unnoticed. "Republic or no republic," she wrote to her mother, "people here are more pushing than in any other country." She met with constant difficulties when riding. In her thoughtless way she would ride over cultivated fields, and this led to unpleasantnesses, which the Republican *L'Univers* of August 17, 1875, exaggerated almost into an affair of State. The Empress and the Austrian Embassy in Paris caused all rumors of an alleged insult by some peasants to be contradicted, but there really was something in them, for she frequently complained in her letters to her husband. "The people here," she wrote, "are so insolent and unmannerly. Yesterday they followed me about again, so I drove straight to Fécamp in a carriage and returned here by water. While out riding too, I have often met with unpleasantnesses on the roads and in the villages. The children, the drivers of vehicles—everybody tries hard to frighten the horses, and if, as one naturally would, one turns into the fields, where no harm can be done, the peasants are dreadfully surly. I really do not feel much inclined to go to Paris, but Nopcsa is afraid that if I did not, it might make a bad impression. What do you think?"

Elizabeth had sent to England for Mr. Allen, who had given her riding lessons in the previous year, but the Countess Festetics felt a curious instinctive antipathy for him. It is remarkable how she always guessed beforehand what people were likely to have an unfortunate influence over her mistress. She would confide these misgivings to her diary on the very day when the person concerned entered the Empress' life, so it was not a judgment arrived at after the event. Her intuitions were sharp, and she had a keen gift of observation and remarkable intellectual qualities—in fact, she undoubtedly possessed more brains and intelligence than any other woman in the Empress' immediate circle.

Mr. Allen was first and foremost a horseman, bold and vigorous, or, in the eyes of the Countess Festetics, rough. When he wanted a horse to do something, he would simply force it to obey. Once he was trying to show the Empress how he could ride a horse straight into the surf. The beast tried to refuse, and when Allen used the spur and slashed it with the whip it reared, turned head over heels, and both horse and rider disappeared beneath the waves. The bathing man pulled Mr. Allen out of the water, and the horse managed to save itself, while the Empress looked on speechless, as white as a ghost. As they rode homewards she remarked to the Countess Festetics: "Don't be alarmed, Marie, that is a trick I shall not try to imitate."

Allen was not the right man for Elizabeth, for he was so keen that he expected too much of her. He had a course with obstacles laid out in a park near the château, where the Empress practiced jumping regularly, till one day she, too, met with the inevitable accident. A new horse had just arrived, and on September 11, 1875, Elizabeth wished to try it. Allen had been riding it before her, and it was overtired. They came to a fairly low obstacle, which Elizabeth expected to be easy, but her horse took off far too violently, stumbled, and came down on its knees. Elizabeth was thrown with such violence that the pommel of her saddle broke. Her faithful Bayzand, the manager of her stud of hunters, was standing at the far end of the course, waiting for her to complete the round. Suddenly he saw her horse gallop up riderless, rushed to the spot, and found Elizabeth lying unconscious on the ground. Everybody was bathing except the Countess Festetics, who heard him shouting: "Madame, a doctor! Quickly! There has been an accident in the park." Dr. Widerhofer hurried out half-dressed, while Elizabeth was carried to a garden seat, where she sat with a great stain on her forehead, completely dazed, her eyes fixed and glassy. They sprinkled water on her brow and spoke to her. At last she raised her eyes and seemed to recognize the Countess, for she faltered in a dull, scarcely audible voice: "Don't cry, Marie, please, it hurts me to see you." Then she went on after a pause: "But what has happened?" "Your Majesty has had a fall." "But I have not been riding. What time is it?" "Half past ten, Your Majesty." "In the morning? But I never rode at such a time before!" Then she looked down at her habit and asked wonderingly: "Where is the horse?" They led it up, with its knees cut and bleeding. "Oh! Why is its skin all torn?" "On account of the fall, Your Majesty." "But I cannot remember falling. Have you got any carrots?" She tried to get up, but when she found that she could not move, she began to believe that something had really happened. "Where is Valerie?" she asked, "and the Emperor? And where are we?" "In Normandy, Your Majesty." "Why, what are we doing in Normandy? If it is true that I have been thrown, then I am just a little idiot (*Trottli*). Shall I always be one now? But please do not alarm the Emperor."

Symptoms of slight concussion soon appeared, violent

headaches—for which applications of ice were necessary—nausea, and a sleepless night. Widerhofer came to her bedside and said bluntly: "If the head is not better within twenty-four hours, the hair must come off." The Countess Festetics was horrified to hear this, for to touch those masses of glossy curls seemed to her like murder. Ida Ferenczy never left Elizabeth's side, and when Widerhofer finally banished her from the room she and Marie Festetics sat on the steps outside and kept vigil.

They telegraphed to Francis Joseph, who was badly alarmed and wanted to come at once, though when, two days before, the Empress had asked him to come to Sassetôt, he had said it was impossible for political reasons. As the news improved Andrássy begged him not to go, for fear of possible complications; so he stayed at home and wrote his wife touching letters. "Most heartfelt thanks to Almighty God that things are going on so well. I cannot rid myself of the thought of what might have happened. What on earth should I do without you, the good angel of my life?" The concussion was soon cured, but Elizabeth's pleasure in Sassetôt was spoiled, and she could hardly wait till it was time to leave.* Her answer to the Emperor's letter was as follows: "I am grieved at having given you such a fright, but both you and

* In a book entitled *The Secret of an Empress* (London, 1914) and crammed with inaccuracies, a certain Countess Zanardi-Landi asserts that she is of exalted birth. She invents a story that Elizabeth had a child at Sassetôt, the birth of which was concealed under the pretext of a riding accident. But the authoress of this thick volume of 365 pages did not even take the trouble to ascertain exactly in what year the Empress was there, and alleges that she herself was born there in 1882, whereas Elizabeth only stayed there in 1875. This book, which sets out to prove the authoress' high birth, appeared during the worst days of "war psychosis" in 1914. Any allegation that the Empress Elizabeth ever had a "secret" child must be utterly rejected as a baseless fabrication. There were innumerable witnesses of the Empress' riding accident, but not a single even tolerably credible proof can be produced in support of the Countess' assertion.

I are really prepared for such accidents. I am quite well now. Widerhofer is awfully strict, but he will let me leave here as soon as possible." She was already making arrangements for riding at Gödöllö and wanted all her horses and hunters to be sent there in readiness for her. "I shall be very glad to have some more horses again," she went on. "I had too few here to work properly, and possibly fatigue may have had something to do with Zouave's somersault." She meant to go out riding in public again as soon as possible, she said, for she was proud to show that she had not lost her nerve "on account of a bad jump (*Rumpler*) like that." The Emperor sent an aide-de-camp with instructions never to let her out of his sight, and asked her to visit Paris on her way home, for the whole world was talking about her, and Andrássy considered that if she did not it would be a slight to the President.

On September 26, 1875, Elizabeth arrived in Paris, fully restored to health and in good spirits. The President, Marshal Macmahon, had tried to pay his respects to her at Vernon as she passed through, but she was asleep, so he did not disturb her. Elizabeth rushed about the city from morning till night, looking at the sights, as she always did in foreign towns. She had a horror of anything suggestive of moldiness, dust, physical decay, or gloom, and she loved light, sunshine, art, youth, beauty, and strength. For the same reason she dreaded growing old and tried to postpone it by physical exercise and sport and unremitting care of her health. Her favorite form of art was statuary, especially the Greek. She was in ecstasies over the lovely face of the Venus of Milo and her irresistible grace, though she could not reconcile herself to the classical ideal of beauty, which preferred full forms to slender hips. Of course she visited the Invalides, and since guides made her nervous, she went alone with Marie Festetics to do homage to Napoleon, whose genius filled her with awe. They stood for a long time before Lucien Bonaparte's splendid sarcophagus, imagining it to be the Emperor's, till another visitor overheard their remarks and pointed out their mistake, leading them to Napoleon's simple porphyry sarcophagus, on which was laid a fresh bunch of flowers. Elizabeth knelt before it reverently and afterward remarked: "When people want to say something really withering, they say that Napoleon was great, but ruthless; but I always think how many people are ruthless without being great—for instance, myself." She continued her round of museums and palaces, châteaux and gardens. What amused her most was a fine park in which there were elephants, ostriches, and camels on which people could ride. She did not venture to do so herself, much as she would have liked to, but her ladies and Baron Nopcsa did, while she took a childish pleasure in watching them.

She had quite forgotten her accident and would dearly have liked to go to the Opera House and visit the famous Bal Mabille, of somewhat equivocal reputation, but she dared not do so. She sent Nopcsa with Marie and Ida, who returned home so horrified and indignant at what they had seen that she went into fits of laughter at their accounts of it. On the very next day, however, she was gloomy and upset when she visited the chapel erected on the spot where the Crown Prince Ferdinand Philippe of Orleans, son of Louis Philippe, had been killed in a carriage accident at the age of only twenty-three. "It shows," she remarked, "that what God ordains for any man is bound to happen. He went out quietly for a drive. Who could have supposed that he would never cross his threshold again alive! You would like me never to ride again. But whether I do or not, I shall die just when I am destined to." On the same day she went out riding in the Bois de Boulogne with her husband's aide-de-camp and jumped a few barriers. She was pale and rather tired after it, but had recovered her good spirits.

The King of Bavaria was deeply affected by the news of her accident and wrote to the Crown Prince Rudolf with his usual rhetoric:* "Fortunate and enviable one, to whom it is granted to spend so much time with the august Empress, pray lay me at her feet and beseech her in my name to graciously remember her faithful slave, who always honored her of old and will do so forever. It was a great comfort to me when Louis (the Empress' brother) sent me an assurance from Gödöllö last October that she would curb her impetuosity in riding. Never in my life should I recover from my grief if any accident were to befall her. God forbid such a thing! And may he preserve you and me from such an appalling experience!

"I will have your portrait framed, so that I may always have it before my eyes, together with that of the Empress. For nobody on earth is so dear to me as you and she are. Please remember me most cordially to the Emperor. I am spending these winter days really gloriously among the mountains, absorbed in fascinating books, which are my dearest pleasure."

On returning to Gödöllö, where she was joined by her brother Duke Ludwig and his daughter, Elizabeth picked up the threads of her peaceful country life, diversified only by much riding. Francis Joseph was overjoyed at having the Empress back again "whole and sound," but he warned her to be more prudent. She was next joined by the Crown Prince Rudolf, whose tutors were all loud in his praises, though the court dignitaries pointed to his "exalted" views as evidence that he had not yet digested the teaching of his liberal-minded professors. On November 19, Elizabeth's name day, a

* The letter is now in the State Archives, Vienna.

little dance was arranged in Valerie's apartments with parlor games in which Elizabeth took part so wholeheartedly, that her sudden fits of gloom seemed hardly credible. Yet even so slight a cause as the death of her faithful dog, Shadow, sufficed to bring one on. She mourned him as a dear old friend and had him buried in the garden at Gödöllö, where his grave was marked by a stone.

In November, 1875, Count Grünne was removed from his position as Master of the Horse, and with him vanished one of the last traces of the Archduchess Sophie's régime. The Empress no longer shrank from making overtures to those ladies who had formerly been entirely on her mother-in-law's side; and in 1876 the Landgravine Therese von Fürstenberg took the place of Frau von Schaffgotsch as lady in waiting. Before she had held this position for more than a month or two she had to admit that as soon as anyone came into close personal touch with Elizabeth she could not help falling under the spell of her extraordinary fascination.

At the end of January news arrived that the great Hungarian statesman Deák was lying at death's door. Elizabeth would have liked to visit him on his deathbed, but this was not allowed, and on January 31 she could only pay the last tribute to him as he lay in state. She looked like some lovely genius of mourning, and her tears went straight to every Hungarian heart.

In March she was again seized with a restless desire to travel. It had been one of her great wishes to hunt in England, and now her desire was fulfilled. Early in March, 1876, she started for Easton Neston, Towcester, where Linger had rented a fine old country seat with a park, quite near another attractive hunting box where the Queen of Naples was staying. In addition to her immediate suite she was joined by a little band of horsemen from home who had always been devoted to her, including Prince Rudolf Liechtenstein, Count

Hans and Count Heinrich Larisch, Ferdinand Kinsky, Tassilo Festetics, Baron Orczy, and others.

While in London Elizabeth expressed a wish to be received by Queen Victoria, but the answer was: "The Queen cannot receive her; she is too busy." This was Queen Victoria's little revenge for Elizabeth's repeated refusals of her invitations to dinner in the previous year. Elizabeth had long since forgotten these incidents and was indignant. "Imagine if *I* were so ill-bred!" she wrote to Francis Joseph. "But everybody whom I visited this afternoon was ashamed, for I made myself very agreeable. I have seen them all now."

The Empress proceeded on her way to Easton Neston, where she hunted on the very day after her arrival, going out with the famous Bicester and Duke of Grafton's hunts. Next came a visit to Lord Spencer's country house, full of portraits of his ancestors by Rembrandt, Van Dyck, Gainsborough, Romney, and others, and with superb works of art on every side. In this setting, which suited her so well, Lady Spencer gave a luncheon party in Elizabeth's honor.

The Empress was in the saddle for hours on end, and her suite were always in a state of anxiety. But Elizabeth threw herself into the novel English sport on unfamiliar soil and among complete strangers with spirit and passion. Once again the old rule was illustrated, that what one does well one enjoys doing. The English watched her ride to hounds with some misgivings, for it was hard to believe that such a lovely Empress could jump and gallop well enough to hunt. Two picked horsemen, Colonel Hunt and Captain Middleton, a friend of Lord Spencer, were told off to ride before the Empress and give her a lead—to pilot her, in short. The Captain was by no means pleased with this mission. "What is an empress to me?" he asked. "How can I look after her? I'll do it, of course, but I'd rather go my own way." He was soon to change his mind. He was one of the best riders in

England and soon saw that this Empress was a keen horsewoman and, what is more, made an incomparably charming picture on horseback.

On March 12 Elizabeth was expected at Windsor by Queen Victoria, who, having administered her lesson, was now ready to receive her; but the Queen felt a little uncomfortable with Elizabeth, and the two ladies had not much to say to each other. The visit was as short as possible, and on the thirteenth the Empress went down to Leighton Buzzard to hunt with the Ferdinand Rothschilds. She had been persuaded to do so by the Queen of Naples, who had her reasons for wishing to obtain this honor for that family. A sudden snowstorm made hunting impossible, so the Empress visited the racing stables instead. When evening came, the Queen of Naples even tried to persuade her sister to stay the night, but in spite of all the efforts made by the Rothschilds to keep her, Elizabeth returned to London the same evening, so as to be in the shires again by the fourteenth.

The next time she was out with the hounds it was Colonel Hunt who gave her a lead. He recommended the Empress to try a certain light chestnut which had so far behaved very well. But this time it fell with Elizabeth at the first jump. She wanted to mount again, but the Colonel firmly forbade it.

"Very well," she said, "I will ride another horse today. But I will buy this one, all the same."

To which the Colonel replied: "Oh, no, Your Majesty. I would not sell it to you for the whole of Austria."

There was a field of no less than a hundred. The Empress' presence was a great attraction, and people crowded to the spot not only to hunt but to look on. Elizabeth was in the best of spirits and absolutely untiring. "Other people," said the Countess Festetics, "ride four times a week. We ride every day." "So far," wrote Elizabeth to the Emperor, "I have not known a moment's fatigue. None of your horses are any good, they are slow and spiritless; one wants quite different material here. I am constantly being asked whether you are not coming some time. After all, everybody has a right to a holiday occasionally."

Elizabeth also attended every steeplechase in the neighborhood and would have liked to take part in them all herself. She presented a fine silver cup with the inscription, "Presented by the Countess of Hohenembs," which to her great joy was won by Captain Middleton. This officer, who was then thirty, had won his first steeplechase eleven years before, at the age of nineteen, thus starting upon a brilliant career of victories. His Christian names were William George, but everybody called him "Bay," either on account of his red-brown hair and dark complexion, or after the famous horse Bay which won the Derby in 1836. Elizabeth admired his skill and observed with a critical eye how her own countrymen rode. "Fritz Metternich and Count Wolkenstein were full of fire last Tuesday," she wrote to Ida Ferenczy, "so that they not only jumped everything that came their way, but went out of their way to look for obstacles. The latter fell twice in succession, and came out of a swampy brook in such a state that his grey horse looked black, and he himself like a Moor."

Elizabeth felt particularly well here. She was tanned "like a wild hare" by the March sun and wind. Her face was covered with freckles, but she felt fresh and healthy and enjoyed going about among people without all the "fuss" (*Getu*) which usually surrounded her and made people everywhere show their most boring side. Everybody seemed independent, lively, and interesting here, including the gentlemen from her own country. The burdensome, servile cringing was banished from this circle, which the Empress called her "colony." But all things must come to an end, and she had to go home. On April 5 she arrived in Vienna, where, in his happiness at seeing his wife home again safe and sound, Francis Joseph sanctioned the payment of 106,516 gulden 93 kreuzer for the expenses of her visit without turning a hair. He heard great accounts of Elizabeth's triumphs, and Baron Nopcsa, the Controller of her Household, could only assure his sovereign that "neither in England nor anywhere else in the world was there a lady who could ride like Her Majesty, and very few men either."

On returning to Vienna Elizabeth had to get back "into harness" (*ins Geschirr*). Balls, festivities, and the Corpus Christi festival followed one after the other and are duly recorded in the Countess Festetics' diaries, together with such little incidents as the first appearance of the Countess Paula Széchényi (*née* Klinkosch) at a court party, on which Marie Festetics comments as follows: "Vienna is quite prepared to receive adventurers of doubtful origin, such as Madame Vetsera with her . . . conduct, but turns its back on the daughter of this great and honorable citizen family."

The Queen of the Belgians and the King and Queen of Greece were expected at the beginning of May, which Elizabeth found "horribly disagreeable." At that beautiful season she found "such bothersome court duties even more unbearable." But when the Queen of the Hellenes asked to see her horses, and Elizabeth had them all led out, she decided that the Queen was very nice and sympathetic. Her particular delight at this time was circus horses. She took some with her to Ischl and spent part of every day training them. She even wanted to have a little riding school built, "tucked away in the garden where nobody can see it."

This was the year in which war broke out between Serbia and Turkey, and now that Andrássy found what worries had been brought upon him by his office as Minister for Foreign Affairs, he saw that Her Majesty had lured him into a regular witches' caldron. But by this time Elizabeth no longer exerted the slightest political influence. Her interference was confined to nonpolitical matters, such as, for instance, a difference of opinion which she had with the Master of the Horse. Prince Taxis wished to allow private persons to have charge of horses belonging to the Emperor from the stud farm at Kladrub and to enter them for races during a certain period, but the Empress strongly opposed this. After some discussion he reported that it was absolutely necessary in order to encourage the breeding of thoroughbreds in the country, but Elizabeth retorted that the Emperor would never consent to such a proposal. Furious that anything should be done quite against her will, she sat down then and there and wrote to her husband as follows: "If you give in to him in this matter, I shall be seriously annoyed with you, for it has never happened to me before to be ignored in this way. . . . I no longer interfere in politics, but I should really like to have some voice in matters of this kind, in which the true details never reach your ears."

Francis Joseph was alarmed and gave way to her entirely, especially as this question about horses was a matter of indifference to him in the midst of all the complications of foreign politics. He was just arranging to meet the Tsar at Reichstadt in Bohemia, to discuss the situation developing out of the Serbo-Turkish War and the rising in Bulgaria and define the policy of the two empires in the Eastern Question. "I wonder whether anything sensible will come of this visit to Reichstadt," was Elizabeth's comment in her letter to him on July 5, 1876. "I am afraid the great crash that Néné always prophesied is coming now. . . . I am sending word to Andrássy that he is to persuade you to come to Feldafing. After your great mind has been so much overtaxed in the Empire, you will certainly need to have it relaxed by the family at Possi." The Emperor could not get away, however, and she had to travel to her old home without him, accompanied by her latest pet, a fine sheep dog named Plato, who now took Shadow's place. A brief visit to the King of Bavaria and she could then settle down to "family routine" (*Familiengewurstel*), as she called it. Everybody was in a good humor, and the Landgravine Fürstenberg had to admit that Elizabeth was more charming "than she had ever dreamed before."

Early in September the Empress made up her mind to spend another short time at Corfu, which she had found so enchanting fourteen years before. From there she paid a flying visit to Athens, where she arrived on the *Miramar* on September 9. The aged Austro-Hungarian consul was on the quay to meet her, but behaved most awkwardly, bending the knee before the Landgravine Fürstenberg, whom he took for the Empress, and finally escorting them to the capital amid a whole series of accidents. The Landgravine wondered to see Elizabeth endure all this tactlessness without a word. In the Empress' place, she said, she would long since have lost all patience. At last Baron Eisenstein arrived from the Embassy, and in a trice everything was changed. A plan was devised in a moment, and the diplomat showed them around, explaining and arranging everything, the Empress following him with the greatest interest. All that was modern struck her as wretched and dismal, but all that was antique, however ruined, she took as evidence of a glorious and irrecoverable age.

On the way home from Athens the *Miramar* ran into heavy weather, and everybody was seasick except the Empress, who was amused at all the "sea corpses" (*Meerleichen*) surrounding her. On the thirteenth, after yet another short visit to Corfu, she returned to her residence at Miramar near Trieste, and then went straight on to Gödöllö for the hunting, but she carried away with her from Corfu an overmastering longing for that beautiful island.

There was a large party again at Gödöllö, including Duke Ludwig with his wife and daughter. His wife, the Baroness Wallersee, formerly an actress named Mendel, the daughter of a court manservant, was good-natured, modest, tactful, and quiet. Everybody liked her, but the Duke made her life no easy one with what the Countess Festetics called his incessant "pretensions" (*Faxen*). Although Elizabeth was fond of her brother, she remarked to the Countess: "It is a good thing that Henriette is his wife, for anybody else would long since have left him, and he is happy with her." She took great interest in her brother's daughter Marie, who was now eighteen and was known as the Freiin (Baroness) von Wallersee, because her parents' marriage was morganatic. Elizabeth had romantic views and meant to show that she was above all prejudice. She was very nice to the little "morganatic niece," hoping to find a really faithful and devoted friend in her young kinswoman. Marie Wallersee was introduced to the imperial family, and among others to the Crown Prince, who was now sixteen, but much older than his age both mentally and physically. The Countess Festetics watched the young girl with a distrustful eye. There was something about her—she could hardly say what—that was not sympathetic to her. Here again she displayed that instinct which warned her when something was likely to happen that would not be for the Empress' good. "I find Marie Wallersee pretty," she wrote in her diary on September 28, 1876. "I wish I liked her, I do like her in many ways, but—but what? There is something which pulls me up short, I can hardly trust myself to write it down for fear of doing her an injustice. I have a feeling—I write in the kindest spirit—that she is not true, not sincere, as though she had 'the talent of an actress.' "

Among those invited to Gödöllö that year for the hunting was Captain Middleton, the Empress' "pilot" in the English hunting field. By this time he was as enthusiastic as everybody else about the Empress, both as a woman and a horsewoman. He was an ugly man, but cut a good figure on horseback, thanks to his splendid seat. He was a pleasant, natural soldier, but very deaf. However, the Empress, who liked him, said that it did not matter, for after all she heard what he said and had no need to make conversation herself. Francis Joseph found Middleton very pleasant, too, and everybody laughed at his bad German and way of confusing words. Hunting and shooting occupied every day, accompanied, as usual, by innumerable intrigues. "Everybody wishes to be Master," said Elizabeth, "just as in a ministry everybody wants to be *elnök* (President)." The Empress was on horseback almost all day. She visited the stud farms at Kisber and Kladrub and held regular receptions in her riding school at Gödöllö, where she went when there was no hunting and rode different horses for hours or watched the gentlemen jumping. Marie Festetics played the piano while they rode. Elizabeth regretted having to return to Buda in January. "It is all very well for you," she wrote to her mother. "You can live as you please in Munich, and that is why town is not so distasteful to you as it is to me." In this she resembled Ludwig II of Bavaria, who wrote to her son Rudolf that year: "I long so much to stay in some beautiful spot with fresh, healthy air, for being shut up in town does not suit me at all."

When, in February, 1877, Elizabeth had to return to Vienna, "where nothing but plagues (*Plagen*) awaited her," as she said, she comforted herself with the thought of taking lessons in *haute école* riding in the world-famous Spanish court riding school, the only one of its sort in the world, after which, in March, there would be coursing on the imperial estates at Göding.

All this hunting and riding were the outward signs of that nervous unrest which had been growing on Elizabeth during the last few years and was increased by her exaggerated solicitude for little Valerie. Those about the Empress were worried by her excessive love for the child. If Valerie had a slight cough, all plans were canceled in a moment. Elizabeth's relations with Francis Joseph were excellent at this time and based on deep feeling. The Emperor's love for his wife was touching, and he never ceased to repeat to her: "You are the good angel of my life." Elizabeth had a thousand ways of attaching him to her. Her oddities sometimes disconcerted him, but she never bored him. She knew how to make herself desirable without any pose, for her whole being was instinct with this power, and Francis Joseph was still as susceptible to her charm as a young lover. He smilingly tolerated all her vagaries, except when they were too extreme. For instance, when Elizabeth sent for a pair of negresses who were Siamese twins, he refused to see them, nor could he understand her latest pet, a hideous little negro called "Rustimo," presented to her by the Khedive. Little Valerie, to whom this "black devil" was given as a playmate, was afraid of him and took some time to grow accustomed to him, while the whole household was up in arms, the tutors, masters, and ladies in waiting refusing to ride in the same carriage with him or have anything to do with him. The Countess Fürstenberg always wrote of him as "that grinning little monster," or the "black monkey," and Marie Festetics said he was a little above the beasts, but less than human.

Elizabeth now interested herself in the future of Marie Wallersee. A certain Count Georg Larisch had been attracted to the young girl, and Marie Festetics was instructed to take her to Solza and present her to his family, a mission which was as little to her taste as the Baroness Wallersee herself. "There is something about her," she wrote in her diary, "which I find uncomfortable, though she is very pretty. She seems to take an interest in everything concerned with art. But I am not absolutely sure that this is not art, too." The Crown Prince, who was now nineteen, also showed a marked dislike for Marie Wallersee. She was betrothed to Count Larisch on September 8, though the Countess Festetics' impression was that the Baroness did not care very much for her fiancé; but the Empress' opinion was that if the others liked the marriage, then she was content with it too.

After this interlude riding, hunting, and shooting were resumed at Gödöllö, the Crown Prince taking part in these amusements as indefatigably as his mother. He would rise before dawn to go out after eagles, and preferred shooting to all other forms of sport. Thanks to constant practice and the wide choice of splendid mounts at her disposal, Elizabeth had a perfect mastery of the technique of the hunting field and was now so absorbed in this sport that her one dream was to spend another hunting season in England. Her visit was fixed for the end of the year, and this time the Crown Prince was to accompany her, in order to acquire the final polish. His majority having now been proclaimed and his Household appointed, he was free from the supervision of the innumerable tutors who had crammed him with more knowledge than was good for him. One of his tutors, Max, Baron Walterskirchen, uttered a serious warning:* "You have a splendid, joyous youth behind you, so you have no need to drain the cup of life greedily like one long parched with thirst. Enjoy the pleasures of life, but in moderation. . . ." But Rudolf turned a deaf ear to these well-meant words.

Elizabeth did not want Rudolf to ride to hounds in England. She knew what qualities this required, and dreaded an

* See Mitis, *op. cit.*, p. 310.

accident, for his riding was far inferior to hers. Rudolf promised to respect his mother's wishes, and shortly after Christmas the Empress traveled to London by way of Munich.

This time she had rented a very fine hunting box for six weeks at Cottesbrooke, Northamptonshire, near Lord Spencer's country house, and indulged her passion for riding to her heart's content. Day after day she hunted the fox or the stag, feeling singularly at ease in her new surroundings. To these chivalrous English gentlemen and consummate sportsmen, with their unbounded hospitality, the Empress was simply a beautiful, original, and charming woman, a brilliant rider and sportswoman. In such circles she was far removed from all gossip, envy, and political spite. The only people from Austria-Hungary who were present were personally devoted to her, especially Rudolf Liechtenstein, the "handsome prince," or "*szépherczeg*" as he was called in Magyar. In addition to him there were the Kinskys, Count Franz Clam, old Count Larisch, and of course the doughty Bay Middleton, too, for he was again to pilot the Empress. In the hall of the house hung a fine picture, Gainsborough's "White Lady," a lovely figure which, people said, might almost have been Elizabeth herself. The whole party was a gay one; the Empress was enjoying herself, everybody rode, hunted, and danced, and many were the invitations to countryseats in the neighborhood. The Empress' sunny, lovable, simple nature triumphed everywhere and exerted its spell, for here she was free from all fear of what her entourage might think, and everybody declared her to be "every inch an empress."

At nine in the morning there would be the meet, during which she enjoyed the views of rich green meadows and parks where stood ancient and often historic houses with famous hunting traditions; the members of the hunt in their pink coats, mounted on perfectly groomed horses, quivering with excitement at the prospect of the run; the slender, elegant ladies with their becoming, close-fitting habits; and, as the center of interest, the hounds, held in check with difficulty by the huntsmen, while the Master, cool and composed, saw to it that all was in order. Breakfast would be ready in the hall of the house, and when the Empress appeared everyone fell silent, as though spellbound, and bowed before the "fairy queen." Her host led her to the room set apart for her, where she arranged her habit and hastily took some refreshment. When she came out, Bay would be waiting on his steeplechaser Minotaur, with her manager Bayzand beside him, and behind them her Austrian "colony." Assisted by Bay, the Empress would swing herself lightly into the saddle, and the hunt moved off, while Marie Festetics stood looking after the riders and thinking: "God grant that my beloved Empress return home whole and sound." And this was no baseless fear, as Elizabeth's letters to the Emperor plainly show. During the very first runs in January the most experienced riders were thrown and Count Franz Clam had a fall, breaking his jaw and tearing open his face. The brimming ditches on the far side of difficult hedges were often, as Elizabeth puts it, "peopled" with ladies and gentlemen who had had a fall. But little she minded. The fox gave them runs of forty or fifty minutes over the springy turf. Up and down the gently swelling hills she rode at a good gallop, and over "appetizing" hedges with no ditches. In fact, she was in her element. "I thought of you so much," she wrote to Francis Joseph. "If only we could share and share alike, you one day and I the next. I am always telling Lord Spencer how much you would enjoy it. I like him very much, he is so nice and natural, and I think that if ever he pays us a visit you will like him, too."

Bay Middleton led her skilfully and sensibly, forcibly preventing her from taking jumps that were too much for her.

She would complain to Francis Joseph when Middleton had "a terribly prudent day" and insisted on dismounting, tearing his coat in the effort to break down difficult places in the hedges by pushing through them backwards. Often, too, the Empress' horse was more spirited than his and outdistanced him. On one occasion Elizabeth jumped three gigantic hedges one after the other, while Middleton went at the third so hard that he jumped into it and fell. He was back in the saddle again in a trice, but the Empress had to check her career and a few minutes were lost. She was always eager to get to the front and follow right behind the hounds; for the first rider to be in at the death got the brush, and she meant to earn it honestly and not through favor. At times, when the poor hard-pressed foxes slipped from one cover to another by the most devious ways, the field would split up. "I saw no more of Kálmán Almássy for the rest of the run," wrote Elizabeth to the Emperor on January 25, 1878. "Heini's (Count Heinrich Larisch's) horse was worn out, and Rudi Liechtenstein's kept refusing, so they could only follow along the road when the run was all over. The fox was seen several times, but at last he was lost, which was no wonder, with all those hedges and places to hide in; besides, the last time the huntsman was nowhere about, nor did I see anything more of the whips. The Master, too, a very disagreeable man, was more behind me than in front of me. For the rest, Heini tells me some of the best riders were left behind yesterday, tired out by the heavy going, though it was almost all grass. But thanks to your good Bravo, I did not once notice it; he simply flew and was full of fire. Colonel Middleton was delighted with him. If only you had been riding him! He takes big obstacles splendidly, but he almost came down at two little tangled hedges with ditches. . . . If only you were here! I say it every day I hunt, and how popular you would be for your riding and the way you understand hunting. But it would be dangerous, for you would not allow yourself to be kept in leading strings (*Hofmeistern*) by Captain Middleton, but would go dashing over everything without waiting for him to see whether it were too deep or too broad."

During the hunting season the Queen of Naples also came on a visit to the Empress with her husband, but English society did not find her by any means as sympathetic as her sister Elizabeth. She, too, was undeniably beautiful, with her dark, velvety almond eyes, and equally dark lashes, which made them startlingly effective, but she lacked the Empress' sweetness and kindliness and radiant smile, and her pointed nose and chin gave her a rather satyrlike expression. The Countess Marie Festetics did not care for her much and pitied the King, who deprived himself of everything so that his wife might spend money with both hands. "Pointed nose and pointed chin," she writes in her diary. "There sits the devil in between." The Queen was annoyed with Middleton for declining to pilot her in the hunting field, so she found all the fault she could with him and even hinted to the Crown Prince, whom she met in London, that the Englishman was too much in love with the Empress. For a time the Crown Prince believed this gossip and was positively rude to the Captain, till he was undeceived. The Empress' beauty so completely turned all men's heads that people were only too ready to believe talk of that sort, even when there was not a particle of truth in it. Elizabeth had long been used to this, and no longer let it upset her as it had in earlier days; but this attempt to slander her to her son made her indignant, though she never found out who was really at the bottom of it.

During Elizabeth's stay at Cottesbrooke Pope Pius IX died in Rome on February 7, 1878. Happening to be indisposed at the time, she did not hunt for a week and wrote to Francis Joseph: "Since I am not hunting for a few days people will say it is on account of the Pope. So it is most opportune."

In the middle of February she left for home. The business with Rudolf had upset and annoyed her and spoiled her pleasure in England and hunting. An American dentist named Burridge, whom the Queen of Naples had persuaded her to employ, had played an unpleasant part in this gossip. Some remark made by the Crown Prince, who had a rather hasty tongue, was exaggerated and distorted for the purpose of sowing discord between mother and son. This cut Elizabeth to the heart, and she returned home filled with bitterness.

Meanwhile the Russo-Turkish War of 1878 had come to an end, and victorious Russia had been with difficulty prevented from occupying Constantinople. Strong differences of opinion were felt at the court of Vienna. The Archduke Albrecht, with his sound political sense, was on the side of the Tsar, but again Andrássy got his way. The Congress of Berlin deprived Russia of the fruits of victory, and the hostility between Austria-Hungary and Russia was still further embittered. But Andrássy succeeded in concealing his mistake by acquisitions of territory, and the fateful occupation of Bosnia and Herzegovina took place. Nowadays Elizabeth refrained most carefully from interfering in politics, so she confined herself to a few warning words on hearing of the occupation. "Do not send too many Russophiles to Bosnia," she said to Francis Joseph, "such as Croats, Bohemians, etc." She had small confidence in the trustworthiness of the Slav peoples in the monarchy with whom her husband was inclined to effect a *rapprochement* in opposition to Andrássy's advice.

That summer Lord and Lady Spencer were among her guests at Ischl, after which she went on to Tegernsee, where her parents were to celebrate their golden wedding on September 9. The celebrations were clouded by bad news of King

Ludwig's brother, who was now declared hopelessly insane, while the King himself was growing so abnormal that the whole country feared the same fate for him, too.

On returning to Schönbrunn, Elizabeth devoted herself to visiting the soldiers wounded in the Bosnian campaign. In the middle of September she returned to Gödöllö for the shooting season, and was joined by the Crown Prince, Lord and Lady Spencer, Bay Middleton, and Heinrich Larisch. But Francis Joseph could seldom leave Vienna, in spite of her protests. "You send everyone else away on leave," she wrote to him, "but you never think about yourself, and that is not wise."

Among her beloved horses at Gödöllö were a splendid pair of greys named "Flick" and "Flock" which she was training herself. She would stand in the middle of her little riding school with bread and sugar; the horses were turned loose into it on all sides and galloped up to their mistress, who always had something good to give them. They would stop short in front of her, and her great amusement was to take strangers into the riding school and see how startled they were when the horses suddenly came rushing in.

Elizabeth would sometimes ask her secretary to read her the more striking letters she received, most of which were begging letters. A certain Ferdinand Aufrichtig, for instance, wrote and asked her to wear imitation jewelry, for if she made it the fashion, this would help industry and relieve the pockets of husbands in general. Another person, this time a Frenchman, alleged that he had discovered a remedy for cancer, and promised to send it to her on receipt of five hundred thousand francs, paid in advance. And she could not help laughing at a bequest from an Italian gentleman, whose will provided that every year so long as she lived she should be sent a loaf of the famous Milanese fancy bread known as *panettone*.

On December 11 the Empress was seriously alarmed by an accident to the Crown Prince, who shot himself in the left hand with a miniature rifle. "That is because he was never taught any other pastime but that stupid shooting," was Marie Festetics' indignant comment. "Every creature that breathes or has wings is doomed to death. Such men become possessed by a sort of lust for killing, and it seems to me so unnecessary. Even as a child—and a charming little fellow he was—he would shoot bullfinches from his window, and the Archduchess Valerie, who had a tender little heart, would cry bitterly." The wound was not serious and soon healed, but by this time Elizabeth had no influence whatever over her son. His real character was beginning to come out—passionate, uncontrollable, reckless.

The court balls in Vienna in the winter of 1879 and "all the other plagues which one has to endure here" made her long to cross the Channel again for hunting, which had been such a joy to her in recent years. But England was no longer enough for her. She had heard that the hunting there was only a feeble copy of what went on in Ireland. There, and there only, she heard, was the huntsman's paradise, and those who had not hunted the fox and the stag in Ireland did not know what hunting meant. The Empress' headquarters were at Lord Langford's hospitable country house in County Meath, and the trusty friends of former years were again at her side. The country was beautiful, with wide stretches of vivid green grass, but the land was for the most part untilled, quite unlike England. The people lived by breeding cattle, so the pastures were surrounded by hedges, which were excellent for jumping. Hunting here was far more dangerous than in England, and Marie Festetics trembled for her mistress more than ever. "There are such high drops," she wrote, "such deep ditches, and doubles too, and Irish banks and walls and God knows what besides, enough to break one's arms, legs, and neck. Nowhere have I heard so much about broken limbs as here, and every day I see somebody carried off the field. Bayzand had a really nasty fall, Middleton turned head over heels, horse and all, and Lord Langford too, and so it goes on. The Empress has splendid horses. Domino is the best, a magnificent black, which bolted with its mistress on the very first day, to Lord Spencer's horror. The field was surrounded by obstacles, and everybody's hair stood on end as they wondered what she would do. But she had the presence of mind to give her horse its head, and fortunately it came to a few ditches, so that she soon regained control of it and galloped calmly back again. There is only *one* opinion about her, but really, my hair is always on end."

There were often more than a hundred riders in the field, but not in pink coats, as in England, for it was not the custom here. The many falls were to be attributed to the fact that people rode horses which were not fully trained, but the Empress' mounts had been carefully chosen. Horses are like cats, they must be allowed to go as they like, and Elizabeth had always known that. Broad ditches full of water were delicate morsels to her, and when she came to difficult banks and high obstacles she would slacken the reins and let her horse take the jump in its own way, for she had an easy, supple seat, entirely independent of the hands. Once she was riding a magnificent grey mare, which was going splendidly, when she had to jump a sunk fence down in a ditch. On another occasion after a particularly sharp run, in which the best riders in Ireland found it hard to keep up, Middleton was beside himself with pride, for not more than four or five others had finished besides him and the Empress.

Once the kill took place just beyond a high wall. The whole field came leaping across, led by the Master and the Empress, and suddenly found themselves in the presence of an assembly of reverend gentlemen. They had jumped into the garden of Maynooth College. The fathers wrapped a priest's cloak around Elizabeth's shoulders, for she was wet through, and pressed her to enter the refectory, where some fine wine and a delicious lunch were served. Everybody was delighted at this unexpected distraction. Shortly afterwards Elizabeth expressed her gratitude by sending the seminary a statue of St. George. She felt much more at ease here than in England; the Queen of Naples not being present, there were none of the little irritations that had spoiled the previous year. Besides, in this Catholic country the Empress was greeted not only as a horsewoman, but as the first lady in a great Catholic empire. Wherever she went the poorest villagers put on their best clothes and triumphal arches appeared. There was soon such a cult of the Empress that she had to be rather careful, for in view of the antagonism between the English and Irish, between Protestants and Catholics, the jealousy of Queen Victoria and her court might be aroused.

But she was absorbed in horses. Even the most experienced masters of hounds, who were no flatterers, said that she was a wonder, and that they had never seen such riding. Once after a day's hunting Elizabeth and Rudolf Liechtenstein passed a racecourse where one of the great steeplechases had recently taken place. They tried the obstacles, and before the Prince could stop her Elizabeth was over them all.

She took the "stickiest" (*klebrigsten*) jumps as though they were child's play. Even her pilot Middleton was often thrown. Once a fox was started in a park. "I was riding Easton," wrote Elizabeth to Francis Joseph. "Captain Middleton had a very awkward beast, quite out of condition. The pace was sharp and the obstacles high, so he was soon down. He came off a second time at a high, steep bank; the horse went on jumping, but was so pumped that it came down on its head, I had to steady Easton for a moment on top so as not to jump on it, and performed this goatlike feat very cleverly. Rudi Liechtenstein fell at the same bank and had such a frightful appetite in consequence that we laughed at him all the evening. Captain Middleton said he could not give me a lead any longer, because his horse was done for, so we rode slowly to the spot where our carriages were waiting."

Next day there was another mishap. "We came to a bank with a ditch," relates Elizabeth, "and Captain Middleton fell in. While still standing on his head, he called out 'All right' quite cheerfully, and I got across perfectly easily. The ditch was very much overgrown, so his horse had made a mistake and jumped into the middle of it instead of over it, but mine could see the ditch through the hole which he had made."

Everybody came down, one after the other, and at last it was Elizabeth's turn. This was late in March, during one of the last runs of the season, and the Empress was riding her gallant grey mare, which had so often carried her over the worst obstacles. But now she came to an insignificant, overgrown little ditch, and the mare unsuspectingly took off too late and fell on the opposite side. Elizabeth jumped quickly to the ground, the mare struggled to its feet without anybody's help, and in a moment Elizabeth was mounted again and off to join the rest of the field.

In the midst of her enjoyment the Empress received disastrous news from home. The town of Szegedin had been half destroyed by floods. She was deeply shocked and wanted to start for home at once. "Owing to the sad news from Szegedin," she at once wrote to Francis Joseph, "I have decided to leave here. . . . It was not till we saw the latest telegrams and details in the papers that we realized the full extent of the catastrophe. So I feel that it would be better for me to leave now, and you will be better pleased too. It is the greatest sacrifice I can make, but in such conditions it is necessary." She accordingly prepared to start for home, hoping that Francis Joseph would not expect her to make any visits in London. As a rule she had little thought for what her expensive tastes cost—her visit to Ireland, for instance, had cost no less than 158,337 gulden—but now she suddenly turned economical. "The Queen will not be back from Italy when I leave. The Prince of Wales has sent a message suggesting that we might meet somewhere on my way. Do you really want me to stop in London? I would gladly avoid it, to save hotel bills. Then I should have made the whole journey here and back without going to a hotel." But Francis Joseph did not want her to pay any visits; he was only glad that she had realized the necessity for coming home without his having had to give her a hint.

Both the Emperor and the Empress still looked so young and blooming that it was hardly possible to believe they had been married twenty-five years; but now Vienna prepared to celebrate their silver wedding. Elizabeth's dislike of the restraints of court life made her imagine that she was unpopular. She did not realize that outside her own circle there were millions of excellent people of all classes who were far more loyal to their sovereigns than many of those who basked in their grace and favor daily, and these days of rejoicing offered an opportunity for all classes to display their affection.

Unfortunately it rained on the anniversary of their wedding day, and the procession had to be postponed; but this did not damp the enthusiasm of the hundreds of thousands who had crowded to Vienna from every corner of the Empire. It merely meant that the brilliant pageant designed by Makart took place a little later. This tribute offered by the capital developed into an overwhelming expression of the heartfelt affection of the people of the Empire for their sovereigns, and the few critics who could not refrain from trying to depreciate the Empress passed almost unnoticed. In other places, said one malicious wit, it was customary to celebrate a silver wedding after twenty-five years of *ménage* (housekeeping) but this was after twenty-five years of *manège* (riding school). The jest was repeated to Elizabeth, but she only laughed.

After the celebrations in Vienna, the Emperor and Empress went on to Hungary, where they were received with such roars of cheering that the sceptical Landgravine Fürstenberg was stirred by the tumultuous and "almost wild" enthusiasm.

The Jubilee festivities having come to an end, life resumed its customary routine. The Empress was on horseback from early morning till late in the evening, and when she was not riding she brooded over and analyzed the people around her. The Countess Marie Festetics, whose understanding of character amounted to genius, observed with anxiety that Elizabeth was incapable of moderation, not only in activities, into which she flung herself with whole-hearted ardor, but also in her sympathies and antipathies, the trust and confidence, or mistrust and reserve which she showed toward those about her. The Countess never wearied of trying to understand her mistress. "To me," she wrote in her diary, "the Empress is like a book which one never tires of reading; the more one absorbs oneself in it, the more it fascinates one." In spite of all her love, admiration, and enthusiasm for Elizabeth's beauty, Marie Festetics' worldly wisdom and penetrating intelligence were almost prophetic. There could be no more acute analysis of the Empress' character than that which she wrote on September 14, 1878, when the future was, of course, entirely hidden from her: "The Empress is sweet and good, but she makes everything a torment to herself, and what to others is a source of pure joy becomes a source of discontent to her. She seems to me like a child in a fairy tale.

The good fairies came and each of them laid a splendid gift in her cradle—beauty, sweetness, grace, dignity, simplicity, kindness, nobility, intelligence, wit, archness, penetration, and shrewdness. But then came the bad fairy and said: 'I see that everything has been given you—everything. But I will turn these qualities against you and they shall bring you no happiness. I give you nothing, but I deprive you of one supreme good which is too little valued, but is very necessary to preserve the balance of the soul, if one is to enjoy happiness through inward harmony and one's spirit is to know peace. I deprive you of something which a man bears within him unconsciously: of moderation in your actions, occupations, thoughts, and sensibilities. Nothing shall bring you happiness, everything shall turn against you, even your beauty shall bring you nothing but sorrow. Your noble intelligence shall see so deeply into things that it will lead you astray and you will despise humanity; and thus you shall lose your faith in goodness and love, and your trust in those who are best, and give it in those very quarters where it will be abused. And so your soul shall be filled with disgust and bitterness, till you never find peace.' I often hear what is said and see that she is suffering. I am afraid I shall always prove to be right, and yet I would give my life for her happiness."

That autumn saw the resignation of Count Andrássy from the Ministry for Foreign Affairs. Much has been written on the subject, yet the real cause of his resignation remains a mystery. His own explanation was that he did not want to be either one of those ministers who cling to their post at all costs, or who are driven out because people are tired of them, but one of those who retire of their own accord when they have achieved their purpose. It might have been supposed that Elizabeth would be greatly affected by the fall of the minister whose appointment she had urged so eagerly, but she accepted it with equanimity, "for," she said, "in so doing, he remains with us all the same," thus drawing a distinction between his sympathetic personality and his politics. The Crown Prince did not like his mother's attitude. In his eyes his father was too conservative. "There was a time," he said later in the year,* "when the Empress often concerned herself with politics, whether with happy results or not I refrain from deciding, and discussed serious subjects with the Emperor from a point of view diametrically opposed to his own. But these times are past. The august lady now cares for nothing but sport, so that even this channel, through which outside opinions of a fairly liberal tinge had access to him formerly, is closed."

Elizabeth's visit to Gödöllö that autumn was again devoted entirely to horsemanship. In the morning she hunted, and in the afternoon went to her little riding school adjoining the palace, where there was music and her guests were entertained at tea, while she rode one highly trained horse after another, studied her faults, and tried to perfect her technique. She had a little red notebook in which she made daily notes on every horse and entered such rules of riding as: "Throw your body forward at the take-off," or "A firm seat, steady hands, and turn your toes in." She wrote down instructions for the *pirouette* or the *volte,* or noted that she had not succeeded in "changing legs while threading my way in and out of the benches at a gallop." She performed *lançades* and *ruades* on the splendid horse Majestoso from the imperial stud at Lippiza, and practiced all the subtleties of the *haute école.* But she studied the subject in theory as well as in practice. Innumerable works on horses and riding were added to her library at this time, with racing calendars and other books of that sort, besides volumes on gymnastics and

* See Mitis, *op. cit.*, p. 263.

the art of training the body both for sport and for general health, quite in the fashion of the present day.

The Crown Prince was full of *joie de vivre*. "If only I could live till I was a hundred!" he said to Valerie. "It is terrible to think that in the end one has got to die!" But he enjoyed life too much to cherish such thoughts long. He was a universal favorite, "too nice for words," as Marie Festetics noted, but he, too, knew no moderation. He often confided in the Countess, and these little "confidences" brought to her knowledge many things which worried her. "What temptations assail such a young man!" wrote the Countess. "Among others, I find, is Madame Vetsera . . . which ought not to be so very dangerous, for Heaven knows she is not good-looking, but she is so sly and so glad to make use of everybody. She means to get to court and advance herself and her family. Her daughters are growing up, very slowly, it is true, but she is beginning to train them in good time." The Baroness Vetsera also made advances to the Empress' ladies, to the unsuspecting Ida Ferenczy as well as the highly sceptical Countess Festetics; and when the Countess avoided her, she tried to bring the Crown Prince's influence to bear on her. Once Rudolf said suddenly to the Countess Festetics: "The Baroness Vetsera will come and call upon you tomorrow evening if you will allow her." But the Countess replied with a laugh: "Oh, no, Your Imperial Highness, I cannot allow it. She may make assignations with Your Imperial Highness elsewhere, but not in my sitting room. I have no desire for her society. I have kept her at arm's length so far, and shall continue to do so." He laughed and accepted her decision, but the Baroness did not desist from her efforts. The Empress watched the whole thing with great annoyance, and even the Emperor remarked at dinner on December 3, 1879: "The way that woman behaves with Rudolf is unbelievable. She is always in close pursuit of him. Today she has actually sent him a present." And turning to the Countess Festetics, he added: "It seems to me that you have rather an antipathy for her, have you not, Countess?" "Yes, Your Majesty, I have," was the reply.

In February, 1880, the Empress was again overcome with longing for the Emerald Isle and the splendid hunting which had given her such pleasure the previous year. Leaving a bleak winter behind her in Bavaria, where she broke her journey, she arrived in Ireland, at Summerhill, on a warm spring day. The day after her arrival there was a hard day's staghunting. "I rode Domino," she wrote to the Emperor. "Owing to the pouring rain during the night, the going was very heavy. We found at once and were off at a sharp pace, over innumerable obstacles of every sort. Middleton and I kept up for an hour and twenty minutes. Though Bayzand was riding a good horse, which he praises up to the skies, he pitched over a bank into the field beyond and hurt his foot. . . . He is now in bed with an ice bag on his ankle, and desperate at being prevented from riding. Rudi Liechtenstein came down too, but did not hurt himself, and our host, Lord Langford, fell on his face and has not been able to swallow very well since." Lord Langford fell once at a ditch full of water and after that at an insignificant little ditch, where his horse broke its back, so Francis Joseph had every reason to be anxious about the Empress.

On the seventeenth she wrote again: "Staghunting at some distance from here, near Dublin, so there was an enormous field. Thanks to a few big jumps right at the beginning, we got away from the crowd at once and had a wonderful start. Then came a ditch for which one had to take off from the road; it was not so very wide, but the take-off needed a horse better accustomed to this sort of thing, and Middleton's had hunted more in England than here, so it jumped too soon and fell in. He was soon out again himself, though somewhat out of breath, or, as they say here, with the wind knocked out of him, but by the time he had pulled his horse out again, of course the hounds were far away." The same thing happened on the tenth. "The pace was very sharp from the first; there were a number of jumps, and big ones, too, but the ditches were not overgrown, we came to only one double, a bank broken by a ditch in the middle and on the far side of it a boggy ditch, quite green, over which both Middleton and I fell, but well clear of it, on the other side of the bog, so that we did not get wet, and the ground was soft. Several people must have fallen in, so Tom told me later, but I did not see them, for of course I rode on at once. I saw Lord Langford standing by another ditch fishing for his horse."

Middleton's brown horse, which had never hunted in Ireland before, refused so often that he was sometimes left far behind and the Empress had to follow the lead of Tom Healy, who had taken the place of her manager Bayzand after his injury. Elizabeth's horse went splendidly and made no mistakes, so that even Tom Healy had difficulty in keeping up with her. When he too fell for the second time, the Empress gave up hunting for the rest of the day, as by that time the horses were tired out. Everybody was nervous about her. Though she had the best of horses, and rode none in which she had not absolute confidence, she was far too daring. Liechtenstein saw her take a ditch which he considered to be the biggest jump he had ever seen in Ireland. The horses pulled so badly that Elizabeth rode without gloves, and the reins chafed her hands till they were sore. Minor accidents were constantly happening in the field all around her. "Within a few minutes," she wrote to the Emperor on the nineteenth, "we were over some water, and then came a bank, behind which was a full ditch. It was not a very nice jump, so I waited to see how Middleton would take it. But instead of jumping straight, his mare pitched head over heels to the left into the water, where the ditch, with a lot of tangled bushes, formed the corner of the road. Since the way was free before me, I got over safely, and so did Tom, who jumped at the same moment and hurried to help Middleton, who was hanging head downwards, with his foot so fast in the stirrup that he could not have got up again by himself."

Two days later Elizabeth's pilot was again unlucky. "Though we were really invited to hunt the fox with the Kildare, the gentlemen decided yesterday evening that we must go staghunting instead, if only to give the slip to all the inquisitive persons who come out in crowds by special train when I am expected anywhere at a meet. All the evening and early this morning Middleton and Lord Langford were laughing at the thought of taking them in like this. A lady named Miss Hussey fell in front of me, and she and her grey simply rolled over and over. Later on she fell into the water, too, but for all that she was in at the death. Middleton had another fall . . . and remained with his foot caught in the stirrup again, in a way that was almost more alarming than the other day, for his horse wanted to go on, but my Tom saved him again." When Middleton appeared at supper that night at Summerhill, a great cheer went up, and somebody improvised a poem in honor of Elizabeth:*

> *The Queen of the Chase!*
> *The Queen! Yes, the Empress!*
> *Look, look, how she flies,*
> *With a hand that never fails*
> *And a pluck that never dies.*
> *The best man in England can't lead her—he's down!*
> *"Bay" Middleton's back is done beautifully brown.*

* See *British Hunts and Huntsmen* (London, 1909), p. 50.

Hark horn and hark halloa!
Come on for a place!
He must ride who would follow
The Queen of the Chase!

Middleton could take this jest in good part, for he had proved his skill by winning countless steeplechases, and continued to do so afterwards. He won no less than twenty-nine races, eleven in succession, on his mare Lady of the Harem. If such a man as this came down so often, it can be imagined what the country was like. But the keener the sport, the more Elizabeth delighted in it. Here she was on holiday, enjoying perfect liberty, peace, and independence; but here, too, she showed her lack of moderation. For the moment her passion for hunting was uppermost, but suddenly there might be a change and something else would take its place, only to be equally overdone.

"The great advantage of Ireland," Elizabeth considered, "is that it has no Royal Highnesses." It "bored her terribly," she wrote to her mother, when she had to go and see the Queen at Windsor again on her way home; but on this occasion it was all the more desirable, because people in England did not look with much favor on the Empress' second visit to Ireland. Throughout large parts of the island there was discontent with English rule, and distress on account of the bad harvest. Tenants were not paying their landlords, and there was talk of Home Rule. Though nothing of the sort was to be noticed in the neighborhood of Summerhill, the western part of the island was seething with unrest. At such a time the Empress' travels in search of pleasure were hardly timely, so she started for home sooner than usual, leaving Lord Langford's on March 7 in glorious weather.

On March 10, while she was still in London, Elizabeth was brought a telegram, on opening which she turned deathly pale. The Countess Festetics inquired in trepidation what was the matter. "The Crown Prince is betrothed to Princess Stephanie," was the reply. "Thank God," said the lady in waiting, "that it is not news of some disaster." But the Empress answered agitatedly: "Heaven send that it be not one." Her impression was that the whole thing was premature, for the Crown Prince was only twenty-two, and his future wife only fifteen.

When she had luncheon at Windsor, the stateliness of everything impressed her, but the stout little Queen was again embarrassed beside the tall, slender Empress. Lord Beaconsfield was presented to her. She thought him ugly, but interesting and entertaining. On her way home the Empress had to visit Brussels, to make the acquaintance of her son's affianced bride; but, as was her custom, she had asked that there should be no State reception. She and her party traveled by night and were to reach Brussels punctually at eight o'clock in the morning. Everybody on the train was asleep, when suddenly the thunder of cannon, followed by the national anthem and cheering, was heard in the darkness. The whole party started up from their beds. There were no servants in readiness, no clothes, and no lights. Everybody imagined that they had already arrived in Brussels. "What ever is happening?" they asked. "Her Majesty is still in bed." They all pulled on garments of some sort or another, Nopcsa hurried out of his sleeping compartment in full dress and a silk hat, and hastily attired lady's maids ran to and fro. At last the incident was explained. The train had arrived at Tournai, on the Belgian frontier, at four o'clock in the morning, and this welcome was intended for the fiancé's mother. They returned to bed again till eight o'clock, when a similar din was heard, and this time it was really Brussels. The Crown Prince was on the platform with his future bride and all the royal family. Elizabeth appeared, looking exquisite in a dark blue costume trimmed with sable, and the Crown Prince, who was really moved, fell on his mother's neck. Next came his fiancée, young, fresh, and undeveloped, and not very well dressed, a mere child with a child's complexion. Everybody admired the Empress, but there was nothing to appeal to her heart during the visit. She returned home in a rather grave mood and remarked to Francis Joseph: "If only it turns out well!" But he calmed her fears, saying: "You always worry over things far too much."

Rudolf soon became aware of her feeling and confided to Colonel Latour that she was not so nice to him as before.* He did not hesitate to criticize his parents in an outspoken way, and remarked to Latour on one occasion that his mother was "an idle, but thoroughly clever woman."

Once more there were public rejoicings in Vienna. Elizabeth most enjoyed a tournament arranged by the nobility, with costumes in the style of the Emperor Maximilian. She went on to Buda with a sigh of relief, but here another ordeal awaited her, when for the first time in her life she took the chair at a meeting of the Red Cross Society, of which she was patroness. On such occasions she always had to struggle against her inveterate shyness, the extent of which was only guessed by her intimates, and she particularly disliked appearing in public when she felt that it was for the purpose of extorting contributions. Such occasions made no appeal to her vanity, which was of quite a different order. She loved the knowledge that she was beautiful, but being stared at caused her actual physical pain. She took her beauty quite naturally, and would have liked to enjoy this heaven-sent gift without paying for it with discomforts.

During her visit to Bavaria that summer she called upon Ludwig II at Schloss Berg on the Starnbergersee, and, find-

* From a letter in the State Archives, Vienna.

ing him not at home, left a spray of jasmine as a visiting card. King Ludwig was enchanted at this attention and wrote her such a rapturous letter that she sent him a whole wreath of the flowers, with a photograph of little Valerie. The child was not particularly pretty at this time, but had an unusually affectionate, warm-hearted, and thoughtful nature, though she suffered severely from the family malady of excessive shyness or "*Genation*" (from the French *gêne*), as she had already begun to call it in 1877, when she started her diary at the age of nine.

Valerie found it hard to reconcile herself to her brother's betrothal. "Nazi, that boy!" she wrote in red ink—Nazi being the nickname she had invented for him—"Nazi, who only a few years ago used to make a light luncheon of the bullfinches which he had shot himself, Nazi, who used to tease me so . . . betrothed!" Valerie's shyness prevented her from showing much affection to those around her, and this explains why the Empress' "one and only" little girl was often misjudged in early childhood. Elizabeth was the one person who knew her daughter as she really was; she was only happy when with the little girl or on horseback; at other times she felt a strange unrest and had frequent fits of low spirits. On All Souls' Day she said to Marie Festetics: "It is often so sad here upon earth, and hard though it is to pass from life to death, I am sure that nobody would choose to come back, even if he could." But such moods are difficult to reconcile with her outward life.

At the parties given for Valerie, her parents joined in the games as if they had been children themselves and on such occasions their family life was both happy and delightful. But on leaving this atmosphere, Elizabeth was once more tormented by her distrust of humanity. She did not make fun of people or tell unkind tales about them, but if she felt people to be ill-disposed toward her, though this might be due to a misunderstanding, she was far too quick to treat them with coldness, and even contempt. She also showed slight symptoms of that "persecution mania" from which so many people suffer, and then she would seek refuge with her adored Valerie. Her affection for the child brought out all that was deepest in her nature, but even her love was full of exaggeration and consequently lacking in harmony. Her beauty and sweetness surrounded her, as it were, with an aureole. Whether she sat on the throne at the Emperor's side, or bent the knee before the altar, whether she wore a court train or walked about the garden in a short skirt, whether she was riding, playing, or drinking milk, she remained a true empress, and that, as the Countess Festetics remarks, not by reason of artificial etiquette and formality of bearing, but through that infinite grace with which God had endowed her.

The Crown Prince's wedding now began to be discussed at court but his fiancée was still such an unformed child that, though the Belgian side wished to hurry on the marriage, the date which had been fixed had to be postponed.

In the autumn Lord Langford was the guest of the Emperor and Empress at Gödöllö, and he persuaded Elizabeth to cross the Channel again in the following year. She would have preferred to go to Ireland, but it was represented to her that this was not advisable on political grounds. Another visit from a Catholic sovereign might be interpreted by Catholic Ireland as encouragement to the Home Rule movement and a demonstration against the British Government; so this time Elizabeth decided to go to England again, to Lord Combermere's house in Cheshire.

A thick fog was lying over the country when she arrived on February 15, 1881. She went at once to the stables to visit the horses she had left there during the winter. She was homesick for Ireland, but was more likely to get back to

Austria again safe and sound from a place where the country was not so rough. Middleton had been very ill during the winter, but was now recovered and staying at Lord Combermere's. The house had originally been an old abbey, built in the year 1132 and altered for William of Orange in 1682, the room in which he had slept being painted orange in his honor. This room was allotted to Marie Festetics. Even the furniture was orange, and the bed in which the Prince of Orange had slept was hung with curtains of the same shade. The bed was so high that, to Elizabeth's great amusement, the Countess had to climb on a chair and jump up at the risk of breaking her neck. She felt as if she were living in an orange rind turned inside out. The house was surrounded by splendid woods of oaks and lime trees. The master of a neighboring pack with which the Empress hunted was Lord Stafford, and the field was much larger than in Ireland, as many as a hundred and fifty people turning out; but Elizabeth found the jumps insignificant, though neither Rudolf Liechtenstein nor Middleton considered them so very harmless, and even with such a big field barely twenty were in at the death. It amused Elizabeth to see how the children of one Master of Hounds—"Sir Whyn,"* as she calls him, nicknamed "the Prince *in* Wales"—two dear little girls of eight and fourteen, joined in the hunt. When the Countess Festetics asked in alarm: "But who looks after the children?" the Master replied: "Oh, everybody does."

The Empress would often ride three horses in the course of the day, and would not get home till half past five in the afternoon, in addition to which she did not neglect her usual gymnastics morning and evening. She was excessively slender and ate too little, and all this had a bad effect upon her

* Sir Watkin Williams Wynn of Wynnstay, 6th baronet, who was descended from the Princes of North Wales, and had his own hounds. *Translator's Note.*

nerves. Though she tired herself out, or perhaps because of this, she often had little refreshing sleep. But she delighted in the countryside with its deep, clear lake, rich, velvety lawns, meadows, cedars and cypresses, cork oaks, and conifers. The English gentry vied with one another in their hospitality, yet she no longer found so much pleasure in riding as in past years, and became more and more difficult to please in the matter of horses. Her fondness for hunting was severely judged by many people. A certain Herr Friedrich of Rotterdam, for instance, wrote her an ironical letter, requesting her to advance him the cost of one day's hunting in England to enable him to carry on his business. A malicious article in a Socialist newspaper gave great offense to the Controller of her Household, but Elizabeth had long since grown accustomed to such attacks. "The only thing that surprises me now," she wrote to Frau von Ferenczy from Combermere Abbey, "is when anybody says or writes anything nice about me."

But now came the news of the murder of the Tsar Alexander II in St. Petersburg. Elizabeth was deeply shocked and remarked to the Countess Festetics, referring to the proposal she had had from Prince Dolgoruki: "Isn't it better to be with me at Combermere than in that savage country?"

Her departure had been fixed for March 28 and she had to keep all manner of engagements in a hurry at the last moment, including the Grand National and visits to the Duke of Westminster and to the Queen at Windsor. Then she went on to Paris, where her sisters, the Queen of Naples, the Countess of Trani, and the Duchess of Alençon, were staying. The President of the Republic, Jules Grévy, called upon her at her hotel, and made an odd impression upon her because of his self-conscious behavior. Among other things, he congratulated Elizabeth upon her son's approaching marriage, adding clumsily: "When one sees you, Madame, one might almost think you"—he seemed hardly able to get out the words "Your Majesty"—"to be the bride yourself." Her ladies had great difficulty in not smiling, but Elizabeth blushed to the roots of her hair and looked at him in such astonishment that he was embarrassed, and, fearing that she might dismiss him, jumped up in a hurry and left.

While she was in Paris a telegram came fixing the date of Rudolf's wedding for May 10. The court of Vienna was rather uncomfortable at all the delays and postponements, but Elizabeth had insisted most seriously that the marriage must not take place while the bride was still a child. Now, however, it was celebrated with all the traditional splendor. For the Empress this meant, in a sense, bidding farewell to her son; now that he had a wife, he would no longer be so near to her. All she hoped was that it would make him quieter and more settled. "He is clever," wrote Marie Festetics in her diary on June 9, 1881, "but after all, he is young still and has had no guidance. But what will happen now? I feel a little anxious."

The Crown Prince was still very unbalanced, and his mind fermented with exaggeratedly liberal opinions. He had contempt for mankind, for he saw how everybody deferred to him and every woman made advances to him, from the princess to the chambermaid. He was gifted and remarkably intelligent, but he lacked moderation. Elizabeth was unaware of this, since she did not see how Rudolf behaved when he was with other people. In fact, the Emperor and Empress knew little enough about his real life; it had never been his habit to confide in anybody.

In July, while the Empress was staying with her family at Garatshausen, the King of Bavaria sent her a huge bouquet and asked when he might call upon her. He added that it must be in the evening and nobody else must see him. When little Valerie heard this she made up her mind to find out what he was like. She watched his arrival from a hiding place, but was disappointed to see how stout he was and what a fuss he made. Elizabeth wanted him to know Valerie, so she sent the child to fetch some jasmine, which was her own favorite flower and the King's too. Valerie offered him the flowers, and he had to accept them with what grace he could, but he thanked her hurriedly and indistinctly, and it was hard to say whether he or Valerie was the shyer and more embarrassed. One thing is certain: everybody was glad when the King had gone.

The rest of the summer was spent in the usual way, in riding and country house parties. In September Elizabeth was pleased to hear that Francis Joseph proposed to build a house in the Tiergarten (deer park) at Lainz, in which they could spend their "old age." In the middle of September the court moved to Gödöllö for the shooting season. Duke Ludwig was there again with the Baroness Wallersee, and Elizabeth remarked to the Countess Festetics: "I cannot treat her with enough consideration, for I cannot but be grateful to her. I am fond of my odd brother, yet even I cannot get on with him for a single day, and with a nature like his, who could? Nobody! Yet she makes him happy. It does not matter to me who she is, she suits him, so I am not in the least uncomfortable about the 'citizen's daughter of Augsburg,' but esteem her for her husband's sake."

The Empress was also very fond of her brother's daughter, Marie Larisch, but the Countess Festetics could not "swallow" her now any more than she could before.

Occasionally outsiders would find their way into the Empress' world. For instance, on one occasion some gentlemen sent an English manufacturer to her to show her a new invention. "Can you ride?" she asked him; and the manufacturer answered rather hesitatingly that he could. He had to borrow riding clothes in a hurry and follow the Empress, showing her his goods as he rode. For forty minutes Elizabeth kept him galloping hard through the forest of Haraszti, and we may well wonder whether she took in much of what he had to explain. The Englishman dismounted, bathed in perspiration, and said: "Those were the fastest forty minutes I ever went through," which remark Elizabeth triumphantly repeated to the Emperor.

But her visit to Hungary was prematurely broken off. On October 11 Andrássy's successor, Baron Haymerle died of a heart attack, and on October 27 Elizabeth went to see his widow, who tottered toward her looking the very picture of woe, and when Elizabeth held out her hand for her to kiss, collapsed at her feet as though lifeless. Elizabeth helped her up and almost carried her to her apartments. Tears streamed down her cheeks, and nobody who saw the expression of tender pity on her lovely face ever forgot it. She left the house in a state of great agitation. "It is terrible," she said, "to think that this poor woman, who adored her husband, should have said good-bye to him quite casually and unsuspectingly, only to come home a few hours later and find him dead. Her hasty farewell was to be forever."

Those who had once seen the Empress in such circumstances as these were less severe about her vagaries, which were beginning to be the talk of the whole Empire. She was too much given to hiding her face behind her fan when she appeared in public, and this gave offense to people. Somebody wrote an article entitled "The Strange Lady" (*Die seltsame Frau*), omitting, however, to mention her visits to the cholera hospitals, and it is significant that a comic paper, called the *Kikeriki*, was the only one to rebuke people by publishing some verses under the same title, the gist of which was as follows:

Truly this woman is strange, who, fearless of danger and moved only by love of humanity, bears consolation to the house of tragedy; who, regardless of her beauty, goes and talks to smallpox patients, hurries with tears in her eyes to the dying man's bed, and stays there by the side of those whom all others have abandoned. You patronesses, see now how humane a woman can be, not only while listening to Strauss's music, but also in the hospital, drying people's tears where death in all its forms threatens. Learn this noble humanity from our Empress!

At the end of October King Humbert of Italy arrived on a visit with Queen Margherita. Elizabeth liked the Queen, though she was not exactly good-looking; the Italian visitors were enchanted with the Empress, and a mutual sympathy alleviated the burden of the exhausting days during which fête followed fête, tea parties, state concerts, and theatres, till Elizabeth was worn out with changing her dress five times a day. She was glad when she could return to Gödöllö, which Francis Joseph, too, had come to like more and more.

On December 8 the Emperor was already at supper when an urgent telegram was handed to him. He read it hurriedly and then let it drop from his hand. "The Ringtheater is on fire," he said hoarsely. "Taaffe telegraphs that the audience is safe, but who knows whether it's true?" He rose from the table at once and hurried to Elizabeth, who did not dine with him, for her evening meal consisted of nothing but a glass of milk. They soon heard that Taaffe's hasty telegram was untrue. Hundreds of people had tried to fight their way out of the doors, which only opened inwards, so that the pressure of the crowd made it impossible to open them, and the whole audience was crushed or burned to death. Francis Joseph and Elizabeth were deeply shocked, all hunting was stopped, and everything possible was done for the bereaved. Among the victims was a son of the Baroness Vetsera.

Elizabeth only felt really at ease in a limited circle. A court ball was a misery to her, but the children's dances given for her daughter Valerie were her delight. On one occasion seventeen little girls belonging to the greatest families had been invited. The Emperor danced with them gaily and Elizabeth presided like the most gracious of mothers. She enjoyed it all enormously, especially the delicious naïveté of the youngest child present, "Do" Hohenlohe. The party had begun at four, and by nine o'clock the little girl was sitting in a chair, very sleepy, when Elizabeth went up to her and asked gently: "Do, would you like something to eat?" It had been carefully impressed upon the child that she must behave beautifully, so she looked up at the Empress and replied, in accordance with the strictest rules of etiquette: "I thank Your Majesty a thousand times, no." The Empress offered her ices, jam, tea, lemonade, cake, but still the little girl declined politely. At last the Empress said kindly: "Tell me, Do, is there anything you *would* like?" Whereupon the child suddenly lost patience and answered: "I should like to be left in peace and go to bed." To which the Empress answered laughingly: "You are a clever little person. That is exactly what I should often like." And Do was allowed to go home.

In the year 1882 carnival was not yet over when the Empress left for her visit to England, which had now become an annual event. Ireland was avoided for the same reason as in the previous year, and she again stayed with Lord Combermere at the Abbey. This time Bay Middleton did not pilot the Empress; he was engaged to be married and this was the eve of his wedding. His position as pilot and the charge of the Empress' horses were taken over by Captain Rivers-Bulkeley. Rudolf Liechtenstein was there, too. Both the hunting and the weather were excellent, yet after the first few days in the field Elizabeth was very tired. Her former high spirits had abandoned her. Her moodiness and a thousand little trifles betrayed that hunting was now an effort to her, and she did not enjoy it as she had done before. The month was hardly finished, therefore, before she left for home. She lunched with the Queen at Windsor again, and went on to her three sisters in Paris. Eager to enjoy all she could, she wandered about on foot from early in the morning till late in the evening, when her ladies could walk no more. Hair-raising rumors reached Vienna that the Empress had ridden in an omnibus. "If only she would!" was the Countess Festetics' comment. "But we always have to walk!" During her short visit to Paris the Duke of Aumale arranged a stag-hunt at his Château of Chantilly, at which the ancient costumes were worn. The Duke, as Master of the Hounds, came out to meet her at the entrance to the château, followed by the whole hunt, including all the royal princes. Once more the horns sounded the old traditional hunting-calls, and after a long gallop the trophy was presented to Elizabeth in state.

Yet the whole thing seemed to her like a theatrical performance, a copy of something past and gone. It seemed almost symbolic, for the Empress' hunting fever had now cooled too, her joy in wild gallops had passed away. They were a thing which had been, but would never be again. Never again would Elizabeth ride in England.

XI
LONG WALKS AND DANGEROUS EXPEDITIONS
1882–1886

THE EMPEROR MET ELIZABETH AT THE station in Vienna. As always on these occasions, his eyes were shining and his joy was deep and genuine. But the happy reunion was almost immediately interrupted by a visit from the Russian Grand Duchess Vladimir, who was on her way to Italy. She had disturbing things to tell about St. Petersburg, where the anarchists were terrorizing everybody since the murder of the Tsar and nobody belonging to the imperial family or holding high office was safe. Every time she spoke of St. Petersburg tears came into her eyes. "I cannot get well there," she said. "The anxiety about my family is killing me. Whenever my husband goes out, I wonder whether he will return to me alive."

Since leaving England, the Empress had ridden less, even at home. But she now began to take four-hour walks at the pace of a quick march. The only one of her ladies who could keep up with her was the Countess Festetics or occasionally the Landgravine Fürstenberg. "I was walked off my feet," wrote the Countess in her diary after one such excursion, though she tried not to show it. It could hardly be called walking, she added, but was more like running without a stop.

During April there was shooting again at Göding, after which, on April 19, 1882, the Empress appeared at the spring review of the troops on the Schmelz, looking magnificent on her finest horse, Nihilist, a rare honor which roused both officers and men to enthusiasm. On her return home it had to be broken to her that the famous circus rider, Emilie Loisset, a brilliant horsewoman and excellent person, to whom she had taken a great fancy, had been killed in the circus when her horse fell. Marie Festetics purposely gave the Empress a detailed account of the accident, in the hope of inducing her to be more careful; but the warning was no longer needed, for Elizabeth now rode more prudently as well as less often. She had to satisfy her craving for physical exercise in other ways.

On April 23 there was another long walk, on which she was accompanied by the Emperor's aide-de-camp, Freiherr von Gemmingen, a professor, and the Countess Festetics. The expedition lasted five and three-quarter hours. Elizabeth went faster than ever, for she fully intended to tire Gemmingen out. On the way home he remarked: "With all due respect, Your Majesty, that was something of a walk, yet as a sportsman I am used to walking." The Emperor was anxiously waiting for them in the Burg. "So you are still alive!" he said to Marie Festetics. "This is really beyond words!"

"We are quite well, Your Majesty," she replied, "only hungry, for we have had absolutely nothing to eat."

Whereupon Francis Joseph laughed heartily, exclaiming: "What? That on top of everything else? I never heard of such a thing! And poor Gemmingen has had to endure this so-called pleasure as well! Go and have something to eat at once."

Shortly afterwards they moved to Buda, but here too the walks went on. On May 1 Elizabeth spent four hours walking at top speed. After all this, it was most tiring to have to appear at some court party in the evening, as the Empress often had to do, though always unwillingly. These expeditions often lasted till six o'clock in the evening. The Emperor shook his head when the police reported to him that it made the task of providing for Her Majesty's safety very difficult, for since the Empress preferred to start out without any definite object in view, nobody ever knew beforehand which way she was going.

During her annual visit to Bavaria in June the Empress tried to walk from Feldafing to Munich, and went on for four and a half hours, during which, as the Landgravine Fürstenberg wrote to her sister, her attendants had perforce to cease "attending" her; but this time even she did not manage to cover the whole distance on foot. The same thing happened at Ischl, where the expeditions were, of course, into the mountains, and none but good walkers could join in them. The eighty-year-old German Emperor, who arrived on a visit on August 9, excused himself with the words: "Unfortunately I am no longer able to accompany Your Majesty on such tours, on account of my too advanced youth."

A visit of the Emperor to Trieste and Dalmatia had been planned for September and was strongly desired by the Minister President, Count Taaffe, to create a diversion after the crushing of a rising that year in the Krivošije, the southernmost part of Dalmatia, and to counteract the Italian irredentism which was gaining ground in Trieste. In court circles this tour was regarded as most perilous, and everybody was sure that an attempt would be made to assassinate the Emperor. Francis Joseph therefore desired to go alone. But Elizabeth insisted upon standing by her husband in any danger, though she was furious with Taaffe and the Governor of Trieste for suggesting such a hazardous scheme.

Her instinct was not at fault. On September 14 two conspirators, one of whom was Guglielmo Oberdank, left Rome in the hope of finding an opportunity to settle accounts with the alleged tyrant of their native city of Trieste. The Emperor and Empress arrived at melancholy Miramar in pouring rain on September 16. Meanwhile the departure of the conspirators had been reported by the watchful Austrian Legation in Rome, and they had hardly crossed the frontier before the more dangerous one was arrested.

In spite of the rain and mud, Elizabeth and Marie Festetics walked along the high road from Miramar to Trieste and back, returning home "soaked like bath sponges." On the seventeenth the reception of the Emperor and Empress in Trieste took place in reasonably good weather. There was much talk of plots, the suite looked about anxiously, and the atmosphere was decidedly unquiet, but the opening ceremony went off without accident, and everybody was glad to reach home safely again in the evening.

On the following day Elizabeth was one of the first to rise. On going out of the house she read the words: "Pereat Francesco Giuseppe," "Evviva Oberdank," scrawled in black paint on the pedestal of a statue. Francis Joseph wanted to go alone to inspect the barracks and hospital, but Elizabeth spiritedly insisted upon accompanying him and was waiting with her dog Plato when the carriage came round. She told the Emperor that she must sit on the landward side, on his left, so as not to be incommoded by the sun, her real intention being to shield him the better. Francis Joseph would only take the smallest possible suite with him, for, he said: "We cannot expect anyone who is not absolutely indispensable to drive in with us. Here one is really in danger everywhere."

In the evening a ball was to take place on a Lloyd steamer, but there was a violent storm with torrents of rain. The Emperor and Empress descended the wet marble steps at Miramar with their suite, just as Maximilian and Charlotte had done when they started on their voyage into the unknown. The whole scene was like some strange masquerade, for all, including the Emperor, wore mackintosh capes with the hoods drawn up over their heads, while footmen lighted them with torches. They entered the boat tossing at the foot of the steps and met with a heavy sea as they left the harbor. The Empress sat like a marble statue, brightly illuminated by a lantern, and with the calm, pensive expression which she always wore in the presence of danger. Francis Joseph chatted cheerfully to keep up the others' spirits, but Marie Festetics thought of Taaffe, the Minister President, who was responsible for the whole rash expedition, and who was probably at that very moment sitting comfortably in his armchair with a cigar while the Emperor and his consort were putting out to sea on this wild night in a mere cockle-shell. In the background was Miramar standing out against the darkness with its bright lights like a fairy palace. The gunboat *Luzifer,* which was to take them off to the Lloyd steamship, was brilliantly lit up, hung with flags, and decorated. But as the launch drew alongside, it tossed up and down so violently that the imperial party had to leap on board at the risk of their lives. The national anthem was struck up, and a roar of cheers went out into the night, but everybody was shivering with cold and nerves. The gunboat at once started for Trieste, which rose like an amphitheatre illuminated with thousands of lights. Elizabeth admired the picturesqueness of the scene, saying with a smile: "It reminds me of Valerie when she was quite a little thing. Like all children, she loved everything that was dangerous, and I always said to her: 'You may look, but not touch.' "

But the smile faded from her lips as a flash of lightning was followed by a terrific roll of thunder. By the time the *Luzifer* reached the Lloyd steamship *Berenice,* on which the ball was to take place, the storm was at its height, and now it was impossible to get from one boat to the other. They waited patiently for hours, while the fireworks were let off in spite of the storm. Hundreds of rockets failed to go off, but others succeeded in mingling their stars and balls of fire with the flashes of lightning. At last the Governor managed somehow to get on board the *Luzifer* and begged Their Majesties not to expose themselves to the dangers of the storm any longer. He did not mention a still graver reason for their not coming on board the *Berenice:* a leak had just been discovered and all hands had been ordered to the pumps.

Slowly the *Luzifer* returned toward the glittering lights of Miramar. The storm was beginning to abate, and the whole adventure had a sort of wild romance. But Francis Joseph, whose poetic side was not very highly developed, suddenly dispelled the romantic atmosphere by observing in a matter-of-fact tone: "The Countess Festetics looks so pale, she is surely going to be sick."

The next day was such a contrast that it hardly seemed credible, with bright sunshine, a smooth, deep blue sea, and the garden a riot of flowers. The sea was like a mirror as they crossed to Duino to a great dinner given by Prince Taxis, at which the notables of Trieste were present. One of the guests drank the contents of his finger bowl, then suddenly fell strangely silent, and Elizabeth, who had noticed the incident, struggled to control her laughter till the tears came into her eyes.

Soon all was over and forgotten; but when Their Majesties got back to Gödöllö and Elizabeth related their experiences to Valerie, she poured out all the vials of her wrath. Her daughter had never seen her in such a rage. Tears of indignation came into her eyes as she spoke of their reception and Taaffe's lack of forethought. When the Minister President waited upon Their Majesties and spoke complacently of the careful measures which had been taken for their protection, Elizabeth's exasperation came to a head, and she cut him short by saying icily: "We owe it to God, and God alone, that everything went off well." And with a slight inclination of her head she turned and left him.

Once she was home again, Elizabeth resumed her ordinary way of life, though her long walks were now diversified by fencing, which she practiced daily. When she was in Vienna she would walk far into the Wienerwald. On one occasion a policeman, seeing the Empress and the Countess Festetics hurrying so, and failing to recognize them, imagined that two ladies of position were being pursued by somebody. He was just about to question them when he recognized the Empress and said nothing, but followed them panting till they got back to the palace.

Dr. Widerhofer now declared that the Landgravine Fürstenberg could no longer take part in these expeditions without grave risks to her health, and they soon became too much even for the Countess Festetics, so inquiries were made for a young and hardy maid of honor to act as "*promeneuse*" to the Empress, for, as the Archduchess Valerie wrote in her diary about this time: "Soon nobody will be able to go for walks with her." By Elizabeth's own wish the new maid of honor was again to be a Hungarian, and this is how it was that Sárolta (Charlotte) von Majláth entered her service.

The Empress took a growing pleasure in her daily fencing practice. A fencing master was engaged for her at a regular salary, and in a short time she had made great progress in the sport, which she took as seriously and practiced as ardently as everything she undertook. The little cuirass, the fencing gloves, and the short grey tunic, quite in the modern style, suited her splendidly, and her masters soon had to summon up all their skill if they were to remain victorious in these little contests.

This year the Empress expressed a desire to spend her "leave" at Baden-Baden. She took some horses with her, and her life there was an orgy of exercise: gymnastics in the morning, then fencing, and after that a six hours' walk in the surrounding country, or long rides into the mountains or on the plain. By this time Valerie was fifteen and old enough to accompany her mother frequently. Elizabeth took a keen interest in her daughter's intellectual development, followed her simple little entries in her diary, and was vastly entertained by the small girl's remark on Napoleon's Russian campaign after she had had a history lesson: "The Russians were artful (*pfiffig*) ; it would certainly never have occurred to me to burn Moscow like that."

Other royal personages the Empress did her best to keep at arm's length. Prince Alexander of Hesse, whose son was struggling against serious difficulties in Bulgaria, of which he was now Prince, tried to find an opportunity of putting in a word in his favor. He asked for an audience, but days and weeks went by without his receiving any invitation. When he ventured to remonstrate, Baron Nopcsa at last admitted to the Prince that he was in the greatest embarrassment. Even he hardly saw Her Majesty, he said, for she was off riding or else roaming about on foot in the mountains from early in the morning till eight o'clock at night. She ate no dinner, so no guests were invited. Prince Alexander persevered, and at last the Empress received him, when he found her impossibly slender owing to her "beauty regimen" and "excessive physical training." She answered his questions absent-mindedly with a mere "yes" or "no," and he had hardly made a move in the direction of the door when she dismissed him curtly and hurried out. Elizabeth was in good spirits during her visit to Baden-Baden, for it amused her to compare her own powers of endurance with those of her entourage.

The early summer saw her once more in Bavaria, and this time she did succeed in walking all the way from Munich to Feldafing on June 8 along the almost shadeless military road, covering the distance in seven hours, though even this performance was soon improved upon. Everything was done secretly, and nobody ever knew when she started or what she did, for she always acted on the inspiration of the moment.

She heard with anxiety of King Ludwig's peculiarities, which were increasing every year. Since the death of Richard Wagner in Venice on February 13, 1883, King Ludwig's passion for solitude had become still more intense, and Elizabeth had to defend her cousin against imputations of insanity, which she resented.

In July she went on to Ischl, where her walks developed into what can only be called forced marches. Seeing that she could no longer expect her ladies in waiting to walk for seven and three-quarter hours, which was now her daily allowance, she made men follow with carrying-chairs for them and a kind of climax was reached on an expedition to the Langbathseen and the Ammersee, when she was on her feet for almost nine hours. Everybody began to be anxious about her health, for she was getting more and more thin and pale. It was not surprising that her feet began to pain her again, so that by the end of July she had to set some limit to her walks. She now took up riding again, but the country was not well suited for it near Ischl or even at Mürzsteg, where she spent some time in a shooting lodge at the end of August. She would sometimes ride in the direction of the "Tote Weib," a beautiful but steep climb. Once her pony put his foot through a hole in a bridge across a gorge at the bottom of which flowed a torrent. She felt herself going down and her pony was already toppling toward the abyss when a workman who happened to be passing rushed up and saved both horse and rider.

Deeply though she loved her mother, Valerie did not share her love of Hungary; on the contrary, it was very painful to her always to have to talk Magyar with her, and even, by her mother's wish, with the Emperor. She kept intending to ask him whether she might not be allowed to speak German to him, but being very conscientious she shrank from doing so, for fear this might not be behaving properly to her mother.

The winter passed by uneventfully, and in April Elizabeth once more went abroad, this time for reasons of health; she had begun to be troubled with sciatic pains, though this did not prevent her from continuing her long walks and rides. Even at Wiesbaden, where she stayed at the beginning of April, 1884, she would walk for seven hours on end, while once she rode all the way to Frankfurt and back, which took all day. But her incessant restlessness only made her sciatica worse, till at the beginning of May she began to be worried and abruptly made up her mind to go to Amsterdam, to a famous doctor named Metzger. He alarmed the Empress by saying that she would become a cripple if she did not start upon a cure then and there, though he could not guarantee that it would be successful. A consultation took place at which a specialist on muscular affections from Heidelberg maintained that Metzger's diagnosis was incorrect. However, it was decided that Elizabeth should undergo a six weeks' cure, though she only consented when Metzger gave her permission to walk, ride, and fence. Baron Nopcsa, the Controller of the Household, watched the whole business rather doubtfully, remarking: "I fear Metzger has no idea what Her Majesty means by walking, riding, and fencing." In spite of her cure she would walk along the seashore through wind and rain, and when her ladies could no longer keep pace with her, she would allow herself to be escorted by Linger, who was in charge of her traveling arrangements, for she found his simplicity pleasing. But she had to spend such a long time in Amsterdam for her massage that she was forced to send her daughter home in charge of the Landgravine Fürstenberg.

She was most unhappy at the separation, the cure was tedious, and no improvement could be expected, as she was again indulging to excess in walking, riding, and fencing, her record being a walk lasting for ten hours. Metzger's manners were uncouth. He was very curt with her, and though she was quite unaccustomed to this, for that very reason it impressed her. She had recently got into the habit of eating nothing, but drinking a great deal of milk, which in the long run was bad for her digestion. She wrote to Valerie every day, telling her that she had only to telegraph and she would break off her cure and come at once. "I had a thousand times rather continue to put up with my sciatica," she wrote,* "than that you should suffer in any way." She faithfully reported progress to her daughter. "My knee was swollen after my march," ran one letter. "I rode four horses, only one of them any good, Achilles is howling across the waves, now I am going to fence. It is only simple practice with the little lieutenant. . . . I love the sea, it is the last thing I look at before going to bed. . . . As I walk along the shore, I could cry aloud, for never was anything so beautiful. But I enjoy the prospect of Heidelberg, for it means that we shall soon meet again, and I never know any peace without my Valerie. Now I must go to Metzger again. He finds that I have aged and grown wrinkled."

Elizabeth arrived at Feldafing in the middle of July. She was sunburnt and looked very well, but was still nervous and "fidgety" (*zappelig*), as Valerie puts it, and in ecstasies over Metzger and his blunt ways. He had at least succeeded in making the Empress eat good, regular meals again instead of starving herself as she had done for the last few years for the sake of preserving her slender figure. Not even her most faithful and devoted admirers had succeeded in this

* The Empress' letters to the Archduchess Valerie are now at Schloss Wallsee.

before; but when Metzger told her that if she went on as she was doing she would be an old woman in two years' time, she began eating again. Her persistence in walking or riding in the pouring rain for hours on end, however, was too much for her health. Little Valerie's shoes were often, she said, "like boats," and it was quite usual for the Empress to ride into Munich and back again in the rain to see her friend Irene Paumgartten, now an ailing, half-crazed old maid, who had gone in for spiritualism and talked excitedly of her dealings with spirits.

Elizabeth returned to Ischl, where a visit from the Archduchess Stephanie was announced, but instead of "moping at home" with her, as the Empress put it, she determined to make an expedition up the Hutteneckalm. She ascended the Salzberg, to use Francis Joseph's phrase, at such a "senseless pace" (*sinnlosem Tempo*) that all the others were left behind, completely out of breath. Soon she was out of sight of them all, and not till then did the Crown Princess unbend, for in the Empress' presence she was always overwhelmed.

As Valerie grew up the intimacy between her and Elizabeth became even deeper. She recognized how like her mother she was and got on very well with her. "But all the same," she wrote in her diary, "there are so many impassable barriers between us, which would not exist if we had not the same unyielding, erratic (*fahrig*) character, the same passionately uncompromising, impatient judgment, and the same capacity for exalted enthusiasm, arising though it does from such opposite motives in the two of us." "Mamma talked to me about the poetry of her life of ideas, which nobody suspects, nobody understands," she wrote on another occasion, and she implored her mother to give expression to this inner life in poetry. This suggestion was a ray of light to Elizabeth. She was now in her forty-eighth year, but had written scarcely any verse for nearly thirty years past. She seemed to welcome Valerie's suggestion, and rejoiced to find that her daughter understood her so well, though she still railed against mankind in general.

"Oh, this shrinking from contact with people (*Menschenscheu*)," wrote Valerie. "How Mamma could be adored if she only wished it!" The Empress discussed with her daughter all those forming her entourage. While in attendance on the Archduchess Sophie the Landgravine Therese had been strongly disposed to criticize Elizabeth, but the Empress had now taken her to her heart and considered her the only one of her Austrian ladies who was worth anything, finding far greater "resources" in her than in Sárolta Majláth or Aglaë Auersperg. She recognized that the Landgravine did not gossip or say unpleasant things about others and was always bright and responsive.

On August 6 the old German Emperor William I, who was still incredibly hale and hearty at the age of eighty-seven, paid a visit to the Emperor and Empress at Ischl. Happening to be left alone with Valerie for a moment, he asked her in his Berlin accent whether she accompanied her "Frau Mama" on her "Jewalttouren" (*Gewalttouren*, or violent expeditions). Shortly afterwards Gisela and Leopold arrived on a visit, and Francis Joseph felt, as usual, some impatience at seeing how Elizabeth seized every opportunity of showing how much she preferred Valerie to her elder daughter.

On September 11 the Empress made an excursion to Mariazell, for she had vowed to make a valuable offering to the Church if she recovered from her sciatica, and though the pain was not much better yet, she made an offering of a medallion set with diamonds, emeralds, and rubies, and a head of Christ in mosaic. Once as the Empress and Valerie were walking out into the country they met a disabled soldier with only one arm, dressed in tattered clothes and with a little bag at his side. Without stopping he pointed heavenwards, saying: "Don't you see Mary up there with the Child?" The Empress was struck by this, hurried after the man and began to talk to him. He rambled on about Radetzky, the Emperor, and the Fatherland, impressing on her all the while that she must pray a great deal, and constantly pointing up to the heavens. Suddenly he recognized the Empress, and fell on his knees weeping, but then he again confused her with the Blessed Virgin and talked so disconnectedly that Elizabeth hardly knew whether to laugh or cry. She rewarded him handsomely, and he went off blessing her. A few days later the greys drawing her carriage, which had been kept standing too long, bolted when both she and Valerie were in it. Fortunately no harm was done, but Elizabeth was upset all day because Valerie had been in the carriage, and kept attributing their good fortune to the disabled soldier's blessing. She was always on the lookout for omens and favorable signs, especially when they concerned her daughter's welfare. "The less there is wrong with me," the child wrote in her diary, "the more anxious Mamma often is, and it is so boring."

The autumn found Elizabeth once more at Gödöllö and Buda, where on November 11 she received a visit from Queen Carmen Sylva, who was still youthful and active, with a fresh, kindly, red face. She got on very well with Elizabeth and encouraged her to write poetry, for, she said, it is an excellent lightning conductor for so many things in life. Valerie observed Carmen Sylva with interest, but was annoyed because Andrássy escorted the Queen and sat next her at table; the Emperor's daughter hated the Count and believed that he returned her hatred with at least equal intensity.

After this visit they returned to Vienna, where the imperial family had lately taken to appearing more frequently at the

Burgtheater. Elizabeth did not go very often, except when Lewinsky was acting, and she would occasionally summon him to the palace to read to her; but Francis Joseph often went. Since November, 1883, there had been a new actress there named Katharina Schratt, whom the Emperor admired, regarding her as a true daughter of Vienna, simple, ingenuous, and natural, at the opposite pole from all the tedious ceremonial with which he was always surrounded. In some respects he found affinities between her nature and Elizabeth's, though she was less complicated and unusual and, above all, was never unhappy or afflicted with *Weltschmerz.* He did not know her personally yet, but that was how she appeared to him on the stage. The Crown Prince did not like her so much, for his tastes were different. At that time he was going through a phase of lofty aspirations and enthusiasm for liberty such as Elizabeth had once experienced, though he now found her far too lukewarm. Another thing which tended to make the Empress and her son drift apart was that she did not feel particularly drawn toward the Crown Princess Stephanie, and they avoided each other's company by mutual consent for fear of friction. Rudolf was attached to his wife, wrote her affectionate letters, and was always glad to return to her and his child, though he was certainly not meticulously faithful. He allowed himself, in fact, the greatest license, but concealed this carefully from his parents and even his own Household.

In January, 1885, Elizabeth started the year valiantly by being present at the first of the usual court and public balls in Budapest, but she was seized with such a "court-ball headache" afterwards, as Valerie called it, that on January 19 she withdrew to Miramar to recover for a few days by the seaside. She took with her the works of Heinrich Heine, in which she had become more and more absorbed lately, for they appealed to her critical and satirical side as well as to her love of lyric poetry. Homer's *Iliad* had also become her inseparable companion, and during the last year she had become so enthusiastic about Achilles that she ordered a copy of Herterich's statue of the dying Achilles and had it set up in the garden at Miramar. In March, after a short stay in Vienna for the Industries Ball, she had a return of her sciatica, due to the usual exposure and overindulgence in exercise, and felt bound to go to Dr. Metzger again for the same cure as in the previous year. This time she did not take Valerie, but traveled to Holland with only one lady in waiting. Remembering her conversation with little Valerie, and under the influence of Heine and the poetry of the sea, she now began to compose verses again, the main themes of which were the heroic figure of Achilles and the sea, whose changing aspects she admired so much from her villa at Zandvoort that on hearing of this a builder proposed to build her a house on the same site. Elizabeth, however, rejected the proposal.

Out, out across the sea so wide a mighty longing drives me!

she might write in one of her poems; but none the less her mind was busying itself with the thought of building a palace. Soon, however, she came to the conclusion that no one spot on earth could bind her for long. And she composed a "Reply to the Master Builder," which ran as follows:

A palace they would build me
Here on the North Sea strand,
With lofty domes all golden
And all that's gay and grand. . . .

Ah, greatly do I love thee,
Thou harsh tempestuous sea,
Thy wildly tossing billows,
Thy storms that rage at me.

KATHARINA SCHRATT IN *VERSPRECHEN HINTERM HERD*

From a photograph. National Library, Vienna.

But love endures no fetters—
Must needs go wandering,
To nothing constant ever—
Palace or wedding ring.

O'er thee, like thine own sea birds,
I'll circle without rest;
For me earth holds no corner
To build a lasting nest.

On returning to her villa from Amsterdam after her treatment, Elizabeth would often go out in a boat, usually at sunrise or sunset, and her impressions of the sea, with its myriad waves and aspects, inspired her with innumerable poems.

O had I songs as many
As thou hast waves, my sea,
I'd write them in these pages
And bring them all to thee.
All that I feel and ponder,
These errant thoughts of mine,
How gladly I could sink them
Deep in thy crystal shrine.
How happy to be near thee,
On thee to feast mine eyes,
My first joy in the morning,
My last when daylight dies.

For hours Elizabeth would watch the flight of the gulls, and she developed a fanciful idea that in her whole nature and mind she really resembled a sea gull, thirsting for liberty on the broad ocean. She remembered how Ludwig II of Bavaria had compared himself to the eagle, which loves to make its home high on the steepest crag and is king of the mountains just as the sea gull is queen of the seas, and she wrote a little poem in his honor while she was at Zandvoort.

Thou Eagle high-throned on the mountains,
The sea gull swift circling below
Sends greetings from foam-crested billows
To thee in thy kingdom of snow.

Looking back over her life, she next composed a little autobiographical poem entitled "The Butterfly" (*Der Schmetterling*), describing her young days from her childhood to her flight to Madeira, and comparing herself to the butterfly, as it unfolds its fragrant wings, enjoying the beauty of life and seeing the world as a paradise.

The Empress surrendered herself entirely to her dreams. She often saw a stranger at Zandvoort whose well-proportioned form and fine head fascinated her, as did everything that was beautiful. She was capable of going into ecstasies over a handsome person, whether man or woman, and this stranger to whom she had never addressed a word, and never would, cast such a spell over her that she poured out her heart in the following verses:

Away, away from thee! No more can I endure it! My frenzied heartbeats stun and send my sick mind reeling. I close mine eyelids fast. No more will I gaze on thee. . . . Peace, peace at any price, ere all my senses fail me! For when this day I saw thee, I strove myself to master—else—as though God were nigh me—clasping my hands imploring, I could have called upon thee and kneeling sunk before thee. . . . And ah! the pain and anguish! The storm that raged within me! Is this, then, Nemesis? Because my heart for earthly love did fickle and unfaithful prove?

But her dreams were rudely interrupted when, on the very day that she had written these verses, a well-dressed Dutchman named Leon Bindshuyden struck aside her fan with his umbrella in the streets of the city. He was immediately arrested by one of the detectives in attendance on her, and nothing more came of the incident. The man alleged that he did not know who the Empress was, but had only been curious to see the face of the lady who always hid it behind a fan. The Dutch Government expressed its regret, but this was a little warning to Elizabeth, who wandered about with the utmost unconcern on her travels abroad, usually without any male escort.

Her cure was now nearly over, and this time Metzger's massage had been more successful, for the Empress had not gone for so many exhausting walks or rides as in the previous year. She decided to return home by way of Heidelberg and Feldafing, and wrote farewell verses addressed to the sea and concluding as follows:

When o'er thy lonely wastes of sand
Shall break another day,
On swiftest pinions borne afar
I shall have soared away.

The snowy cloud of circling gulls
Still on their way will speed;
One will be gone—but which of them
Thou wilt not even heed.

She critically reviewed the poems of which, as she puts it, she had been "guilty" during the last month, and came to the conclusion that she would leave poetry alone in future and go in for fencing, riding, and walking again—now that the pain in her feet was less acute. She knew perfectly well that her poems were not masterpieces, so she went out in a boat and dropped most of them overboard, as a present "to the codfish and soles," to quote her own ironical little verses.

At Heidelberg she found Valerie waiting for her, with a fencing master and a collection of horses. It was fine weather and the meeting was a happy one, for Valerie was proud of

Elizabeth's poems, which had occupied her mind and acted as a safety valve for her varying moods. From Heidelberg the Empress had meant to go on to Switzerland with her mother and visit the ruins of Habsburg, but inquiries through diplomatic channels in Bern elicited the fact that the Swiss Government would not care to see the Empress of Austria visiting the former seat of the House of Habsburg. There had been persistent rumors that the Emperor wished to purchase it, and this would not have pleased the Federal Council.

By the end of May Elizabeth was at Feldafing, where she had leisure for reading. By now she knew almost the whole of the *Iliad* by heart. World-wide interest had been aroused by Schliemann's remarkable excavations and romantic finds at Tiryns, and the Empress longed to look upon the scenes of her favorite epic with her own eyes. She absorbed herself in the ideas of the Homeric world. "My body is still here," she wrote on June 10, 1885, "but my soul has flown on ahead of it to Troy. If only I could go there!" On June 20 she visited King Ludwig's palace on the Roseninsel with her daughters Gisela and Valerie. She took with her the poem which she had written to the King at Zandvoort, copied it out, placed it in a sealed envelope addressed to him, and left it in one of the rooms in the castle.

About this time she recalled her adventure at the masked ball in 1874, and wondered what the young man with whom she had had such an interesting conversation was now doing. She had never seen him again, but had occasionally run across his name in the papers; and since 1876, when her ladies in waiting had made an unsuccessful attempt to get her letters back from Fritz Pacher, she had neither seen him nor written to him. She now composed a poem entitled "Long, Long Ago," which she called "The Song of the Yellow Domino," and would have liked to send it to him. But in order to be sure that it would reach his hands safely after so long a time, she wrote to him as before under the name of Gabriele, asking him to send her his address and photograph. This letter astonished Pacher and caused him some perturbation, for though it really seemed to come from the "yellow domino," he was afraid he might be the victim of a practical joke. He was therefore cautious and did not send his portrait, but gave his address and replied in the following terms:

Vienna, June 9, 1885.

DEAR YELLOW DOMINO,

I hardly know what could have surprised me more than receiving this sign of life from you (*dir*).

To say that I was thunderstruck is a mild way of expressing my feelings—far too mild. How much has happened during the last eleven years! You are probably still as radiant as of old in your proud beauty—while I am a bald, respectable, but *happy* husband, with a wife resembling you in height and figure and a dear little girl.

After these eleven long years you can, if you think fit, lay aside your domino and throw light upon the mysterious adventure which has interested me more than any other I have experienced.

You see that I still have my honest old "German" nature, with its same old faults. Anything coming from you must needs be good, so do send what it is that you have to send. Whatever it may be, it will give me the same heartfelt pleasure as any news from you does. . . .

On October 14 Pacher received an inquiry from the "red domino" as to whether he had been induced to have his "fatherly bald head" photographed in the meantime, for they would like so much to see him as a husband. The letter was quite inoffensive and contained no suggestion that the writer felt any distrust of Fritz Pacher, but he took it in the wrong spirit. He really believed now that he was being made fun of, so he lost his temper and answered as follows:

Vienna, October 22, 1885.

HONORED REDDISH-YELLOW DOMINO!

I am really sorry that you still find it necessary to play at hide-and-seek with me after the lapse of eleven years. It would be great fun to unmask after such a long time, and a nice ending to that Shrove Tuesday in 1874, for in the long run an anonymous correspondence loses its charm.

Your first carnival letter was a pleasure to me, but the latest one an annoyance. A man does not like not being trusted when he knows he has given no cause for distrust. Farewell, and no offense meant! . . .

When Frau Ferenczy showed Elizabeth this letter, she threw it aside in some pique, for she was not used to being addressed in such a tone and quite forgot that she was nothing to the writer but an unknown masked lady. She was about to say something sharp, but laughed it off, merely remarking: "Very well, then, he simply will not get what I had intended for him," and the poem was not sent off for the present.

The Empress felt it acutely that she could no longer take such liberties with her health as in earlier years. In addition to the pain in her feet, she now suffered from frequent headaches, and seldom rode, for the shaking was too much for her. Her incessant headaches depressed her so that she gave way to melancholy very easily, though to all outward appearance her forty-eight years of life had left no trace upon her.

Meanwhile the political situation in the Balkans had taken a critical turn. The state of affairs created by the Congress of Berlin could not last, and some modification was urgently necessary. Count Kálnoky's efforts were directed toward maintaining some sort of stability in the relations between his country and Russia, strained though they were, and he did not want to make matters worse by active intervention in the Balkans, as Andrássy still desired, though his counsels no longer possessed their former weight. A meeting with the Tsar was arranged for August 25 and 26 at Kremsier, and Elizabeth accompanied Francis Joseph. The theatrical company which had been delighting everybody at Ischl and, among other actors from the Burgtheater, included Katharina Schratt, also went to Kremsier, where it gave a gala performance; afterward the leading actors were presented to the Emperor and Empress and received their cordial congratulations. From Kremsier Elizabeth returned to Ischl, where she resumed her long walks with Valerie. When it was impossible to go far, she would walk in all weathers as far as the neighboring Jainzen, which Valerie called "Mamma's magic mountain." This was where Elizabeth liked best to spend her time, writing poetry, dreaming, and pouring out her heart to her daughter, who was her dearest and most intimate friend, and whose diary is a reflection of the Empress' inmost feelings from day to day.

On September 6 Elizabeth took Valerie up a side of the mountain which she had persistently avoided before and showed her a little chapel she had had built there as a surprise for her. It contained a beautiful image of the Virgin, beneath which were the opening verses of one of Elizabeth's poems, calling down blessings on the house and neighborhood where they had been staying. The rest of the poem she gave to her daughter, who was now seventeen years old. In it she commended Valerie's future children to the Blessed Virgin, for she was already looking forward sadly to the day when Valerie would marry and leave her. "I have a feeling," she said, "that your eldest boy will be a cardinal, and the second one a poet." Elizabeth continued to write verses, though she often made fun of her own productions. She only hoped that the world at large would not laugh at her as it did at Queen Carmen Sylva of Rumania, who had just sent Valerie a portrait of herself looking perfectly ridiculous, with her "untidy hair like a bluestocking's," wearing the Rumanian national costume and writing poetry in a forest, "just like an actress," Elizabeth said.

On September 9 the Empress, accompanied by Valerie and Gisela, who was visiting her, drove to the sporting estate of Eisenerz, to a shooting box near Radmer. Gisela and Valerie differed very much in taste, appearance, and feelings, but got on very well together, and Valerie admired Gisela as a model wife and mother.

Elizabeth's health was still far from good, and since she could no longer walk as much as she desired, she thought of going on a long sea voyage in September. Sharing as she did her family's Greek sympathies and enthusiasm for the antique, she longed to see the excavations at Tiryns and Mycenæ, at the same time paying a visit to Constantinople and Suez. It was arranged that on October 5 she should leave on the yacht *Miramar* for a month's cruise in the Ægean and the Levant. Her route lay past Lacroma, Lissa, and Corfu, which again fascinated her. The Austrian Consul there, Baron Alexander Warsberg, was a specialist in Greek antiquities and had published a history and description of Corfu in his two works entitled *Odysseische Landschaften* (Scenes from the Odyssey) and *Das Reich des Odysseus* (The Realm of Odysseus). It was he who received the Empress and acted as her guide. She had not yet read his books, so he promised to have them sent to her at once. Elizabeth was particularly enraptured with an expedition to a little island which, according to the *Odyssey,* was formerly a ship, but had been turned to stone by the wrath of Neptune just before reaching port. On it stands a little Greek church in a cypress grove. A sad, taciturn monk received the Empress and conducted her to a grave in which, twelve years before, he had laid his only companion, a man of seventy-nine. The voyage continued past Santa Maura, the island hallowed by the death of Sappho; then round the mainland of Greece to the Dardanelles, where the *Miramar* arrived on October 21.

Meanwhile complications in the Near East had grown more acute, and the antagonism between Russia and Austria was reflected in their policy toward Bulgaria. There were two parties in Austria; one, toward which the Crown Prince and Andrássy inclined, was in favor of a vigorous attitude, while the other, led by Kálnoky, the Minister for Foreign Affairs, was anxious to avoid becoming involved in a serious war. "In my opinion," wrote the Crown Prince about this time to Count Latour, "much might be done even now. But there is an utter lack of decision here; they are (*man ist*) even more irresolute than ever before. . . . The Empress is absent on a cruise in the East; the moment is most unfortunately chosen."

Elizabeth had wished to visit Constantinople, but in view of the grave situation Francis Joseph had to telegraph that he could not consent to her going through the Dardanelles or landing at Smyrna. Accordingly, she merely visited the ruins of Troy, where she was deeply moved as she stood before the mound indicated by tradition as the grave of Achilles. The Landgravine considered it "a lack of respect" that this supposed grave should be a mere heap of stones with a deep hole in it, but Elizabeth celebrated it in a poem, in which she represents the sun, moon, and stars as pausing on their daily or nightly round to pay their tribute to the lonely tumulus.

In spite of the Emperor's orders they had to touch at Smyrna for the purpose of taking in coal. The news of the Empress' arrival ran round the town like wildfire. The Austrian Consul donned full dress in readiness to receive her, the soldiers turned out with their bands, the local authorities put on their best clothes, and the whole population of the city assembled. Elizabeth now ordered the State launch to be got ready, and her hairdresser, Frau Feifalik, entered it and was rowed up and down the harbor, being greeted with cheers every time it drew near the shore. Meanwhile a little boat landed some distance away. Elizabeth and the captain of the *Miramar* stepped ashore in their everyday clothes without attracting attention, wandered through the whole city undisturbed, visited the bazaar, had coffee at a public coffee-house and returned to the yacht safe and happy, so that, as the Landgravine Fürstenberg remarked in her diary, the wishes of both the Emperor and the Empress were gratified.

They next went on to Rhodes and Cyprus, the consuls, to their disappointment, being always sent on ahead with the ladies in waiting, while the Empress wandered through the town as she had done at Smyrna. If the two parties met, as they did in the street of the Knights of St. John at Rhodes, the other party, by the Empress' express wish, had to take no notice of her. But by the time she reached Port Said Elizabeth had had enough of her voyage, and described in an ironical poem in the style of Wilhelm Busch how the sea gull from the North Sea, having come on a visit to her sisters in the south, did not find that spot particularly beautiful. The verses ended as follows:

And now that I have seen you,
My sisters all, bon jour.
For I admit quite freely
I long for the retour.

On November 1 the *Miramar* returned to its haven near the palace of the same name, and all the officers were invited to dinner and cordially thanked. That very same afternoon, however, Elizabeth took an umbrella and went for a walk in pouring rain. On seeing a girl go by thinly clad and shivering with cold, she threw a shawl round her shoulders and gave her her own umbrella, saying: "There, I make you a present of them," and walked home through a perfect deluge.

Elizabeth hoped that her sea voyage would have cured the sciatic pains in her feet and on returning to Vienna was at first free from them. She found Francis Joseph worried and upset by the Balkan crisis, which in November led to war between Serbia and Bulgaria. Since both Russian and Austrian interests were involved, all such developments seemed to indicate a clash between the two great empires. While the Empress was at Gödöllö in December her sciatica returned, and was so acute at times that she could not even go out in the garden, till on December 26, 1885, she declared in despair that she must leave at once for Amsterdam to consult Dr. Metzger. Valerie endeavored to calm her and pointed out that there was a famous sciatica specialist in Vienna. She was very sorry for her mother, but felt that her anxiety was out of all proportion to the gravity of her illness. At times the Empress went so far as to say that it was a torture to live and hinted at suicide. But Francis Joseph did not take this seriously, merely rejoining: "Then you will go to hell." Whereupon Elizabeth would reply: "One already has hell upon earth." Having always done all he could to anticipate his wife's every wish, this made him most unhappy at times. It was painful to him, on returning home in search of relaxation from his political anxieties, to be met with nothing but lamentations. He anxiously discussed with Dr. Widerhofer what was to be done, and resigned himself with a sigh to the likelihood that further cures would continue to be necessary, involving frequent absences on the part of the Empress.

In spite of her health Elizabeth did fulfil her public duties that winter and was present at the court ball on January 28, 1886. She took a greater interest in these festivities now that Valerie was grown up and suitors for her hand were already beginning to appear. At this ball the Archduchess Valerie danced a quadrille with the Archduke Franz Salvator of the Tuscan line of the House of Habsburg. The same thing happened at the next ball, and Elizabeth noticed that the young Archduke was paying marked attentions to her daughter. Her relation to Valerie was like that of an elder to a younger sister, and she now discussed her future with her for the first time, promising that she would never allow any pressure to be put upon her to take the most important step in life against her will. "If you are bent upon marrying a chimney sweep," she said bluntly, "I will place no obstacles in your way. But I have a sort of inkling (*Spurius*) that one day Franz Salvator will be your husband." At first this did not quite fit in with the Emperor's plans. His idea was that the Crown Prince of Saxony, the nephew of his great friend Albert, would be the right husband for his daughter, and it was said that the Prince was shortly coming to Vienna.

This news gave Elizabeth food for deep and unhappy reflections. Till now she had not seriously faced the thought that one day she would have to lose her daughter, but she felt it would not be so hard if Valerie did not have to leave her own country. When it seemed that she might have to go abroad, Elizabeth was in despair, and Valerie once more realized, to her alarm, that she was really the only link attaching Elizabeth to life, for since his work occupied him from early morning till evening, Francis Joseph was unable to devote himself exclusively to his wife. The older the Emperor and Empress grew, the more the differences between their characters came out. On the one side were a matter-of-fact spirit, devotion to duty and hard work; on the other passionate surrender to the idea prevailing at the moment, introspection, and an everlasting struggle between imagination and reality; and though Elizabeth longed for occupation she had really nothing to do. The Emperor was naturally suited for his functions as a ruler, but Elizabeth was entirely unsuited for her rank.

The Crown Prince was growing increasingly independent and able to stand on his own feet, and was passing through a period of political storm and stress such as Elizabeth, too, had experienced in her day. The curious thing was that, when Rudolf was expected at his parents' table, Elizabeth dressed more beautifully than when some stranger was coming. The Princess Gisela said laughingly that the whole family regarded Rudolf as a person to be treated with particular respect. The Crown Prince did not much care for his Bavarian relatives, considering himself superior to them, which was bound to annoy Elizabeth, and this unfortunately caused her to "efface herself." Her headaches and sciatica made her escape from the court of Vienna as often as she could. On February 6, 1886, she left for Miramar, intending to take a short sea voyage, but on February 11 the Crown Prince had what was said to be a severe attack of peritonitis and cystitis, so she did not venture to sail from Miramar, but returned home to see her son, who was shortly afterwards sent to Lacroma. Thus it was not till March 2 that she started out with Valerie for her usual spring cure, which was to take place that year at Baden-Baden. The days there hung heavy on her hands; she could not ride or even walk, but would sit in the woods reading, for preference, Heine's descriptions of his travels, with their blend of ruthless irony and poetic feeling. She found much that was akin to her own nature in these writings, or imagined that she did. She would turn eagerly to passages of world-weary discontent and apply them to herself, and she even coquetted with the scoffing and atheistic ideas which are to be found scattered about this writer's works.

She had long discussions with the Princess Gisela, who was far from sharing her passion for Heine. Elizabeth would wonder why mankind should have to suffer so much for one sin of Eve's, and was, indeed, born to nothing but suffering. The poison which Heine himself admits to be present in his poems was beginning to have its effect upon her and her belief in God, though she had so far stood firm in spite of all her doubts and liberal tendencies which were so much opposed to rigid clericalism.

At the beginning of June Elizabeth returned home through Munich and Feldafing, to find better reports of Rudolf's health. His visit to Lacroma seemed to have done him good, although it was said that the cure was not complete. Outwardly, however, he appeared quite well and began to resume his former way of living, so that Elizabeth thought his condition less serious than it really was.

At the same time she heard that Andrássy was ill and commissioned Baron Nopcsa to write and tell him that he must take care of himself and go to Karlsbad. Nopcsa took this opportunity to tell the Count something about his mistress' state of mind. "Her Majesty," he wrote on June 10, 1886, in a letter still preserved in the archives of the Andrássy family, "expects you to do whatever the doctors tell you, if not for your own sake, then at least for hers. Live prudently! . . . Her Majesty, thank God, is going on well, but unfortunately her state of mind is not such as I should wish to see it. There is no reason for it that I can see, yet for all that she has a mind diseased. And she leads such an utterly isolated life that she makes herself worse."

Nopcsa's cool, practical mind took a grave view of the future, for while he was only the Empress' servant and desired what was best for her, he was not unaware of her weaknesses. The Empress had never suffered any really serious misfortune yet, and many were in store for her. But she had little or no suspicion of this. The seriousness of the Crown Prince's illness was made light of to her, and though she watched his intellectual development uneasily, she could not foresee what results might be produced by such ideas as he had in the head of one destined for a throne; for she, too, had dallied with ideas of liberty and the cosmopolitan theories of the literary men and journalists who influenced the Crown Prince.

Elizabeth withdrew more and more into herself, till, as she put it, she became "too lazy to talk" (*redefaul*), even omitting to repeat her remarks when the Emperor failed to understand her. Valerie had usually to fling herself into the breach on these occasions, so that Francis Joseph remarked to Elizabeth with a laugh: "It is really fortunate that we have this speaking trumpet. But," he added sadly, "what will it be like when we no longer have her?"

In spite of his wife's changed frame of mind Francis Joseph remained devoted to her. It was he who had the villa built in the Tiergarten at Lainz, for which his wife's love of luxury has been held responsible. This villa ministered, so to speak, to the special weaknesses of the Emperor and Empress. The Emperor was an enthusiastic sportsman, and the Tiergarten had been renowned for its game since the eleventh century; while the Empress loved its quiet solitude, as contrasted with the Burg and the imposing "pleasure palace" of Schönbrunn, where she always went into residence with the greatest "displeasure." The palace at Lainz was built in a French-Italian Renaissance style in keeping with the taste of the age. The interior decoration designed by Makart was characterized by a heavy and pompous splendor—especially in the Empress' bedroom—which seems incredible nowadays. The finest thing in the palace was the Empress' gymnasium, decorated in the Pompeian style and containing every possible form of apparatus, including an accurate pair of scales, which Elizabeth consulted daily. Of course there were magnificent stables and an outdoor riding school, for when building operations had been started it was not foreseen that Elizabeth would almost have given up riding. Orders were now given to dispose of her stables at Vienna, Ischl, and Gödöllö, keeping only a few of her favorite horses.

On May 24, after her return from Bavaria to Vienna, Francis Joseph drove her out to see the Villa Hermes, as the new house at Lainz was called. The Empress shook her head over her bedroom, and Valerie remarked that it was grand and up-to-date, but not homelike (*gemütlich*), and Francis Joseph said: "I shall always feel afraid of spoiling things." But then he looked out of the window, from which a whole herd of game could be seen, and felt as pleased as the Empress did when she found that she need only take a few steps outside the villa to find herself in the midst of the woods. She was particularly delighted at being able to reach her own apartments by a little spiral staircase. But the house had not turned out what the Emperor and Empress had originally intended it to be, a small, modest but comfortable "Buen Retiro" for their old age. It had grown into a palace which would involve considerable expenditure and a large staff of servants.

In June, 1886, Elizabeth again departed on a long visit to Feldafing. On the eighth her brother-in-law, Count Trani, had died in Paris, and she now took his widow and little daughter to her heart in the most affectionate way. From this time onwards she paid her widowed sister an annual allowance of 40,000 marks, half of which came out of her own resources, while the Emperor Francis Joseph made himself responsible for the rest. For she was always faithful to her family and loved ones.

ELIZABETH'S BEDROOM IN THE VILLA HERMES AT LAINZ

From a photograph.

XII

DEATH OF LUDWIG II. HEINE AND THE HOMERIC WORLD

1886–1887

IT WAS NOW REALIZED IN BAVARIA THAT the problem presented by King Ludwig's condition defied any simple solution. The members of the ruling house were already alive to the fact that its prestige would be endangered if a change did not soon take place. As early as 1871 a Munich doctor had predicted complete insanity, and the last few years seemed only to confirm his diagnosis. The King's utterances were often incoherent, he carried on long conversations at table with unseen guests, and thrashed his servants and officials. Though due to his taste for the arts, his extravagances had led to an accumulation of debts amounting to ten million marks, and he was demanding a further ten million for his architectural schemes and his theatres. He raved at the ministers when he presented them with demands for money, and if they could not supply it, he would intrust the raising of it to his menservants. Scandalous episodes took place at court in which soldiers in his Chevaux-légers were involved—in short, matters could no longer go on as they were, and on May 8, 1886, the Ministers resolved to force the King to abdicate. But it came as a surprise to everybody when on May 17 a proclamation was issued to the effect that Prince Luitpold, the heir presumptive, would assume the Regency, while an army order declared the King incapable of governing owing to mental derangement. A deputation now waited upon the King at Neuschwanstein, but, though only commissioned to inform him of these measures, it proceeded to treat him as totally insane. The first attempt failed, for everybody about the court—footmen, peasants, workmen, and such loyal officers as Count Dürckheim, supported the King, and on June 10 the deputation fled back to Munich. It was not till the eleventh that a fresh commission succeeded in gaining possession of his person. This time it was accompanied by two doctors with warders, police, and soldiers who could be depended upon, and they took the King to the Castle of Berg on the Starnbergersee, which had been fitted up like a regular prison. Here he was to remain under the care of Dr. Gudden, a specialist in mental diseases.

The whole business had been managed both irresponsibly and injudiciously. Only two days previously the King had been treated as a sovereign, yet now he was suddenly informed that by Dr. Gudden's orders ropes and a straitjacket were to be kept in readiness. He kept repeating to Count Dürckheim that he feared another attack. "But I am not a madman," he said, "so why should I be put under restraint?" The abrupt contrast between his situation now and what it had been only a day before was calculated to produce the most alarming effects.

Elizabeth was staying with her mother at Garatshausen when news of all this arrived. The Duchess Ludovika was greatly agitated, and though she had never forgiven the King for breaking his engagement, she pitied the poor Queen of Bavaria, both of whose sons had now been declared insane. But when Elizabeth expressed doubts of Ludwig's total insanity, she said it was to be hoped that he was mad, for they must be thankful if he could not be held guilty of having brought his flourishing country and loyal people to their present pass by his criminal irresponsibility. Sadly Elizabeth returned to Feldafing, where she heard of Ludwig's confinement in the Castle of Berg.

The end came after dinner on the evening of Whitsunday, June 13. No one will ever know what really happened; the King and Dr. Gudden were both found drowned in the lake at about half past ten at night. Close investigation pointed to a preceding struggle, but whether it was suicide or an attempted escape which the doctor tried to frustrate will remain a mystery forever. What is certain is that since Elizabeth was at Feldafing, entirely unconscious of what was going on, she cannot possibly have lent any assistance to an alleged attempt at escape by providing a carriage or anything of the kind.

On Whitmonday, June 14, the Empress Elizabeth and Valerie were on their way to breakfast when the Princess Gisela suddenly entered the room looking distraught and drew the Empress aside: "I have something to tell you and must see you quite alone." Elizabeth accompanied her into the adjoining room, and an agitated conversation was heard. Then she came back as pale as death, saying: "Only think, the King has thrown himself into the lake!"

The Empress was deeply distressed as she described the King's death, for in spite of all, he had had brilliant abilities and she had many happy memories of this friend of her youth. "The King was no madman," said Elizabeth, "only an eccentric who lived in a world of ideas. They might have treated him more gently, and so, perhaps, spared him such a fearful end." She passionately upheld this point of view in speaking to her mother, but the Duchess Ludovika contradicted her irritably, and mother and daughter parted on a note of discord. That same evening when Valerie was about to say her prayers in her mother's room before going to bed, the Empress suddenly threw herself full length on the floor. Valerie screamed with terror, for she thought her mother had seen some terrible vision, and she clung to her in such alarm that in the end both of them could almost have laughed. "All I wanted," said Elizabeth, "was to pray God in repentance and humility to forgive me my rebellious thoughts. I have lacerated my mind (*meinen Verstand wund gedacht*) by brooding over the inscrutable decrees of God, over time, eternity, and retribution in the world beyond, and, wearied with fruitless, sinful meditations, I mean in future, whenever doubts beset my mind, to say in all humility: 'Jehovah, Thou art great! Thou art the God of vengeance, Thou art the God of grace, Thou art the God of wisdom!' "

Elizabeth was haunted by some old monk's ancient prophecy that the year 1886 would be a year of disasters, because Easter came so late. She could not recover from the blow she had suffered, and excitedly condemned the steps taken by the ministers in the severest terms. She did not go and see Ludwig's dead body, but sent a wreath and a bouquet of jasmine, with orders that the jasmine was to be laid on his breast and buried with him.

The Crown Prince Rudolf visited Feldafing on his way to the funeral and was shocked at his mother's condition. It flashed across his mind that one day, perhaps, a similar fate might be in store for her, so he questioned Valerie very closely. Yet, charming though he was on this occasion, when they visited the old Duchess at Possenhofen Valerie again felt that he was far too prone to set himself on a pedestal of haughty dignity and had not learned, as his father had, to be first and foremost a man, and only in the second place a prince.

On the morning of June 21 Elizabeth had a solemn Requiem Mass said in the King's memory, after which she went to Munich and laid a wreath on his grave in the family vault of the Wittelsbachs. The visit did her good, and she returned home in a calmer frame of mind, remarking that Ludwig II

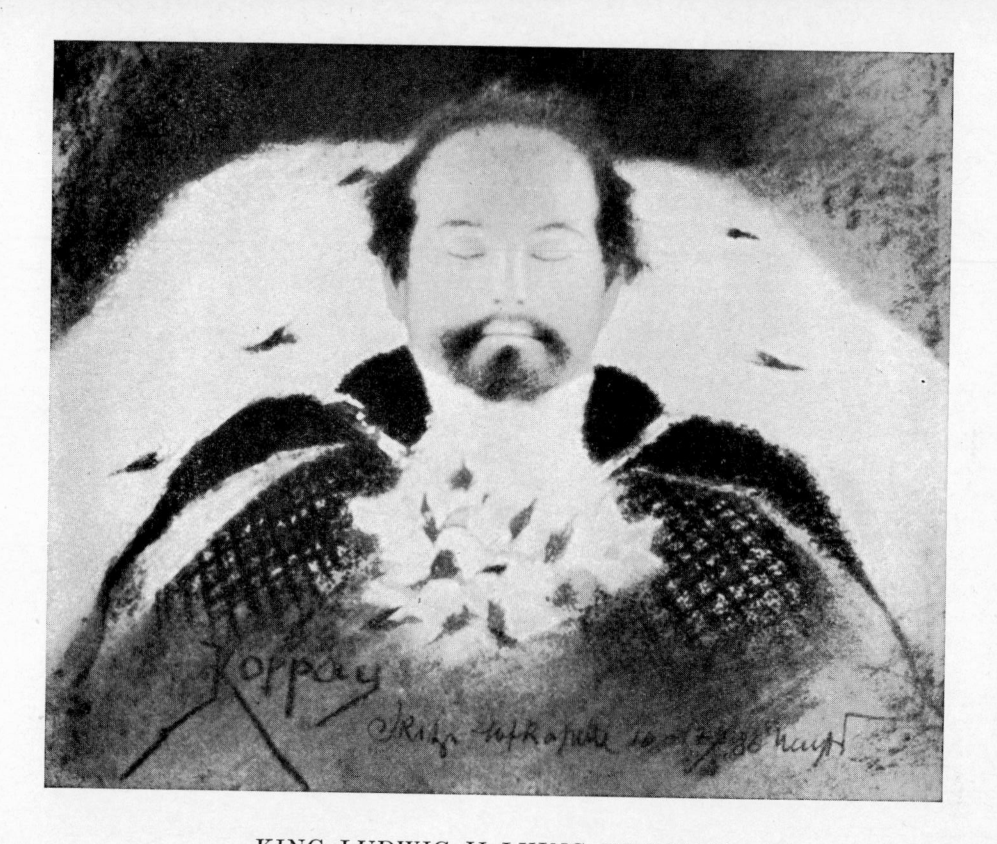

KING LUDWIG II LYING IN STATE

From a sketch in oils by Koppay made on June 16 and 17, 1886. In the Villa Hermes, Lainz.

was better off in his grave than if he had gone on living under the new Government.

Everyday life and family visits now claimed her attention, but she could not shake off the nervous agitation which had troubled her even before the disaster. In whatever company she found herself her comments on the leading men in Bavaria and their recent behavior toward the King were scathing and unrestrained, and she quite agreed with the Countess Festetics, who wrote to Frau von Ferenczy that all the waters of the ocean could not remove the stigma of disgrace attaching to them for their brutal treatment of the King. In this unbalanced state Elizabeth had become virtually estranged from her mother, and now an unfortunate incident occurred which threatened to cause a total breach with her family. Her sister Sophie, the Duchess of Alençon, who was staying at Possenhofen with her daughter Louise, caught scarlet fever, and by some oversight no warning was sent to Feldafing, with the result that Valerie unwittingly went over to Possenhofen and asked her cousin to go for a walk with her. She had gone inside when Louise said: "For heaven's sake, leave the house, Valerie. You ought not to have come in. Mamma has scarlet fever." The Archduchess rushed home in alarm and met her mother hurrying to meet her, white with terror. "Surely you have not been to see Aunt Sophie!" she said. "I never heard of such a thing! It is scandalous! That doctor has no conscience whatever, nor have any the rest of them. They knew yesterday evening that she had scarlet fever and never sent us word."

Dr. Kerzl, physician to the imperial family, declared that in the circumstances there could be no question of infection, but poor Valerie had to keep gargling with carbolic. The Empress decided then and there to go home, naturally without saying good-bye to the household at Possenhofen. She left her old home in a state of exasperation, though she did not omit to write the usual little poem, the closing verses of which show how violent was the reaction of her outraged sensibilities: "Farewell, my lake," they ran, "this day I cast my home into thy depths and go forth once more into the world restless and homeless." The doctor's assurances were powerless to allay her fears of infection, and she vowed that if Valerie did not catch the fever she would go on a pilgrimage to Mariazell and make an offering to the shrine. She succeeded in making Valerie share her own nervousness, till the Archduchess kept imagining that she had a sore throat. "I saw myself already on my deathbed," she wrote in her diary, and added in brackets: "which I found vastly unpleasant."

From Feldafing the Empress went to Gastein, hoping that a cure might relieve her sciatica, but Dr. Widerhofer declared that in her present condition it would be dangerous for her to take the baths, so they drove on to Ischl, Elizabeth walking beside the carriage while Valerie rode in it, her usual companion being Colonel Latour, the Crown Prince's former tutor, who never stopped talking. He had nothing very intelligent to say, and Valerie's comment in her diary was: "His stupidity is a comfort to me, for I believe the fact that Rudolf is what he is, and not what he might be, is due to no more than that." They were all annoyed because the Crown Prince called their beloved Ischl a "frightful hole" (*schreckliches Nest*), though Elizabeth considered that it was already getting too fashionable.

The Empress' verses at this time were full of morbid preoccupation with the ideas of death and her own death in particular, and Valerie was alarmed at the extent to which this melancholy and disgust with life which, she had to admit, were really unreasonable, were gaining control of her mother's mind. She wondered what would have happened if she really had caught scarlet fever and died of it. "It is appalling," she wrote, "to think that I should be the only link binding my mother to earth."

Valerie having escaped infection, Elizabeth had now to fulfil her vow. On July 21 she went to Mariazell, where she had a Mass said at the altar of Our Lady of Grace for the late King Ludwig. She confessed and went to Holy Communion, pouring out her whole heart to the priest and describing the painful effect produced upon her by the King's death. On August 12 she went to the Villa Meran at Gastein, where the venerable German Emperor was also taking the cure, and called upon him unannounced. She also took Valerie with her to call upon Prince and Princess Bismarck, and the little Archduchess said to herself: "You are now in the presence of the cleverest man of your day." The Empress had met the Imperial Chancellor in earlier days and remembered having been struck by a certain hardness in his face; but what she now saw was a hale and hearty old man with an expression of mild benevolence in his pale blue eyes, while Valerie was "sorry" to admit that she found him "positively congenial." The old Grand Duchess of Weimar also came to call upon Elizabeth, who pointedly invited her to sit immediately opposite the clock, in the hope that she would soon leave. The visitor was very hard of hearing, and when Elizabeth remarked: "I am afraid the illuminations tonight will be spoiled by the rain," replied with a stately inclination of the head: "I hope so!" at which both mother and daughter restrained their laughter with difficulty. At last the Empress said: "My Valerie has a very severe cold. I wonder whether it is infectious"—whereupon the Grand Duchess made a hurried departure.

At the end of August they returned to Ischl, where the members of the Tuscan branch of the family, including the young Archduke Franz Salvator, were frequently their guests, rather to Francis Joseph's annoyance. "Surely Valerie is not going to make yet another marriage inside the family!" he said. "What will be the end of us if she does? The Saxon (the Crown Prince of Saxony) is coming to Vienna during the winter. Now that would be a good thing and in every way appropriate."

From Ischl they went on to Gödöllö, where the Empress led a very different life since she had given up riding. Rising at half past five in the morning, she would do gymnastics for a long time after breakfast. Then the Emperor would join her and walk up and down discussing the events of the day—a time which he enjoyed above all others. Elizabeth now had leisure to think over past events, and once more recalled the episode of the masked ball and the poem which she had written about it. About this time one of her relatives went on a long tour in South America, and she gave him a letter containing the poem to post to Herr Pacher.

Elizabeth was still studying Heine with her characteristic ardor and thoroughness, and found Robert Proelsz's recent book on him most absorbing. "Heine is my companion always and everywhere," she wrote to the Archduchess Valerie. "Every word, every letter in Heine is a jewel." But most of all she loved his poems, and her pocket edition in its dark green linen cover never left her. She considered that Heine had been misunderstood and unjustly judged in his own country, for a poet ought not to be estimated by the same standards as ordinary men. She had pictures or busts of him put up everywhere, at Lainz and Gödöllö, in the Burg and at Schönbrunn, and even at Ischl. Hearing that a nephew of the poet's, Baron Heine-Geldern, was living in Vienna, she commanded him to wait upon her, for she had heard that he owned certain pictures and other things which had belonged to Heine. She talked to him about the great man's other surviving relatives, especially his sister, the venerable Frau Emden of Hamburg, and made up her mind to pay that lady a visit in the course of her travels.

Since the death of Ludwig II Elizabeth had known no rest. It was now quite clear to her that the King had been really insane, and in view of the other cases of insanity in the House of Wittelsbach and the many characteristics which she shared with Ludwig II, she again began to dread the same fate, and to interest herself in the arrangements made for the care of the insane, which were very defective at that time. On December 11, 1886, after her return to Vienna, she visited the chief lunatic asylum for lower Austria at Bründlfeld, appearing there quite unexpectedly with her sister-in-law, the wife of Duke Karl Theodor. The director was hastily summoned and appeared just as he was, in white overalls. Elizabeth spent some time examining a group of fantastic oil paintings in the manner of the two Breughels by the insane artist Kratky, which represented in a confused but not altogether unsuccessful way the basic fact of nature that one form of being can only exist through the death of another.

At first the staff intended to show Elizabeth just those parts of the establishment in which there were no violent cases, but she insisted upon being shown the dangerous cases, too, and did not hesitate to address remarks to the patients. When she came to the department for the "quiet" cases, the women patients were all sitting together in a large room, talking, embroidering, or working at handicrafts, and rose and curtseyed as she entered. Among them was a Fräulein Windisch, an attractive woman of twenty-eight, who had occasional attacks of mental derangement which had begun after an unhappy love affair. The moment the Empress entered, this young woman, who was usually subdued, suddenly shrieked, darted toward the Empress, and before anybody could prevent her, tore off her hat. Elizabeth turned pale and shrank back, but the doctor had already seized the patient. "Why, good heavens, Fräulein Windisch," he exclaimed, "you are usually so good."

"What!" cried the unhappy patient, "does that woman pretend she is the Empress of Austria? I never heard such insolence! Why, *I* am the Empress!" Elizabeth left the room, and her sister-in-law helped her to put on her hat again; yet, in spite of this shock, she insisted upon seeing the part of the establishment where the violent cases were kept, for she wished to convince herself that they were not badly treated. Just as she was on the point of leaving she abruptly said: "I should like, please, to pay another visit to the ward where that happened."*

"Your Majesty," replied the doctor, "I cannot be responsible for the consequences if you do. I strongly advise you not to go back."

"No, please," she urged. "I must go up again." The director had to give way. Fräulein Windisch was still sitting in the room when the Empress entered, and approached the Empress again. But this time she fell on her knees before her and begged her forgiveness. Tears ran down Elizabeth's cheeks as she waved aside the doctors and wardresses who had formed a protecting ring between her and the patient, and, raising the young woman to her feet, took her by the hand and soothed her.

The Duke Karl Theodor had been trying for some time to make peace between Elizabeth, her mother, and the Duchess of Alençon, but the Empress had not yet forgotten the scarlet fever incident. "Such stupidity and callousness are inexcusable," she said, and for once the Crown Prince agreed with Valerie, who said this was an exaggeration. Rudolf heard rumors of Valerie's approaching betrothal and

* From personal information given the author by Dr. Weiss, at that time on the staff of the asylum.

asked his mother what truth there was in them, expressing his disapproval in a cold, sarcastic manner. He was growing more and more estranged from his family, with the exception of the Archduke Johann Salvator, who shared his negative, critical, and bitter view of life. Elizabeth worried about what might happen if Rudolf became Emperor and the Archduke Franz Salvator her son-in-law, for, she believed, it might be very uncomfortable. Her idea was that, if war were to break out between France and Germany before it did between Austria and Russia, the Archduke might volunteer to serve in the German Army, and thus put all those who were against him to shame. One day while Elizabeth and Valerie were walking up and down in the park at Schönbrunn talking over the future, they met Frau Schratt, who had had many conversations with the Emperor and Empress since the first meetings at Ischl and Kremsier. It happened to be March 1, and the actress offered the Empress a bunch of violets, since, she said, on that day of the year they brought luck. As an acknowledgment of this little attention Elizabeth and Valerie went to the theatre that evening for the first act of a comedy by Ohnet in which Frau Schratt was playing, though as a rule Elizabeth did not go to see modern pieces or lively comedies, preferring, for instance, Sophocles' *Œdipus at Colonus*.

In the spring of 1887 Elizabeth elected to visit Herkulesbad in Southern Hungary, which had been described to her as very lovely. She walked for hours in that picturesque region with Sárolta Majláth, going as far as the Rumanian frontier, where they ate a picnic lunch in the forest and drank some sheep's milk brought them by a handsome Rumanian lad. Elizabeth would sit dreaming and writing poetry by moonlight till late into the night and insisted upon sleeping as usual by the open window, though her room was on the ground floor.

The inhabitants of the place, who had expected to see a proud, unapproachable sovereign, found instead a simple-mannered lady who disliked all pomp and associated with people of all classes on equal terms, and not only loved nature, but enjoyed it as few people were capable of doing. One of the poems which she wrote here in Magyar maintained that truth and fidelity are to be found only in nature, to whose consolations she could always turn without fear of disappointment. Here, too, she kept her Heine always at her side and became so deeply imbued with his works that she felt herself to be living in a sort of mystic communion with the poet's spirit.

On April 28, Queen Elizabeth of Rumania ("Carmen Sylva") appeared at Herkulesbad,* and one day the conversation turned upon Heine. "I have rather got over my admiration for him," said Carmen Sylva, "for there are many things in his poems which affect me unpleasantly." She saw that the reason why Elizabeth thought so highly of him was because, like herself, he had "a contempt for all externals, a bitterness, but at the same time a touch of impishness such as characterized Elizabeth and so often drew original and startling remarks from her"; but also because he felt the same despair as she did at the falseness of the world and could not find words strong enough to castigate its emptiness. That evening Elizabeth in bed was thinking over her conversation with Carmen Sylva when suddenly she saw the poet's profile quite distinct and clear-cut before her, as she knew it from pictures, while at the same time she experienced a curious, unpleasant feeling as though his soul were trying to draw her own out of her body. "The struggle lasted for some seconds," she said afterwards in describing it to her

* She afterwards described her impressions of Elizabeth in an article entitled *"Die Kaiserin Elisabeth in Sinaia,"* in the *Neue Freie Presse* (December 25, 1906).

daughter, "but Jehovah would not permit my soul to leave my body. The vision faded, and in spite of the disappointment of continuing to live, it left me happy in the confirmation of my sometimes wavering faith, my increased love of Jehovah, and my conviction that He sanctioned the intercourse between my soul and that of Heine." In response to an incredulous observation from Valerie, Elizabeth assured her that she could swear to the truth of it, and that she had seen the apparition with her own eyes, while fully awake.

Next day the Empress and Carmen Sylva went for a walk in the forest and Elizabeth talked of building a country house in those lovely surroundings. Each of the two ladies was obviously interested in the other and curious about her, but certain antagonisms could be felt between them.

"Carmen Sylva," said Elizabeth to her daughter Valerie, "is very sweet, amusing, and interesting, but her feet are firmly planted upon earth. She could not possibly understand me, though I could her. I am fond of her. She is so fond of narration and making up stories, it is what she enjoys, and the King is so prosaic that an abyss separates them spiritually. Of course she does not put it so bluntly as this, but I managed to get it out of her."

The Empress Elizabeth was rather mistaken, for Carmen Sylva had formed quite a fair estimate of her. She recognized that Elizabeth's character was genuine and natural, without the slightest trace of artificiality, and that that was why she could not tolerate court ceremonies and formalism. "People had tried," said Carmen Sylva, "to harness the fairies' child (*Feenkind*) to the torture of etiquette and stiff, dead forms, but the fairies' child cannot endure bolts and bars, restraint and servitude. The fairies' child has hidden wings, which it spreads and flies away whenever it finds the world unbearable."

She also saw that Elizabeth had no desire for "the recognition of the world, which she despises, but there is a prodigious force latent in the Empress, which has to work itself off (*austoben*) somehow. The excess of it has to find expression in riding and walking, traveling and writing, and she has to do everything with all her might, if only to escape the crushing pressure of circumstance."

After Carmen Sylva's departure Elizabeth continued to enjoy her carefree life, except for the snakes—some of them poisonous—which she found everywhere. Her daughter Valerie had sent her a live salamander, so she thought of sending her one of the larger harmless snakes in return, but when one of them tried to bite her, she gave up the idea, merely sending one specimen to the menagerie at Schönbrunn, and another to her friend Ida Ferenczy, who started back in terror when she opened the curious cagelike box.

On May 13 Elizabeth went to Sinaia to return Carmen Sylva's visit, and, as the Queen understood her tastes, no receptions or solemn festivities were arranged for her. What impressed Carmen Sylva about Elizabeth was the way in which she looked people straight in the eyes and was quite incapable of "draping the truth with even the slightest cloak of convention." At her first dinner at Sinaia Elizabeth lamented the etiquette and ceremonies that were inseparable from her rank.

"But is not your beauty a help to you?" said the Queen. "Does not that cure you of your shyness?"

"I am not shy any longer, only bored!" replied the Empress. "They dress me up in fine clothes and all sorts of jewels, and then I go out and say a few words to people for hours on end, till I can bear it no longer. At last I hurry back to my room, tear it all off and write, while Heine dictates to me." The Queen's impression was that Elizabeth never said anything commonplace, but as a rule something totally unexpected, and the Empress confided all sorts of things to Carmen Sylva which she usually said only to her daughter, especially her reflections on the underlying essence of Nature. The insane artist's picture which she had seen at the lunatic asylum had made an impression upon her, and she considered it perfectly true that all forms of life are cruel, the stronger devouring the weaker, and the clever striking down the stupid, without pity, justice, or law, simply because they are the stronger.

"Do you mean to publish your poems and writings?" asked Carmen Sylva. But the Empress replied: "I write and I compose poetry, but I do not want anybody to see what it is like yet. Later, after many years, when we are long dead, it shall all be published."

For a long time after Elizabeth had left Sinaia, Carmen Sylva could not cease musing over the character of her namesake and fellow sovereign. "We are apt," she wrote, "to accuse a person of forgetting his duty so soon as he is unwilling to turn the wheel, the treadmill, the old water wheel, which custom has devised for this or that caste or category of mankind. A man has only to have the courage to be different and think and act differently, to be stoned by those who can only get on by going round and round on the treadmill. . . . I always say that fashions exist for women with no taste, etiquette for people with no breeding, church for people with no religion, and the treadmill for those with no imagination or elasticity."

Elizabeth returned to Vienna, and Valerie was astonished at the change in her, noting that her mother had become unusually devout since King Ludwig's death, more so than she had ever known her to be before. Elizabeth now submitted everything to the great Jehovah's guidance and committed everything to His charge. "But," wrote Valerie, "Mamma's piety is of a kind all her own, unlike that of other people, not so much communicative as ecstatic, introspective, and abstract—for instance, that cult of the dead in which she has recently indulged, especially over Heine and Ludwig II."

At the end of May the imperial family went into residence again at the new Villa Hermes, but both Elizabeth and Valerie were still unable to feel at home there.

"These marble reliefs, these luxurious carpets," wrote Valerie, "these fireplaces of chased bronze, these innumerable angels and Cupids, the carvings in every hole and corner, this mannered rococo style! How I wish we were back at home again!"

They were joined by the Crown Prince, who seemed to be on bad terms with his wife, and, as Valerie remarked, "behaved as though he wished to be taken for a man of a hundred." When they were discussing the question of peace or war and mentioned the risk to his life, he merely said with a disdainful gesture: "When one has known every enjoyment, there is nothing left to interest one."

Elizabeth was also worried about her sister the Duchess of Alençon, who was interested in a doctor of middle-class origin and for a moment even contemplated obtaining a divorce and marrying him. What the Empress feared was that she might be declared mentally deficient, for she had been taken to Graz to Dr. Krafft-Ebing, who had declared treatment to be necessary. The state of her nerves proved, however, to be due to the aftereffects of scarlet fever, and the peace and quiet of the sanatorium effected a cure; but the whole thing had been a shock to the Empress, and she often irritated the Archduchess Valerie by her excessive solicitude. Besides, they did not agree about politics, Valerie taking a more optimistic view of the future of Austria than her mother, who said on one occasion: "The old, rotten stock is diseased." She would often say that Francis Joseph was the last Emperor but one of the House of Habsburg and repeat the ancient prophecy that it had started with a Rudolf and would end with a Rudolf. These gloomy predictions about the future of the Empire naturally brought her into conflict with Francis Joseph, and at such moments she would even say that it was hard to get on with him. "For my part," commented Valerie, "I find it far easier to get on with him than with her, God forgive me."

As Carmen Sylva had said, the Empress must be "forever traveling, traveling, traveling," and the world was almost too narrow and small to satisfy her. She had hardly returned from Herkulesbad, where she had felt so well, and now, in July, she was starting out for England again, passing through Hamburg.

About this time Herr Fritz Pacher received a letter with a Brazilian stamp on it. He opened it in surprise, and out fluttered a printed page, on which he found, to his amazement, some verses entitled "The Song of the Yellow Domino," and headed in English "Long, Long Ago." They ran as follows:

Thinkest thou still of that night in the glittering hall?
'Twas long, long ago, long ago.
Of the night when two souls to each other did call?
'Twas long, long ago, long ago.
'Twas there that our friendship so strangely began.
Dost thou think of it, friend, if but now and then?
Of those heartfelt avowals, so true and profound
That we exchanged while the dance went round?
Too soon, alas! those hours went by.
A clasp of the hand and away I must fly.
Though my face must needs be veiled from thy sight,
On my soul's hidden depths I turned a light.
Friend, what greater thing could I do than this?
Years passed by and faded away,
But we never knew such another day.
By night I question the stars on high,
Yet never have they vouchsafed a reply.

Now near, now far methinks thou dost roam
On some other star hast thou found a home?
If thou livest, ah! send me but a sign,
Though I scarce can hope it may yet be mine.
For 'twas long, long ago, long ago!
I would wait it no more,
Wait no more!

No address was given, and not a word was written by hand. But Fritz Pacher resolved to show her that he knew perfectly well who she was. He had never attempted any poetic flights before, but he determined to reply in verse and penned some stanzas "To the Unknown Lady":

'Tis long ago, yet I think of thee,
Remote though thou may'st be.
For, as I think, within me stirs
Youth's roseate memory.

Recall'st thou with what haughty mien
Thy hand thou did'st refuse
At first—yet as I turned to leave,
Did'st condescension choose?

How all that evening, arm in arm,
We jested, laughed, conversed?
And how I nearly guessed the truth—
But thou hadst vanished first.

Yes, all of this was long ago—
But simple were thy wiles,
For majesty was written in
Thy form, thy voice, thy smiles.

The great ones of this world are not
From all caprices free,
And now, it seems, it is thy whim
To learn who I may be.

Not that my fortune 'twas to please—
No flattering dreams are mine—
But from my lips the honest truth
To hear thou did'st incline.

Mankind, prostrate before thy feet,
Filled thee with naught but scorn.
Its lies, its flattering words too long
Thy noble heart had torn.

While life is his he will look back
With gladness on that day,
For thou hast feeling, wit, and heart,
Whatever men may say.

"What!" thou dost cry indignantly,
"Insolent! dost thou dare,
Divining my exalted rank,
To stand unbending there?"

With deference I answer: "Nay,
Whatever thou may'st be
To others, witty fair, thou'rt but
A domino to me."

Too well I know, unless this world
Shall to disorder yield,
Forever must my humble lips
Remain discreetly sealed.

Yet I will venture this farewell—
This right at least I claim,
Praying that thou wilt evermore
Greet with a smile my name.

And think when thou dost lay aside
All grandeur and all sham:
"One faithful soul at least there is,
Knows me for what I am."

The letter was addressed as usual, *poste restante*, but months went by and it was never claimed. After a while Pacher himself called and inquired for it, and it was returned to him untouched. Nobody had asked for it. And so the adventure, which was no adventure, was at an end.

Meanwhile Elizabeth had stopped in Hamburg for the purpose of making herself known to the poet Heine's sister, Frau Charlotte Emden. The aged lady received her with enthusiasm and showed her a number of letters and manuscripts, but the Empress, to her disappointment, was not presented with a single specimen of Heine's writing. She was merely asked to accept a little seal which, she was told, he had always used. "Let us hope that that at least is genuine," was her private comment; but she promised the poet's old sister that the first member of the imperial house who went to Paris should lay flowers upon his grave—a promise afterwards fulfilled by the Crown Princess Stephanie. After the Empress' visit to Hamburg, her love of Heine became generally known, and whenever it was desired to pay her some attention, it generally took some form connected with the poet.

From Hamburg Elizabeth went on to England, where she stayed at Cromer in Norfolk for the sea bathing. At the end of July she wrote to her husband that she was going on a visit to the Queen in the Isle of Wight, and shortly after that would be coming home; to which he replied: "*Edes, szeretett lelkem* (Dear, beloved soul), my infinitely beloved angel, your dear letter made me very happy, for it was another proof that you are fond of me and are glad to come back to us. . . ."

This time Elizabeth had arranged to meet her husband and daughter at Kreuth on the Tegernsee, where the marriage of her parents had taken place nearly sixty years before. During Mass Elizabeth called her daughter's attention to the fact that over the altar-piece before which her parents had stood on that occasion was inscribed in large letters: "Father, forgive them, for they know not what they do"—a discouraging omen which had unfortunately been only too completely justified. From Kreuth the party made an expedition along the shores of the Achensee as far as the Achen Pass, and Elizabeth reveled in the scenery. "This beautiful region," she remarked, "is a poem of Jehovah's and His poems are inexhaustible in their beauty, variety, and number." At Kreuth, too, Elizabeth read Valerie the poems she had written at Cromer, and her daughter was amazed at the ease and copiousness with which Elizabeth composed verse, and considered much that she wrote both beautiful and original, though much, again, was too original to be really beautiful. Elizabeth's brother Karl Theodor also considered her poems good, but warned her against following too far the exaggerated ideas among which she lived, and remarked anxiously to Valerie that this imaginary communion with the soul of Heine would overtax her nerves to such an extent that they might end by "snapping." But Valerie thought otherwise. In view of the disturbing ideas which so often came into her mother's head, she believed that creative work brought her happiness, for she had spent so many years without any serious occupation at all. "My mother's life is a strange one," she wrote, "her ideas are occupied with the past, her efforts with the distant future. To her, the present is an unsubstantial, phantomlike thing, and her chief pride is that nobody guesses her to be a poetess. . . ."

Elizabeth confided to her daughter that it was her object to have her poems published long after her death for the benefit of those unfortunates who had been branded as criminals on account of their political activities and liberal tendencies. The poems continued to show strong traces of the influence of Heine, who entirely dominated the Empress' mind at this time. She felt it most unjust that no monument had yet been set up to him, and wished to do something about it, though she did not quite know how. Her idea was to issue an appeal to the German people, asking them to subscribe to a monument which she wanted to have set up in Düsseldorf, Heine's birthplace, and she questioned the actor Lewinsky about how this could best be done.

The Emperor's birthday was celebrated at Ischl by a large family dinner party, at which twenty-five members of the ruling house were present, among them Franz Salvator's uncle Ludwig Salvator, the eccentric Archduke who lived in the Balearic Islands. He wrote learned and charming books about his home and always sent them to Elizabeth, for whom he had a great admiration. Neither the Archduke nor the Empress was an ordinary person, so they got on well together, though Ludwig Salvator was regarded as a family joke. He was unmarried and lived as he chose, cared nothing for appearances, and was always dressed in a baggy coat, having only a single military tunic in his possession, so that everybody felt uncomfortable when he appeared at court. His yacht was a kind of communistic state; complete equality prevailed on board. He shared the crew's sleeping quarters and meals, performed the same menial duties, and dressed exactly as they did. Apart from this, however, he was a highly cultured man, with scientific interests which he used his property and rank to forward.

At this dinner Franz Salvator sat next the Archduchess Valerie, for the Emperor was slowly coming round to the idea of their marriage. On August 21, when Rudolf's twenty-ninth birthday was being celebrated, Francis Joseph was just raising his glass at the end of a short speech proposing his son's health, when Elizabeth whispered to him that it was Franz Salvator's twenty-first birthday, too. After a moment's hesitation, the Emperor raised his glass for the second time and added with a good-natured glance: "Very well, then, to the other one's health, too!"

Elizabeth now discussed things frankly with Franz Salvator. "You know," she said, "Valerie is so conscientious. I believe she is really fond of you already, but you are both quite free, and so young. You must meet often, you cannot get to know each other too well. You must not think, as so many people do, that I want to marry Valerie to you in order to keep her near me. When she marries, it is the same to me whether she goes to China or remains in Austria. In any case she will be lost to me; but I have confidence in you and your love and character, and if I were to die today, my mind would be perfectly at rest if I were leaving Valerie to you." "If that man is false," said Elizabeth to her daughter afterwards, "then I will never trust anyone again!" She was already making up her mind that she would not be like so many other mothers-in-law. She knew from her own experience what they could be like, and once when a newly married man was presented to her, she asked him, to his amazement: "Is your mother-in-law objectionable (*zuwider*)?" "Oh, no, not in the least," was the reply. Upon which Elizabeth said calmly: "Only wait! Mothers-in-law are always charming at first—but after that!"

Though Elizabeth's mind was full of her daughter's anticipated betrothal, even now she could not resist her overwhelming love of travel. She knew no peace, though she had already been to Herkulesbad, Hamburg, and England that year as well as to Bavaria. Francis Joseph was alone a great deal and was really pained to find that his wife now took hardly any interest in his political cares, still less in her ceremonial duties as Empress. Unable, as a rule, to settle down anywhere, she had found only one spot for which she cared enough to want to build a villa there, and that was

Corfu. During that winter her Controller of the Household, Baron Nopcsa, had already written to Baron Alexander von Warsberg, the great authority on ancient and modern Greece, asking him to look about and see whether he could not find a property for sale there. Elizabeth had been reading Warsberg's *Odysseische Landschaften* and now invited the author to accompany her to Corfu on the yacht *Greif* (Condor). He was none too pleased at this, for he had a "weak chest" and knew quite well that those in attendance upon the Empress could not take much care of themselves, though he had small idea how exhausting it would really be to travel with her. She had a thirst for knowledge and plunged into the Homeric world with her usual ardor. The Consul Warsberg showed her the island as she had never seen it before, and she felt as though she were seeing it through the eyes of Homer himself. "Corfu," declared Elizabeth, "is an ideal place to stay in, with its climate, its walks through the unending shade of the olive groves, its good roads and glorious sea air, and over all the splendid moonlight." After a short excursion to Albania, they went to Leucadia and on past Sappho's headland to Ithaca, the island of Odysseus, and Elizabeth walked with Warsberg where the hero of the *Odyssey* had trod. On the voyage she had read the Consul's books in which these idyllic scenes on Ithaca were reconstructed, with copious quotations from Homer; and now, on October 30, she went down to the shore as Odysseus had done and plucked a whole basketful of flowers to send to her dear ones at home. Her escort took pains to make her expedition upon classic soil enjoyable, and she found it so profitable that, thanks to Warsberg, she said, it was "quite an educational voyage." She was enthusiastic about the Consul, but he found it hard to keep up with her. "The exhaustion exceeds anything I ever experienced on my travels in the East," he wrote in his diary,* "and they were not devoid of exertion."

The officers of the *Greif* observed this odd-looking scholar, as he seemed to them, with a jaundiced eye, for the Empress expected everybody to share in her mania for Odysseus. It was no light matter to serve her, and the joys of cruising round Ithaca in the worst of weather in an old tub like the *Greif* involved serious responsibilities. But Elizabeth cared nothing for this. She was entirely absorbed in the Homeric world and followed Warsberg's every word, and whenever he mentioned any place of interest, the *Greif* had to visit it at once. Elizabeth had originally meant to be away for only a fortnight, but by this time she was so lost in her Hellenic dreamland that she did not want to go home till her name day, November 19, and sent Francis Joseph this unwelcome news from Ithaca. "However," he wrote to her from Vienna on October 29, "if you consider it necessary for your health, I will say no more, though since the spring of this year we have not spent more than a few days together." Francis Joseph was entirely incapable of entering into his consort's sympathy with Greek antiquity. "I simply cannot imagine," he wrote, "what you are doing in Ithaca for so many days. However, the main thing is that you should be well and contented, and this seems to be the case."

Warsberg took Elizabeth to the village of Staoros, supposed to be the site of the ancient Homeric city, and they ate their light lunch in a simple dwelling house standing roughly on the same spot as Odysseus' palace. Elizabeth was delighted beyond words with the island. "I should like to be buried here one day," she said to the Landgravine Fürstenberg, and showed her a poem on this theme.

* Now in the possession of his grand-nephew, Alexander Freiherr von Warsberg.

Francis Joseph was growing impatient at Elizabeth's absence. "My longing thoughts are always with you," he wrote to her from Gödöllö, "and I sorrowfully reckon up the time—unfortunately such a long one—between us and our next meeting. . . . You are missed everywhere, and naturally most of all by me."

Bad weather awaited Elizabeth at Ithaca, with incessant wind and rain, and it was impossible to make any excursions, so on November 4 the yacht returned to Corfu. The officers of the yacht blamed the learned Warsberg, with his "classical ecstasies" over the "bones of Ulysses," for the whole thing. They had to be careful, however, to avoid ribald allusions to the subject before the Empress, for she took the whole thing in deadly earnest, and Warsberg's words of wisdom were gospel to her.

During her stay in Corfu, Elizabeth would go out sailing in a cutter all day, and while Francis Joseph was counting the days to her return, she was regretting that her visit would so soon be over. The Emperor followed his wife's doings from afar in a sceptical spirit, and when at last she wrote that she was preparing to sail for home, his reply was: "How happy I am that tomorrow is your last expedition in the cutter and that your jaunts (*Promenaden*) in disturbed Albania will at last be at an end, but I shall not be quite cheerful again till you have made a safe voyage home and are with us once more."

Elizabeth arrived home punctually in time for her name day. She now felt quite sure that her daughter's betrothal to Franz Salvator would soon take place, but when she developed to her husband her idea that an officer who was persecuted and snubbed in the Austrian army could always turn to the great and glorious German army—not, she insisted, the Prussian one—Francis Joseph exclaimed: "Well, that is a nice thing to say!" She pressed this suggestion upon Franz

Salvator and he, too, raised objections: "But if I were to enter the German army," he said, "I might find myself forced to fight against my own country." "Oh, no!" replied Elizabeth. "Never again will it be possible to induce Germans to draw the sword upon Germans."

The Archduchess Valerie was really overwhelmed by her mother's "vast, indeed crushing, love," which she felt she did nothing to deserve. She faithfully records in her diary one of her mother's passionate protestations of love, which may be taken as typical: "I really love nobody but you," said Elizabeth. "If you leave me my life is at an end. One can only love like this once in one's life. All one's thoughts are of the beloved one, it is entirely one-sided—one requires and expects nothing from the other person. And for that reason I cannot conceive how anybody can love a number of people. Sophie took the place of a mother toward my other children, but from the very first moment I said to myself that things must be different with you. You had got to remain my own, my ownest child, my treasure, over whom none but myself must be allowed any right, and the whole of that capacity for loving which had hitherto been imprisoned in my heart I have poured out upon you."

With equally unrestrained passion she threw herself into her poetry, which again occupied all her thoughts. In memory of her recent visit to Hamburg, she sent some beautiful presents to Ludwig von Emden, the husband of Heine's sister, who replied by sending her a portrait of Heine and some manuscripts, which particularly delighted Elizabeth—her disappointment at the time of her visit had obviously become known to the family. Elizabeth's poems were now legion. A niece of the Baroness Wallersee was summoned to Gödöllö and commissioned to make a fair copy of them all under seal of the utmost secrecy. In the evening she would read the poems to the Empress, who corrected and improved them, after which they went off to the State printing press, where a special staff of compositors and other officials was intrusted with the business of printing them. The pages were then locked up in an iron box with an inscription on the lid, stating in what circumstances it was ultimately to be opened.

Every evening Valerie would read the *Odyssey* to her mother, and the Emperor's anxieties about home and foreign politics fell into this idyllic inner life like echoes from a distant world. Valerie describes how the prospect of war was anxiously discussed in the family circle—which had been joined at Gödöllö that winter by the Duke Karl Theodor—for the tension between Austria and Russia was becoming still more acute. "With compulsory military service and our present armaments, nobody can really desire war," said Francis Joseph: "but if it really were to come, Austria-Hungary would presumably be on the side of Germany, Italy, and perhaps England too, while Russia would be the ally of France; but even without France, the preponderating power would be on the side of Russia." "But what is the real, fundamental reason of it all?" asked the Archduchess. "Oh! nobody knows," replied Francis Joseph. "There *is* no real reason."

On December 20, 1887, Baron Warsberg appeared at Gödöllö on a visit to the Empress. He was tall and emaciated, with rather sharp features, a red-gold moustache, and hair turning grey, but his eyes were intelligent and piercing. Elizabeth revered him as "a superior in mind," and, to quote Warsberg's own words, overwhelmed him with favors. She was "more than gracious, she was positively familiar," he says. "Perhaps nobody has ever stood in such a close relationship to her," he wrote in his diary, "as she has assigned to me about her person." This was an illusion which he shared with many of those who came in close contact with the Empress.

On December 24 Elizabeth celebrated her fiftieth birthday in no very happy frame of mind. She was oppressed by the thought that half a century had passed since her birth—not that age had impaired her beauty, as was alleged by those who did not know her well, but because she had spent her life in a state of inward discontent, nervousness, and dreariness.

Elizabeth's frequent absences and lack of interest in the destiny of the Empire or her court duties hurt the Emperor, so it is quite understandable that he should have been increasingly charmed and amused by such a simple, sensible, normal woman as Katharina Schratt, with her dry humor and *joie de vivre*, and her unselfish and disinterested nature, who talked to him freely, saying whatever came into her head. Elizabeth's conscience was not altogether easy at having left her husband alone so often, so she encouraged this friendship, seeing no more in it than a friendly camaraderie which helped to distract the Emperor's mind from the cares of government when she herself was away. She commissioned the painter Angeli to paint a portrait of the actress, and pointedly went to call upon Frau Schratt during her visit to the Wolfgangsee in July, 1886, when the gossips had begun to talk of the Emperor's infatuation.

The Crown Prince Rudolf and his wife were present at the birthday celebrations, and Duke Karl Theodor summed up the uncomfortable atmosphere which seemed to pervade Rudolf's personality as follows: "He is undoubtedly remarkable, but not so remarkable as he himself imagines. He has rather too little heart. Rudolf's good qualities have been stifled by his entourage, and he has been turned into what is often an unsympathetic, and indeed, sinister person."

The Empress had a return of her sciatica on her birthday and began to long for the south, as she always did when the winter arrived. Valerie was greatly perturbed and had recourse to a discreet confidante, the Mother Superior of the Convent of the Sacré-Cœur in Vienna, Mère Mayer, to whom she had also confided her love for Franz Salvator. She poured out her heart to her, bewailing her mother's state of mind and the strong influence still exerted over her by earlier circumstances—the way, for instance, in which the shadow of the Archduchess Sophie continued to darken the relations between the Emperor and Empress.

"Ah!" said Mère Mayer, "if only the Empress knew how she is loved and adored! If only she were willing, if only she would let herself be seen a little more, she would have all hearts at her feet. In more favorable circumstances Her Majesty might have been a Maria Theresa; she possesses all the necessary qualities. But one question: Is the Empress pious?"

"Oh, yes, she is pious, but in her own way; she is not a good churchwoman."

"Try to bring influence to bear on your mother, Your Imperial Highness, to submit to the discipline of the Church, and also to become reconciled with her relatives at home, from whom she has often been estranged since the unhappy events of the year 1886."

"That is very difficult, reverend Mother. There is nothing more hopeless than to induce Mamma to change an opinion once she has formed it for what she considers sound reasons."

Elizabeth had noticed that her husband was a little put out at her long absence during the year 1887, so in spite of her sciatica and her longing for the south she decided to stay at home till the time came round for her usual holiday in March, and to take part in the carnival celebrations in both Vienna and Budapest for her husband's sake. On January 18 she talked to people for four hours on end at the court ball in Vienna, and in spite of the many political misunderstandings between Austria and Hungary was present at a similar function in Budapest. A few days later, on February 23, news arrived that the gay and talented young Prince Ludwig of Baden, whom she had known well at Kissingen, had died of pneumonia. "It looks as though the curse on the House of Baden were being fulfilled," she said, "which says that it will die out because it came into power through the crime against Kaspar Hauser. We are as nothing in the hand of God! Jehovah is the greatest of philosophers; we cannot understand His decrees, but we must bow before Him."

In March the Empress started out on her usual spring holiday, first visiting England for the instruction of the Archduchess Valerie. Sárolta Majláth was in attendance on her, as the Landgravine Therese Fürstenberg had had to resign her position owing to increasing deafness. Elizabeth stayed at Claridge's Hotel, and at once began "racing" from one museum to another and seeing all the sights. They paid another visit to Madame Tussaud's, where their fingers itched to destroy the exasperating caricatures of Francis Joseph and Elizabeth herself. She and Valerie made frequent expeditions to the shopping districts of the great city, which amused Elizabeth enormously, because she was entirely unknown there. In one shop a young married couple looked them up and down and the wife remarked to her husband: "Most extraordinary people those!"

During her visit to England the Empress heard that Count Andrássy was dangerously ill and that his sickness was incurable. She still regarded him as her best friend and that of her House, and sent her warmest wishes for his recovery, together with a watch which, though not of great value, was a token of remembrance. Andrássy was deeply touched. "You will understand," he wrote to Ida Ferenczy, "you, who know Her Majesty even better than I do and are well aware that she never does anything for the sake of appearances or out of caprice, but that everything she says or does is full of truth—you will understand how happy and proud Her Majesty's present and letter make me. . . . This watch is all the more precious to me because I feel, as I look at it, that this is no court favor, no formal grant of an honor, but an affectionate remembrance sent me by a person, who, even if she were not our Queen, would be the most interesting being I have ever seen, whether in mind, exterior, or character. I only wish most ardently that everybody were able to know and love her as we do."

Ida Ferenczy hastened to show this letter to the Empress, who had meanwhile returned to Munich from England and there seen Countess Irene Paumgartten, whose spiritualism had become a subject of diplomatic correspondence. The Prussian Minister at the court of Munich reported her séances to Bismarck, because he considered that Elizabeth's belief in communications from the spirit world, conveyed to her by the Countess by means of automatic writing, might in some circumstances assume considerable importance. But the diplomat exaggerated their significance. It is true that Elizabeth frequently visited her old friend, but she was amused at her assumption that when she was writing "automatically" in a state of trance, her hand was guided by spirits. Elizabeth could not quite make out whether it was all humbug or whether there was something in it after all. But she saw at least that the Countess was acting in perfectly good faith and never abused this faculty for personal ends. Sometimes she felt doubtful, sometimes she believed in it all, and then again she would turn the whole thing to ridicule.

From Munich Elizabeth went to Lainz, to the Villa Hermes, where she met with a warm, joyous welcome from Francis Joseph, but a cool reception from the Crown Prince which grieved her. "So this is what they call coming home!" she said bitterly. "But one is only at home where Nature is lovely and men happy." During the lengthy festivities connected with the unveiling of the monument to Maria Theresa on May 13, 1888, she brooded over Rudolf's possible treatment of Valerie in days to come and made up her mind to talk it over with him. "Never be nasty to Valerie," she said to him during the great court banquet, "for it would bring you bad luck yourself." Elizabeth knew what a deep effect everything mystical and uncanny produced upon Rudolf's impressionable, superstitious soul and determined to influence him through this side of his character. "I am a Sunday's child," she said, "so I am in communion with the other world and can bring good or bad luck to others. And so I remind you of May 13."

"I shall not do Valerie any harm, Mamma," he replied, but Elizabeth looked him full in the eyes and was struck by his restless, wavering glance, the dark shadows under his eyes, and the pallor of his face.

"Are you ill?" she asked.

"No," was the reply, "only tired and nervous."

During June, when Elizabeth and her daughter were living in very close companionship, they would philosophize during their country picnics. Elizabeth believed more in a God of vengeance and Valerie in a God of love. The Empress' poor opinion of humanity often saddened her daughter. "What I should most like," said Elizabeth, "would be to retire to Corfu altogether, since I have to give you up. I must accustom myself to this bitter medicine in good time."

At the end of July, after a visit of a few weeks to Gastein, they moved to Ischl, where they were joined by Francis Joseph. The actress Frau Schratt was also spending the summer there, and now made frequent visits to the imperial villa and went for walks with the Emperor and Empress. On August 4 Valerie accompanied them, and found this lady unaffected and sympathetic, but she had an uncomfortable feeling, for people were talking and refused to believe that the

Emperor's attitude in the matter was what it really was. For this reason it pained Valerie that Elizabeth had encouraged the friendship so much. The Empress had always been fond of associating with theatrical people, and now that she spent so much time reading, she would have her favorite poetry and plays read to her by actors and elocutionists such as Emmerich Robert and Alexander Strakosch. From Heine, whose *Belsazer* and *Wallfahrt nach Kevlaar* always moved her to tears, she had gone on to Byron and Shakespeare, and was forever reading, translating, and declaiming.

On August 15 the King and Crown Prince of Portugal arrived at Ischl, apparently in search of a crown princess. They naturally did not know how far Valerie's word was already pledged, and Elizabeth listened with amusement when the Crown Prince of Portugal asked Valerie about her poems and told her how he and his father translated Shakespeare together.

When the guests from abroad had gone, Elizabeth suddenly announced one day that she was going to the Langbathseen quite alone. "I am going into seclusion for a few days," she said, "and am taking nobody with me, for I do not want to talk." Her maid of honor, Sárolta Majláth, was alarmed. "Provided only that she comes back contented and calmer," she wrote to Ida Ferenczy. "But the more she broods, the unhappier she is: God grant that she find rest for her soul in something, but I do not believe Heine or Byron is capable of giving it to her. It is really sad."

On her return Elizabeth went to Bayreuth for the Festival performances of Wagner's operas. The Empress was not musical, but she was so deeply affected by *Parsifal* that she wished it would never come to an end. Between the acts she had Frau Cosima Wagner summoned to her. Tall and distinguished, uncommonly attractive, with obvious traces of past beauty and a calm dignity, this lady entered the Empress' box. She assured Her Majesty that but for Ludwig II all this music, which to her, at least, was the realization of everything that is most desirable here below, would never have been created. With tears in her eyes she spoke of her husband and of Liszt, her father.

"I now live for the past alone, in retirement with my children," she said. "Music is my only happiness."

"You are quite right," replied Elizabeth. "I, too, never go to the theatre, where people stare at me, and I prefer not to be among people at all."

"I understand that so well," replied Frau Cosima, "and always understood King Ludwig, for in our age something so strange, so coarse has come over mankind that anyone with delicate sensibilities and lofty aspirations can hardly live among them."

Elizabeth was so delighted with the performance that she expressed a wish to see the conductor, Mottl, and Van Dyck and Reichmann, who were taking the parts of Parsifal and Amfortas, but their unpoetic appearance rather destroyed her illusions. "I should like to hear the whole thing all over again at once," she said, and Reichmann's answer was: "I should be on the spot immediately."

From Bayreuth she went on to Kreuth, to share in celebrating her mother's eightieth birthday, and then to Ischl, where on September 10 the Duke of Oldenburg appeared with his wife, a Baroness not of royal birth, who was cold-shouldered in royal circles. Such things always aroused Elizabeth's spirit of contradiction, and she received the Duke and his wife with particular cordiality and friendliness.

Already, however, she was dreaming of foreign travel again. Warsberg had taken the Villa Braila at Gasturi, Corfu, for her, and she rejoiced at the thought of visiting her beloved island once more. At the beginning of October she informed the Emperor of her intention of going there.

"*Édes szeretett lelkem,*" he replied gloomily, "I am in very low spirits at the thought of your departure for the distant south and your long absence, especially after our recent meeting, which was so cosy and congenial, though unfortunately so short and rushed. You were particularly gracious, charming and sweet, too, for which I again send you my very best thanks. . . . Think often of your boundlessly loving, sad and lonely Little One."

But soon the world at large began to say unpleasant things about the Empress' mania for travel. The newspapers took up the theme, and before long the English papers reported that Elizabeth was contemplating a voyage to America and the West Indies, even around the world. For the present, however, she started out from Miramar for Missolonghi, where Byron, whose works she read constantly on the voyage, had died for Greek freedom. Her voyage was spoiled by terrific wind and rain, but in spite of this her boat anchored off the island of Santa Maura and in a rainstorm she climbed the rock known as "Sappho's leap."

On returning to her beloved Corfu, she resumed her sailing expeditions in the cutter *Lizzy*, and also began to study both ancient and modern Greek with Professor Romanos of Corfu, recommended to her by Warsberg. At first she would study alone, walking up and down the garden, or write exercises on the terrace, with its view of the sea and the Albanian mountains. Yet her whole way of living was a source of uneasiness to the Countess Festetics, and this lady poured out her doubts to Ida Ferenczy, who had not accompanied the Empress. "What I see and hear in this place, dear Ida," she wrote, "weighs upon my mind. Her Majesty is always sweet when we are together and talks as she used to do in the old days. But she is no longer her old self—a shadow has fallen upon her spirit. I can find no other words to express my meaning, for when a person represses and denies all fine and noble feeling out of indolence or for the sake of amusement, one can only ascribe it to bitterness or cynicism! Believe me, my heart weeps tears of blood. And then she does things which make not only one's heart, but one's understanding, stand still. Yesterday morning the weather was bad from the first, yet she would go out sailing. By nine o'clock it had begun to pour, and the deluge, accompanied by thunder, lasted till three in the afternoon. And all that time she went on sailing round and round, sitting on deck holding an umbrella and getting drenched through. Then she landed somewhere or other, sent for her carriage, and wanted to spend the night in some strange villa. So now you can imagine what a pitch things have reached. Thank God the doctor accompanies her everywhere. . . ."

Wherever Elizabeth went, people were struck by her characteristically light tread, which made her seem to float along the ground. Romantic spirits expressed their admiration by comparing her walk to that of a goddess advancing to victory, though to others her rapid pace caused her to be known as "the railway." This was not intended sarcastically, for in the eyes of the Greek peasantry of Corfu a railway stood for all that was most grand.

Elizabeth was treated with every consideration, special roads being planned and entirely reconstructed for the convenience of some of her drives about the island. She was appreciative of this, but declined to receive any visitors in Corfu, on the ground that she had gone there for the express purpose of living in absolute quiet. When King George of Greece announced his intention of visiting her, she merely sent word that she would be away for the next few days. Shortly afterwards she heard that the King intended to arrive during the following week, but she again had him informed that she expected to leave Corfu for a few days, and after that no more was heard of the royal visit.

But now bad news arrived from Munich. The Empress' father had had a stroke during the summer, and on November 10 he had another and far more serious one. Word reached the Empress on the twelfth, and she wanted to leave for home at once. She telegraphed her intention to Francis Joseph, but he advised her not to come, since he wished to obviate the effect which such an event was sure to produce upon his wife's spirits. In any case she would not have arrived in time, for on November 15 the Prince died at half past three in the morning. Toward the end of his life he had become more and more lonely as his friends died, and he had spent his last days in cheerful acceptance of his deprivations. The news was announced to Elizabeth in an affectionate telegram which she received from the Emperor during the afternoon of the fifteenth: "Deepest and most loving sympathy with you on Papa's death." The Empress was greatly affected and reproached herself for having troubled so little about her father while he was still alive, though it had seldom been possible to see him during her visits to her home.

Warsberg tried to distract the Empress' thoughts from her grief by discussing with her the plans for her projected villa on Corfu, where the mild climate was proving beneficial to her sciatica. "I mean to spend my name day by the sea," she wrote to the Archduchess Valerie on November 16. . . . "I intend to be at Miramar by the first so as to meet Póka* there, of which I shall be very glad. It will surely get warmer now. I feel that I suffer more from the cold as time goes on. . . . The day before yesterday I walked on and on through olive groves and along the seashore as far as the Villa Capo-

* Once when Francis Joseph was in a lively mood he had told his wife and daughter that his position in the Empire made him feel like a turkey cock (in Magyar *póka*) in a poultry yard, which amused Elizabeth so much that the name stuck to him and she always used it in her letters to her daughter when she did not wish to mention the Emperor's name.

distria, two hours' walk away. It stands in a very wild spot, like an enchanted fairy castle, but all crumbling away, among great orange, lemon, and mandarine trees which have grown into a tangle in the neglected garden. Loveliest of all were the camellia trees. It would be hard to find such fine ones in Madeira. . . . I have seen much that is beautiful before, but there is nothing lovelier upon earth than Scheria (the Homeric name for Corfu). Under a starry sky it is even lovelier. Yesterday evening this world of wonders glittered before me, and my heart could hardly contain itself at the sight of so much eternal glory."

With a heavy heart Elizabeth at last tore herself away from her beloved island, and the only thing that gave her any pleasure was the meeting with her husband, who joined her at Miramar. There she discussed with him her intention of building herself a villa in Corfu, and Francis Joseph, who had never denied his wife a wish, consented, though not altogether gladly, for the building of a house in a foreign land so far away meant that she wished to live at a distance from him and her home, and he could hardly be pleased at that.

Elizabeth now sent for Warsberg, and he was formally commissioned to build her villa, combining in himself the functions of architect, gardener, and everything else. Though sceptical as a general rule, the Consul was delighted at this. "The Empress is enchantingly kind," he noted in his diary, "I cannot resist the lady. And I really like the task, for it is an artistic one." But Warsberg noticed Francis Joseph's reserve and felt that something was amiss in that quarter. "This favor on the part of the Empress," he remarked, "really does me harm in Vienna." And as a matter of fact people there held him responsible for having instilled in Elizabeth's mind this "Greek mania" which encouraged her tendency to forget her family, husband, and position as Empress. Nor did Warsberg quite know how he was to rise to the occasion, as his health was poor and he had not desired all these duties.

December 2 was the fortieth anniversary of Francis Joseph's accession, and he went to Miramar not only to see his wife, but to escape from any celebrations of this event. The Emperor and Empress had a long and intimate conversation in which they poured out their hearts to each other, for Valerie had joined them, and Elizabeth was worrying more than ever about her future. "My advice to you, Valerie," she said to her one day, "is to confide in Papa once and for all. For my part, of course, I give my consent to your betrothal, though I shall then be left utterly alone and everything will be changed. The best time to choose would be Christmas Eve." At this moment Francis Joseph came into the room. "Have you been crying," he said to his daughter, "at the hideous surprise of finding that Mamma has had a blue anchor tattooed on her shoulder?"

"Oh, no," said Elizabeth, "it is *I* who have been crying, at quite a different surprise."

"Why, what is that?"

"She wants to tell Franz that he is the husband of her choice."

"Why, what is the meaning of this?" asked Francis Joseph in his curt way. Upon which Valerie said hesitatingly: "Why, I should like to be betrothed."

Elizabeth laughed, but the Emperor nodded as though he had long regarded the matter as settled, and then said in a businesslike tone: "Now we must make arrangements for the wedding."

Elizabeth made a show of indignation at the Emperor's matter-of-fact way of taking the news, but it was only a pretense. He walked across to the window and looked out in order to hide his feelings.

Shortly after this the Emperor and Empress went back to

Schönbrunn. Elizabeth was still full of the beauty of her beloved Greece, which, she told her daughter over and over again, she regarded as her future home. She had brought a Greek lawyer with her from Corfu, a Dr. Thermojannis, with whom she now took a daily walk in the garden of Schönbrunn, eagerly studying Greek, at which Francis Joseph and Valerie were highly amused, for the man was a comical sight and quite out of place among the courtiers.

Valerie still felt afraid to tell Rudolf her secret. The Crown Prince was strangely altered and had become so taciturn and aloof that the Landgravine Fürstenberg, who had not seen him for a long time, said that she would hardly have taken him for the same person. Elizabeth invited him and his wife to dinner on December 16, 1888, adding that she wanted to tell him a secret. At first he seemed excited and upset, but not unfriendly, so "for the first time in her life," she says, Valerie ventured to throw her arms around his neck and tell him everything. Rudolf was touched at this confession of love, which had been so long restrained by shyness and nervousness, and embraced and kissed his sister with warm brotherly affection.

"Please," said Elizabeth, "be good to Valerie and her husband, if ever they are dependent upon you."

"I promise and swear it," replied Rudolf simply and cordially, whereupon Elizabeth hurried up to him and made the sign of the cross on his brow.

"God will bless you for it," she said, "and it will bring you happiness. You are my son and I do love you so."

Rudolf kissed her hand with deep feeling, and then Valerie ran up to them, gathered them both in her arms, and said almost without thinking what she was saying: "This is how we ought always to be."

This affectionate evening made Elizabeth quite happy, and her fears were now set at rest.

"Yes," she said to her daughter, "I am quite ready to trust you to Franz's love; but all the same he is a robber, and in taking you away he is depriving me of the only real joy of my whole married life."

And so Christmas Eve, 1888, came round, and with it Elizabeth's birthday. Rudolf and his wife were among the guests, and the Crown Prince presented his mother with Hugo Wittmann's edition of Heine's letters, at which Francis Joseph cast an ironical glance but made no comment. When the Crown Prince and Princess had gone off to their own Christmas tree, Francis Joseph sent for the Archduke Franz Salvator and the formal betrothal took place. Elizabeth embraced the young fiancé with sisterly tenderness, saying: "I am so fond of you. I am giving you my all. Make my Valerie happy!" Then Valerie took her mother in her arms and begged her to forgive her all the occasions upon which she had offended her. "I only wish," said Elizabeth, "that there were more to forgive. Then it would not be so hard for me to give you away."

That evening Elizabeth had laid aside her mourning for her father and was looking dazzlingly young and lovely in a light-colored dress. Francis Joseph addressed some kindly words to his future son-in-law, looked at the young couple happily, and said at last, hiding his tears: "Valerie looks as jolly as can be." The Countess Tornis, who had been Valerie's governess for many years, now came in to offer her good wishes, and Elizabeth greeted her by saying mischievously: "Ah, we two are on the shelf now."

On December 26 Elizabeth accompanied the newly betrothed couple to Munich to present them to her mother, whom she had not seen since her father's death. On New Year's Day she received an affectionate and feeling letter from her husband: "My best wishes to every one, but above all to you, my beloved angel. I hope, too, that all your wishes which are practicable and not too inconvenient to myself may be fulfilled, and I beg you always to show me the same love, consideration, and goodness. The blessed feeling that your love, too, increases with the passing years, instead of growing colder, causes me the warmest gratitude and makes me infinitely happy. I received the inclosed telegram yesterday from our friend (*die Freundin*)." Francis Joseph added this reference to Frau Schratt, whom he always called "*die Freundin*" in writing to Elizabeth, because he wished to have no secrets from his wife. She must know everything, for there was nothing to hide from her. He hoped that Elizabeth's enthusiasm for Greece and her mania for travel would pass away as so many of her crazes had done, so that in the end she might be recovered for home, family, and the Empire.

XIII

THE DEATH OF THE CROWN PRINCE

1888–1890

ELIZABETH SPENT NEW YEAR'S DAY, 1889, at her old home, and wrote to her mother from Munich on her way back in the following terms: "Well, we leave here with heavy hearts, myself especially, for Valerie is in love and consequently stupid. I so much enjoyed this lovely quiet time with you, dear Mimi. I was so happy at being able to have it with you, that today I feel very sorry for myself (*einen wahren Katzenjammer habe*)." On arriving in Vienna the Empress had to receive belated New Year's visits, from Franz Salvator's mother among others. Elizabeth was very nice to her, addressed her as "thou," and closed the conversation with the words: "All I want to say is this: it is always best for mothers-in-law not to interfere with a young married couple, so I mean never to visit them unless I have to." And the Archduchess replied amiably: "Oh, yes, one must be a mother, not a mother-in-law."

The imperial family were all on the best of terms, and the future appeared to lie rosy before them. But a terrible blow was in store for the Emperor and Empress.

The Crown Prince was very different in reality from what he had recently seemed to be. The Empress had had little opportunity of observing him, for during the last two years she had been absent a great deal from Vienna and even when at home had been far too much wrapped up in her daughter Valerie. The Emperor, engrossed with the cares of govern-

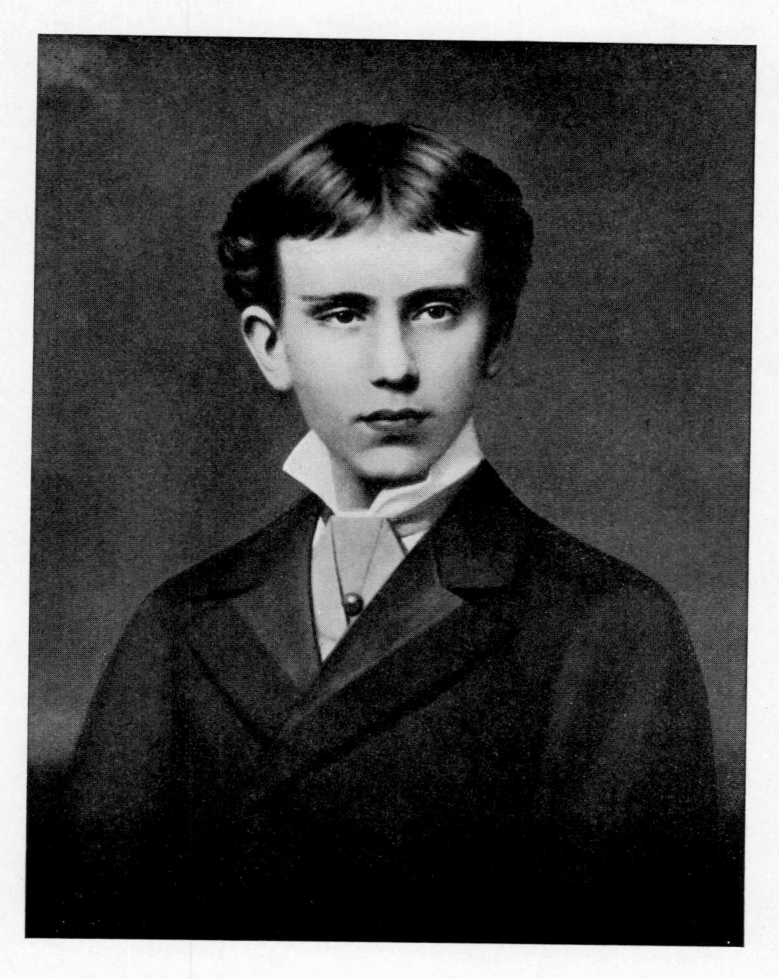

THE CROWN PRINCE RUDOLF OF AUSTRIA

From a photograph.

ment, had few really intimate friends at court, perhaps because he would admit of no intimacy. The Crown Prince managed to keep his private life a secret even from his closest entourage, and the few who had any knowledge of it were either unwilling to lose the future Emperor's favor or found it to their advantage that Francis Joseph should not be warned of the danger that threatened. The only persons who really knew anything about Rudolf's private affairs were those in a menial position, such as his coachman Bratfisch and his valet Loschek, but the principal members of his Household were in complete ignorance.*

During the last two years this clever and talented Prince, who really had an excellent disposition, had become a mere shadow of himself. He had never quite recovered from his illness in 1886, and the resulting low spirits made him grasp at anything that would stimulate his nerves and stifle his lurking dread of the future. He drank more than was good for him and gave himself up to pleasure without restraint, as though eager to get the most out of his last years. He had affairs with women very much beneath him, and with ladies in society as well, and then he would reproach himself bitterly and ask himself whether these things which he was driven to do by some obscure and uncontrollable impulse were compatible with his honor as an officer and the Emperor's son. His character was essentially noble and chivalrous. His unbridled dissipation was undoubtedly the result of an abnormal mental condition. At times he was overcome with disgust at his life and said to himself that he could only expiate it by death. In his anxiety to hide his way of living from his kind and irreproachable parents, he naturally could not admit what large sums of money he was spending, so he

* There is a detailed description of the Crown Prince's later years in Oskar Freiherr von Mitis', *Das Leben des Kronprinzen Rudolf,* especially in the Memoir by Count Josef Hoyos printed in that book (p. 385, *seq.*).

found a complaisant Jewish banker who secretly lent him large amounts, looking forward to reaping his reward in the shape of railway concessions in the East.*

But when he dallied with the thought of death, he was faced with the unanswerable question of what comes afterwards. He was terror-stricken, and felt that he could not venture to take such a step without somebody to help him on his passage into the world beyond. He appealed to a woman who was in many respects quite unworthy of him, and proposed that she should accompany him to the Husarentempel, a belvedere on a hill near Mödling, and there die with him. But she confessed everything to the President of Police, and so the plan failed. But it seems that Francis Joseph was not informed of the matter, though unmistakable proof of it exists in the shape of a letter.

Rudolf now looked about him for another companion in death. About this time the daughter of that Baroness Vetsera who had tried to enmesh him in her toils years before came into his life. The girl had grown into a beautiful, romantic person of seventeen, and long before meeting the Crown Prince had heard him spoken of at home in exalted terms. No wonder, then, that this young girl idealized the heir to the throne and fell in love with him at their first meeting. Rudolf, in the frame of mind he was then in, could not resist the spell of her charm and passion. They soon became lovers and in his anxiety to conceal this intrigue, as he had concealed so many others, Rudolf made use of the Empress' niece, the Countess Larisch-Wallersee, as a cover for the girl's visits. The part played by the Countess, who had received many kindnesses from the Empress, was indeed highly equivocal.

The young girl who was now in love with him was a very different type from the other woman to whom the Crown

* See Mitis, *op. cit.*, pp. 396 and 429.

Prince had proposed a suicide pact. Not till she had given herself to him did she hear all kinds of reports. In an exaltation of love, finding herself involved in an intrigue with the heir to the imperial throne, who was a married man, and dreading the consequences which might result, she, too, fell into an overwrought state. It seems probable that at this moment Rudolf made the same proposal to her that he had to the other lady, and she did not draw back. She was genuinely in love with him and resolved, if necessary, to expiate her love with her life.

On January 29, 1889, Francis Joseph and Elizabeth gave a family dinner party, from which Rudolf had excused himself on grounds of indisposition. The Emperor and Empress planned to start for Buda on the thirty-first, and their preparations were already made. The Crown Prince had arranged for a day's shooting at Mayerling early on the morning of the thirtieth, but when his valet Loschek went to call him, his knocks and calls brought no answer. Count Hoyos joined him, and they knocked and knocked again. No movement was to be heard. They tried to force the door, but it would not give way. At last Loschek smashed in a panel with an axe, and broke into the half-dark, shuttered room. The Crown Prince was sitting motionless by the side of the bed, leaning forward and bleeding from the mouth. Before him on the bedside table stood a glass and a mirror. Without examining things more closely, the servant jumped to the conclusion that Crown Prince had drunk poison from the glass, for strychnine, he knew, causes bleeding. On the bed lay the body of a young girl, the Baroness Mary Vetsera. She was white, ice-cold, and already quite rigid.

In his alarm Hoyos did not look closer, but rushed to the station and took a special train to Vienna. There he hurried to the Emperor's Adjutant General, Count Paar, and requested him to break the appalling news to Francis Joseph.

"I cannot possibly. Her Majesty is the only person who can tell His Majesty such a thing," declared the Count, and at once sent for Baron Nopcsa, Controller of the Empress' Household. Nopcsa hastened to Ida Ferenczy and asked how Her Majesty was to be told the news.

Elizabeth happened to be having her Greek lesson. Her master was reading her passages from Homer. Ida Ferenczy appeared at the door, white to the lips, and announced that Baron Nopcsa had something urgent to tell Her Majesty.* Impatient at the interruption, Elizabeth replied: "Well, he must wait and come back again later." But Ida insisted with unwonted agitation that Nopcsa must be received at once, and was at last compelled to add softly: "He has bad news, grave news from His Imperial Highness the Crown Prince."

Elizabeth signed to the Greek to withdraw, while Ida Ferenczy pushed Baron Nopcsa into the room. He performed his painful duty with the utmost delicacy. When Ida entered the room again a few moments later, she found Elizabeth in floods of tears. At this moment a quick, light step was heard outside. It was Francis Joseph. "Not yet! Do not come in!" cried Elizabeth. Ida Ferenczy rushed to the door. "I implore Your Majesty most earnestly to wait a moment longer."

Francis Joseph stood outside with Nopcsa, who was controlling himself with great effort. Meanwhile Elizabeth dried her tears. "Is anything noticeable?" she asked. "No? Very well, then, show him in, and may God help me."

Francis Joseph entered with his elastic tread. God alone knows how the Empress told her husband the dreadful news. Francis Joseph left the room with drooping head, a broken man.

* This account is based on the stories of two eyewitnesses who heard everything at first hand, the Archduchess Marie Valerie and Frau Ida von Ferenczy, to whom the Archduchess herself dictated her memories of what happened, besides describing it in detail in her diary for February, 1889.

"Come with me, Baron Nopcsa," he said.

Meanwhile Elizabeth went downstairs to Ida Ferenczy's rooms. It was just time for the visit of Frau Katharina Schratt, who had often come to see Their Majesties lately, and always went straight to Ida, the Empress' most intimate and confidential attendant, as though to demonstrate that nothing secret or doubtful was afoot. That day the young actress' composure and sincerity were particularly welcome to Elizabeth. She felt that at such a moment the Emperor stood more than ever in need of wholehearted consolation from some outside person, such as a grief-stricken mother could hardly give. The Empress herself accompanied Frau Schratt to her husband. Then her first thought was for her daughter Valerie. To talk with her, though she knew nothing as yet, was the only thing that might perhaps to some extent assuage her own despair. Valerie was not in her apartments, so Elizabeth sent to fetch her. She came running in, merry and unsuspecting, and found her mother weeping in her bedroom.

"Rudolf is very, very ill," sobbed Elizabeth. "There is no hope."

Valerie threw her arms around her and sat on her knee.

"It will blanch your cheek with horror. The worst has happened. . . ."

"Has he killed himself?"

Elizabeth started. "Why do you think that? No, no. It seems probable, even certain, that the girl poisoned him."

There were steps outside.

"There is Papa," said Elizabeth. "I entreat you to be as calm as I am."

Francis Joseph entered the room. Both women threw their arms around his neck, and the three clung together in a close embrace. The two ladies tried to be calm, in order to give him strength. But now they saw that, in the depths of his own sorrow, it was his example that was sustaining them. "Send for Stephanie," said the Emperor.

The Crown Princess came upstairs sobbing. Elizabeth went to meet her lovingly, without the least bitterness. Then Valerie's fiancé hurried in, too, saying: "At such a moment as this, one must surrender oneself entirely to the will of God."

But Elizabeth answered: "The great Jehovah is terrible when he goes forth like a destroying storm"—the words she had uttered once before, when Ludwig II of Bavaria met his death.

Meanwhile Ida Ferenczy had returned to her apartments. She opened her door, and there was the old Baroness Vetsera sitting on a chair waiting. Ida Ferenczy addressed her sharply: "What do you want here, Baroness?" she said. "I cannot see you now. Kindly go away."

But the Baroness only repeated persistently: "I must speak to Her Majesty the Empress."

"But, Baroness, that is impossible."

"I must, I must. I have lost my child, and she alone can restore her to me." The Baroness had as yet no idea of the true state of the case. Even before the catastrophe she had been to the President of Police and Count Taaffe, the Minister President, in search of her daughter, and since the Crown Prince was involved, their advice had been: "Go to Her Majesty, she alone can do anything."

Ida Ferenczy returned to Elizabeth.

"Does she know everything yet?" asked the Empress.

"No."

"Poor woman! Very well, I will go to her."

But Ida replied anxiously: "Will Your Majesty not wait a moment? I will get Nopcsa to speak to her first."

He accepted the mission, but did not tell her all. The Baroness persisted in her request. "Very well, then, fetch Her Majesty," decided Nopcsa.

Elizabeth entered, Nopcsa withdrew, and Ida Ferenczy stayed in the next room with the door open, where she could see everything and hear a great deal, and would be at hand if Her Majesty had anything to command.

The Empress stood quietly before the agitated woman who was demanding her child and saying that the Crown Prince must have taken her away with him, and in a gentle voice she said: "Collect all your courage, Baroness; your daughter is dead."

"My child!" the Baroness cried wildly: "My dear, beautiful child!"

"But do you know," continued Elizabeth in a firmer voice, "that my Rudolf is dead, too?"

The Baroness reeled, fell to the ground before the Empress, and clung to her knees.

"My unhappy child!" she cried. "What has she done? Can this be her doing?"

So the girl's mother had interpreted the situation in the same way and believed, as the Emperor and Empress did for a long time, that her daughter had first poisoned the Crown Prince and then herself. After a silence Elizabeth left the Baroness, saying as she went: "Remember! Rudolf died of a heart attack!"

Meanwhile a commission had arrived at Mayerling, headed by the court physician, Hofrat von Widerhofer. He was the first to enter the room since Hoyos and the valet Loschek had been there, and now he came in with them and had the closed shutters thrown open. There he saw the young girl in all her beauty, but deadly white, lying on the bed with her hair loosed about her shoulders and with a rose in her folded hands. The Crown Prince was still in a half-sitting position, and on the floor lay a revolver which had fallen from his hand. Now at last they looked at him in full daylight. There was no poison in the glass on the night table, only brandy.

The doctor raised the tall, cold form and found the skull perforated, the bullet having entered at one temple and gone out at the other, while the girl was similarly wounded. Both bullets were found in the room.

Francis Joseph spent Thursday night in a state of painful agitation, waiting for the result of the commission's examination. Neither he nor Elizabeth was yet sure whether the Crown Prince had killed himself. Others were told that it was a heart attack. The people of Vienna stood in thousands on the Burgplatz, full of deep sympathy. Calmly Francis Joseph waited for more detailed information. Elizabeth had to promise him that she would not be there to receive Rudolf's body, which was to be brought to the Hofburg by night. But as she and Valerie lay awake, they heard the hollow roll of drums and the guard turning out when the somber procession entered the courtyard of the palace at two o'clock in the morning. Early next day the Emperor sent for Widerhofer. He was still certain that the girl had poisoned his son and all he expected from the doctor was confirmation of this and the exact details.

"Tell me everything frankly. I want to know all the details."

Unaware of the Emperor's mistaken idea, Widerhofer started his report, as a doctor would, with the consoling words: "I can assure Your Majesty that His Imperial Highness the Crown Prince did not suffer for a moment. The bullet entered his temple absolutely straight, and death followed instantaneously."

But Francis Joseph turned on him, saying: "What do you mean? The bullet?"

"Yes, Your Majesty, the bullet. We found it—the bullet with which he shot himself."

"He? He shot himself? That is not true. She poisoned

him. I repeat, Rudolf did not shoot himself. If you say that, you must prove it."

Reluctantly Widerhofer had now to describe, first, how carefully the girl had been laid out and, then, how Rudolf shot himself; for, in order to obtain greater accuracy of aim, he had done it before the mirror which stood on the night table, thus removing all doubt that he had taken his own life.

And now for a moment the Emperor Francis Joseph almost collapsed and sobbed heartbrokenly. Then he asked: "Did Rudolf leave a letter of farewell?"

"Several letters. But none for Your Majesty."

On the table in the bedroom at Mayerling there lay a telegram from Rudolf to the Prior of the Cistercian monastery of Heiligenkreuz, asking him to come to Mayerling at once and pray over his body with the monks. Besides this there were several letters—among them one to his wife Stephanie and one to his sister—all of which, the one to the Archduchess Valerie most certainly, had apparently been written beforehand in Vienna. Only the one to Elizabeth seemed to have been written at Mayerling, where Rudolf had felt a longing to turn to his mother in his last hours. According to the testimony of the Emperor Francis Joseph, all the letters were more or less variations on the same theme, which was that Rudolf had to die because his honor demanded it. They were all very brief and concise; only those to Elizabeth and Valerie contained certain remarks of greater importance.

To his sister Rudolf definitely confessed: "I do not die willingly," and he advised her to go abroad with her husband when the Emperor died, for it was impossible to foresee what might then happen in Austria.

In the letter to Elizabeth were words of love and gratitude

to her and the Emperor, to whom he did not dare to write. "I know quite well," he said, "that I was not worthy to be his son." Then Rudolf spoke of the survival of his soul and referred to the girl who had died with him as a pure, atoning angel. He asked the Empress to have him buried at Mary's side in the monastery of Heiligenkreuz. It is evident that without her perhaps he might not have dared to face death, but that it was not on her account that he died. No definite reason is mentioned in any of the Crown Prince's letters. It is to be sought in his whole physical and mental state during the last two years.

The Crown Prince was laid out on the bed in his room in the Burg. Immediately after his conversation with Widerhofer, the Emperor entered the room, where nobody else was present but the Crown Prince's aide-de-camp, Arthur Freiherr von Giesl, and a priest.

"Where has the Crown Prince been laid?" asked Francis Joseph.

"Where he lived as a bachelor, Your Majesty."

"Is he much disfigured?"

"No, Your Majesty."

"Please cover him up well. The Empress wishes to see him."

With these words the Emperor left the room. Giesl laid the white blanket over the Crown Prince's folded hands and drew it high up to his throat. This was what afterwards gave rise to the absurd reports that the Crown Prince's hands had been covered with cuts. On the contrary they were absolutely uninjured. Giesl himself had drawn the white gloves on them. About seven o'clock in the morning the Emperor arrived, wearing gloves and a saber, and entered the room where his dead son lay. He stood before the body in silence for a quarter of an hour. At noon came the Empress Elizabeth, Valerie, and the Archduke Franz Salvator. A priest was praying in the chamber of death. The windows were draped, and at the foot of the bed candles were burning to right and left of a crucifix. There lay Elizabeth's only son, covered up to the breast with a white sheet and surrounded with flowers. The light bandage around his head did not disfigure him, his cheeks and ears were still rosy with the healthy hues of youth, and the changeable and often bitter expression which was so characteristic of him in life had given place to a happy smile. He seemed to sleep and to be content. Sobbing aloud, Elizabeth sank down at the foot of the bed, for Francis Joseph was not present, and so for a moment she could let herself go. During the last terrible twenty-four hours she had made superhuman efforts to control herself for her husband's sake and had fought down her own grief. As always in crucial moments of stress Elizabeth was at her post. All her play acting and fantastic imaginings fell away from her. In the moment of bitter need the greatness, nobility, and goodness of her nature stood forth and she was ready for every sacrifice. And so, during the sad meals with her husband, she pulled herself together in order not to show how terribly this trial had affected her. They were joined at meals by Stephanie, too, with her child, little "Erzsi," at the sight of whom the Emperor burst into tears. For the first time the Empress lost her composure for an instant in the presence of her husband and began to weep unrestrainedly.

It was very hard for the Emperor to have to admit publicly that Rudolf had committed suicide, but his ministers pressed him to make the truth known, because nobody now believed in a natural death. And so a medical certificate was published in the *Wiener Zeitung* of February 2, 1889, stating, among other things, that on examination the Crown Prince's brain had revealed "pathological symptoms which are shown by experience to be the usual accompaniment of abnormal mental conditions, and justified the assumption that the deed took place during a state of mental derangement."

Though this explanation was a consolation to the Emperor Francis Joseph, Elizabeth received it with very different feelings. She believed in predestination and, paralyzed with grief as she was, began to tell herself that it was her Bavarian Palatine blood that had been the cause of these appalling phenomena in Rudolf's brain. "Why did Francis Joseph ever enter my father's house?" she exclaimed in despair. "Why did I have to see him and why did he have to know me?"

Since her short interview with the Emperor and Empress immediately after the news had been received, Frau Schratt had hardly been able to rest. But her profession did not allow her to remain idle even on that terrible day, and she was fully engaged by rehearsals. On the evening of the thirty-first, however, she begged Ida Ferenczy for news of Their Majesties. On the following day the actress appeared again and did all she could to find words of consolation. "Your Majesty has three angels about you," she said, "the Empress and Their Highnesses Valerie and Gisela, to watch over you, love you, and console you."

"Yes, you are right," replied Francis Joseph, taking Elizabeth's hand in his, while the Empress gazed long and sadly at him.

"If I could have Rudolf back again," she said on another occasion, "I should like him to be a daughter, not the Crown Prince again. Yes, from his very childhood he was kept away from us too much and brought up so differently from an ordinary child."

Meanwhile the King and Queen of the Belgians had arrived from Brussels. Their coming was only a burden to the Emperor and Empress, and especially to Elizabeth, who had never been on good terms with them. She would have preferred to be alone with those most closely related to her. The Princess Gisela had hurried to Vienna from Munich and the Empress led her to the Crown Prince's bedside when for the last time she kissed her son's cold lips. On the third night she suddenly entered Valerie's room. "It is not true," she said; "it is impossible that Rudolf is lying up there dead. I must go up and see if it is true." And Valerie only restrained her with difficulty. The self-control which Elizabeth had managed to maintain during the last few days was soon transformed into wild grief. After all, the Emperor Francis Joseph had stronger nerves, and his work helped him over the hardest trials. "Throughout all these sad days," writes the Prussian military attaché in Vienna, "the Emperor did not sign a single military report a day later than usual, even on January 30, and since then he has been working exactly as he did before. Only a few people, even here, suspected their monarch of possessing such strength of mind. Never, not even now, has His Majesty lost his firm faith in the future of Austria and her high mission, or in the love of his army and people."

It was no empty phrase when, in his address to the deputation of condolence from the Austrian Parliament, the Emperor said: "I can find no words warm enough to express how much I owe to my dearly beloved wife the Empress during these sad days, and what a great support she has been to me. Only tell people this; the more widely you make it known, the more grateful I shall be to you."

But when Francis Joseph looked at his wife now, he could not but be alarmed for her; and for this reason he implored her not to attend the funeral, for he well knew how painful it was for her to appear in public at all, and this occasion would be excruciating. So before four o'clock on February 5 Elizabeth and Valerie entered the Josefskapelle, so as not to see the funeral procession crossing the courtyard, and there they remained praying during the whole of the gloomy ceremony. Not till half past five in the afternoon did Francis Joseph and the Princess Gisela return.

"I bore up well," said the Emperor in a trembling voice. "It was only in the crypt that I could endure it no longer. But never did a funeral take place in such circumstances as today."

At five o'clock in the afternoon of the following day, vigils were read for the Crown Prince. The chapel in the Burg was hung with black. There were crosses everywhere with the name Rudolf above his coat of arms. In the middle of the chapel was the great catafalque with his orders and gloves, and the service was accompanied by solemn music. The effect was awe-inspiring and gruesome. Elizabeth was pale as death under her heavy black veil. She racked her brain in the endeavor to understand how and why the whole thing had happened. Neither she nor the Emperor really knew for what reason Rudolf had taken his life. He had never been frank with them, and the bitterness of earlier days rose up once more before Elizabeth's mind, revived by her present grief. On returning from the service she went to her dressing room, remarking to Valerie: "Now all these people who have spoken so much evil of me from the very moment of my arrival will have the consolation that I shall pass away without leaving a trace behind me in Austria."

Such reflections as these disquieted Valerie. Once when Francis Joseph remarked: "One grows docile beneath the weight of misfortune;" Elizabeth said to Valerie, "I don't know. I only feel hardened and can scarcely pray." But during the Requiem Mass in the Burg chapel on the following day, when the deeply moving *Libera* was being sung, Elizabeth burst into tears and said in Magyar: "Ah, how deeply I love and worship the great, great Jehovah. I cannot say how much."

When she heard this remark, Valerie thanked God that her fear lest Elizabeth might entirely lose her faith had not been justified. But the Empress was always thinking about how she might be brought into communion with her dead son. Only in the spirit world, she thought—supposing such a thing existed—would this be possible.

When the Empress retired on the evening of February 9, she undressed and washed as usual and dismissed Valerie, Ida Ferenczy, and the servants, saying that she wanted to go to bed. Toward nine o'clock she got up again secretly, dressed herself, left the Burg through a side door, and, so closely veiled as to be unrecognizable, hailed the first cab that came along. Then she drove with all possible speed to the Capuchin monastery on the Neuer Markt, where Rudolf lay buried. The chill crypt of this monastery, where the coffins of the Habsburgs lie in rows like goods stored up in a warehouse, was repellent to Elizabeth, and she had never felt any desire to descend to it. But on this occasion it was as though some inner voice were calling her. She hoped Rudolf might appear to her and tell her why he had taken his own life and whether he wished to be buried in the place where he lay. Dressed in deep mourning, she rang the bell at the monastery door. When it was opened, she asked to be taken to the Father Superior. She raised her veil, greeted him, and said simply: "I am the Empress—please take me down to my son." The crypt was hastily illuminated by a few torches placed beside Rudolf's grave, and then the Father Superior offered to conduct Elizabeth downstairs. At the iron door of the crypt she requested him to accompany her no further. When he ventured upon a respectful remonstrance, Elizabeth cut him short with the words: "I wish to be alone with my son," and descended the steps to the somber hall, ghostly in the pale illumination of the torches. She walked straight toward Rudolf's coffin. The draught stirred the leaves on the withered wreaths. Fallen flowers rustled here and there like light footsteps, so that Elizabeth often turned her head, but she saw nothing. Then, twice in succession, she called: "Rudolf!" Her voice echoed through the hall, but nobody appeared and nobody made answer.

She returned to the Burg disappointed, yet the visit had consoled and calmed her. Spirits, she said to her daughter next day, on telling her the whole episode, may only come if the great Jehovah allows them. When Francis Joseph heard of this visit to the crypt, he resolved then and there to remove the Empress from the melancholy environment of Vienna, which reminded her perpetually of their tragedy.

The departure of the Emperor and Empress for Hungary was fixed for the tenth. At noon on February 11 their special train steamed into the station at Budapest. All those present raised their hats, but without the customary shouts of "*Eljen!*" The road to the royal castle was lined by vast crowds of people, who saluted the imperial pair in silence, only uncovering their heads. There could have been no more moving expression of their sympathy.

The Emperor Francis Joseph had the business of government to occupy his attention, but grief and despair began to overwhelm Elizabeth when she resumed her too monotonous and quiet life, occupied chiefly by her Greek studies. About a fortnight after the catastrophe she remarked that she felt as though she had been struck on the head and was still dazed. "From youth up," she said to Valerie, "I have always had the feeling, which has now become a conviction, that the great Jehovah means to lead me into the wilderness, where I am to spend my old age as a hermit, entirely consecrated to Him, in contemplation and worship of His divine glory. This is my appointed lot, and God is leading me to it whether I will or no."

Rudolf's words in his last letter to Valerie made a remarkable impression upon Elizabeth. She was now of the same opinion, that Austria-Hungary could endure no longer. "It will fall to pieces," she said, "when the Emperor ceases to hold it all together by the might of his stainless character and self-abnegating fulfilment of duty. Nothing else will avail to support the decaying state."

"It is hard," writes Valerie in her diary, "to imagine a greater contrast than that between Mamma and Papa. Yet I often ask myself which of them is the nobler in bearing this sorrow. My mother often causes me such anxiety. She is capable of everything great, yet incompetent in small things. Now that agitation has given place to the monotony of everyday life, and Papa at least appears outwardly the same and works as he always did, life seems to her oppressive and cheerless. Besides, she is afraid that her ever-increasing grief may become burdensome to Papa and lead to misunderstanding between them." Valerie saw with alarm that this was becoming a fixed idea with Elizabeth, from which she could no longer be distracted, and she had to listen while her mother said: "If only Jehovah would take me to Himself, so that Papa would be free, and you undisturbed in your future married happiness by the thought of the disconsolate life I shall lead without you!"

In the midst of her lamentations Elizabeth would often begin hysterically to laugh aloud and talk of the madhouse to which she would yet come. When Valerie begged her to take care of her health, she only answered "Why?" After such outbreaks she would say things which revealed her utter apathy, in which even her favorite interests—Heine, Greece, and all the rest—would be completely lost sight of. The committee for the Heine monument at Düsseldorf, which was, after all, formed at her own initiative, was told, on making inquiries, that Her Majesty had ceased to act as patroness. She had already spent 12,950 marks on models and preliminary sketches for the projected monument. The model was left in her possession and it was not till much later that she took up this once cherished idea again.

The Empress spent a good deal of time in trying to discover the causes of the catastrophe. Rudolf's letters, even the one to his mother, had been couched in general terms and allowed scope for all kinds of hypotheses. Their Majesties could not make up their minds. At first, Francis Joseph inclined toward the view that the tragic affair with the Baroness Vetsera was solely responsible for what had happened. But then he adopted Widenhofer's opinion that the Crown Prince had died as the result of mental derangement, just as one might die of any other disease. This enabled him to bear up, but it was impossible to refer to it often before Elizabeth. The whole family was left with a vague sense of horror, which was generally shared.

Francis Joseph anxiously watched the progress of his wife's depression. "Make every effort," he said to Valerie, "to persuade Mamma to take her cure in March as usual, for the pain in her foot is worse again." But when Valerie mentioned the subject, Elizabeth replied: "No, I will not and cannot hear of such a thing. I cannot leave Papa alone at the present moment before the eyes of the whole world. For Frau Schratt is not there to distract him either, as she is away on leave. I should like to go away, but I will not, even if staying were to drive me mad."

The deep mourning into which the court was plunged only encouraged the Empress' usual tendency to shut herself off from everything, and even the return of spring suggested melancholy thoughts. "How could Rudolf part from the spring?" she asked. At last she was persuaded to spend Easter with the Emperor at Ischl, after which she went on to Wiesbaden. Newspapers all over the world were already filled with rumors of the Empress' insanity. Even the *Ber-*

liner Tageblatt of April 21, 1889, contained a long article on the subject. The *Matin* of April 12, the *Gaulois* of the following day, and the *Matin* of the seventeenth represented the Empress' physical and mental condition as highly disquieting. They alleged that she was the victim of what they called a "*folie raisonnante*," that she dandled a pillow in her arms and asked those about her whether the new Crown Prince was not lovely. They were full of abominable stories in which the King of Bavaria played a part, and much more of the same sort. Other papers took up these fantastic reports, and immediately the press of the world was flooded with them.

The reports were contradicted, and it was pointed out that the Empress was to be seen daily in Wiesbaden with her daughter and other persons, taking walks in the town and the surrounding country. But it was no use—the world believed what was served up to it with its breakfast, and henceforth, in its eyes, the Empress was insane, though she was only different from the general run of humanity and crushed for the time by her bitter grief. About this time Ida Ferenczy felt it her duty to draw the Empress' attention to the sort of rumors that were being circulated about her. Elizabeth then began to show herself again in Wiesbaden and afterwards in Vienna on occasions when she would not otherwise have appeared, so as to make the fabrication of these reports a little more difficult. Her stay at Wiesbaden had a calming effect upon her. One of her ladies, Sárolta Majláth, remarked that the Empress' former sweet expression was coming back and she looked fairly calm, but that there was something sad in her expression. This effect was naturally increased by the heavy crepe veil which the Empress did not lay aside even in Wiesbaden.

Elizabeth continued her Greek studies, and had her feet massaged by Metzger, though she at once counteracted the treatment by taking too much exercise. She discussed her plans for the future with Baron Nopcsa in a way that betrayed her intense mental agitation. Her restless love of travel was still further increased by the misfortune that had overtaken her. "Our stay at Lainz," writes Nopcsa to Ida Ferenczy, "will last till at least the middle of June, and then comes Ischl. The following are our plans, which I tell you in confidence. At the beginning of September we mean to go to a Dutch seaside place, where Her Majesty will be treated for a fortnight by Metzger. From September 15 till the end of October we go to Meran. The Archduchess and her fiancé will join us there. After Meran there is some idea of Corfu. As you see, our wandering life is extending, and God knows where we shall go next. Her Majesty is well, thank God, and much calmer, and is already speaking Greek fluently. This seems to me to occupy her mind fully, which is a favorable sign. Warsberg is very ill. Her Majesty and I are much worried about the building operations in Corfu, for we do not know what Warsberg has already ordered, or where."

Unhappily, the good effects of the Empress' cure at Wiesbaden were to some extent undone by an accident in which her special train was involved between there and Frankfurt on her way back to Lainz on May 22. One of the baggage cars was derailed, and the train began to rock violently, at which the Empress exclaimed in great alarm: "This is really quite uncanny. The engineer must be drunk!" At last the coupling broke and the train stopped with a jerk which almost threw the Empress to the floor as she tried to look out of the window to see what was happening. All was in confusion, but as the Empress hurried from the train with Valerie, her first question was: "Is anybody hurt?"—while the Archduchess cried distractedly: "Where is Franz?" Fortunately little damage was done and only one person slightly injured, but while waiting for the train to start again the

Empress paced nervously up and down the platform and said to her daughter: "Life is gruesome with its dangers. Men are born to nothing but misfortune. I shall never have a quiet moment when I know you are traveling by train."

There was too little to distract the Empress at Lainz, for it had nothing to offer but riding, which she had given up, and shooting, which had never interested her. She became completely absorbed in her broodings. Her meditations about God and the world often made her religious faith very precarious, but she always returned to her dominating idea of the mighty Jehovah, before whose destroying power and greatness she would abase herself. Yet she doubted whether he listened to the prayers of his creatures, "for," she said, "everything has been foreordained from the beginning of the ages. Man is powerless against this predestination from all eternity, due solely to Jehovah's inscrutable will. In His eyes everything is but as the tiniest fly—and of course, I myself, too. How, then, could I matter to Him in the least?"

The Empress' growing apathy was gradually destroying every chance of her recovering any happiness and inward peace. "I am too old and weary to struggle," she would say, though she was only fifty-two. "My wings have been singed and now all I long for is rest."

On May 28 news arrived that Freiherr von Warsberg, known rather bombastically in Vienna as "the last of the Greeks," had died at Venice in his fifty-third year. Elizabeth was much affected; that she had had the highest esteem for this fine Greek scholar was shown by her intrusting him with the building of her palace in Corfu, which was to bear the name of her favorite hero, Achilles. It had now to be confided to other hands, and a retired naval officer, Freiherr von Bukovich, who, though practical and competent, had none of Warsberg's scholarship, was appointed as his successor.

The court now moved to Ischl, where the Empress again

made long expeditions to her favorite places and often went to pray in the chapel of the Virgin which she had had built for Valerie on the Jainzen. In July she went on to Feldafing, for grief had drawn her closer to her own relatives, whom she had not visited for the last three years. Her mother was careful not to mention Rudolf during the whole visit, and her family were so much concerned at her state of mind that when she left for Gastein, Gisela whispered in her sister's ear: "For heaven's sake, be careful of Mamma by the waterfall at Gastein!" Nor were her fears entirely groundless, for Elizabeth's mind ran on the subject of death. "How I envy Rudolf," she would often say. "But there! one does not know what comes after. If one knew that, then it would indeed be easy."

She now heard from Nopcsa that Count Andrássy was suffering from cancer of the bladder, and sent him a kindly message through Nopcsa, who added on his own account, yet certainly in accordance with his mistress' wishes, that Andrássy owed it to them all to take care of his health, for he was the last hope of Austria-Hungary. The Count replied on August 6 in a letter which ends with a deeply felt vindication of his Queen:

"I can find no words," he wrote, "to describe Her Majesty's graciousness in thinking of me at such a distance. It is more than sweet of her. You know what a high opinion I have always had of her mind and heart, but since reading some of her poems this has been transformed into the greatest admiration. When I consider that in addition to as much intelligence as would do honor even to a very great man, there is also room for so much heart, I can only say that *there is no other such woman upon earth.* The only thing that grieves me is that so few people know what she is. I should like the whole world to know it and admire her as such a rare personality deserves. Perhaps she is right in not wishing to concern herself with politics. It is not always a grateful task, but with her wide understanding it would be. I can only regret that she hides her superior intelligence and great heart, in comparison with which the famous Maria Theresa's were only those of a good housekeeper, as though it were not meet to display such things. I simply console myself with this one thought: that I am one of the few fortunate people who have had an opportunity of learning to know and admire a woman of whose true nature so many millions of her subjects have no real idea."

Nopcsa showed the letter to the Empress, who requited it with the words: "Yes, he is one of my few true friends in this world."

From Gastein the Empress returned to Ischl, where Francis Joseph paid her occasional visits. In spite of all his love, reverence, and sympathy for her, he had so many cares upon his shoulders already that his wife's alarmingly disconsolate state made him irritable at times; but if ever he answered rather curtly, or made an impatient gesture, the Empress' feelings were wounded at once, and she would contrast it with his bearing toward Frau Schratt. She would weep bitterly to Valerie, saying: "Why was I born? My life is a useless one, and I only come between the Emperor and Frau Schratt. I really play an almost ridiculous part." "Marriage is a nonsensical (*widersinnig*) institution," she said on one occasion; "one is sold as a child of fifteen and takes an oath which one does not understand, but can never undo."

On August 26, while she was taking a walk with Valerie, she said suddenly: "I love the great Jehovah and abase myself in the dust before Him, without hope of any reward." And so saying she threw herself full length on the ground. "Only thus," she said, "can one pray to the great Jehovah, and one can only worship Him, for what is the use of prayers, when everything is foreordained?" Yet on the next day she was praying to Jehovah again and vowing to go to Mariazell if her prayers were granted.

This year, seeing how matters stood with his wife, Francis Joseph encouraged her plans for travel in the hope that a visit to Madonna di Campiglio and Meran would do her good. Avoiding the railway as much as possible, she traveled on horseback or walked, and to the Emperor's relief Dr. Widerhofer was included in the party, riding along the narrow mountain paths behind the Empress on a mule. For these long walks Elizabeth would kilt up her skirt to the knee and on the march would sometimes retire behind a bush and take off her petticoat. When Widerhofer saw this, he discreetly tried to turn his mule back on the narrow path, but on one occasion it slipped, and though it saved itself at once, the doctor, who was not much of a horseman, fell off heavily, breaking his collarbone and seriously damaging his ribs. This was quite enough to make Elizabeth repeat that bad luck pursued her in all she did, and spread to her companions, too.

They crossed the Mendel to Meran, where they stayed at the Schloss Trauttmansdorff. The Empress was now comparatively free from sciatica, so she went on long tramps among the mountains with an excellent guide named Buchensteiner, who noticed how differently from other people she was affected by beautiful views, for they always left her sad and depressed. During her wanderings she would often be seen standing for a long time before the wayside crucifixes with their clumsily carved figures.

Elizabeth received affectionate letters from Francis Joseph regularly, telling her about the smallest details of his life, and especially all that concerned Frau Schratt. "Low though my spirits were on the morning of October 4" (his name day), he wrote, "they brightened up a little when I received your letter and one from our friend, with a pot of four-leaf clover, and when an unusually splendid, sunny day lit up the woods and snow-covered mountains with the most magnificent and varied coloring. You are right. After all, Nature is the best comforter."

Toward the end of October Francis Joseph came on a visit to Elizabeth at Meran, but he found his wife's spirits in no way improved. She still shrank from seeing people and had almost ceased appearing at meals. It was now evident that at the moment the only thing that united the Emperor and Empress was their common grief, and the realization of this made them even more disconsolate.

"I could go mad," said Elizabeth, "when I look forward and see life still stretching before me for years more!"

In such a mood as this the Empress took leave of her family and went to Miramar, where the yacht of the same name awaited her under the command of Count Cassini and bore her to Corfu. She wished to see how the building of her house was progressing, hoping that the beauty of the island might alleviate her gloom and despair. But she did not intend to remain in Corfu, knowing that too long a stay in any one place would only encourage her broodings.

The little Greek, Thermojannis, now left Elizabeth's service and wept like a child on saying good-bye to her, though by this time the Empress could not endure him. His place was taken by a new master named Rhousso Rhoussopoulos, a somewhat sallow, unkempt-looking person. Elizabeth could already understand and speak Greek, but wished to learn the literary language thoroughly. "Do not think I am joking," she said to her new master. "Quite seriously, I wish you to be strict with me and draw my attention to every mistake, for one ought to learn a thing thoroughly or not begin it at all."

While the Empress was in Corfu, the Emperor William II expressed a wish to visit her on his way to the wedding of his sister with the Crown Prince of Greece. He was on his yacht the *Hohenzollern*, escorted by a squadron of warships. But Elizabeth excused herself on the ground that she was not yet in a fit state to receive visits. She fled from the villa to another place near by and remained hidden there all day. The Emperor William, assuming her to be at Gasturi, sailed close by the cliffs on which the villa stood, with his squadron of nine gigantic vessels in review order, and the whole squadron fired a salute of twenty-one guns. When the squadron entered the harbor, Baron Nopcsa went on board to bear the Empress Elizabeth's excuses to the German Emperor and Empress in person. They were both most sympathetic and gracious, though no doubt inwardly disappointed, for they would have liked to see for themselves how Elizabeth was, and her behavior seemed to confirm the rumors in circulation about her. As a matter of fact, her stay in Corfu quieted Elizabeth's nerves and did her a great deal of good. The expression in her eyes was noticed to be calmer, and she joined quite eagerly in planning her travels for the winter.

From Corfu she went on to Sicily, passing through the Straits of Messina to Palermo, then touched at Malta and Tunis, and visited the ruins of Carthage. She did not celebrate her name day or receive any congratulations. She had, indeed, instructed the Ministry for Foreign Affairs to intimate to all foreign courts that in future she did not wish to receive any more congratulations (*Glückwünsche*), for the word *Glück* (happiness) had no further meaning for her.

On December 4 the Empress returned to Vienna and was met at the station by Valerie, but on stepping off the train she recalled how Rudolf had always been there to meet her before, and burst into tears. "Do you know, my child," she said, "if it had not been for the sake of seeing you, I should hardly have had strength to return. The Hofburg in Vienna weighs upon my spirits. Here one not only feels what has happened, one is reminded of it every day and sees it all over again, and it is impossible to shake off the burden. Do you know, I often feel as though Rudolf's bullet had killed my faith. I worship the great Jehovah, but apart from that . . ."

Elizabeth reviewed her wardrobe. She meant never to wear colored clothes again in her life, so she put aside everything brightly colored and gave away dresses, parasols, hats, shawls, and gloves. Valerie begged her father not to spend Christmas Eve in the Hofburg, fearing the effect which it might have upon her mother; so Francis Joseph and Elizabeth with the Archduchess and her fiancé spent the day at Miramar. For the first time there were no Christmas tree and no presents, and Elizabeth wore a light grey dress for a few minutes only, in memory of Valerie's betrothal the previous year.

On New Year's Day all the usual courts were canceled, and nobody was admitted to Elizabeth's presence but Valerie and Franz Salvator. Even Valerie now longed to escape into a healthier atmosphere and find a sphere of her own, as she hoped to do through marriage. She confessed to herself that there were many things which the Empress need not have taken so much to heart. Too often she retired into herself in wounded pride instead of saying what she felt, with the result that she had ended by becoming estranged from almost everybody.

January 30 was the first anniversary of Rudolf's death, and Elizabeth arranged with the Emperor to go to Mayerling, which she had never seen. The little shooting box had been turned into a Carmelite convent, and the room in which Rudolf had died, into a chapel. The Emperor and Empress drove out with Valerie through the lovely woods, but nobody spoke a word during the whole drive. Their chaplain from the Burg chapel read mass at an altar built on the very spot where Rudolf's bed had once stood. Elizabeth listened with dry eyes, as though in some terrible dream, while the Emperor was calm and full of Christian resignation. Elizabeth thought bitterly of all those who had played such a sinister part during the last months of Rudolf's life. After such experiences, she thought, it is impossible to retain any belief in life, love, and friendship.

On February 18 she was shocked to hear that Count Julius Andrássy had died at Volosca. "My last and only friend is dead," she said. And now it seemed as though she could find no rest. Though this death was not unexpected, it was another devastating blow, for, according to the Archduchess Valerie's testimony, "she clung to him with true and steadfast friendship as she did, perhaps, to no other person."

"Now that Andrássy is dead," said Elizabeth to Valerie, "I realize for the first time what he was to me. Not till now have I felt utterly deserted, without a single counselor or friend. Andrássy's spirit will not dwell either in his sons or in any other person." She went and laid a wreath of lilies of the valley on his coffin as he lay in state in the Akademie, and once again Hungary saw its Queen kneeling in prayer beside a great patriot.

In the middle of March Elizabeth started on her usual spring holiday, this time going to Wiesbaden and Heidelberg. As they walked together, she would say to her daughter: "Only through you can an occasional gleam of brightness still come over me. I can hardly conceive what my life will be after we are parted by your marriage. The time between now and your wedding is like a condemned man's last hours."

Gradually, however, she began to emerge from the complete retirement in which she had lived since her son's death. On April 11, 1890, she received a visit from the Emperor William, and a little later, one from the Empress Frederick, whom she loved and found not only simple and sympathetic but also very clever. The Empress Frederick had been crushed by the death of her husband and she too felt very bitter toward the world.

"My loss is no less hard than yours (*das deine*)," she said to Elizabeth. "People's ingratitude toward me is more than flesh and blood can bear."

"All that happens is foreordained," replied Elizabeth sadly.

"Ah, no! I believe that in the long run God in Heaven orders all things for our good. For the rest, I simply wait, for no man can know what comes after death."

Shortly after this visit Elizabeth returned to Vienna, where her life resumed its accustomed routine, though a new person now formed part of her intimate circle. Frau Schratt was often the fourth person at dinner with her and the Emperor and Valerie, for instance on May 7, 1890, when the Archduchess notes that she finds the situation rather an awkward one and cannot understand how Elizabeth can call it so "*gemütlich*" (homelike).

More bad news arrived, this time from Ratisbon, where Néné Taxis, the Empress' eldest sister, was seriously ill. It seemed as though everything was conspiring together that year to prevent Elizabeth from shaking off the effects of the Crown Prince's death. By the time she reached her sister's bedside she found her dying, though unconscious of the gravity of her condition and delighted to see her "old Sisi" again.

"We have both had to bear some hard knocks in our lives," said Elizabeth.

"Yes, because we have hearts," replied her sister.

A few days later she died in agony, and Elizabeth returned home shattered and once more at odds with God and the world.

"I can understand now," she said, "how a man might be capable of committing suicide merely out of dread of such a lingering end."

The Emperor Francis Joseph had hoped that he might gradually accustom the Empress to appearing in public again, but this fresh grief undid what progress she had made. "The Emperor," wrote the German Ambassador to the Emperor William on May 12, 1890, "is the person who suffers most from his consort's isolation, and the whole social burden falls entirely upon him. The very idea of an imperial court is vanishing, and the relations between him and court society are becoming more and more precarious."

Every possible device was resorted to in the hope of tempting Elizabeth out of her retirement now that eighteen months had elapsed since the disaster; but without success. Even at Ischl she was surrounded by a prohibited zone, the Emperor's aides-de-camp being only admitted to certain stated places in the immediate neighborhood of the imperial villa, so as not to come in Her Majesty's way. Once only, when King Alexander of Serbia, then but fourteen years of age, arrived at Ischl, could the Empress be persuaded to appear at dinner, which she never did now. She came in a few moments late, entering through a curtained door at the very moment when a footman was going out. They bumped into each other violently, but all the Empress said was: "How clumsy!"

Valerie's approaching wedding now occupied all Elizabeth's thoughts. "I cannot understand," she would often say, "how people can look forward to marriage so much and expect so much good to result from it. But if it makes you happy, I will gladly make every sacrifice."

During these months Elizabeth tried to make her little daughter's last days in her old home as pleasant as possible. She took a personal interest in every detail of her trousseau and was always arranging small surprises for her. For example, she had one of her poems, of which Valerie was fondest, set to music.

It began as follows:

O ask not of tomorrow
So fair it is today.
Scatter our care and sorrow,
May winds bear them away.

One evening at Ischl this song was suddenly heard being sung beneath Valerie's window by a men's choral society. Elizabeth joined her daughter, and both of them listened with deep emotion, then the Empress threw her arms around her daughter and with tears in her eyes said: "I thank you for always having been a good child to me." And this, says Valerie, was the most beautiful moment in her life.

And so the morning of the wedding day came round, July 31, 1890. Elizabeth was very pale as she drove to the church alone with Valerie in the last carriage of the bridal procession through masses of cheering people. The ceremony went off with due pomp and dignity, and when the bride changed her clothes afterwards, the Empress helped her, weeping bitterly. This depressed Valerie so much that she took her Uncle Karl Theodor's hand and said to him earnestly: "I beg you to promise me that you will always be a true friend to Mamma in all life's contingencies. She will certainly have need of one in future." The Duke clasped her hand warmly and gave her his promise. A long separation from Valerie awaited Elizabeth, for the Empress had announced her intention of going on a cruise all around Europe.

And now the moment of parting arrived, and as the young couple drove off, the Empress felt as though her heart were being torn from her body.

XIV

THE EMPRESS' ODYSSEY

1890–1897

ELIZABETH WAS NOW LEFT ALONE WITH her unrest and could hardly endure to stay at home for a single day. First she went to Bavaria, but even there she did not remain long; she felt she must go far, far away over the sea. She embarked on a cutter, the *Chazalie* (Star of the Sea), which was waiting for her at Dover. On her very first trip the boat ran into the worst gale the sailors had ever experienced and had great difficulty in fighting her way back to harbor. But Elizabeth had herself lashed to a mast and thoroughly enjoyed the spectacle of the warring elements, while the foam-crested sea broke over the deck and drenched her to the skin.

This experience caused consternation among the members of her suite, as their letters home testify. "All I can say about this sea trip is that it was appalling," wrote the Countess Festetics, whose criticisms grew sharper as the years went by, to Frau von Ferenczy. "It was a miracle that we reached land at all. Nobody can imagine what it was like. . . . What I suffered during the first eighteen hours beggars description. . . . The idea of going on board again is horrible. I pray that my strength may not fail me. . . . For me, too, this sort of thing is far too much."

The *Chazalie* had been damaged by the storm and had to be repaired before the voyage proper began. Since she was on an English yacht, the Empress did not travel as the Countess of Hohenembs this time, but as Mrs. Nicolson.

Owing to the prevalence of cholera, they were not allowed to touch at any Spanish port, which pleased the Empress, as it gave her a good excuse for not visiting the Queen of Spain at San Sebastian, which she would otherwise have been unable to avoid. The yacht sailed straight for Portugal, meeting with very rough seas, and all the ladies in waiting were so sick that they could not attend the Empress, so the Greek tutor was all the more in request. But he, too, was often so ill that he could not perform his duties, and the Empress, who was the hardiest of the party, complained of losing time from her Greek studies. But the gigantic waves were inexorable and wreaked their will upon even the Empress at last.

The yacht, with its "passengers half done for (*halbkrepiert*)," to quote Marie Festetics, had hardly berthed in the harbor at Oporto before Elizabeth was on shore, where, in spite of the great heat, she spent two whole days walking about the city and its countryside from morning till night. Only in such circumstances did she feel entirely in her element. "Her Majesty," wrote Marie Festetics, "is so contented at such times that it helps one to endure the fatigue." On receiving an invitation to dinner with the royal family, however, the Empress sent regrets at being compelled to decline. The reigning Queen, whose consort was not in Lisbon, affected to consider the excuse valid, but the Dowager Queen Maria Pia, a proud princess of Savoy, who had signed the invitation, replied curtly and imperiously: "Tell Her Majesty that I particularly desire to see her, and that if she does not come to us at Cintra, I shall have to pay her a visit on her yacht." Thus the Empress could hardly do otherwise than call upon the two Queens, but the moment this was over she resumed her rapid walks. "Her sole object," wrote the Countess Festetics to Ida Ferenczy, "is to keep moving. When we got home I collapsed on my bed with weariness."

A projected excursion to Alhandra, on the estuary of the

Tagus, was abandoned owing to an outbreak of cholera, for, as Elizabeth said to Rhoussopoulos, though she was quite ready and willing to die, she had no desire for a long and painful death. "But," she added, "I am responsible for the lives of my suite, so the trip must be omitted." On September 15, 1890, they sailed from Lisbon for Gibraltar, where Elizabeth spent eight hours on the first day and ten on the next wandering about the town and fortress with the Countess Festetics, afterwards crossing on a rough sea to Tangier. Here, after walking about the town for seven hours, the Empress asked the Countess if she could go on a little longer, and on receiving a hesitating "yes," went on for another hour. The voyage continued along the north coast of Africa, the same story being repeated at Oran, where the Countess Festetics held out with difficulty. Baron Nopcsa shook his head over it all. "This mania for movement of Her Majesty's is on the increase," he wrote to Ida Ferenczy. "God knows what it may lead to."

On September 25 the yacht was forced by stress of weather to put into the port of Tenéz. "The storm has driven us into this little harbor," wrote the Countess to Ida Ferenczy, "and here I take up the tale of our sufferings once more. . . . Even on board it is becoming more intolerable every day, the hairdresser growing more and more insolent and giving herself the airs of a great lady. The yacht is so small that one cannot escape from her. . . . Her Majesty tells us the most intimate things. She is very sweet and kind, but I often tremble for her beautiful soul, foundering in egoism and paradox." Her impression was, however, that Elizabeth's state of mind was on the whole better, for she indulged less frequently in eccentric views and severe strictures and showed more concern for other people. But whatever happened she continued to insist on perpetual change of scene. She had hardly reached Algiers before she was hurrying on to Ajaccio in

Corsica, to see Napoleon's birthplace. "What a great man he was!" she said. "But what a pity that he aimed at an imperial crown." And so the voyage continued, ever further and further afield, to Marseilles, the Hyères Islands with their pine woods, and finally to Italy, the first place she visited being Florence.

The Italian Prime Minister, Crispi, had not yet come to terms with Pope Leo XIII, and when he heard of the Empress' arrival he was afraid she might go to Rome and pay an ostentatious visit to the Vatican—which shows how little he knew her. As for the Emperor Francis Joseph, his wife's vagaries were a perpetual source of disquiet and alarm, and for political reasons her visit to Italy was most unwelcome to him. But her lack of any fixed plans and her erratic wanderings to unknown destinations made it almost impossible for him to arrange anything with her by correspondence. Elizabeth went on, however, to Pompeii and Capri without visiting Rome, merely writing a polite letter to the King and Queen of Italy, so that all friction was avoided.

At Naples she was met by the *Miramar*, in which she set sail for Corfu, arriving on November 25. She had brought a number of marble statues with her from Italy to adorn her villa, including one of a peri, a "kindly light fairy in Milton's *Paradise Lost*," and another of Sappho, together with busts of Homer and of Greek philosophers. Her spirits had improved, but she dreaded going home, for she feared that she had entirely alienated the Emperor and disliked the idea of being a burden to her newly married daughter and son-in-law. On December 1, 1890, she met the Emperor at the palace of Miramar. It was indeed high time for her to return, for even in Hungary, where she was idolized, there had been open references in the Chamber of Deputies to the growing infrequency of royal visits.

Valerie had hurried to Vienna to greet her mother, and

though Elizabeth once more assured her that since the parting at Ischl her heart was dead and she had become a different person, the Archduchess found her mother far less bitter and hoped that in time she would reconcile herself to the change. The same expectations were felt at court. It was already being intimated semiofficially that the Empress would give some large dinner parties for the diplomatic corps and attend certain evening receptions. "That will make a good impression," reported Prince Reuss, the German Ambassador, "for the comments upon this exalted and sorely tried lady have really gone to extremes."

Elizabeth made this effort because she was anxious not to reveal her actual state of mind to the Emperor too plainly, knowing what effect it would have upon him. In her relations with Francis Joseph she followed a "fixed program," which she had thought out on the *Chazalie* during the storms. Her conversations with him were mainly about Frau Schratt or the theatre; for the rest, she did only what she was absolutely obliged to do. "I am like a log," she wrote to Valerie, "and even more fatalistic than I used to be."

She declined an invitation to spend Christmas with her daughter and son-in-law at Lichtenegg near Wels, where the Archduke Franz Salvator was in garrison with his regiment, the Fifteenth Dragoons, for, she said, she never wanted to see a Christmas tree again. When Valerie proposed to come and spend Christmas Eve with her at the Hofburg, she declined this too. "On December 24," she wrote, "people should stay at home in their own nest and celebrate the festival with a tree and everything in as beautiful and homelike a style as possible. It will be my joy to think of you from a distance on that evening. For happiness exists only in the imagination."

Elizabeth mastered her feelings in the New Year, and appeared in society for the first time at a great reception on

January 17. She was dressed in deep mourning, with crepe, and many of the ladies were in tears, so that in spite of the gay dresses and flashing jewels the whole affair was more like a funeral than a carnival celebration. Eight days later, accompanied by the Countess Festetics, Elizabeth paid her first visit to her daughter and son-in-law at Lichtenegg, where, contrary to her expectations, she felt thoroughly at home. The Archduchess Valerie begged her to stay a little longer, but she would not. "It is precisely because I like being here that I must not stay," she said, "for the sea gull is out of place in the swallows' nest. I will take a photograph of your home at Lichtenegg back with me; I am content with that, and I will commend the swallows and their nest to the protection of the great Jehovah."

Valerie had actually persuaded the Empress to eat normal, and even substantial, meals—a difficult matter, for at every mouthful Elizabeth was afraid that she would grow as fat "as a tub." There was certainly no danger of this, for she continued to be excessively slender; but her terror of becoming stout was now a fixed idea against which, as Valerie said, there was no contending. In the middle of March the Empress invited the young couple to go with her to Corfu in the *Miramar* and see her villa. As the Countess Festetics had suffered severely from the strain of the previous journey, her place was taken by a new maid of honor aged twenty-five, the Countess Janka Mikes, who had previously been subjected to a medical examination as a test of her capacity for walking.

The *Miramar* arrived at Corfu on March 18 and anchored directly in front of the high ridge, near the hamlet of Gasturi, on which the villa was being built. It could be seen from far out at sea and, in accordance with the ideas of the late Baron von Warsberg, was intended to represent a royal palace of the golden age of the Phæacians. The terrace was already completed, and from this the Empress showed Valerie the view out to the open sea between two lofty cypresses, saying: "This is where I should like to be buried."

Next they went on to Corinth and Athens, where no notice had been given of their visit. They found nobody in the royal palace but the Princess Sophie, the Emperor Frederick's pleasant, simple daughter. The Empress tried to talk Greek to her, but the Crown Princess preserved an uncomfortable silence, for she did not understand a word of her country's language. The Empress found this amusing, just as she did talking Greek with Rhoussopoulos about the Countess Mikes when she was present, and then talking Hungarian with her about the Greek. In the evening they visited the Acropolis by moonlight, after which the Archduke and Archduchess returned home, while Elizabeth sailed for Sicily. But despite her enchantment with its beauty, she wrote to Valerie from Gasturi on April 22 that it could not be compared with Corfu. "Though I have seen so many lovely places," she said, "I prefer this to them all. Wherever I may go, I say on my return: This is the loveliest spot on earth. The English claim that Tasmania is equally beautiful. But that would be rather a long expedition. . . . I pray for you to the great Jehovah. May the Almighty take my turtledove and her beloved one under His protection and send them in due time some little turtledoves. I am now going to Mass and will pray with this special intention. Today the sun is shining, the sea is blue, and the island shines green as an emerald in all the freshness of spring after the warm, abundant rain. If only Póka and you could be here!"

Valerie always showed the Emperor letters like this containing a little good news, and he responded with news of Frau Schratt. He had gradually formed a habit of taking a walk with the actress every day in the park at Schönbrunn by way of distraction, or meeting her at the house of Frau von Ferenczy, previous to which the latter always received a note in his own hand asking if she would "perhaps be so gracious as to allow his friend (*die Freundin*) to come about one o'clock."

Elizabeth was preparing to return to the Villa Hermes at Lainz at the end of April. Meanwhile she had been learning not only ancient, but also modern, Greek, into which she translated *Hamlet*, *King Lear*, and *The Tempest* almost without help. The *Iliad* had ceased to attract her, for she found the clash of arms repellent, and the *Odyssey* was now her favorite poem. But she was bored with Rhoussopoulos, while the little Corfiote, Janko Kephalas, was not intellectual enough and was, moreover, apt to collapse after a long walk. A search was therefore made among the young Greeks studying at the University of Vienna, which led to the discovery of two brothers named Christomanos, who could speak German and, like so many other Greeks of the commercial class, came from Macedonia. One of these, Constantine Christomanos, was now temporarily attached to the Empress' service. He was small and hunchbacked, with a poetic and extremely sensitive nature. From time to time the Empress would invite him to Lainz, where he would accompany her in all kinds of weather on one of her now famous walks. For the young man, who had always before been painfully conscious of his deformity, this was an overwhelming experience.

Elizabeth was no longer the transcendent beauty of former days; the years had left their traces on her. Wind and weather had tanned and wrinkled her skin, while now and again something cold and somber in her expression would reveal the hardening process within. Yet the indescribable dignity of her presence, her slender figure, her gliding walk, and her soft, musical voice remained, and occasionally a gleam of her former loveliness would break like sunshine from her eyes.

Added to this was her unusual conversation, with its mournful scepticism, its cynical irony, and then again its poetry and aspiration. Her attitude toward the young Greek's enthusiasm was a little mocking, but he never noticed this. On the whole Elizabeth found him entertaining, for he was not at all ordinary, so she contemplated taking him with her on one of her longer journeys.*

In July Elizabeth spent some time with the Emperor Francis Joseph at Gastein, where she took pains to conceal her melancholy and once more proved a pleasant and agreeable companion. At the same time she made long excursions into the mountains with the Countess Janka Mikes and would pass the night sleeping on hay in Alpine huts. She showed some consideration for her maid of honor, however, for she had heard that it was being bruited about that she had half killed Marie Festetics.

At Gastein the Empress lived in the Helenenburg. Her amiability was a comfort to Francis Joseph, and he was extremely grateful to her for the understanding view which she took of his inclination for Frau Schratt. "My inexpressibly beloved angel," he wrote to her shortly after his departure, "I am in a melancholy mood, with an aching heart and a feeling of homesickness for Gastein. Yesterday as I drove down the hill below the Johannespromenade and looked sadly and longingly back at the Helenenburg, I thought I recognized your white parasol on the balcony, and my eyes filled with tears. Once again my warmest thanks for your love and goodness during my stay at Gastein. It is seldom now that I pass such happy days." When Elizabeth replied that

* In his *Tagebuchblätter* (1st ser., Vienna, 1899) Constantine Marie Christomanos published an account of the time he spent with the Empress in 1891 and 1892. The book bears sufficient witness to the rapturous admiration which the Empress inspired in the young hunchback, but the facts are enveloped in a sentimentality that makes it difficult to disentangle what the Empress actually said and did.

he was right in thinking he had seen her, he replied: "The certainty that after our parting at Gastein you really did wave your white parasol to me makes me very happy, and I am deeply touched and grateful."

But no sooner was Elizabeth alone again than she relapsed into her moods of melancholy. Now, however, she heard that her daughter was expecting a child. Valerie's letters bubbled over with joy but the answers she received were always in the same mournful strain. "The birth of another human being always seems to me a misfortune," wrote the Empress. "I feel the burden of life so heavily that it is often like a physical pain and I had far rather be dead." Valerie was unhappy that her mother should doubt God's mercy, and for a moment had the idea of sacrificing her child in order that Elizabeth's noble and richly endowed soul should not be lost to the Lord. "May He take it," she thought to herself, "and in return for this save my mother's soul." But then again she repented, for she felt that in the depths of her heart she had never honestly meant it, so she prayed that, after all, God would spare the child.

Soon Elizabeth began to feel unsettled again and moved restlessly about from Gastein to Feldafing, and thence to Miramar and Corfu. But she wanted to go still further. She consulted the eccentric Archduke Ludwig Salvator, who was a great traveler, on the subject of Tasmania, which the English praised so highly, and he too described it in glowing colors. But the suggestion of a voyage across the ocean, or even a trip to America, about which Elizabeth had often dropped hints to her husband, had hitherto fallen on deaf ears, in spite of the Emperor's complaisance in granting her every other wish.

On arriving in Corfu Elizabeth went straight to her new palace in Homer's "far-gazing spot." The most beautiful thing about her new home was its situation. The palace itself was a not very successful blend of the classical and Pompeian styles with the comfort and dubious taste of the day. Much of its contents, for example, the furniture in the ancient Roman style and the stucco reliefs of cupids and glass fruit glittering with colored electric lights, appeared shoddy and pretentious. The cost had been enormous. With his usual chivalrous generosity, Francis Joseph had given orders that such part of the building expenses as was not covered by the Empress' current income was to be charged to his privy purse. Statues were now being set up embodying the ideal of human beauty adored by Elizabeth, including one of the dying Achilles, while on the wall of the staircase hung Professor Matsch's gigantic and effective painting of "Achilles Triumphant." As feminine pendants to these there was a copy of Canova's so-called "Third Dancer," supposed to represent the Princess Pauline Borghese, Napoleon's favorite sister, with her exquisite figure. In addition to these Elizabeth proposed to erect imperishable monuments in the "Achilleion" to Heine and to her son, the two poles upon which her life revolved.

In a letter to Ida Ferenczy dated from Corfu on November 26, 1891, Baron Nopcsa described the whole "fairy palace" as most beautiful and unique of its kind. Elizabeth was pleased with her new home, too, for every little detail was original. Everything in the "Achilleion" was to be dedicated to the dolphin, the sacred creature under whose form Neptune had disguised himself. So the dolphin, surmounted by the Austrian imperial crown, appeared upon everything used in the house, whether china, glass, linen, or writing paper. It was all beautiful, and yet she did not feel well or contented. She was tortured by sciatica again and could not settle down. Though she did not take much exercise now, she bathed in the sea every morning and afternoon and in the evening was packed in sheets soaked in sea water to prevent her from getting stout, which, the Countess Festetics wrote, was bad for her nerves and spirits.

A life-sized statue of Heine was brought from Rome and solemnly set up in a little open temple. It represents Heine seated wearily in a chair, with a sheet of paper in his drooping hand on which are inscribed the famous verses: "*Was will die einsame Träne,*" which may be roughly rendered as follows:

What means this tear so lonely?
It dims my vision so—
Still in my eyes it lingered
From days of long ago.
Thou tear so old and lonely
Flow down like all the rest. . . .

The erection of this monument was intended to mark Elizabeth's contempt for the world which, for political reasons, had denied the poet such honors. Yet even in this earthly paradise, where everything was arranged to suit her own ideas, Elizabeth was as restless as ever. And so in November the palace in Corfu was deserted and the yacht *Miramar* sailed for Egypt. Here the Empress spent nearly three weeks at Shepherd's Hotel in Cairo and, as soon as her sciatica was relieved by the hot climate, began her endless walks again. The Austrian representative in Cairo, Herr von Heidler, was amazed. "Her Majesty's pedestrian feats are so marvelous," he reported to Count Kálnoky on November 23, 1891, "that the secret police said it was intolerable to have to follow the all-highest lady except in carriages."

From Egypt the Empress returned to Vienna, where Francis Joseph was glad to discuss with her the political complications caused by Count Taaffe's policy of playing off the Slavs and Germans against each other. She stood so entirely outside politics that she was often able to judge matters calmly and in a detached spirit. Once he came in just as Elizabeth was about to start her Greek lesson with Christomanos, who had resumed his service in December, 1891. The Emperor spoke Magyar so that the tutor should not understand him, and when he had gone Elizabeth remarked: "I have just been discussing politics with the Emperor. I wish I had been able to help. . . . But I have too low an opinion of such things. Politicians always think that they are directing events, while in reality events always take them by surprise."

The little crippled Greek student with the almost uncannily clever face and burning eyes was a source of amusement to the Empress. She liked to see his startled expression when she made fun of herself, as for instance on one occasion when she asked him whether he thought she felt very imperial while her masseuse was kneading her. She was fond of laughing at herself and equally fond of poking quiet fun at the little student for his love of scent and the overelegant clothes with which he did his best to make up for his personal imperfections. And he was quite spellbound in her presence. Everything about him seemed to be done for effect, but he was widely read and stimulating on account of his general culture and his feminine appreciation of stuffs, colors, and flowers.

On January 26, 1892, the Empress heard that her mother had died very suddenly of pneumonia at the age of eighty-four. On the following day Valerie was safely delivered of a little daughter, who was of course baptized Elizabeth, but called Ella for short. Torn by these conflicting emotions, Elizabeth left hurriedly for Corfu, where she took frequent walks with the unfortunate Christomanos, whose deformity made them a severe ordeal. Some of their conversations are recorded in his diary: "If one is to come to terms with life," she said to him once, "one must ultimately retire to an island. For it is always people who spoil things; only where things are left alone do they preserve their eternal beauty. Only think that a hundred years hence not a single person belonging to our age will still be in existence, not one, and probably not a single royal throne either. A constant succession of new people, new poppies, new waves. They are like us, we are no more than they are. The first time I was in Corfu I often visited the Villa Braila; it was superb because it was quite deserted among its great trees. That attracted me so much that I had it made into the Achilleion. . . . And now I quite regret it. Our dreams are always fairer when they are not realized."

In time the Empress came to feel Christomanos' rather fulsome ways and dreamy unworldliness as oppressive "as a relaxing south wind (*Föhn*)." At the end of April, 1892, a new tutor arrived from Alexandria, a Mr. Frederick Barker, who was half Greek and half English. Absorbed in her Greek studies, the Empress seldom troubled her maid of honor, the Countess Mikes, though she would feel impelled now and then to talk frankly with one of her ladies, and at such times, the Countess records in her diary, it was hardly credible how outspoken she would be. "Poor lady!" wrote the Countess, "I do not think anyone on earth feels so unhappy and misunderstood, but nobody can do anything about it now."

After another short expedition to Athens the Empress returned home at the beginning of May and went on a visit to her daughter at Lichtenegg. But though the sight of Valerie's happy home life rejoiced her heart, she confessed that since the death of her mother had broken the last link between her and her youth, even joy now gave her pain.

In June the Empress went to Karlsbad for the cure and could be seen walking for hours in the woods with her white sunshade and fan, till Christomanos could hardly drag himself after her. Since she ate nothing on these walks, on one occasion she had a fit of giddiness, and a few days later she fainted while her hair was being dressed; upon which the Countess Festetics told her plainly that if she went on as she was doing she would have a stroke. This impressed Elizabeth for a time, but soon she relapsed into her old ways again. "Her Majesty looks so ill," wrote the Countess Festetics, "that it goes to one's heart. . . . She is obsessed with the idea that she is getting stout. I believe that if I did not insist so often, she would long since have died of starvation. Yet with it all she is unbelievably gentle and kind." From Karlsbad Elizabeth went on to Bavaria and Switzerland, where she ascended the Rigi and visited Zürich, Rigi Kaltbad, and Lucerne, spending the whole day on her feet, whether she was exploring the countryside or wandering about the streets of the cities, as she did for nine and a half hours at Lucerne on September 6. "Her Majesty is in excellent spirits," wrote Baron Nopcsa to Ida Ferenczy on September 1, 1891, "and races about even more in consequence." Barker now took the place of Christomanos on these walks, being younger and better able to stand the strain. Francis Joseph wrote to his wife every other day, and it is touching to see how exactly he kept her informed of everything important, though she was so indifferent to politics that the *Indépendance belge* actually printed a story alleging that on September 16, Kossuth's ninetieth birthday, the Empress caused a Mass to be said and sent him her greetings. The report was contradicted at once, but this did not prevent many people in Hungary from believing it.

At the end of September the Empress went straight from Switzerland to Gödöllö, where she spent the beautiful autumn quietly, though she grieved to see how the last remnants of the hunting stables were now being disposed of. But a political demonstration in Budapest caused the court to move from Gödöllö to Vienna, where the Tsarevitch arrived on a visit in November. As a special courtesy to him, the Empress was induced to appear at dinner, though, until this was explained to him, the Grand Duke hardly realized what an event the presence of his hostess was.

The relations between Elizabeth and Francis Joseph were very cordial at this time, and when she left for the south Nopcsa wrote to Ida Ferenczy that she felt the parting almost more deeply than she ever had before. This time she meant to escape the cold by going to Spain, touching first at Sicily and the Balearic Islands. "I can quite understand," wrote Marie Festetics to Ida Ferenczy from Messina, "that anybody should want to go in search of warmth, but it is peculiar taste to spend three months on board ship in the winter. As for where we are going, not even Her Majesty really knows that." Even Francis Joseph had to wait uneasily for a telegram to inform him that the Empress had safely arrived somewhere.

Once again Elizabeth celebrated her birthday on Christmas Eve away from home. "Today," wrote Francis Joseph, "I want to send you my most heartfelt wishes, together with a petition that you will be as kind and sweet to me during the future which is in store for us—which may be only a short one—as you have been more and more up to the present. And I should like, too, to put into words what I cannot do enough to show you—for it would bore you if I were always trying to show it—how enormously (*unbändig*) fond of you I am. May God bless and protect you and send us a happy reunion, we have nothing more left to desire or hope for. . . ." The letter is signed "your little one" again, which had been less frequent during the last few years.

But though the Emperor and Empress were on such excellent terms, growing discontent was felt within the monarchy at Elizabeth's incessant absences and neglect of all her duties, and the ambassadors of foreign powers referred to this feeling in their dispatches. Elizabeth, however, had long ceased to care what people said about her. She spent Christmas Eve visiting every hole and corner of Valencia, afterwards going on to Malaga and Granada, where she admired the Alhambra. Here she received an invitation from the Queen Regent of Spain to visit her at Aranjuez, but declined it on the pretext of her sciatica, thus giving offense in Madrid, where it was considered that the reports of the Empress' travels and long walks were hard to reconcile with all this talk about her health.

Passing through Seville and Cadiz, she returned to Gibraltar. "Such a nice, congenial place," she wrote to Valerie on January 23, 1893. "I like it best of anything in the whole of Spain, chiefly because it is English and everything in the town is so clean. . . . There are some most amusing shops here kept by negroes. I visit one every day, so it is only thanks to Marie Festetics that I am not now lying in a debtors' prison. But she is so good at bargaining that we get things fabulously cheap." This was the Empress' latest craze. "Her Majesty is buying such quantities of miscellaneous objects," lamented Nopcsa to Ida Ferenczy, "that the ship is already full of them."

The erratic journey went on, past Majorca to Barcelona, then on to the Riviera, and afterwards to Turin, where news was received that the Archduchess Valerie had had a son, which delighted Elizabeth as much as it did Francis Joseph. "I do not know why," wrote the Emperor on February 18, 1893, "but I cannot help thinking of Rudolf. It is a poor substitute, but still a substitute of a sort."

From Italy the Empress decided to make an expedition to Geneva and Territet, and begged her husband to allow himself a little relaxation for once and pay her a visit in Switzerland. She had a bad conscience at having left the Emperor alone so long, and was always asking Ida von Ferenczy to take an interest in her husband and the little things which pleased him. Frau von Ferenczy would often arrange special lunches for him with all sorts of sausage, pork, and delicious bread from her native Hungarian plains, which the Emperor was particularly fond of. Yet when the Empress and Frau Schratt were away at the same time, Francis Joseph became quite melancholy, and this was reflected in all his letters. At Territet Elizabeth took her usual walks. Baron Nopcsa was now seventy-eight and found it more and more difficult to stand being constantly on the move, while Marie Festetics had a bad attack of catarrh and had to take a rest, so it was fortunate that Francis Joseph arrived on a visit at this moment.

The whole world was astounded to see the Emperor traveling to Switzerland, which was known to be a haunt of Nihilists and Socialists; and ingenious journalists tried to explain it by saying that the Empress had lost her reason and believed that Francis Joseph too had shot himself, so that she had tried to throw herself into the lake, and the Greek Barker, who, they said, was no more nor less than a clever nerve specialist from Athens, had declared it necessary to prove to her that her husband was still alive. The *Secolo* of Milan for March 16, 1893, which retailed all these fables, even added that the Empress could no longer bear the Achilleion and was afraid to go back there, because she believed that the famous Macedonian bandit Athanasio intended to descend upon the place, take her prisoner, and hold her for an enormous ransom. These wild tales in the Italian press caused anxiety at home, and the *Magyar Hirlap* for March 11, 1893, complained that nobody in Hungary ever heard a word about their queen. In spite of these reports, however, Elizabeth's state of mind had improved. During the Emperor's visit she behaved with a little more restraint, but to her genuine regret he soon had to leave again. Marie Festetics was in ecstasies over the Emperor's graciousness and kindness, but observed once more that the Empress' charm enabled her to "put the Emperor completely in her pocket."

He had hardly gone before Elizabeth moved on to the Lake of Como, and then by way of Milan and Genoa to Naples, where she plucked up courage to confess to Francis Joseph by letter something as to which the newspapers had already anticipated her. Though the Achilleion was hardly completed, she now told him that she took no further pleasure in it. What she had said in the past was still true: "Wherever I might happen to be, if anyone were to tell me that I had to stay there forever, even Paradise would become a hell to me"; and the Achilleion had now become a trammel to her restless spirit. She accordingly wrote to the Emperor that she would like to sell the villa, for Valerie would be able to put the money to a better use now that her family was increasing so rapidly. Visions of a fantastically rich American who would pay a fabulous sum for her fairy palace, floated before her eyes. For some time Francis Joseph had noticed that the Empress no longer took any pleasure in the Achilleion, but he had hardly expected that she would want to part with it, and suggested that she should think the matter over again. "Even without the sale of your house," he wrote on April 6, 1893, "Valerie and her probably numerous children will not starve. . . . The matter would, in any case, have to be approached with great caution and tact if a reasonably decent face is to be put upon it, and even then people will raise a dust over it. . . . Your intention has its sad side for myself, too. I had cherished a secret hope that after building Gasturi with so much pleasure and zest, you would remain quietly in the place which is your own creation for at least the greater part of the time which you unfortunately spend in the south. Now even that is to come to nothing, and you will only go on traveling and roaming about the world." The

Empress therefore postponed her intention for a time, but the idea remained in her mind.

In May Elizabeth returned to Lainz for the betrothal of her granddaughter Augusta, daughter of the Archduchess Gisela, to the Archduke Joseph August, and at the end of the month held a court again after this long interval. The German Ambassador, Prince Reuss, did not think she was looking well and said she had aged greatly, but he hoped that her appearance in public might silence the rumors of her mental derangement which were no longer to be prevented. Comparisons were being drawn between her and the unhappy King Otto, now hopelessly insane; but those closest to her read her character more truly. "She must be measured by a different standard from that applied to other people," wrote the Countess Janka Mikes, who went with her to Gastein in July; while the Archduchess Valerie, who visited her there, noted that "there are in Mamma perhaps the greatest contrasts which could possibly be combined in the same character." When the faithful Ida Ferenczy drew Elizabeth's attention to the reports which were going the round about her mental condition, she was eager to prove how false they were.

But the gossip about her made her all the more desirous of going far away. "I am now preparing myself to become a great-grandmother," she said to the German Ambassador, "and then perhaps people will allow me to retire from the world for good." This time she meant to take Christomanos with her on her travels again. Nopcsa's place was now filled by Major General Adam von Berzeviczy, who had a great reputation in the army for horsemanship. In the year 1863 he had made a bet that he would take his half-trained charger over all the eight obstacles in the army riding school with his back to the horse's head. He was to be allowed one fall, but even this did not prove necessary, and the smart hussar officer won his bet without falling once. This feat won him Elizabeth's highest admiration. Moreover, he had a dry, wholesome humor and a military terseness of expression and did not mince matters even in speaking to Her Majesty, and this Elizabeth particularly appreciated. She laughed heartily at his homely Viennese expressions and imperturbable manner when, for instance, on hearing that he was to accompany her on board the notorious *Greif*, he only replied: "I am always sick on that old swing."

Elizabeth bade a sad farewell to the Emperor, the Archduchess Valerie, and Frau Schratt, "the only three roots binding me to earth," as she remarked to the Countess Mikes, and on December 1 sailed from Miramar for Algiers. Francis Joseph found the parting hard too. "I am only slowly growing accustomed to my loneliness," he wrote. "What I miss so much are the moments I spent with you during your breakfast and our evenings together. I have already been twice into your rooms on my way to the Bellaria, and though all the furniture is in covers, everything reminded me so mournfully of you."

On arriving at Algiers Elizabeth wrote to the Archduchess Valerie: "Military order now prevails among us, for Berzeviczy is most intelligent and useful." They went on as far as Madeira, where Elizabeth thought sorrowfully of her former visit thirty-two years ago, when she had first gone forth into the wide world as a young and lovely woman, disillusioned and burdened with care. She received affectionate letters from the Emperor at Christmas and the New Year. "With all true love I wish you happiness and the blessing of Heaven," he wrote, "and I beg you still to show me the same kindness and consideration in the future. Happiness is hardly the right word for us; we should be satisfied with a little peace, a good understanding between us, and fewer misfortunes than we have had hitherto. Show consideration for my age during the coming year, too, and my increasing idiocy (*Vertrottelung*). Your kindness and solicitude and the friendship of *die Freundin* are the only bright spots in my life. I think of you continually with boundless longing and am already beginning to look forward to our next meeting which is, alas! still so far away."

Elizabeth spent her time in Madeira taking long walks, now with her Greek master and now with the Countess Janka Mikes. Christomanos was becoming much too conceited and self-important and could not get on with any of her party. There was a scene between him and the officers of the *Greif*, and everybody was glad that the Empress did not intend to keep him after the month of March. She continued to study and translate with him regularly, but often felt impatient with the "spiritual veneration" which the young man professed for her.*

Elizabeth would have liked to visit the Azores, but renounced the scheme, for the *Greif* was hardly seaworthy enough, besides being difficult to navigate. On one occasion the boat ran aground on a flat, sandy coast and had to be floated off again by the high tide. She touched at Alicante, where the Archduke Ludwig Salvator was waiting to meet the Empress. He came on board, as usual, with tousled hair, wearing the same seedy-looking suit which he had had for years, but he was as interesting as ever, and Elizabeth was pleased to see him.

From Alicante Elizabeth went on to Cap Martin, where her husband met her. She was in comparatively good spirits and went for many walks with Francis Joseph, but did not appear at table, for her meals were most irregular and her diet extraordinary. The Emperor was stupefied when he heard that Elizabeth would often eat a violet-flavored ice

* At the end of March, 1894, Christomanos was relieved of his post and appointed Reader in Greek at the University of Vienna.

with oranges instead of a proper meal. On March 15 he had to return to work, but the Empress remained behind and was thus unable to avoid Napoleon III's widow, who was also staying at Cap Martin. The Empress Eugénie's society was not very good for Elizabeth, for Eugénie, too, was a most unhappy woman, whose life was spent mourning for her husband, her son, her rank, and all that had once filled her life. She was, however, better balanced than Elizabeth and had managed to achieve some degree of peace of mind.

Elizabeth liked at times to pay unbidden visits to private gardens which particularly attracted her. This soon became known in Nice and its neighborhood, but occasionally she was not recognized, and once there was an unpleasant encounter with the indignant owner of a villa, upon which Francis Joseph observed that he was only thankful "the old hag did not give you a thrashing." It might come to that yet, though, he added, for to go pushing into people's houses like that really was not done.

The summer of 1894 was occupied by visits to Bavaria and southern Tirol. At Madonna di Campiglio Elizabeth heard of the assassination of President Carnot, which Francis Joseph begged her to regard as a lesson that it was not quite so easy as she imagined to go about safe and unmolested. Her own fears, however, were not for herself but for the Emperor, and she continued her travels with the utmost unconcern.

After a visit to Corfu she went to Gödöllö, but even in Hungary her holidays failed to refresh her now, for she was conscious of having alienated not merely court society but also the people at large. She attended none but the largest court functions, and those only by an effort, and put them off as long as possible. She was glad when on December 2, 1894, she could once more sail from Trieste for Algiers in the *Miramar*. This time she was attended by the Countess

Irma Sztáray as a temporary maid of honor. What surprised this lady most were the Empress' fads on the subject of diet, for she was always worrying about her weight, which varied between 101 and 110 pounds, and had "milk days" or "orange days," quite in the present fashion, on which she would partake of no other food; however, when she felt inclined she would eat quite a good dinner. Every day after her gymnastics she would consult the scales and settle her diet accordingly. Though she was now in her fifty-sixth year, dieting and exercise had kept her incredibly supple. To prove this to the Countess Sztáray, on one of their excursions when nobody else was near, she suddenly went through a complicated exercise which would have done credit to any professional gymnast. Yet she was now a great-grandmother, for on January 4, 1895, the Archduchess Gisela's eldest daughter Elizabeth (who on December 2, 1893, had married Otto, Baron, and afterwards Count, Seefried) had a little daughter.

The new Greek master, Pali, soon incurred Elizabeth's contempt because of his inability to endure hardship. "Yesterday," she wrote from Algiers to the Archduchess Valerie on January 10, 1895, "I went for another walk with Pali, but soon returned home, for he is still so weak; these Greeks are such mollycoddles. He is now trembling at the prospect of the voyage and saying it would be better to stay here till the wind drops."

As a pleasant surprise for Francis Joseph at Christmas, Elizabeth had commissioned the painter, Franz Matsch, to paint a miniature in oils and a three-quarter-length life-size portrait of Katharina Schratt as Frau Wahrheit in Hans Sachs' *Frau Wahrheit will niemand herbergen* (*Nobody Will Entertain Mistress Truth*). The Emperor was touched at his wife's kind thought, but added in his reply: "I am only depressed by the thought of the gnawing hunger which you punish by fasting, instead of appeasing it as other sensible people do, but the case is beyond all remedy, so we will pass it over in silence."

Now that the Empress lived so largely on milk she insisted that it must be the purest obtainable, and in order to ensure this special cows were bought for her and in due time sent home, where Ida Ferenczy was instructed to set up a model dairy. The extraordinary regimen which Elizabeth followed naturally had its influence upon her general health. Just as she had suffered from sciatica in earlier days as the result of her excessive walks in the wind and rain, so she now began to suffer from digestive disorders due to her ill-regulated diet. She was always trying new cures, usually with so little moderation that they did her constitution more harm than good.

About this time Queen Victoria was expected at Cap Martin. "It is said," wrote Elizabeth to Valerie, "that the English Queen has taken the whole hotel . . . and two villas as well, for she is bringing seventy people, among them a number of Indians. . . . It must be a great pleasure to travel like a circus." In February Francis Joseph again visited his wife at Cap Martin and tried in vain to persuade her to adopt a more normal regimen. On his departure Elizabeth at once left the sunny Riviera and sailed for Corsica, where violent snowstorms awaited her. Francis Joseph could never understand why the Empress did not remain quietly on the Riviera instead of roaming about the world in all weathers; but nothing could be done to prevent it. On resuming her journey to Corfu, she found that it had not lost its old power to charm her. "We have just had two fabulously lovely days," she wrote rhapsodically to Valerie on April 8, 1895. "Everything was so beautiful that it was almost unnatural, the scent of the olive trees was so strong in the evening, and the setting sun surrounded them with an aureole like golden roses. The sea was like a great sheet of pale blue glass, on which the little ships with their white and rose-pink sails floated as though motionless. The hillsides are covered with golden blossoms, and beyond are the Albanian mountains, still with their covering of snow, which turn first rosy pink, then gradually begin to blaze with a ruby glow, while everything is pervaded by a heady perfume, countless swallows swoop to and fro as though drunk with ecstasy, and above all this glory the silvery moon, almost at the full, floats overhead in a deep blue sky. Achilles turns up toward it his face as pale as death, and his eyes fall as he gazes on all the splendor. It was too lovely—in fact it made me so nervous that I could not sleep after it. I lay gazing out from my bed into my moonlit room and listened to the mournful note of the owls."

On April 22, 1895, Elizabeth had the statue of her son by the Italian sculptor, Chiattone, set up amid all this loveliness. When it was unveiled she spoke not a word, but stood absorbed in tearful contemplation of his face. Her emotion was so violent that on the following day she fled from Corfu and sailed for Venice, quite unaware of the fact that Their Italian Majesties were there. She had therefore to call upon them and was received in the very rooms which she had once occupied when Venice was still under Austrian rule. Then she went on to Lainz for a month, and after that to Bártfa, a watering place in the Carpathians surrounded by magnificent forests, in which she could enjoy the seclusion she desired more than anything on earth. She had recourse more than ever to the protection of her inevitable sunshade and fan, but those who managed to see her face felt a pang of heartache, for now it was scored with deep wrinkles, and sun, wind, and rain had left their mark upon it. Only her eyes retained all their fire, and her tall, proud, slender form and incomparable step remained unaltered. When on August 6 Carmen Sylva visited Ischl with her consort, and tactfully inquired whether she still rebelled against fate, the Empress replied: "No, I have turned to stone."

In September, 1895, her travels began once more, first to Aix-les-Bains for the cure, then on to Geneva and Territet, then back to Gödöllö and Vienna for the month of October, and then, at the end of November, to the Riviera, this time attended by the Countess Sztáray, for the young Countess Mikes was about to be married. The Empress was now drinking Karlsbad water, because she considered her weight of not much over 110 pounds excessive. Francis Joseph was quite justified in writing to her on December 14, 1895: "I am happy to hear that your constitution, which is so excellent (*unberufen*), still opposes such a successful resistance to all your slimming treatments and the racing about in which you indulge to excess."

Early in March Elizabeth felt unusually unwell and at once attributed this to her weight. "When I am not feeling well," she wrote to Valerie, "my weight goes up, and of all my ills this upsets me the most." It was rather dangerous to mention any new cure to her, for she immediately wanted to try it. At that time everybody was reading a book by a doctor named Kuhne, who recommended a sand cure as a means of reducing stoutness. Elizabeth had to give it a trial at once, and so did Frau Schratt, on whom the Empress' continual cures had made quite an impression. "It is extraordinary," wrote Francis Joseph to Elizabeth, "how you two are always making the same medical experiments, though without taking any particular harm from it, thank God."

The spring was spent chiefly in Corfu, where Elizabeth occupied most of her time translating Shakespeare into Greek, in which she was assisted by a new master, a dandified young man, whose habit of perfuming himself—a thing which she had always disliked, even in women—got on her nerves. But her stay in Corfu was broken off at the end of April, for

Hungary was about to celebrate the millenary of its existence as a state, and Elizabeth did not want to miss the occasion.

On April 30 she arrived in Budapest and on May 2 accompanied the Emperor to the opening of the Millenary Exhibition, at which they were received with storms of applause. She appeared in deep black, though her dress had the fashionable puffed sleeves. Everybody was eager to see the Queen, about whom such contradictory reports had recently been heard, but Elizabeth hid her face behind her fan both during the drive to the Exhibition and during the open ceremony. She was moved as she listened to the Cardinal Prince Primate's words at the *Te Deum* in the Coronation Church, when he spoke of the nation's boundless love and gratitude to her. But everybody in the Hungarian capital remarked on the heart-rendingly sad impression made by the Empress' black-robed form amid these spring festivities.

The most painful thing to Elizabeth was the way in which these festivities recalled the vanished past: "The opening ceremony," she wrote to her daughter from Buda on April 3, 1896, "was very sad. To think of appearing again amid all that splendor and pomp! The last celebrations of the sort at which I was present were those at the unveiling of the Maria Theresa monument, with Nazi (as Rudolf was called at home). The whole thing brings back that day to me. The singing, the national anthem, it was all exactly the same."

On returning to Schönbrunn Elizabeth often went for walks with Frau Schratt, whom she still found congenial, pleasant, and amiable, now that her embarrassment in the Empress' presence had disappeared and been replaced by simpler and more natural relations. Next the Empress went to Budapest for the opening of the new wing of the royal palace on June 6, the building of which she had so warmly advocated. On June 8 the coronation insignia were borne in solemn procession from the Coronation Church to the Parliament House and the royal palace, after which there was a state reception of the Hungarian Parliament, finely described by Kálmán Mikszáth in the *Pesti Hirlap* for June 10, 1896.

"There she sat in the throne room of the royal palace," he wrote, "in her Hungarian costume of black, adorned with lace. Everything about her was somber. From her dark hair fell a veil of black. Black were the ornaments in her hair, black her pearls, everything black, only her face was marble-white and ineffably sad . . . a *mater dolorosa*. It was the same face as of old, well known from her bewitching portraits; the free, noble features, with the hair cut short in front and waving round her brow like a silken fringe, and above this her luxuriant braids, the loveliest of all crowns. She was still herself, but sorrow had left its mark upon her face. The picture was still the same, but as though shrouded in mist. The lashes drooped over her sweet eyes, so full of life. Still and impassive she sat, as though seeing and hearing nothing. Only her soul seemed to range far and wide. Not a movement, not a glance to betray her interest. She sat like a statue of marble pallor. And now the President of the Parliament, Desider Szilágyi, began to speak. Slowly and cautiously, full of reverence for the throne. The King listened. A word, an idea riveted his attention, and his eyes rested upon the face of the Hungarian nation's great orator. Still nothing could be read in the face of Elizabeth. It remained pale and impassive. But now the orator pronounced the name of the Queen. She did not move an eyelid, till suddenly a cheer broke forth such as the royal palace at Buda had never heard before, as though a storm of emotion burst from every heart with a ring of wondrous sublimity which can be neither described nor told. In it mingled supplication, the tone of bells, the roar of the sea, tenderness, emotion, perhaps even the fragrance of flowers. And now that majes-

THE KING AND QUEEN OF HUNGARY AT THE HUNGARIAN MILLENARY CELEBRATIONS, JUNE 8, 1896, IN BUDAPEST

From a picture by Julius von Benczúr.

tic head, till then unmoved, was seen to stir. Gently, almost imperceptibly, it bowed in gratitude. A wondrous grace was in this gesture. Louder still rang the cheers, and for minutes they refused to be silent. As roar after roar went up the vaulted roof quivered.

"The magnates of the realm waved their hats. Still the cheering would not abate. The orator was forced to pause, and the Queen inclined her head. Her snow-white cheek showed a faint flush. Its milky whiteness was tinged with pale rose, then a crimson wave surged up, flooding it with a living red. As though by magic, a Queen appeared in all the hues of life seated at the side of the King. Her eyes dilated and flashed with their former splendor. Those eyes, whose captivating smile had once had power to console a sorrowing land, now filled with tears. Once more the current of sympathy flowed back and forth. The land, now happy, had succeeded in consoling its Queen, but only for a moment. Majestically she raised her lace handkerchief to her eyes to dry her tears. The orator resumed his speech. Slowly the flush of life faded from the Queen's countenance, and soon by the King's side there sat once more the woman shrouded in mourning, the *mater dolorosa.*"

Elizabeth, too, was overcome by the emotions of this sacred moment. She divined this to be no ordinary homage, and for a moment her feeling that every Hungarian was conscious of her sympathy for his country broke down the wall of gloom which she had set up between herself and the rest of the world. But the emotion was too much for her. She immediately withdrew to the seclusion of the villa at Lainz, and nothing more was heard of her in public for weeks to come.

Elizabeth now proceeded to make a new will, for the one which she had made before the death of the Crown Prince had embodied her original intention, which was to leave her whole estate to Valerie. She divided her property into five parts and bequeathed a fifth to each of her daughters, Gisela and Valerie, and a fifth to her granddaughter Elizabeth, the daughter of the Crown Prince. Pensions and jewels were allotted to all those who had served her faithfully. Nor was Katharina Schratt forgotten; she was left a large gold coin (a *Georgstaler*) mounted as a brooch. Then Elizabeth proceeded to arrange for the disposal of her great secret, her writings. Ida Ferenczy was instructed to hand over the casket containing her poems to the Duke Karl Theodor. By Elizabeth's express order, everything was sealed with her private seal, which bore the device of a sea gull.

Elizabeth had next to do violence to her feelings by receiving the Tsar and Tsaritsa; then she retired to Ischl, where she once more withdrew into absolute seclusion and began to diet again, this time eating hardly anything but milk and eggs. Her weight was now about 101 pounds, which was little enough for a woman five feet six inches in height. Yet such was her terror of growing stout that she would take frequent steam baths, immediately followed by a very cold plunge bath. This treatment made her anæmic and more nervous, which led to a fresh bout of cures, and so the vicious circle continued.

Valerie's family was still increasing, and Elizabeth now meditated how she might secure the children's future. Long before this Ida Ferenczy, her faithful woman of affairs, had persuaded Elizabeth to accumulate a sum which should provide her an independent fortune. This advice she had followed, with the result that by October, 1896, she was in possession of a sum in cash of a nominal value of 3,873,510 gulden, though its actual value amounted to 4,483,991 gulden.

No sooner did the first signs of the cold season appear than the Empress grew impatient for the day when she would start on her yearly winter travels. Early in December, 1896, she set out for Biarritz, where she spent most of her time on the shore. On the whole the weather was bad. "Nobody has any conception," she wrote, "of how grand the sea is here, but with these gales it is hardly possible to walk. . . . The wind and sea roar all night, till one's head is quite dazed."

Francis Joseph now heard very bad accounts of his wife's health. She ate no meat at all, only the juice of half-raw steak, so he sent his own physician, Dr. Kerzl, to Biarritz to see what was really going on. Dr. Kerzl was horrified when he heard of the Karlsbad cure which she had adopted on her own initiative, and he prescribed more food and a little wine. His report to the Emperor was accompanied by a request that His Majesty would bring pressure to bear upon his consort to follow medical advice, with the result that on December 15 and 17, 1896, Francis Joseph wrote to her as follows: "I had hoped that the bad, stormy weather would have disgusted you with Biarritz and brought you to Cap Martin before long, but you have got yourself into such a desolate state of mind by now, and are encouraging yourself in it more and more by listening to the roaring of the sea and the howling of the storm. . . . I fear you will refuse to follow Kerzl's advice and will continue to do all you can to undermine your own health till it is too late and nobody can help you any more. I am unfortunately powerless to do more than beg you, out of pity for me and Valerie, to take good care of yourself and live as Kerzl advises you to do, and, above all, to eat. . . ."

The doctor succeeded in frightening the Empress a little, and for a time she followed his advice and gave up her exhausting walks. Her spirits immediately showed an improvement, as was noted by the Baroness Marie Sennyey, who was in attendance upon her. But she was still haunted by the same obsession as to her weight. She would weigh herself three times a day, which annoyed Dr. Kerzl: "If it were not for those damned scales!" he said. "Devil take the man who advised Her Majesty to weigh herself all the time!" But the improvement in her spirits was only temporary, and before long her letters to the Emperor revealed the same melancholy as before. "You should not let yourself become so much absorbed in your moods of depression," he wrote in January, 1897, "or shut yourself away from other people so much. It will only make it more and more difficult for you to tear yourself away from your solitary life. The Greek and Baroness Sennyey would surely be pleasant and cheerful company."

After the storms of Biarritz Elizabeth enjoyed the Riviera, where she arrived on January 19, 1897, and she would have been very glad if the Emperor could have met her there. "Could you not get here for four weeks this year?" she wrote. "It would be so good for my health and spirits. Only see for what a long time other potentates stay away from home. . . . I hope that *die Freundin* received my New Year's telegram, though the number of her house was not on it. Please send me her numbers in the Nibelungengasse and the Gloriettegasse and that of the Villa Felizitas, and I will put my money on them at the Casino."

Even at Cap Martin Elizabeth's spirits responded to every fluctuation in her physical condition. She continued to doctor herself, this time with sulphur and iron pills. She had to live without Greek for a time and began to lead a completely solitary life. The Emperor was so much perturbed that he sent not only his own physician but also the Archduke Franz Salvator and his wife on a visit to her. Valerie found her mother very pale, thin, weak, and tired, and Elizabeth asked her daughter to write to the Emperor and tell him that she was now absolutely incapable of discharging any duties which involved appearing in public.

Finally the Emperor arrived in person and was in the utmost consternation when he saw his wife in such a low state.

She refused all normal nourishment and could no longer endure any attempts to force her to eat. Valerie found her more inconsolable than she had ever been before, even in the darkest days. She ought to have eaten and slept a great deal and done very little walking, but she did the exact opposite. If a change did not take place soon, wrote the Archduchess, the results might be dangerous. Once again Elizabeth's mind seemed to be haunted by thoughts of death. In former days she had expressed a wish that her body might be sunk in the sea or else had asked that when her time came to die she might be buried by the seaside. But now she desired to lie beside her son. "I feel such a vast longing to lie there in a good large coffin and simply find rest, nothing but rest. More than that I neither expect nor desire. You know, Valerie, in the spot where there is the window overhead, where a little light and greenery peep into the vault and the sparrows can be heard twittering."

On his return to Vienna the Emperor said to the German Ambassador, Prince Eulenburg, who reported his words to the Chancellor at home: "My whole visit to Cap Martin was ruined by anxiety about the Empress' health. My wife was in such a state of nerves that our life together was seriously deranged."

Elizabeth shut herself up from everybody, even refusing to see her amiable lady in waiting, the Baroness Sennyey. To escape the observation of curious eyes, she would often slip out into the park through the underground service rooms of her hotel. But soon she could bear Cap Martin no longer and went on to Territet on the Lake of Geneva, of which she was so fond. It so happened that the Archduke Franz Ferdinand was there, too, with his physician, Viktor Eisenmenger, and the Emperor desired the latter to examine the Empress. Owing to her repeated cures she had conceived an antipathy for doctors and would no longer listen to their advice; but at last she allowed herself to be persuaded. Eisenmenger's examination disclosed the fact that, though her general health was good, the skin was puffy, especially in the region of the joints, and in his opinion this edema was of the kind typical of a state of starvation. He found that she would often eat nothing all day but half a dozen oranges. "Yet for all that my weight is increasing," she added. "Naturally, Your Majesty," replied the doctor. "That is because water accumulates in the tissues as a result of undernourishment." Elizabeth shook her head sceptically and would only promise to drink a few glasses of sheep's milk every day.

Her stay at Territet did her so much good that in May she was able to return to Lainz for a short time. But now the improvement in her condition which had been achieved at such pains was swept away at a single blow. On May 5 news arrived of the appalling tragedy which had befallen the Empress' sister, the Duchess of Alençon, who had died in a fire at a charity bazaar in Paris. The details were of the most shocking nature, the unfortunate Princess' charred remains having been quite unrecognizable until her dentist was able to identify her, and the shock to Elizabeth was crushing. She would admit nobody to her presence but the Emperor, who had hurried to Lainz to console her. He pressed her to go to Kissingen in the hope that it might do her good; but though his hopes were so far realized, on her return to Lainz, and afterwards to Ischl in July, her spirits sank lower than ever. The Emperor complained to the German Ambassador that his consort talked to him so much about death that his depression was overwhelming. On August 29 she left for the Karersee and Meran, where she tried the grape cure. Her indifference to political matters was now complete, except for an occasional gleam of interest where Hungary was concerned. Thus when on September 21 the Emperor William visited Francis Joseph in the Hungarian capital and proposed the health of the chivalrous Hungarian people in one of his eloquent speeches, which the Countess Sztáray afterwards read to Elizabeth, she was so enthusiastic about it that she telegraphed to the Emperor William then and there thanking him for his "splendid toast," which "did so much good to a heart with Hungarian sympathies."

At the end of September Elizabeth left Meran and paid a visit to Valerie in her new home at Wallsee. Here she was in comparatively good spirits, and even cheerful at times; but, as usual, it was impossible to persuade her to make a long stay, for she could never forget that she was a mother-in-law.

Francis Joseph was growing older, too, and his political cares were as pressing as ever. Every indisposition of the Empress' agitated him, and though their relations were excellent, each of them increased the nervousness of the other. This being so, the monarch clung more and more to his friendship for Frau Schratt, in which he was so exacting that it often became burdensome to the actress, especially as the scandalmongers did not fail to make the most of the subject. When this came to her ears she was indignant, for she had nothing with which to reproach herself. But so long as she was shielded by the Empress' protecting hand, nothing worse than gossip could molest her; it was not for anybody to speak ill of her so long as the Emperor's consort esteemed her and distinguished her with her favor. Such was the position of affairs when, at the end of November, 1897, Elizabeth once again left home.

XV
ELIZABETH AND LUCHENI*

PASSING THROUGH PARIS, ELIZABETH again visited Biarritz, for though it had done her no good earlier in the year, she was haunted by a longing for the sea, which is so magnificent there. Once again she wandered for hours along the shore watching the great rollers break with a thunderous roar and often getting drenched through, with the result that her nervous disorders and neuralgic pains only grew worse. She would have liked to go to Lourdes, but this was impossible, and all her conversation now ran on the subject of death. She did not wish to survive the Emperor, she said, but neither he nor her children must be present at her death, for fear it might cause them pain. "I wish to die alone," she told the Countess Sztáray.

Despairing of her health, she abandoned her projected trip to the Canaries, and even thought of returning to Metzger, who was now in Paris, though she had decided by this time that he was a charlatan. This news reached Francis Joseph at a time when serious clashes were taking place in Bohemia between Germans and Czechs over the language question, and it depressed him still further. "Provided only that Metzger does not handle you too roughly," he wrote to Elizabeth on December 17, 1897, "and get you back into his unscrupulous

* The account of Lucheni's antecedents and trial is based upon the official records in the office of the Procurator General, Geneva, supplemented by information personally communicated to the author by the former Procurator General, M. G. Navazza, and M. Fernet, Director of the Prison of Saint Antoine, Geneva.

and grasping clutches and use you as a means of advertisement. There was only one ray of light in your letter, and that was the prospect that you may give up your ocean voyage. I should be endlessly grateful to you if this decision, which is still in the balance, became a certainty. For on top of all my cares and grief, it would be more than my nerves could stand if I had to endure anxiety about you as well, knowing you to be out at sea, cut off from all news. Besides which, it really seems to me risky for you to be so far away just at present, quite out of reach, in view of the events with which we hope we shall not be confronted, but possibly may be."

The Emperor's words had some effect. Elizabeth, now in Paris, was disgusted by Metzger's attitude, for he went so far as to insist that she should place herself entirely under his care for six whole months. Other doctors said precisely the opposite and recommended a warmer climate, so Elizabeth gave up the idea of massage and, after laying wreaths on the graves of Heine and her sister, the Duchess of Alençon, went on by way of Marseilles to San Remo. She was now so broken by weakness and pain that, to quote the Countess Sztáray, she had become "as biddable as a dear child who is ill, listening to well-meant advice and visibly benefiting by it." Yet as soon as she felt any return of strength, she at once wanted to resume her long walks. She even contemplated buying a villa at San Remo, but the Countess Sztáray managed to dissuade her from this, for she was sure to grow tired of it as she had of the Achilleion. Negotiations for the sale of the Corfu villa were now in progress with the Byron Society of London, though the price which was asked—two million gulden—was considered too high.

And now the year 1899 was approaching. "What shall I have to inscribe upon these empty pages?" wrote Valerie in the new volume of her diary. January found the Empress suffering from an inflamed nerve in the arm and shoulder, which made it impossible for her to practice her gymnastics or sleep at night. "Even this will come to an end, however," she wrote to Valerie, "and eternal rest will be all the more welcome." She was most unhappy at losing that physical fitness on which she had prided herself all her life, and longed for her husband, pressing him to pay her a visit. But conditions within the monarchy were too critical for the Emperor to absent himself for so long. "It is an exaggeration," he wrote to her in February, "to say that you feel as though you were eighty, but come what may, one is growing weaker and less energetic all the time, and the nerves gradually lose their powers of resistance. I feel exactly the same thing myself, and the progress of decay in me this year is particularly noticeable. . . . It is depressing to think what an endless time our separation is going to last. When and where shall we meet again?"

On March 1 Elizabeth traveled from San Remo to Territet. Her health was not much improved, and she was still weak, yet again she made long expeditions into the mountains, till, hearing of this from Barker, the Emperor implored her to stop subjecting her enfeebled constitution to such a strain and systematically ruining her health by her own act. Territet was now too much for her, and she hoped to regain strength by a cure at Kissingen, of which she was very fond. "It is not beautiful in the grand style," she wrote to Valerie, "but so lovable, so nice and quiet. Exactly like real country, and the air is like balm." Here she sent congratulations to her daughter Gisela on her silver wedding day, and added: "On this day you will sadly miss our Rudolf, whom we can never forget, for he was so full of life and happiness at your wedding twenty-five years ago, and saw you depart with such a heavy heart. How we miss him, but I envy him for being at rest."

THE EMPEROR AND EMPRESS AT KISSINGEN, 1898

From a photograph by Kolb.

On April 25 the Emperor joined his wife at Kissingen, and as a pleasant surprise told her how he had got two fine cows for her dairy from an English lord in exchange for two horses from the stables at Lippiza. He had been prepared in advance to find Elizabeth looking ill and worn, but what impressed him most was the fact that she, who had once been so rapid and tireless a walker, now dragged slowly and wearily along. She controlled herself in his presence by an effort and managed to some extent to conceal her depression, so that this week passed by in complete harmony; but the Emperor saw that she was in a very serious condition. He induced Valerie to join her mother at Kissingen and try to exert a reasonable influence over her. Once again mother and daughter were reunited as in the happy days of Valerie's girlhood; but in those days the Empress had had only occasional attacks of melancholy, while now she was never free from it and said to her daughter: "You know, the words 'hope' and 'rejoicing' have been struck out of my life forever."

In spite of being tired and languid, Elizabeth refused to give up her walks, though her expeditions to Klaushof and other places were now made at a more leisurely pace. Occasionally a brighter mood would momentarily alleviate the gloom, recalling happier days, only to be immediately succeeded by melancholy and physical prostration. "I long for death," she remarked to Valerie, "and I have no fear of it, for I refuse to believe that there is a power so cruel that, not content with the sufferings of life, it would tear the soul from the body in order to go on torturing it." "But man is far too small and wretched to meditate on the nature of God," she would say. "I have long ceased to do so." Of one thing alone she was sure: that God was strong and in the right. Might, she said, is always right.

Soon Valerie had to return to her family, which Elizabeth felt most keenly. "We had some extremely good times together," she wrote to her from Bad Brückenau, where she went for her aftercure, "as in the old days. But it is not good for me to get used to them again for such a short time."

She next joined her husband at Ischl, where Widerhofer was to prescribe her future regimen. Francis Joseph had arranged that he was to make an official pronouncement on the state of the Empress' health, if only to prepare the public to hear that she would not be present at the celebrations of the Emperor's jubilee. It was hoped that in this way Elizabeth might be influenced indirectly and submit with a better grace to the doctors' advice. On July 3, 1898, an official bulletin was therefore issued which spoke of anæmia, inflammation of the nerves, insomnia, and a certain dilatation of the heart, which, it said, gave no cause for serious anxiety, but called for thorough treatment at Bad Nauheim. On July 16 the Empress left Ischl. Her husband was never to see her again alive. Though he had no premonition of the coming tragedy, he felt the parting more than ever this time, and on the very next day wrote to her as follows: "I miss you here unspeakably, my thoughts are with you and I think sorrowfully of the endless time for which we are to be parted; your empty, dismantled rooms make me particularly sad." And this separation was indeed to have no end.

Elizabeth had traveled to Nauheim by way of Bavaria, where she visited the scenes of her childhood. But she disliked this watering place. She wrote Francis Joseph that the air was not good, there were few walks, and numbers of unattractive Berlin Jews whom it was impossible to avoid; and besides, she felt the separation from home and all her loved ones. Francis Joseph was pleased that she had thought of him at once and written to him so lovingly. She would soon get used to Nauheim, he wrote, but for the present all she had to do was to take serious measures to restore her health. He had two patients, now, he said, for "*die Freundin*" was often ill.

She was being attended by Widerhofer, who found her as intractable as Elizabeth, and remarked to the Emperor that in this respect she was "an Empress number two."

Elizabeth was examined by Professor Schott of Nauheim, and the first thing he wanted to do was to take some X-ray photographs of her heart. But the Empress flatly refused. When the doctor explained how important it was, she replied: "Yes, for you or my brother Karl Theodor, perhaps, but not for me. I will not be dissected while I am still alive." And as she went out she remarked to the Professor's assistant: "You know, Fräulein, I greatly dislike being photographed, for every time I have had a photograph taken, it has brought me bad luck."

Her spirits still left much to be desired. "I am out of humor and depressed," she wrote to Valerie, "and the family may be glad that I am far away. I have a feeling that I shall never be able to pull myself together again." The Empress preserved the strictest incognito and received nobody. "Tell Widerhofer," she wrote to her daughter during that hot August, "that I had never supposed it would be so horrible here. It makes me morally ill (*gemütskrank*). Even Barker finds little difference between this place and Alexandria in summer. I go on from day to day merely vegetating, dragging myself to the few shady places and taking an occasional drive with Irma, but I am plagued by the dust and flies." She could hardly wait for the day when she could return to the fresh mountain air of Switzerland. She wanted to leave for Caux, and asked the Emperor to be sure and visit her there. But conditions at home would not allow of his absence at that particular moment.

On escaping from Nauheim Elizabeth managed by a little ruse to evade the tiresome ceremonies of a formal leave-taking. She gave out that she was going on an expedition to Homburg by way of Mannheim, but her intention was never to come back, her suite following with the luggage. She drove into the courtyard of the Schloss at Homburg in an ordinary cab. The sentinel on guard sprang forward and stopped her, whereupon Elizabeth replied that she was the Empress of Austria. The man merely laughed and took her before his officer. An orderly was sent to the Schloss to say that there was a lady in the guardroom who claimed to be the Empress of Austria. A chamberlain came rushing out and recognized Elizabeth, who was released with a flood of apologies, upon which a smile lit up the face which so rarely laughed now. The Empress Frederick hurried to receive her; but fond though Elizabeth was of her, she found this visit to one who, like her, had known hideous trials, rather an ordeal. Indeed, she had increasing difficulty in conversing with anybody who was not one of her intimate circle. On the return journey she passed through Frankfurt, where a crowd was waiting to see her at the station. But since she had preferred to drive, she was able to mix with the crowd unrecognized and listen smilingly to the remarks people were making. Then she went on to Switzerland, where her destiny awaited her.

Fearless and unsuspecting, Elizabeth pursued her wanderings regardless of the political and social tendencies in the lands she visited. A republic surrounded by monarchies, Switzerland had become a refuge for conspirators of all nationalities, anarchists and advocates of political outrage, bent upon realizing a new ideal of government based upon some theoretical system, and overthrowing the existing social order by any means in their power. In free Switzerland they were comparatively unmolested and pursued their aims in greater security. It was the foreign workmen living in Switzerland who were especially permeated by the spirit of anarchism. Those who chanced to mix with these elements were all too easily dazzled by the glittering rainbow visions conjured up by these eloquent and subversive philanthropists, who enjoyed comparative immunity from police interference.

A new post office was being built in Lausanne, for which a number of skilled workmen had been engaged, including many Italians. One of these happened to injure his foot slightly. He was taken to the hospital in Lausanne, where an official questioned him as to his name and origin. He was a man of medium height, but healthy, and of very powerful build, with dark, curly hair, a bushy blond moustache, and gleaming grey-green deep-set eyes like those of a cat. His name was Luigi Lucheni and his age twenty-six. Among the belongings which he deposited at the hospital was a notebook containing anarchist songs. On one page was a drawing of a bludgeon with the legend: "Anarchia," and written beneath this in Italian, "For Humbert I." He was reported to the police as a suspicious character, but it was not considered necessary to keep him under particularly close observation on the strength of these facts alone, still less to arrest him. During his long hours in hospital he told the hospital orderly stories of his life. The orderly had just received a letter from his mother.

"I never knew mine," remarked Lucheni. "She was a day laborer from Albareto in the Ligurian Apennines and left her native village at the age of eighteen on discovering that she was with child. She wandered westward till she reached Paris, where she hoped to bring the child into the world unnoticed among the millions in that great city. It was born in a hospital, but after a few days she disappeared, leaving the baby behind, and was never seen again. A search was instituted, but when she reached America all trace of her was lost, and she troubled no more about her son."

The boy was brought up first in the foundling hospital of Saint Antoine in Paris and then at Parma, and a year later was entrusted to foster parents. The records say that he was intelligent and industrious, and by the time he was nine he was already working on the railway between Parma and Spezia. He earned good opinions everywhere, had no bad marks against him, and provided for his own support. During the years 1891 and 1892 he was seized with a desire to travel. Having neither kith nor kin the lad wandered from one country to another, working in the canton of Ticino and Geneva, then going on to Austria, and finally tramping from Fiume to Trieste, where he arrived without a penny in his pocket. The laboring classes there were kept under particularly strict police observation on account of the irredentist agitation. Before long he was deported as being unemployed and destitute and had to cross the frontier into Austrian Italy. He had become liable for military service in the previous year and was now drafted into the Cavalleggeri Monferrato Regiment No. 13 as a private. He took part with his squadron in the Abyssinian campaign of 1896, in which he acquitted himself well. In fact, his squadron commander, Prince Raniero de Vera d'Aragona, singled him out as the best soldier in the regiment in the opinion of all his officers. He was promoted to the grade of lance corporal (*Gefreiter*), but was demoted immediately afterwards, his offense being that he had procured civilian clothes for a sergeant major condemned to confinement to barracks. Though contrary to discipline, this was generally regarded as a mere act of kindness toward a comrade.

Lucheni was an excellent rider and particularly good at jumping, and his liveliness made him popular among his fellow soldiers. For the rest, he was miserably poor, having nothing to live on but his pay. His captain never had cause to complain of him, though he was well aware that Lucheni was ambitious and inclined to be stubborn. On the completion of his military service on December 15, 1897, it was entered on his discharge sheet that his behavior during that period had been good and that he had performed his duty loyally and honorably. Having no resources whatsoever, Lucheni was now faced with the problem of his future and applied to his captain for assistance. The original intention had been to engage him as a warder in the state prisons. But since this came to nothing, his captain, the Prince d'Aragona, proposed that he should enter his own personal service. For three and a half months Lucheni acted as manservant in his captain's house. There were occasional differences of opinion, but here, too, he worked well and honestly on the whole. One day, however, he presented himself before the captain and asked for an increase in wages. The officer considered this a little premature and refused, whereupon Lucheni said that he would leave.

A few days later he regretted his action and begged to be taken back into the Prince's service, but his master replied that he was too insubordinate for domestic service, and Lucheni had once more to go out into the wide world and look for work with very little money in his pocket. However, he kept in touch with the d'Aragona household, and especially with the Princess, who was sorry for him and would, he hoped, succeed in persuading her husband to take him back.

On March 31 he finally gave up domestic service and made his way over the St. Gotthard into Switzerland. He now thought of entering the Foreign Legion, but nothing came of this idea, and he went on to Lausanne, where he arrived in May. Meanwhile he had come in contact with a number of furtive characters, and resentful at the Prince's readiness to let him go and oppressed by poverty, he proved a fertile soil for their doctrines. He greedily devoured the revolutionary newspapers, which pointed indignantly to the Dreyfus Case as a proof of how rotten bourgeois society was. It needed but a blow, they said, to upset this house of cards and set up in its place a new ideal state based on social justice, in which all would be equally well off and there would be no princes and no outcasts. All that was needed was a single great man to change the face of the world as Christ had done before. Such a man must have courage to commit a deed which would bring the whole structure crashing down; in so doing he would cause his name to be exalted to the skies. This obscure workman dreamed of singling himself out from the mass of people by some heroic act and thus proving his worth. If only he could find André, he thought, who had made an ascent in a balloon from Spitzbergen the year before with the object of reaching the North Pole, but had never been heard of since: at a single stroke he would find himself world-famous. But any means would do so long as his name got into the papers and was on all men's lips.

The anarchists with whom Lucheni now began to mix observed their new associate with interest. He was not affiliated with any of their societies, but he was vain, and for this reason, they thought, might possibly be used as a tool in the hazardous policy of political outrage which they considered necessary, but from which so many were deterred by the possible consequences to their own person. This man seemed eager for action. They persuaded him that it was necessary for some prince or emperor to die, no matter which one, so long as the world was shown that these idlers who do nothing but oppress others, who raise themselves above other people, travel by trains de luxe, and dwell in splendid hotels and palaces, are as nothing before the will of the people or a dagger wielded by a bold hand. All this went to Lucheni's head. What if he could send the King of Italy or some other king to his death? He sent letters and newspapers of an anarchist tendency to a soldier in his old squadron in Naples: "The anarchist ideal," he wrote, "is making giant strides here. Pray do your duty by our comrades, too, who know nothing about it."

Yet all the while he was begging the Prince d'Aragona and his wife to take him back into their service. The captain, however, had heard of his sending these subversive newspapers and refused. This only increased Lucheni's bitterness. But if he was to kill someone, he must have a weapon. He had seen a good stiletto, but the shop wanted twelve francs fifty for it, and he did not possess that sum. Next he tried to borrow a revolver, but without success. Every day he read the Italian newspaper, *Il Socialista*, published at Neuchâtel, and the *Avanti* of Milan. One day he heard that there had been a brawl among the workmen at Delmarco and one man had been left on the spot nearly dead; upon which Lucheni remarked to an acquaintance: "Ah! How I'd like to kill somebody; but it must be somebody important, so it gets into the papers."

He still lacked a weapon, however, so he would have to make one himself. He happened to see in the market a sharp, rusty iron file, costing only a few sous. It could not be used as a dagger, for it had no handle, but that did not matter. A bit of rough firewood, a pocketknife, and a bradawl, and he made a handle himself. Now that he had the weapon, all he needed was a victim, and that would not take long to find. For instance, there was Prince Henry of Orleans, who so often stayed in or near Geneva, or some other prince. Perhaps he might even get to Paris and figure in the Dreyfus trial about which the whole world was talking. But that would involve a journey and its attendant expense.

And now, in the week of August 22 to 28, the papers began to speak of Elizabeth's approaching visit to Caux. The Empress of such a mighty land would be a victim worth having. Through her he would strike at the whole governing class and see his name blazoned abroad through the whole world. He was hypnotized by the idea.

Meanwhile, toward the end of August, the anarchists were

holding secret meetings in various towns. First at Lausanne, in the house of one of the comrades, then at Neuchâtel, where various well-known Italian anarchists were to be found, among them the editor of *L'Agitatore.* A *coup* was planned for somewhere in Switzerland or Italy, possibly against King Humbert. Lucheni was never present at these gatherings of regular members; but his name came under consideration, for it was desired to use him as an instrument.

On August 30 Elizabeth of Austria arrived in the "enchanting land of Switzerland" in glorious weather, as her Greek reader Barker reported to the Archduchess Valerie. The countryside soon suggested excursions and parties. First, on September 2, they went to Bex, where the views reminded Elizabeth of the Dachstein and the country near her home. On the way back to Caux in the evening the Empress enjoyed a splendid sunset with unusual effects of light and color. The whole day was so fine that Elizabeth felt exceptionally cheerful and fresh. Yet all was not quite well with her. As she walked rapidly up the steps to the station at Caux to escape the curious crowd following her, she was seized with an attack of heart palpitations. On September 3 she went up the Rochers de Naye by the mountain railway and enjoyed the view over the whole Lake of Geneva from a height of 6,500 feet. She had taken some peaches and grapes with her which the Baroness Rothschild had sent from her villa at Pregny on the Lake of Geneva, together with a pressing invitation to the Empress to visit her there. The Baroness had suggested this visit several times before through Elizabeth's sisters, and this time the Empress thought of accepting, especially since hearing how lovely that property had been made by the wealth of the Rothschilds. On the fifth she made a trip by steamer to Evian with which she was a little disappointed, though the journey back to Territet was beautiful. There were some Italian musicians on the boat who

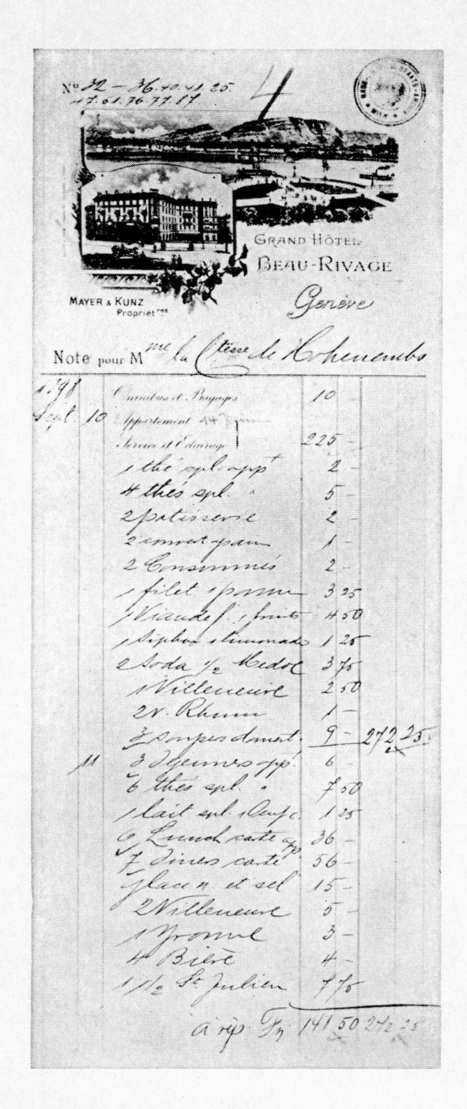

N° 32 – 36.40.41.25.
47.61.76.77.87

GRAND HÔTEL
BEAU-RIVAGE
Genève

MAYER & KUNZ
Propriet^res

Note pour Mme la Ctesse de Hohenembs

1898 Sept.	10	Omnibus et Bagages	10 –	
		Appartement [illegible]		
		Service et Éclairage	225 –	
		1 thé spl. app^t	2 –	
		4 thés spl.	5 –	
		2 pâtisserie	2 –	
		2 [illegible] pain	1 –	
		2 Consommés	2 –	
		1 filet [illegible]	3 25	
		[illegible]	4 50	
		1 siphon 1 limonade	1 25	
		2 Soda ½ Médoc	3 75	
		1 Villeneuve	2 50	
		2 V. Rhum	1 –	
		[illegible]	9 –	272 25
	11	3 [illegible]	6 –	
		6 thés spl.	7 50	
		1 lait [illegible]	1 25	
		6 Lunch carte	36 –	
		7 Dîners carte	56 –	
		glace [illegible]	15 –	
		2 Villeneuve	5 –	
		1 [illegible]	3 –	
		4 Bière	4 –	
		1½ St Julien	7 75	

à rep. Fr. 141 50 272 25

THE LAST BILL AT THE
HOTEL BEAU RIVAGE,
GENEVA

State Archives, Vienna.

played melancholy Italian folksongs. Elizabeth discussed with the Countess Sztáray a plan for going to Geneva but wished to travel without any gentleman in waiting, attended only by the Countess and the necessary servants. General von Berzeviczy begged the Empress to take at least one gentleman with her, if only the private secretary, Dr. Kromar. For a long time Elizabeth would not hear of it, but at last she said: "Tell Berzeviczy that I will take the doctor with me to please him, for I know he has a certain responsibility to Vienna, though it is vastly unpleasant to me." It was now decided that the Baroness Rothschild's invitation should be accepted. On her return Elizabeth received a letter from Francis Joseph dated September 1:

"I went to the Villa Hermes," it said, "to enjoy a breath of air. . . . A great flock of swallows had collected before the gate of the Tiergarten, evidently preparing to start on their travels. . . . Several times I looked up at your window with feelings of great sadness and went back in thought to the days which we spent together in our dear villa. In the evening I had both sour and sweet milk from the farm. . . . *Dein Kl.* (Your little one)."

Reading this letter made Elizabeth feel homesick. She wrote an affectionate letter to Valerie—the last she was ever to write—telling her about her excursions and remarking in passing that her face had grown a little fuller and that she was afraid of becoming too stout, like her sister the Queen of Naples. General von Berzeviczy now appeared and handed her a letter written him by Count Paar, the Emperor's Adjutant General, to whom he had mentioned Elizabeth's desire that Francis Joseph might visit her there.

"To come to Caux after the maneuvers," ran the letter, "would undoubtedly do the Emperor no end of good, but it is entirely beyond the bounds of possibility." Paar gave a detailed account of the Emperor's heavy program of engagements in the near future. "It would certainly agree with him," he continued, "to be able to draw breath where everything is good and beautiful and peace reigns, but to His Majesty consideration for himself comes second to everything else, and he will certainly not allow himself the trip." Francis Joseph himself regretted this most of all. "How happy I should be," he wrote on September 9, "if I could enjoy all that with you quietly as you wish, and see you again after such a long separation; but unfortunately I cannot think of it. Apart from the difficult political situation at home, the whole of the second half of September is already booked up with jubilee festivities, dedications of churches, and visits to the Exhibition . . ."

Her Greek reader, Barker, was very congenial to Elizabeth, and she often discussed serious problems with him on her walks. Once she described her visit to the Capuchin monastery after Rudolf's death, adding that it had caused her to realize that there is no life after death. But of this, too, she felt doubtful, so she proposed that they should both promise that whichever of them was to die first should give the other a sign from beyond the grave.

The Baroness Rothschild had offered the Empress her yacht to take her to Pregny, but Elizabeth considered that she could not accept such a courtesy from anyone but a sovereign, certainly not from the Rothschild family, whose servants they might not tip; and so the offer was declined. September 8 was spent in short walks in the neighborhood. Elizabeth telegraphed congratulations to her daughter Valerie on her name day. She was feeling better than ever, she said, and looking forward to her visit to Pregny; and she brushed aside the warnings of General Berzeviczy and the Countess Sztáray against going to Geneva. Having consented to taking a gentleman with her, she felt that to be enough.

And so September 9 came. It was a beautiful sunny autumn morning. Elizabeth had not slept well, for she had not yet received any answer to her telegram to Valerie. But the glories of nature soothed her and she gazed out tranquilly across the blue lake which reminded her of the sea. She talked of her plans for future travel, about Corfu and the Achilleion, which was now standing half empty and which she would not visit again, she said, till it had been turned into a good hotel. The state of her health would not allow her to take her usual long voyage that winter, so she spoke of going to Nice or Cairo. She was in a gentle mood that day and had a kind word for everybody. The voyage from Territet to Geneva lasted four hours. The Empress wandered up and down the deck and was amused at a mischievous little boy of three whose parents could not keep him in order. She sent him fruit and cakes, and when he came stumbling over shyly and awkwardly to thank her, she said: "How pleased Valerie would have been if she could have seen that." At one o'clock the boat arrived at Geneva, where Dr. Kromar handed her Valerie's telegram of thanks. Her mind was now at rest, and she at once continued on her way to the Baroness Rothschild's house. Her hostess, a lady of fifty-eight, had made all preparations to do honor to the occasion. In the dining room was a table splendidly decorated with old Viennese porcelain and magnificent orchids. There was a dish of costly fruits which were out of season. Innumerable footmen in handsome liveries waited at table. Elizabeth thought it all beautiful, but the servants embarrassed her, for it was impossible to say anything before them; they all seemed positively to hang on her lips. One choice dish followed another, accompanied by iced champagne. The *déjeuner à trois* went off most pleasantly, accompanied by subdued music, soft enough not to interrupt the conversation. At the end Elizabeth drank her hostess' health and gave the Countess Sztáray the menu to enclose with an account of the luncheon to the Emperor, instructing her to underline the *petites timbales*, the *mousse de volaille*, and the *crême glacée à la hongroise*, the last-named to be underscored twice because she had liked it best.

After luncheon they went over the villa. It was a little museum of art treasures, all tastefully arranged and without ostentation. And now came the best part of it all—aviaries full of exotic birds from every quarter of the globe, aquaria with strange kinds of fish, while what most enchanted Elizabeth were some tame miniature porcupines from Java. Last came the fairylike conservatories, full of flowers. Elizabeth stayed longest of all in the orchid house, almost speechless with admiration. Next they walked under the mighty cedars of Lebanon in the park and through the well-laid-out rock gardens with dwarf conifers and alpine plants. The Countess Sztáray was instructed to note three special varieties of flowers which Elizabeth wished to have planted at Lainz. The Baroness Rothschild asked whether the Empress was not tired.

"Oh, no! Why, we have still to visit the little Swiss chålet which I can see over there, and the private landing stage where the sailing yacht and the steam yacht are lying."

The hostess next escorted Elizabeth to the visitors' book, where she wrote her name. Fortunately she did not turn back to the earlier pages, for there, on a page by itself, was the name of her dead son, Rudolf. The Baroness Rothschild expressed a desire to visit the Empress at Caux, and was so insistent that Elizabeth could not help inviting her.

The visit lasted three hours, after which Elizabeth started back to the Hotel Beau Rivage at Geneva. On the way she talked gaily at first to the Countess Sztáray, but then, as so often happened, the conversation turned to religion and death. The Countess Sztáray was deeply religious. "I am a believer," said Elizabeth, "though perhaps I have not so much faith as you; but I know my own nature, and it is by no means an impossibility that you may yet see me extremely religious. You do not fear death, but I do, though I often long for it. It is the moment of passing and the uncertainty that make me tremble." "But in the world beyond are peace and bliss," said the Countess Sztáray. "How do you know that? No traveler has ever returned to tell us."

On arriving Elizabeth retired to her own apartments. An hour later she appeared again and took a little walk around the town. It was half past six on a fine evening. They went into a few confectioners' shops on the way. By a quarter to ten at night Elizabeth was back at her hotel. She had a large corner room on the second floor with two little rooms besides and a view over the lake. It was a splendid moonlight night, and the Empress could not sleep. First she had to listen to an Italian singer bawling out his songs into the night. The street was very noisy and the room flooded with moonlight, besides which the lighthouse illuminated it with shafts of changing hues; but Elizabeth insisted upon leaving the window open and would not have any curtains drawn, and it was two o'clock in the morning before she fell asleep. The moon shone full in her face, so that shortly afterwards she suddenly started out of her sleep in alarm. On other days she was usually up by seven o'clock and had generally gone out for a walk by that time, but on September 10 she lay in bed a little longer on account of her bad night. At nine o'clock the Countess Sztáray appeared and asked what were the Empress' commands. "I want to go into the town at eleven o'clock and hear an orchestrion, a new sort of musical machine, and then, at one-forty, as arranged, we take the boat for Caux. I shall not require anything before then."

Punctually at eleven the Empress was ready for her walk, fresh and cheerful in spite of her restless night. They went to Bäcker's music shop in the Rue Bonnivard. The orchestrion was wound up and played Elizabeth's favorite airs. Elizabeth next chose a large automatic musical machine known as an Ariston for Wallsee, hoping that not only Valerie and the children, but also the Emperor and Franz Salvator, would enjoy it. Meanwhile a lady came in, stared obtrusively at the Empress, and then asked the Countess Sztáray whether she might be presented to Her Majesty, on the ground that she was a well-known Belgian countess and knew her sisters well; but the lady in waiting could not consent. Everything was now concluded as quickly as possible, and they left the shop to avoid being pestered by this lady. By now it was quite late. Elizabeth returned to the hotel barely twenty minutes before the boat was due to leave, and hurriedly drank a glass of milk.

Meanwhile another meeting of anarchists had taken place at Thonon-les-Bains on September 6, at which the death of the Empress was presumably decided upon, and Lucheni, who was always boasting that he was a man of action, was probably summoned before it, though there is nothing to prove this or to show where Lucheni had been staying in the meantime. He had obviously heard something about the Empress' visit to Evian on the fifth. At any rate, he had in his pocket an official list of foreign visitors between the third and fifth of September. The Duke of Orleans and the Duke of Chartres had not, as is sometimes alleged, been at Evian or even in Switzerland. But the whole Lake of Geneva was talking about the Empress Elizabeth, and Lucheni knew for certain that she had visited Evian. By September 8 he was already in Geneva making plans of some kind, for on that very evening he sent a picture postcard to the Princess de Vera d'Aragona, his former mistress, saying: "I cannot explain to you, my lady, the reasons why I did not go to Paris. . . . In the next letter I write you I will tell you why it was. I feel well in every respect. . . . I do not expect any answer, but merely inform you that I shall leave Geneva on Saturday."

Luigi Lucheni very likely knew that the Empress was coming to Geneva on September 9. He hung about in the neighborhood of the Hotel Beau Rivage and the dock from which the boat started. He did not obtain his information about the Empress' probable visit from the newspapers, but from some other quarter; for not till the morning of the tenth did the papers contain a notice that Elizabeth was staying at the Hotel Beau Rivage incognito, under the name of the Countess of Hohenembs. The people at the hotel had been earnestly requested to respect her incognito, yet on the very day of the Empress' arrival the hotel management had informed three Geneva newspapers, the *Journal de Genève*, the *Genevois*, and the *Tribune*. When the Empress arrived on the evening of the ninth, Lucheni was probably no longer near the hotel; but if he was not yet certain whether she was coming, on September 10 he knew it from the morning papers. By nine in the morning he was already at his post of observation, and at ten o'clock he was seen on a seat in front of the hotel talking to a well-dressed man with a white beard, who looked like a person of means. When Elizabeth went out at eleven, Lucheni had already gone to get something to eat, so that her walk passed off without accident; but then he returned again.

It was now time to leave for the boat. Indeed, it was already late. The servants and Dr. Kromar had gone on ahead. The Countess Sztáray was pressing Her Majesty to start, for she was afraid she might be late. Elizabeth gave her some more of her milk to drink, and then at last the two ladies left the hotel, five minutes before the boat was due to depart. On the way to the dock the Countess Sztáray noticed two chestnut trees in bloom. "Yes," replied Elizabeth in Magyar, "the King, too, writes that there are a few chestnuts in bloom at Schönbrunn and in the Prater, though it is autumn." And now the bell on the boat rang, and the two ladies hastened their steps, but the Empress said: "We shall still be in time.

Only see how slowly and quietly the people are walking on board."

Lucheni had watched closely while the Empress' manservant took the luggage on board, so he was sure that Her Majesty was going to take the boat which left at one-forty. He felt with his right hand for the stiletto in his pocket. Then suddenly he saw Elizabeth and the Countess Sztáray coming out of the hotel and walking across the Quai Mont-Blanc toward the steamer. He fell back a little, for there were still too many people around the two ladies. The hotel proprietor and porter were taking leave of them with deep bows, but at last they were left behind. The women walked down the quay quite alone, for it was the lunch hour, and there was hardly a soul about.

The moment had come. Lucheni cleared the street with a bound, ran swiftly across the path where Elizabeth was walking till he reached the balustrade next the lake, then turned at a sharp angle and rushed at the two ladies. They both stopped to make way for him and avoid a collision, whereupon Lucheni pulled up short in front of the Countess Sztáray, as though about to stumble; then, raising his right hand high in the air, he sprang at Elizabeth, stopped, as though to peep beneath her parasol, and with a swift blow plunged his three-edged weapon into her breast. Silently, without uttering a cry, Elizabeth fell backwards on the ground like a felled tree; her head struck the pavement, and only her luxuriant masses of hair broke the force of the blow. So rapidly had it all taken place that the Countess Sztáray, hardly aware of what had happened, uttered a shriek and, with the aid of a cab driver who had hurried up, tried to assist the Empress to rise, while the assassin made off at a run. Elizabeth rose to her feet again, crimson with agitation, and tried to tidy her hair which had been disarranged. The Countess Sztáray, who had only seen the man strike her

ARREST OF LUCHENI, THE MURDERER OF THE EMPRESS

From a photograph.

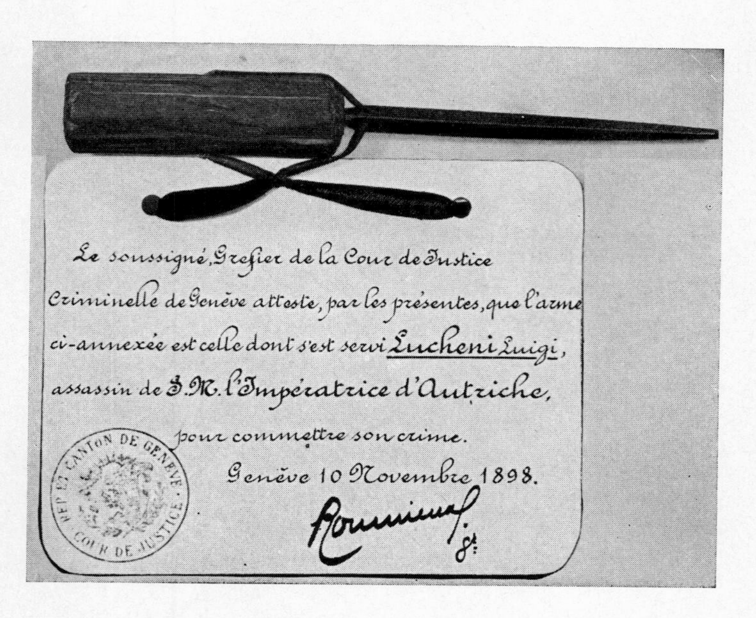

Le soussigné, Grefier de la Cour de Justice
Criminelle de Genève atteste, par les présentes, que l'arme
ci-annexée est celle dont s'est servi Lucheni Luigi,
assassin de S. M. l'Impératrice d'Autriche,
pour commettre son crime.
Genève 10 Novembre 1898.

REP. ET CANTON DE GENÈVE
COUR DE JUSTICE

THE FILE WITH WHICH THE MURDER OF THE EMPRESS WAS COMMITTED

Photographed from the original, preserved in the offices of the Procurator General, Geneva.

with his fist, exclaimed: "Is Your Majesty hurt? Do you feel a pain anywhere?" And an Englishman who had come up made the same inquiries.

"No, no, thank you," replied the Empress, "it is nothing."

The hotel porter had hurried to the spot and asked the Empress to return to the hotel.

"But no, I am not hurt."

"But Your Majesty must be frightened."

"Oh, yes, I was certainly frightened."

Elizabeth straightened her hat, the dust was shaken from her dress, and then she asked the Countess in Magyar: "What ever did that man want?"

"The porter?"

"No, the other one, that horrible person."

"I do not know, Your Majesty, but this I do know, that none but a vile creature could have done such a thing. Is Your Majesty really not hurt?"

"No, no."

And now the two ladies walked rapidly from the scene of the outrage on toward the steamer. But suddenly all the color drained from Elizabeth's face, and was followed by a deadly pallor. She must have felt this, for she turned quickly to the Countess, who had slipped her arm around her mistress, fearing she might be suffering from shock.

"Have I turned very pale now?" Elizabeth asked.

"Yes, Your Majesty, very. Your Majesty feels no pain?"

"I think my breast pains me a little."

At this moment the porter came running up again, shouting from a distance: "The criminal is caught."

Elizabeth walked lightly as far as the narrow gangway, when the Countess Sztáray was forced to withdraw her hand from her mistress' waist for a moment. Elizabeth crossed the gangway; but she had scarcely set foot on the deck before she turned abruptly to the Countess Sztáray:

"Give me your arm now," she said, "but quickly."

The Countess threw her arm round her and a manservant hurried up, but the two of them together could no longer hold the Empress upright. She sank slowly to the deck and lost consciousness, her head drooping on the breast of the Countess, who knelt beside her.

"Water! Water!" cried the Countess, "and a doctor." They brought water and she sprinkled it on Elizabeth's face. The Empress opened her eyes, but they were those of a dying woman. There was no doctor on board, only a lady, Madame Dardalle, who had been a nurse and who now took charge of the suffering lady. Captain Roux came up. The ship had not yet started, and, hearing that a woman had fainted and not knowing who she was, he advised the Countess Sztáray to have her carried on shore at once and taken back to the hotel. The answer he received was that it was only a fainting fit brought on by shock. All this had taken place just beside the engine room, where it was very hot. The captain offered them a reserved cabin, but they preferred to remain in the open air. Three gentlemen carried the Empress to the upper deck and laid her on a seat, where Madame Dardalle tried to revive her. The Countess Sztáray undid Elizabeth's dress, cut her stay lace, and pressed a piece of sugar soaked in alcohol into her mouth. She could be heard crunching it between her teeth. She now opened her eyes and tried to sit up.

"Does Your Majesty feel better?"

"Yes, thank you."

The Empress sat up, looked about her as though waking from a deep sleep, and asked with a touching expression:

"Why, what has happened?"

"Your Majesty has not been very well, but you are better now, are you not?"

No answer came. Elizabeth sank back and never regained

consciousness. "Rub her breast," said someone sharply. The fastenings of her coat were torn open, and suddenly, to her terror, the Countess Sztáray saw a brownish stain about the size of a florin on the violet batiste undergarment, with a little hole in the middle, and then a tiny wound in the breast above it to the left, with some clotted blood. "Look, Madame, for heaven's sake," she exclaimed, "she has been murdered!"

Meanwhile the ship had started and was turning eastwards. The Countess sent for the captain. "I beg you, for the love of heaven," she said, "to return to the shore at once. The lady whom you see here is the Empress of Austria. She has been wounded in the breast. I cannot let her die without a doctor and a priest. Please land at Bellevue; I mean to take the Empress to the Baroness Rothschild's at Pregny."

"But," replied the captain, "you are not likely to find a doctor there, or even a carriage." It was decided to return to Geneva at once. Meanwhile, as there was no proper stretcher on board, they improvised one out of two oars and some deck chairs. The Countess Sztáray knelt beside her mistress in desperation, dried her white face, from which drops of sweat were trickling, and listened to her breathing, which began to rattle more and more ominously in her throat. Elizabeth was laid on the stretcher, covered with the cloak which she had named after her sister, the Countess Trani, and six people lifted her, while a gentleman held a parasol over her head. With anguish in her heart the Countess Sztáray walked beside the Empress and watched how she lay with eyes closed, turning her head restlessly from side to side. But she still lived, so some hope yet remained.

Elizabeth was carried back to the hotel where she had spent the previous night. They laid her on the bed, a rattling sound was still perceptible, then nothing but profound silence. A doctor named Golay was on the spot, and another gentleman named Teisset. The doctor had his probe in his hand and tried to insert it into the wound. Anxiously the Countess Sztáray questioned him:

"Is there still hope?"

"No, Madame, none," was the reply.

"Oh, perhaps there may be. Try everything, do everything to bring her back to life."

Her clothes and shoes were removed with the assistance of the hotel proprietress, Madame Mayer, and an English nurse. A priest appeared and pronounced the absolution. All those present fell on their knees and prayed, but this was the end. Another doctor arrived, but could do no more than confirm the death. A slight incision was made in the artery of the right arm, but not a drop of blood appeared. The Empress lay there peaceful and happy, looking lovely and almost youthful, with a faint flush on her cheeks and a slight smile, her face as subtle and charming as in her lifetime when it had captivated so many.

THAT day the Emperor Francis Joseph had remained at Schönbrunn, and, having a little more time than usual, profited by it to write to the Empress. His wife's letters to Valerie were always sent on to him, too, so that he should have more news of her, and he was glad to read in her letter to Valerie on her name day a favorable account of how she was. "I rejoiced greatly," he wrote to his wife,* "at the better state of mind reflected in your letter and at your contentment with the weather, the air, and your quarters on the terrace, which must afford you a wonderful view over the mountains and lake. I was touched at your having felt a twinge of homesickness for our dear Villa Hermes in spite of this." He described how he had been there again the day be-

* This letter, which never reached the Empress' hands, is now at Schloss Wallsee.

fore and had thought about her a great deal. He told her about the weather and the deer, which were now on the move. Then he gave her a detailed account of his "*Freundin,*" who was also away on a tour in the mountains and rushing about so much that he marveled at the amount she could do in a day. "I am spending today here," he said in conclusion, "and leave the Staatsbahnhof at half past eight. *Isten veled szeretett angyalom* (I commend you to God, my beloved angel). Embracing you with all my heart. *Dein Kleiner.*"

Francis Joseph spent the following day looking through State papers and making preparations for his departure on maneuvers. At half past four in the afternoon Count Paar arrived from the Hofburg and urgently requested an audience. He was deathly pale and held in his hand a telegram from Geneva, which ran: "Her Majesty the Empress dangerously injured. Please break the news to His Majesty."

The Count entered the Emperor's study. Francis Joseph looked up from his writing table. "What is it, my dear Paar?" he said. "Your Majesty," stammered the General, "Your Majesty will not be able to leave this evening. Unfortunately I have received very bad news." Francis Joseph sprang to his feet.

"From Geneva!" he exclaimed instantly, and hurriedly took the telegram from the Count's hand. He swayed backwards, overcome with emotion.

"There must be more news soon," he said. "Telegraph, telephone! Try to get some more details."

And now footsteps were heard in the corridor. It was an aide-de-camp with another telegram from Geneva. The Emperor seized it in the utmost agitation. In his hurry to open it, he tore it right across. "Her Majesty the Empress has just passed away," he read with horror. "So nothing at all is to be spared me upon earth!" he exclaimed, and with a sob he sank down on the chair before his writing table and laying his head on his arms, wept. Then he started up, pulled himself together, and said: "First of all, the children must be informed." The evil tidings were soon on their way to Valerie at Wallsee and Gisela in Munich, who both started for Vienna.

IMMEDIATELY after the crime Lucheni had made off as fast as he could, confident that the weapon had struck deep. As he ran he threw away the file and the point broke as it fell. It remained lying there unnoticed, and was not found till much later. The assassin was at once pursued. A policeman, Antoine Rouge, threw himself in his way and was the first to seize him. Gendarmes and passers-by hurried to the spot, and Lucheni was taken into custody. While Rouge was holding him he exclaimed: "All right, I was on my way to the police."

Nobody knew yet that it was a case of assassination. He was supposed to have struck the Empress with his fist. As they led him to the police station he was asked whether he had used a knife, and replied: "If I had had one, you would have found it."

Lucheni was taken to the police station by two gendarmes, to whom he remarked, "I am only sorry I did not kill her." "So that was what you wanted?" said one of them named Lacroix; and though he did not yet know the truth, he added: "Well, you have murdered her."

"All the better," retorted Lucheni. "I thought it would do for anybody to be stabbed with a thing like that."

The gendarme now plied him with questions, and Lucheni described quite calmly how he had stabbed her with a small three-edged file, such as carpenters use for sharpening their saws. He showed not a trace of remorse, but walked along between the two gendarmes with a smile on his face, and even sang as he went through the streets, till he was told to stop. The first thing they did at the police station was to search his clothing thoroughly; they found on him a very worn purse containing six francs thirty-five, two photographs of himself in military uniform, the list of visitors at Evian, the certificate stating that he had won the Military Medal in Africa, and three letters in Italian from the Princess de Vera d'Aragona.

Lucheni was immediately questioned. He was giving an account of his doings when the telephone rang, and the examining magistrate heard to his horror the news of the Empress' death. When Lucheni was informed of it he cynically expressed his satisfaction: "Well, I meant to kill her," he said. "I struck straight at the heart, and I am delighted at what you tell me."

"What are you?"

"An anarchist."

"Have you ever served a sentence before?"

"No."

This ended the first interrogation, and at his own request Lucheni was driven to the prison of Saint Antoine in a cab, for which he himself paid. He had started life in Saint Antoine's home for foundlings in Paris and was to end it in Saint Antoine's prison in Geneva. On the way there he remarked to Lacroix:

"I am sorry there is no death penalty in Geneva. I have done my duty. My colleagues will do theirs. It is necessary for all the great ones of the world to be convinced of this."

The Procurator General Navazza, the most distinguished jurist in the canton of Geneva, was intrusted with conducting the inquiry. He made a close study of Lucheni, subjected him to countless questionings, and saw that he was only too anxious to assume entire responsibility for his deed in order to enjoy the full "renown" for it.

"I have never belonged to a socialist or anarchist society," he said. "I am an 'individual' anarchist, and, wherever I have been, have always associated with those of the same way of thinking."

Lucheni kept insisting that he cared nothing for his life and was indifferent to punishment.

"Well, then, why did you try to make off afterwards as fast as you could?" he was asked.

"I was not trying to escape. I was only running to the police station."

In reply to the question why he had murdered the Empress, Lucheni said: "As part of the war on the rich and great. A Lucheni kills an empress, but would never kill a washerwoman."

In a state of deep emotion Navazza left the assassin. Here, he thought, is a modern Herostratus, like him of old who set fire to the temple of Artemis at Ephesus, one of the most splendid works of antiquity, and afterwards confessed under torture that his reason for doing it was to make his name immortal.

"Lucheni," he said, "is inspired by the true megalomania of crime. I have never come across such a criminal before in the whole of my career. He is proud of his action and never ceases to lament that he cannot be brought to the scaffold for it." Once again in Lucheni's case it was proved that vanity can delude people even more and move them to even wilder actions than starvation or love can. What Lucheni wanted was to drain the cup of fame to the last drop. The whole world was reading his name and talking about him, and he wanted it to hear from his own lips why he had acted as he had. As he wondered how this could be accomplished, he remembered the Naples paper, *Don Marzio,* which he had often read during his military service and knew to be tinged with liberalism. On the day after the outrage he resolved to write to the editor in chief.

First and foremost Lucheni desired this paper to combat

the theory that he was a born criminal. Lombroso's contention that an individual could be born into the world a predestined criminal was, he said, nonsense. "I further request you," he wrote, "to contradict those who have taken it upon themselves to say that Lucheni did this deed out of poverty. That is absolutely false. I proclaim in conclusion that . . . unless the ruling class attempts to curb the greed with which it sucks the blood of its fellow men, then, within the shortest possible time, the just blows of the undersigned must fall upon all royalty, presidents, and ministers, and everyone who attempts to bring his fellow men into subjection for his own profit. The day is not far distant when true friends of humanity will have extirpated all the laws at present in force. One law will more than suffice: he who does not work shall not eat. Yours obediently, Luigi Lucheni, the most convinced of anarchists."

When the venerable editor of this newspaper was informed of the letter by the prison authorities, he could not imagine why it should have occurred to the assassin to write to him, for Lucheni was entirely unknown to him, and in the issue of the newspaper which appeared on the thirteenth he expressed his abhorrence of this beast in human form. Meanwhile Lucheni had sent a petition to the President of the Swiss Confederation, requesting that he might be tried according to the laws of the canton of Lucerne, where the death penalty was still in force, and not of Geneva, where it was not. He signed himself "Luigi Lucheni, anarchist, and one of the most dangerous of them." He next wrote some private letters, first to the Princess d'Aragona: "As a true Communist," he said, "I could no longer survive such injustices, and as a true friend of humanity I have thus made known to the world that the hour is not far distant when a new sun shall shine upon all men alike. I know that nothing remains to me in life. In the twenty-five years during which I have lived in it, I have learnt enough about the world. I assure you, Princess, from the bottom of my heart, that never in my life have I felt so contented as now. If only I could have the good fortune, for which I have petitioned, to be tried by the laws of the canton of Lucerne, then I should bound up the steps of the beloved guillotine and require no compulsion from the assistants." A few days later there was another letter to the Princess in which occur the words: "My case is comparable to the Dreyfus Case."

How proud the criminal would have been had the prison authorities allowed him to see the innumerable letters congratulating him upon his deed which were sent him by members of the underworld in Vienna, Laibach, Florence, Lausanne, Naples, Sofia, Prague, Baltimore, London, Rumania, and Spain. We may read in them how all who were fighting for the good of humanity endorsed his "noble deed," how he had proved that there were still "heroes" among the people, and how he must endure without losing heart till, when the great day of victory arrived, the people would throw open his dungeon.

But if these letters of enthusiastic approval were not shown to Lucheni, neither were the messages of hate which arrived in even greater numbers. Chief among these was one from the women and girls of Vienna, which filled the whole of a great roll and contained no less than sixteen thousand signatures. "Murderer, monster, ravenous wild beast," it runs, "the women and girls of Vienna sigh to avenge the fearful crime which you have committed against our beloved Empress. Do you know, ravenous beast, what you deserve? Listen, monster. We should like to lay you on a table—yes, kind-hearted though we are, we could look on with pleasure while both your arms and feet were cut off. In order to sweeten your sufferings, we would wash your wounds with vinegar and dry them with salt. If you survived it and recovered, they could do something of the sort again. Or we would make another proposal to you: let the same instrument be driven into your heart as you plunged into that of our beloved Empress—but slowly! Won't you try the experiment? Accursed be the whole of your remaining life, miserable, cruel monster. May what you eat do you no good. May your body be a source of nothing but pain to you, and may your eyes go blind. And you shall live in eternal darkness. Such is the most ardent wish of the women and girls of Vienna for such an infamous wretch as you."

ELIZABETH's body was lying in state in the hotel. Inquiries were made in Vienna as to whether it was to be subjected to a *post-mortem* examination as required by Swiss law, and Francis Joseph replied that the law of the land was to take its course; so on the afternoon of September 11 Professor Reverdin, Dr. Gosse, and Dr. Megévaud appeared to conduct the autopsy. They examined the body, noted the excellent teeth, measured the height, and then examined the wound minutely. Fourteen centimeters below the left collarbone and four centimeters above the nipple of the left breast, there was a v-shaped wound. Next, the heart was laid bare and a slight dilation noted. The weapon had entered it to a depth of eighty-five millimeters, breaking the fourth rib and piercing the lung and the whole of the left ventricle: but the incision was so narrow and the wound so small that the blood could only drip from the ventricle into the pericardium slowly, so that the action of the heart stopped gradually. This explained why Elizabeth's extraordinary energy and amazing force of will had enabled her to walk another hundred and twenty-five paces before she collapsed on board the boat.

To their horror the Countess Sztáray, Count Kuefstein, the Austrian Minister in Switzerland, and General von Berzeviczy had to be present at the autopsy as witnesses. The body was next embalmed, during which process the face changed greatly, becoming swollen, but the doctors said that before long the lovely features would regain their former contours. She was now dressed in black, with her hair arranged as she had usually worn it, and then laid in her coffin. On the table lay the things which the Empress had always carried on her person. There were the plain little gold chain with the wedding ring, which Elizabeth never wore on her hand but around her neck beneath her dress; the simple leather fan which she always carried; her electroplated watch, on which was engraved the word "Achilleus," with its worn leather strap and buckle; and the bracelet with its many charms, most of them having some mystic meaning, including a skull, the three-footed emblem of the sun, the gold hand with forefinger outstretched, medals of the Blessed Virgin, and Byzantine gold coins. There were also two lockets, one containing some hair of the Crown Prince, and the other the ninety-first psalm.

And now Elizabeth started upon her last journey homewards. The whole Empire was plunged in grief. In Hungary the news had at once thrown the whole country and its capital into mourning. Portraits of the Empress draped in black were to be seen everywhere. In Budapest not a house was without a black flag, and even the humblest hovel displayed its scrap of crepe. Francis Joseph was deeply moved when he heard of the grief in Vienna and the tears of Hungary. "Yes," he said, "they may well weep. They do not know what a warm friend they have lost in their Queen."

The funeral was celebrated with all the stately traditional pomp of the Spanish ceremonial, against which Elizabeth could now no longer revolt. The procession arrived at the entrance of the imperial vault in the Capuchin monastery. The crypt was closed. The Controller of the Household struck three times on the door, and the voice of the Father Superior was heard from within asking: "Who is there?"

"Elizabeth, Empress and Queen, desires admittance."

The Emperor and his children stood sobbing beside the coffin. Then suddenly Valerie's eyes fell upon that spot in the crypt which Elizabeth had described to her, where a little light and greenery peeped in through the narrow window. She heard the birds twittering outside, just as her mother had described, and sent up the heartfelt prayer: "May she at last find the peace for which she so ardently longed!"

The Empress' most faithful friends were also present: Ida Ferenczy, whom Elizabeth had loved for her bright, frank, straightforward nature, her sound judgment of people, her tact and high-mindedness and simplicity of heart. She had carried out the Empress' last wishes, one of which was that she should destroy the Crown Prince's last letter to his mother. She turned sobbing to a friend: "I have lost everything," she said, "husband, children, family, happiness, contentment; for my dear Queen was all these to me." Marie Festetics stood beside her in tears. "We shall often mourn together, Ida," she wrote to Frau von Ferenczy a little later. "We have had the best of her. We have long, long enjoyed her heart and her soul. Nobody can deprive us of that, it is our treasure. We have always loved her, not like so many who first came forward after the dagger had pierced her heart." But she and Frau von Ferenczy were in despair at not having been with their mistress in the critical hour.

But the irony of fate did not cease its manifestations even at her grave. The funeral of this woman to whom politics had been odious gave rise to a conflict which projected, as it were, a lurid light ahead of it into the gloomy future of the Empire. According to traditional custom the Empress' coat of arms was placed by her coffin and under it the inscription: "Elizabeth, Empress of Austria." On the first day hundreds of thousands of people walked past it, among them many Hungarians, who at once raised a violent protest, so that on the same evening the words, "and Queen of Hungary," were hastily added. But now an objection was raised by the Chief Provincial Marshal of Bohemia, who inquired why the style of Queen of Bohemia should not also be added. Had the Empress herself been living she would probably have answered simply: "Write Elizabeth, and nothing more." But the Hungarian Minister President, Baron Bánffy, lodged a formal protest against the "tendential character" which, he said, had been given to the funeral ceremonies by their "Austrian stamp," for the express purpose of offering an affront to the dignity of the Hungarian State.

Eighty-two royal persons were present at the last obsequies, so that the chapel of the Capuchin monastery was not large enough to contain them all. By a most unfortunate accident one of the court functionaries had to make the deputation from the Hungarian Parliament fall back to make way for the funeral procession. "We are here as Hungarians to witness the funeral of our Queen," retorted a member of the deputation. And the Ministers President of the two countries, the Ministers of the Imperial House, and the Controller of the Household had all the difficulty in the world in appeasing the political storm which arose in consequence of this incident.

Exactly a month after the outrage Lucheni appeared before his judges. Forty jurymen had been empaneled, drawn from every walk of life, electricians, architects, dentists, laundrymen, gardeners . . . The judges entered. There was dead silence in court when Lucheni appeared. Vain and theatrical, his one idea was to impress the public. As he passed the press table he nodded as if to say: "Well, here I am," then turned and smiled at the public thronging the court. He seemed greatly pleased with the whole proceedings. When he spoke, his every gesture was calculated, his every word weighed. He knew that next morning they would appear in print in every newspaper in the world. He was not in the least impressed when he heard that his mother was still alive and in San Francisco. He continued as proudly as ever to plead guilty, citing the poverty of his youth among his reasons for committing the outrage, and repeating what he had said in his article: that he who does not work should not eat. When the president of the court pointed out discrepancies between his statements he answered: "Believe what you like. I am speaking the truth."

"Do you feel no remorse?" asked the president.

"On the contrary," was the reply.

"If you had it to do over again, would you do it?"

"Certainly." And Lucheni turned triumphantly toward the public to enjoy the sensation produced by his words. Nor was he content with that, for he kissed his hand to some unknown person sitting in a corner of the room. Then the Procurator General, Navazza, rose to make his final speech.

"This man," he said, "has sacrificed his freedom for life to the wild joy which he is flaunting today. He considers that all those who have no definite profession should be destroyed. He believes them to be the happy people in this life. And the wretched man has no idea that in every class of society tears follow close upon laughter and joy.

"Ah, Lucheni, great is the satisfaction this has given your ambition. You committed a sensational act when you stabbed a woman of sixty to the heart with your file. But your cowardice was proportionate to the ease with which you struck the blow."

The counsel for the defense found nothing better to say than that, had she lived, the Empress would have begged a pardon for Lucheni. The verdict was imprisonment for life.

When it was announced, Lucheni shouted in a loud voice: "Long live anarchy! Death to aristocracy!"*

The murderer believed himself to have been an instrument of punishment and judgment. But how little he knew his victim! Would he have murdered her had he guessed how often this woman, this "rich" and "privileged" person, had longed for death—a death that should be swift and painless, that should happen far from her loved ones, lest it give them pain, and come to her, not in her bed, but amid the beauties of Nature which she loved so much? And now through his action

* Immediately after his condemnation Lucheni again wrote to the Prince d'Aragona thanking him for the favorable report of him which he had given to the court, and promising that he would be the best of prisoners, just as he, the captain, had once said he was the best of soldiers. "If I was capable of committing a murder, I shall succeed in this, too, now that I am a living corpse," he wrote. And for two years Lucheni's conduct was indeed excellent. He was only indignant at being placed in the same cells as common malefactors. He regarded himself as a political prisoner and was very touchy when he thought he had been unjustly treated, even contemplating suicide. In February, 1900, he had been given a box of sardines, the key of which by an oversight had not been removed, so he made it into a weapon with which he intended to kill himself. On February 20, 1900, he became violent while Perrin, the director of the prison, happened to be with him, and threatened him with this weapon, which had to be taken from him by the warder. He was given ten days in the cells as punishment, after which his conduct was again irreproachable and he was treated comparatively well; but he grew more and more touchy and nervous. One of the warders was often drunk and always smelt of wine. On October 16, 1910, Lucheni said to him as he entered the cell: "You are a boozer (*Saufer*). You always stink of liquor." An altercation arose, and the warder complained to Monsieur Fernet, director of the prison (on a personal interview with whom this account is based). He concluded, on inquiry, that Lucheni was not altogether in the wrong, so both parties were punished. Lucheni was placed in solitary confinement and not allowed to work, which he felt terribly. He kept shouting, "I only told the truth," and threw all the small things in his cell out of the window. He was then placed in a dark cell. About six o'clock a warder going the rounds heard him still shouting. That evening Monsieur Fernet visited his cell and found him dead. He had hanged himself with his leather belt.

this had become a reality, a terrible, tragic reality. Carmen Sylva was indeed right. Elizabeth would have found excuses for Lucheni. With her characteristic irony—an irony sometimes so gay, sometimes so sad—with that charming little hint of laughter in the turn of her lip which always captivated everybody, she would have said: "Well, Lucheni, you have struck a shrewd blow, just as I should have wished it."

BIBLIOGRAPHY

A LIST IS GIVEN BELOW OF ALL THE PRIvate and other collections of unpublished sources on which I have drawn, and also of the books dealing directly or indirectly with the subject of the Empress Elizabeth. I have collected practically all the books obtainable, from the Hungarian professor Dr. Marki's serious work to popular accounts with romantic embellishments. These works I examined and compared with the wealth of original documents placed at my disposal, with the same result in almost every case. Most of them were confused and led to false conclusions, so I was forced to conclude that I could make use of no printed authorities, except for the few serious publications mentioned in the course of the work or specially noted below. Because of the different points of view held by the authors of the original documents, these, too, naturally called for critical treatment. This is particularly true of the highly interesting and important diary of the Countess Marie Festetics, who was under the influence of Andrássy and naturally inclined to see things from an exclusively Hungarian viewpoint. The diary of the Archduchess Valerie, who was strongly Austrian in her point of view, served as a useful counterpoise to it.

The private collections of papers to which I have had access are as follows:

Archives of His Imperial and Royal Highness the Archduke Franz Salvator, Schloss Wallsee.

Archives of Her Imperial and Royal Highness the Countess Gertrude Waldburg-Zeil, Archduchess of Austria, at Schloss Syrgenstein, where the diary of the Archduchess Valerie is also preserved.

Archives of the Royal House, Munich.

Archives of His Royal Highness Prince Konrad of Bavaria at Munich, Harlaching.

Archives of Prince George Festetics, Schloss Keszthely.

Archives of Frau Elizabeth von Farkas, containing the papers of Frau Ida von Ferenczy, at Felsöbabad.

Archives of Baron Alexander von Warsberg.

Archives of the Countess Erna Szécsen-Mikes, at Gyöngyösszentkereszt.

Archives of Frau Mathilde Pacher von Theinburg, Vienna.

Family papers in the possession of Mrs. Violet Borwick, Northampton.

STATE ARCHIVES

State Archives, Vienna. (Indexes of the Empress' private secretariat.)

Foreign Office Archives, Berlin.

Prussian (secret) State Archives, Dahlem.

Bavarian (secret) State Archives, Munich.

Record Office, London.

Archives of the Procurator General, Geneva.

BIBLIOGRAPHY

d'Albon, Eugen. Unser Kaiserin. Vienna, 1890.

—— Vom Kaiser. Vienna, 1909.

Almstein, August von. Ein flüchtiger Zug nach dem Orient. Vienna, 1887.

Andrássy, Julius. Ungarns Ausgleich mit Österreich vom Jahre 1867. Leipzig, 1897.

Anonymous. Am Hofe von Neapel. Vienna.

—— Der Zerfall Österreichs, Leipzig, 1867.

—— Die Ankunft am 22 April und der Einzug Ihrer königlichen Hoheit der durchlauchtigsten Herzogin Elisabeth, Kaiserin-Braut, am 23 April, 1854, in Wien. Vienna, 1854.

—— Erzsébet Magyarok Királynéja. Budapest.
—— Kaiserin Elisabeth von Österreich. Vienna, 1898.
—— Kronprinz Rudolf. Dresden.
—— Kronprinz Rudolfs Tragödie. Vienna, 1923.
BAYERN, ADALBERT VON. Vier Revolutionen und einiges dazwischen. Munich, 1932. English translation: Through four revolutions. 1933.
BEETZ, WILHELM. Die Hermesvilla in Lainz. Vienna.
BELCREDI, FRAGMENTE. Zeitschrift *Die Kultur,* 1906.
BEÖTHY, Z. Erinnerung an Kaiserin Elisabeth von Ungarn. 1902.
BERTELE, CARL, *and* SCHNÜRER, FRANZ. Radmer. Vienna, 1902.
BERTHA, N. DE. François Joseph I et son règne. Paris, 1888.
BERZEVICZY. Absolutizmus kóra Magyarországon. 1849–62. 3 vols.
BIBL, VIKTOR. Der Zerfall Österreichs. Vienna, 1922.
—— Von Revolution zu Revolution. 1924.
BÖHM, GOTTFRIED VON. Ludwig II, König von Bayern. Berlin, 1922.
BREITNER, A. Die Odyssee der Kaiserin. Munich.
BRENTANO, H. Kaiser Franz Joseph I. Vienna.
BURGH, A. DE. Elizabeth, empress of Austria. 1899.

CHANNON, HENRY. The Ludwigs of Bavaria. Leipzig, 1934.
CHRISTOMANOS, KONSTANTIN. Das Achilles-Schloss auf Korfu. Vienna, 1896.
—— Die graue Frau. Vienna, 1898.
—— Die Wachspuppe. Hamburg, 1929.
—— Tagebuchblätter. Vienna, 1899. Detailed references in text, p. 428, footnote.
COBURG, LUISE VON. Autour des trônes que j'ai vu tomber. Paris.
COSTA, ETHBIN HEINRICH. Denkbuch der Anwesenheit Ihrer Majestäten Franz Joseph und Elisabeth im Herzogtum Krain. Laibach, 1857.
CSENGERY, ANTON. Franz Deák. Leipzig, 1877.
(CUNLIFFE-OWEN, MARGUERITE.) The martyrdom of an empress. London, 1900. A mixture of fact and fiction, with no dates, some very bad errors, and no authorities cited.

DAUDET, ERNEST. La chronique de nos jours. Paris, 1912.
DAVENPORT, ADAMS W. H. The Isle of Wight. London, 1882.
DORFMEISTER, F. N. Kaiserin Elisabeth von Österreich. Vienna, 1898.
DREYER, N. Herzog Maximilian in Bayern. Munich, 1909.

ECKHART, FERENCZ. Storia della nazione ungherese. Milan, 1929.
EISENMANN, L. Le compromis austro-hongrois de 1867. Paris, 1904.
EISENMENGER, VIKTOR. Erzherzog Franz Ferdinand. Vienna.
ELMER, ALEXANDER. Aus der Geheimmappe des Kaisers Franz. Vienna, 1926.
EMMER, JOHANNES. Sechzig Jahre auf Habsburgs Throne. Vienna, 1908.
ENGEL-JÁNOSI, FRIEDRICH. Graf Rechberg. Munich, 1927.
EÖTVÖS, JÖZSEF. Költemények szinmüvek. Budapest.
—— Freiherr von. Gedanken. Pest, 1864.
EPON, VIKTOR. Chronik europäischer Fürstenhöfe. Leipzig.
ERMORDUNG IHRER MAJESTÄT DER KAISERIN UND KÖNIGIN ELISABETH IN GENF. Vienna and Leipzig.
ERNST, OTTO. Franz Joseph in seinen Briefen. Vienna, 1924.

FALK, MAX. Krönungsalbum. Pest.
—— MIKSA. Erzsébet Királynéról Visszaemlékezések. Budapest, 1898.
FAYE, JACQUES DE LA. Elisabeth von Bayern. Halle a. d. S., 1914.
FEHMI, JOUSSOUF. Un essai d'apostolat des chevaliers positivistes. Affaire Lucheni, 1898–1910. Paris, 1913.
FORSTER, GYULA. Erzsébet Királyné emléke. Budapest, 1907.
FRIEDJUNG, HEINRICH. Der Ausgleich mit Ungarn. Leipzig, 1877.
—— Historische Aufsätze. Stuttgart, 1919.
—— Österreich von 1848 bis 1860. Stuttgart, 1912.
FRIEDMANN, E., *and* PAVES, J. Kaiserin Elisabeth. Berlin, 1898.

GÁBEL, GYULA. Erzsébet megemlékezés, Magyarország nagy Királnéjárol. Budapest, 1900.

GADOBERT, BENJAMIN. Les drames sous la couronne. Paris, 1899.

GAILLARD, HENRI. L'impératrice idéale. Paris, 1899.

GEORGE, STEPHAN. Der siebente Ring. Berlin, 1922. Contains a poem "Die Schwestern" (Elizabeth and Sophie Alençon).

GILBERT, MARION. Elizabeth de Wittelsbach. Paris. Uses about twenty documents belonging to Frau von Ferenczy; otherwise a light, pleasant popular work.

GLAISE-HORSTENAU, EDMUND VON. Franz Josephs Weggefährte. Vienna.

GOLDSCHEIDER, H. Die Rundreise Allerhöchst Ihrer kaiserlichen und königlichen Majestäten in Ungarn. Arad, 1857.

GOURAUT-D'ABLANCOURT, MARIE. Madame la Duchesse d'Alençon et son temps.

GRIBBLE, FRANCIS. Life of the Emperor Francis Joseph. 1914.

GRIEBEN. München und die Königsschlösser.

HALPERSON, JOSEPH. Das Buch vom Zirkus. Düsseldorf, 1926.

HOCHSTETTER, FERDINAND VON. Madeira. Vienna.

HOFDAMENBRIEFE. Zurich, 1905.

HORN, G. Le compromis de 1868 entre la Hongrie et la Croatie et celui de 1867 entre l'Autriche et la Hongrie.

HORVÁTH, MICHAEL. Fünfundzwanzig Jahre aus der Geschichte Ungarns. Leipzig, 1867.

ILLUSTRIERTES GEDENKBUCH ZUR IMMERWÄHRENDEN ERINNERUNG AN DIE GLORREICHE VERMÄHLUNGSFEIER S. K. K. APOST. MAJESTÄT FRANZ JOSEPH VON ÖSTERREICH UND IHRER KÖNIGLICHEN HOHEIT DER DURCHLAUCHTIGSTEN FRAU HERZOGIN ELISABETH IN BAYERN, VOLLZOGEN IN WIEN AM 24 APRIL, 1854. Vienna, 1854.

D'ISNE, Y. Ferdinand Philippe d'Orléans, *Duc d'Alençon*. Paris.

KELEMEN, BÉLA. Erzsébet Királné és az irodalom. Székesfehérvár, 1908.

KETTERL, EUGEN. Der alte Kaiser, wie nur einer ihn sah. Vienna, 1929.

KIELMANSEGG, MATHILDE. Elisabeth. Vienna, 1902.

KLINGENBERGER, HEINRICH. Kaiserin Elisabeth von Österreich. Vienna.

KOCH, LUDWIG WILHELM. Blüten der Gegenwart und Blätter der Zukunft. Vienna, 1854.

KOHUT, ADOLPH. Kaiser Franz Joseph I als König von Ungarn. Berlin, 1916.

KOWALEWSKIJ. Wahnsinnige als Herrscher und Führer der Völker. Munich, 1910.

KRONFELD, E. M. Franz Joseph I. Vienna, 1917.

KURTH, BETTY. Das Lustschloss Schönbrunn. Vienna.

KUTSCHERA-WOLORSKY, OSWALD. Die Wiener Hofburg. Vienna.

LA FAYE, JACQUES. Elisabeth de Bavière. Paris, 1913.

LAMPEL. Sechzig Jahre Kaiser. Vienna, 1908.

LARISCH, MARIE. My past. London, 1913.

LAUBE, HEINRICH. Erinnerungen. Leipzig, 1909.

LINDE, FRITZ. Schloss Linderhof. Leipzig.

LIPPERT, WALDEMAR. Richard Wagners Verbannung und Rückkehr, 1849 bis 1862. Dresden.

LORM, HIERONYMUS. Die Muse des Glücks und moderner Einsamkeit. Leipzig, 1893.

LUZIO, ALEXANDER. Francesco Giuseppe e l'Italia. Milan, 1917.

MAHAN, ALEXANDER. Famous women of Vienna. Vienna, 1929.

MARCH, RICHARD. Ein Ehrentag in Österreich. Prague.

MARGUTTI, ALBERT. Vom alten Kaiser. Leipzig, 1921. English translation, 1921.

MÁRKI, SÁNDOR. Erzsébet Magyarország Királynéja, 1867–1898. Budapest, 1899. A serious, trustworthy, and good piece of work, based on valuable sources. Deals specially only with Elizabeth's relations with Hungary and her visits to that country.

MÁROSZY, STEPHAN VON. Elisabeth, die Märtyrerin auf dem Kaiserthrone, im Spiegel der Wahrheit. Leipzig, 1912.

MEZÖFI, VILMOS. Anarchisták vagy Szoczialisták. Budapest, 1898.

MITIS, OSKAR VON. Das Leben des Kronprinzen Rudolf. Leipzig, 1928.

Naske, Adolph Carl. Gedenkbuch über die Vermählungsfeierlichkeiten S. k. k. apost. Majestät Franz Joseph I von Österreich mit Elisabeth, Herzogin in Bayern. Vienna, 1854.

Nolston, L. K. Ein Andenken an weiland Kaiserin und Königin Elisabeth. Budapest, 1899. An excellent collection of all the information about the Empress Elizabeth scattered in newspapers, etc.

Oksza, Helène. Impressions et souvenirs. Vienna, 1899.

Paoli, Xavier. Leurs Majestés. Paris.

Penn, Heinrich. Unser Kaiser. Brünn, 1888.

Perquer, A. L'impératrice Elisabeth d'Autriche â Sassetôt-le-Mauconduit en 1875.

Przibram, Ludwig. Erinnerungen eines alten Österreichers. Stuttgart, 1910.

Putnoky, Miklós. Carmen Sylva, élete és müvei. Lugos, 1910.

Radics, P. von. Fürstinnen des Hauses Habsburg. Dresden, 1896.

Rainolder, Johann. Elisabeth. Vienna, 1854.

Redlich, Joseph. Kaiser Franz Joseph von Österreich. Berlin, 1928. English translation, 1929.

Redwitz, Marie. Hofchronik. Munich, 1924.

Reise a. h. Ihrer k. apost. Majestäten Franz Joseph und Elisabeth durch Kärnten. Vienna, 1859.

Ripka, Ferencz. Erzsébet Királyné. Budapest, 1901.

—— Gödöllö. Vienna, 1898.

Roland, A. Kaiser Franz Joseph und sein Haus. Vienna, 1897.

Rostok, Robert. Erinnerungsblätter an weiland Ihre Majestät Kaiserin und Königin Elisabeth. Prague, 1903.

Rotter, Richard. Vaik Stephan und Gisela, Franz Joseph und Elisabeth. Culturgeschichtliche Parallele. Vienna and Troppau, 1879.

Schnürer, Franz. Briefe Kaiser Franz Josephs I an seine Mutter. Munich, 1930. An admirable edition of the Archduchess' letters.

—— See Bertele.

SMOLLE, LEO. Elisabeth, Kaiserin von Österreich und Königin von Ungarn. Vienna, 1904.

—— Fünf Jahrzehnte auf Habsburgs Throne. Vienna, 1898.

SOSNOSKY, TH. VON. Erzherzog Franz Ferdinand. Munich, 1929.

STAVENHAGEN, WILLIBALD. Über die Belagerung von Gaeta. Vienna, 1906.

STEINBACH, GUSTAV. Franz Deák. Vienna, 1888.

(STEINEN, WOLFRAM VON DEN.) Kaiserin Elisabeth.

STEINITZ, EDUARD. Erinnerungen an Franz Joseph I. Berlin, 1930.

STERNBERG, A. Warum Österreich zugrunde gehen musste.

STROHMAYER, W. Psychiatrisch-genealogische Untersuchung der Abstammung König Ludwigs II und Ottos I von Bayern. Wiesbaden, 1912. Important for the ties of blood between Elizabeth and the mentally deranged members of the Bavarian Royal House.

SYDACOFF-BRESNITZ. Ein halbes Jahrhundert österreichischen Hof und Staatslebens. Leipzig, 1900.

SYPNIEWSKI, ALFRED. Fünfzig Jahre Kaiser. Vienna, 1898.

(SZÉCHÉNYI, STEPHAN.) Ein Blick auf den anonymen Rückblick. London, 1898.

SZEKFÜ, J. Der Staat Ungarn. Berlin, 1918.

SZEPS, JULIUS. Kronprinz Rudolf. Politische Briefe an einen Freund. Vienna, 1922.

SZTÁRAY, IRMA. Aus den letzten Jahren der Kaiserin Elisabeth. Vienna, 1909. A valuable authority for the Empress' last years.

TISSOT, ERNEST. Le livre des reines. Paris, 1896.

TOSKANA, LUISE VON (Grand Duchess Louisa of Tuscany). Mein Lebensweg. Berlin.

TSCHUDI, CLARA. Elisabeth. Leipzig.

TSCHUPPIK, KARL. Kaiserin Elisabeth von Österreich. Vienna, 1930. English translation, 1930.

TUWORA, M. J. Aus dem Leben unserer Kaiserin und Königin. Linz, 1898.

UJVÁRY, B. Erzsébeth királyné emlékfüzet. 1898.

VALERIE MARIE. Der Namenstag.
VASILI, PAUL. La société de Vienne. Paris, 1885.
VAUX, BARON DE. Ecuyers et ecuyères. Paris, 1893.
VAY, SÁNDOR. Erzsébet Királnérol és más kronikás földjegyzések. Budapest, 1909.
VELTZÉ, ALOIS. Franz Joseph I im Bilde. Vienna, 1918.
VIVIAN, HERBERT. Francis Joseph and his consort. New York, 1917.

WARSBERG, ALEXANDER. Odysseische Landschaften. Vienna, 1878.
WERTHEIMER, EDUARD VON. Graf Julius Andrássy. Stuttgart, 1913.
WHITEHOUSE, H. The collapse of the kingdom of Naples. New York, 1899.
WOLBE, EUGEN. Carmen Sylva. Leipzig.
WOLF, GEORG JACOB. König Ludwig II und seine Welt. Munich, 1926.
WÖLFLING, LEOPOLD. Habsburger unter sich. Berlin, 1921.
WURZBACH, CONSTANTIN. Das Elisabethbuch. Vienna, 1854.

ZAMORDOWANIE CESARZOWEJ ELZBIÉTY. Caly, dokladny opis, etc. Stanislawów, 1898.
ZANARDI-LANDI, *Countess.* The secret of an empress. London, 1914. See p. 267, footnote.

PERIODICALS

Deutsches Biographisches Jahrbuch, 1922.
Die Zeit, Vienna, September 17, 1898: Die Kaiserin by Hermann Bahr.
Fliegende Blätter, vol. 49, no. 19.
Huldigungsausstellung, Vienna, 1908.
Magyar Salon, October, 1886.
——September, 1898.
Neue Freie Presse, December 25, 1906: Carmen Sylva, Die Kaiserin Elisabeth in Sinaia.

—— March 13, 1880.
—— September 12, 1898: Article by Moritz von Jókai.
Neues Wiener Journal, January 17, 1901: Bei der Vorleserin der verstorbenen Kaiserin.
Neues Wiener Tagblatt, February 19, 1895.
—— April 13, 1933: Friedrich Eckstein, Ahasverus und die Kaiserin.
Österreichische Rundschau, XV: 6, June, 1908.
—— XVII: 5, December, 1908.
Pesti Hirlap, Vasárnapja. January 23, 1927.
Pester Lloyd, September 12, 1898.
Petit Guide de Genève.
Residenzmuseum, Munich.
Stuttgarter Neues Tagblatt, August 12, 1928: Ida Ferenczy über Mayerling.
The golden guide of London, London, 1875.
Uj idök, XIII: 48, Budapest, November 24, 1907.
—— IV, Budapest, September 25, 1898.
Wiener Allgemeine Theaterzeitung, 1854.
Wiener Salonblatt, September 17, 1898.

Lecture published in the *Urania,* Vienna, by Herr Sektionschef Dr. Hans Schlitter on the Empress Elizabeth.

See also the excellent Bibliographie der Habsburgliteratur, 1218–1934 by Dr. Johann Kerterz (Budapest, 1934), s. v. Elizabeth.

INDEX